Southern Living®
complete
quick & easy
cookbook

Southern Living®

complete

quick & easy

cookbook

Oxmoor
House®

ISBN-13: 978-0-8487-3773-3
ISBN-10: 0-8487-3773-3
Library of Congress Control Number: 2009930818

Printed in the United States of America
Second Printing 2012

To order additional publications, call 1-800-765-6400.

For more books to enrich your life, visit **oxmoorhouse.com**

To search, savor, and share thousands of recipes, visit
myrecipes.com

Cover: Sour Cream Pound Cake (page 402)
Back Cover: Beef Fillets With Orange Cream (page 283),
Chicken Noodle Soup (page 244), Southwestern Tabbouleh Salad
(page 110), Thai Coconut Shrimp and Rice (page 166), Roasted
Vegetable Pizza (page 215)

Page 1: Fresh Raspberry-Spinach Salad (page 347)
Page 2: Pronto Chicken Pot Pie (page 80)

Southern Living®
Executive Editor: Scott Jones
Food Editor: Shannon Sliter Satterwhite
Senior Writer: Donna Florio
Associate Food Editors: Shirley Harrington, Mary Allen Perry
Assistant Food Editors: Natalie Kelly Brown, Marion McGahey
Assistant Recipe Editors: Ashley Arthur, Ashley Leath
Test Kitchens Director: Lyda Jones Burnette
Assistant Test Kitchens Director: Rebecca Kracke Gordon
Test Kitchens Specialist/Food Styling: Vanessa McNeil Rocchio
Test Kitchens Professionals: Marian Cooper Cairns,
    Kristi Michele Crowe, Norman King, Pam Lolley,
    Angela Sellers
Editorial Assistant: Pat York
Senior Foods Photographer: Jennifer Davick
Photographer: Beth Dreiling Hontzas
Senior Photo Stylist: Buffy Hargett

Oxmoor House, Inc.
VP, Publishing Director: Jim Childs
Executive Editor: Susan Payne Dobbs
Brand Manager: Daniel Fagan
Managing Editor: L. Amanda Owens

Southern Living® Complete Quick & Easy Cookbook
Development Editor: Susan Hernandez Ray
Project Editor: Vanessa Lynn Rusch
Director, Test Kitchens: Elizabeth Tyler Austin
Assistant Director, Test Kitchens: Julie Christopher
Test Kitchens Professionals: Catherine Crowell Steele,
    Kathleen Royal Phillips, Ashley T. Strickland,
    Deborah Wise
Photography Director: Jim Bathie
Senior Photo Stylist: Kay E. Clarke
Associate Photo Stylist: Katherine Eckert Coyne
Director of Production: Laura Lockhart
Production Manager: Tamara Nall

Contributors
Designer: Nancy Johnson
Copy Editor: Donna Baldone
Indexer: Mary Ann Laurens
Proofreader: Jasmine Hodges

contents

Welcome 6

The Quick & Easy Kitchen 8

Streamlined Southern Favorites 12

One-Dish Dinners 48

Healthy 'n' Quick 94

Quickies from the Grill 118

Slow-Cooker Favorites 148

Quick Nibbles 174

Presto Pizza 'n' Pastas 210

Everyday Soups 'n' Sandwiches 242

Main Dishes in Minutes 280

Shortcut Sides 'n' Salads 320

No-Fuss Breads 356

Desserts in a Dash 378

Index 406

welcome

Dear Friends,

It's a fact: Carpools, soccer practice, work deadlines, and homework have all cut into the time you have to plan and prepare supper. We also know that whether you're a beginner in the kitchen or a seasoned cook, you need practical and delicious dinnertime solutions for your family. That's why we're so excited about *Southern Living® Complete Quick & Easy*. (Take a glance at "Some of Our Favorite Recipes" on the opposite page for a mouthwatering preview.)

Our fast-paced lives have redefined the way we cook. The recipes in this book have streamlined ingredient lists and methods, as well as the use of some convenience products. This collection combines years of expertise, kitchen-tested recipes, and time-saving tips to showcase real recipes for real people like you.

One of the cookbook's most exciting features is this "make ahead" icon. make ahead Because we understand just how busy you are, we tell you what can be partially or totally made ahead and how much time you need to prepare each recipe. And we've made a special notation when a recipe can be made in 10, 20, or 30 minutes or less. You'll find these features to be indispensible. What's more, we include more than 250 taste-tempting photographs (which also include simple ideas for plating and garnishing for entertaining). We hope the more than 600 recipes and ideas in *Southern Living® Complete Quick & Easy* make each day a little bit easier for you.

Happy cooking!

the Editors

some of our favorite recipes

Grilled Southwestern Chicken With Pineapple Salsa *(page 121)*: A spicy rub gives added zip to this favorite entrée that's paired with a fruity make-ahead salsa.

Warmed Cranberry Brie *(page 177)*: This quick spread tastes like you've spent hours preparing it.

◄ Shrimp Jambalaya *(page 23)*: This one-dish recipe calls for some ingredients that you might already have on hand, and it requires only one pot.

▲ Chicken Cannelloni With Roasted Bell Pepper Sauce *(page 83)*: Sure to cure any Italian craving, the stuffed shells can be frozen ahead, so they're perfect for a busy weeknight or casual entertaining.

◄ Tomato-Basil Cream Soup *(page 40)*: A pretty beginning to any meal, this soup can be made ahead (minus the cream) and frozen.

◄ Lemon Squares *(page 384)*: Moist and luscious, this dessert packs loads of flavor with a minimum of fat.

◄ Grilled Shrimp Gyros With Herbed Yogurt Spread *(page 275)*: These tasty sandwiches are great for outdoor gatherings and simple weeknight suppers.

◄ Florentine Artichoke Dip *(page 186)*: Parmesan cheese bubbles over the surface of this scrumptious appetizer that's sure to be a crowd-pleaser.

◄ Beef Lombardi *(page 67)*: Three types of cheese add a rich flavor to this delicious one-dish meal that's ideal for entertaining.

◄ Hot Tomato Grits *(page 27)*: With the mild heat of green chiles, this Southern favorite has a hint of Texas flavor.

the quick & easy KITCHEN

5 HABITS of highly efficient cooks

1 Organize Your Kitchen

- Pick a day to clean and organize your kitchen. Store the utensils you use regularly in a convenient place on your counter so you don't have to dig through drawers to find what you need. Get rid of the equipment and utensils that you never use.
- Use racks, shelves, and bins to neatly store equipment and ingredients.
- Group similar items together in your pantry.
- Group all measuring items (cups, spoons) together near where you prepare foods for cooking.
- Alphabetize your spices and seasonings so they're easy to find. If you have room, dried seasonings keep best in the freezer. If you store them in a cabinet, just place them in a cool area away from heat or light.
- Keep a notepad in the kitchen to jot down ingredients that need to be replaced.
- Clean out your refrigerator and store the items you use the most in the front and in the door racks.

2 Plan Ahead

- Try to plan and shop for a week's worth of meals at one time. It might take a few extra minutes initially, but once you're in the habit of planning weekly menus, you'll save time and reduce the stress of coming up with meal ideas at the last minute.
- Stock your kitchen with quick cooking staples. Many are listed by food category on page 11.
- Read through the recipes you want to prepare and gather everything you need before you start cooking.
- When you're preparing breadcrumbs or toasting nuts for a recipe, prepare extra and freeze in zip-top freezer bags.
- When the price is right, stock up on standard items you know you'll use and have room to store.
- Avoid last-minute stops to pick up an item or two; you'll spend more time and money than you planned.
- Make out a grocery list before you go to the supermarket and stick to the list. You'll buy less and spend less time in the store.
- Make your grocery list according to the order of aisles in the store (see page 11). Follow that order, and you'll backtrack less.
- Microwave to get a jump start on cooking. Use the microwave to thaw foods or to precook casseroles or meat you'll finish cooking in the oven or on the grill.
- Chop and freeze ½-cup portions of red or green bell pepper, onion, and parsley in zip-top freezer bags.

3 Strategize Cleanup

- Get in the habit of cleaning as you cook. You'll be delighted that the dishes are halfway done when you're finished with dinner.
- Soak dirty dishes in hot, soapy water as you prepare meals so you won't have to scrub so much later.
- Use spray-on oven cleaner on extradirty pots and pans to ease cleanup.
- Use a graduated measuring spoon. It's one spoon that adjusts for the measurement you need so you don't have to mess up a whole set.
- Measure dry ingredients before wet ones so you can use the same measuring cups and spoons without washing between measuring.

- Measure or sift ingredients onto wax paper or paper towels for easy cleanup.
- Prevent messy splatters by setting a metal colander upside down over a skillet of simmering food. The colander holes allow steam to escape.
- Use plastic freezer bags to marinate meat or poultry. Turn the bag occasionally to completely coat the food.
- Line baking pans or broiler pans with aluminum foil for quick and easy cleanup when roasting meat, chicken, fish, or vegetables. You'll have very little mess to clean off the pans after removing the foil.
- Chop a small amount of an ingredient with a chef's knife instead of dirtying a food processor.

- Use a zip-top plastic bag to make crumbs for toppings. Place cereal or cookies in the bag; crush the contents of the bag into crumbs with your hands or a rolling pin.

- Beat eggs in a mixing bowl first, and then add the other ingredients to save cleaning an extra bowl.

4 Know Your Grocery Options

- Buy small amounts of shredded carrots, celery sticks, cauliflower or broccoli florets, and sliced mushrooms from the salad bar to save cleaning and slicing time. If you need larger amounts, look for bagged shredded or baby carrots, cauliflower or broccoli florets, and sliced mushrooms in the produce section.
- Buy prepackaged frozen chopped onion and green bell pepper.
- Purchase products that combine more than one ingredient, such as Creole, Italian, Mexican, and Greek spice blends (Mrs. Dash has several good blends). Canned Mexican-, Italian-, or Cajun-style stewed tomatoes (you get tomatoes, onions, peppers, and the seasonings in a single can) are also a good choice. Besides saving on cooking time, these products save you storage space and the time it takes to put away groceries.

- Buy bags of precut, prewashed salad greens, such as spinach leaves, romaine hearts, mixed salad greens, and cabbage, to save cleaning and preparation time. Check the expiration dates.

Continued on following page

• Peeled raw shrimp and peeled cooked shrimp are the quickest cooking forms. Follow the chart below for weight and measure comparisons, which are especially helpful if you want to start with unpeeled fresh shrimp instead.

shrimp choices

Unpeeled, raw		Peeled, raw		Peeled, cooked
⅔ pound	=	½ pound	=	⅓ pound
1 pound	=	¾ pound	=	½ pound
1⅓ pounds	=	1 pound	=	⅔ pound
2 pounds	=	1½ pounds	=	1 pound
2⅔ pounds	=	2 pounds	=	1⅓ pounds
4 pounds	=	3 pounds	=	2 pounds

• Chopped cooked chicken is available in many forms, and we call for it often in our recipes. Below are some helpful conversions when purchasing different chicken products.

chicken choices

Amount and type		Amount chopped, cooked
1 pound uncooked boneless, skinless chicken breasts	=	2⅓ cups
1 (5.5-ounce) cooked boneless chicken breast half	=	1 cup
1 (6-ounce) package grilled chicken strips	=	1⅓ cups
1 (9-ounce) package frozen chopped cooked chicken	=	1⅔ cups
1 (2-pound) deli-roasted chicken	=	2 to 3 cups
1 (3-pound) raw chicken	=	3 cups

5 Be a Speed Shopper

If you want to be a true speed shopper, determine your shopping style by this clever analysis and plan your supermarket strategy accordingly.*

• Dasher: Runs into the store on the way home every night to pick up something for that night's dinner. Frequents the deli and frozen food sections and grabs whatever looks good. Opts for a basket rather than a cart. Generally has less than 8 items; uses the express aisle.

• Gatherer: Travels up and down every aisle grabbing items that might be thrown together for a meal. Subject to impulse buys and advertised specials. Sometimes ends up with a cart full of groceries but still can't figure out what to cook for supper.

• Hunter: Enters a detailed weekly grocery list into the PDA and meticulously searches for each and every item on the list. Not uncommon for this shopper to visit several stores on the quest for one item. Often seen with coupons.

Whatever your shopping style, you can make your selections quickly and move on if you know where to find the foods you need in each section of the store. Our plan on the next page will help you simplify your shopping, whether you're shopping for the month, week, or just for the night.

This is more than a grocery list—it's a strategic plan for shopping. We've identified the key areas of the store where you'll find quick cooking staple products for many of the recipes in this book. Although the specific layouts will be different, most stores will have these same areas. Familiarize yourself with your local grocery, and plan your grocery list around the store's layout.

This sample layout of a grocery store highlights key sections of the store. In each section, there is a list of the products in that section that we recommend you keep on hand to be a superfast chef extraordinaire. Start with the produce section and work your way through the store. The order in which you move through the sections isn't crucial, except that we recommend you add frozen foods and dairy products to your cart last.

The Hunters and Gatherers will probably go to each section. The Dashers may only hit a few. Either way, you've saved yourself the time of going up and down every aisle.

One key point to keep in mind for this strategy to work: Stock up on staples. If you shop once for the staples and condiments that you use frequently, you won't have to spend time doing that each time you visit the store. Use this chart as a general staples guide for items you need to keep on hand for ultimate quick and easy meals, menus, and entertaining.

When you're finished shopping, have your grocer bag like items together (frozen, refrigerated, or pantry products), and put-away time in your kitchen will be quicker.

Based on research done for the national Cattleman's Beef Association.

Speed Shopper's Supermarket Staples

freezer

- ❏ Fruits, whole and sliced
- ❏ Vegetables
- ❏ Onions, chopped frozen
- ❏ Peppers, chopped frozen
- ❏ Seasoning blend (chopped frozen onion, peppers, celery, and parsley)
- ❏ Potatoes, hash browns and cooked mashed
- ❏ Chicken, chopped cooked
- ❏ Shrimp, peeled raw or cooked
- ❏ Ice cream
- ❏ Whipped topping

refrigerated section

- ❏ Butter
- ❏ Cheese, sliced
- ❏ Cheese, preshredded and blends
- ❏ Fresh pasta
- ❏ Milk
- ❏ Bread products
- ❏ Eggs
- ❏ Sour cream and yogurt
- ❏ Fruit juice
- ❏ Potato products
- ❏ Dips and spreads

meat/poultry/seafood

- ❏ Chicken, chopped cooked boneless chicken tenders and breasts
- ❏ Beef, ground chuck
- ❏ Beef, precooked crumbles
- ❏ Pork chops and tenderloins
- ❏ Bacon
- ❏ Shrimp, peeled and/or cooked
- ❏ Premarinated meats and poultry
- ❏ Sausage

condiments & miscellaneous

- ❏ Dressing: Italian, Greek, Ranch, Honey Mustard
- ❏ Honey
- ❏ Ketchup
- ❏ Mustard, Dijon and regular
- ❏ Oils, vegetable and olive
- ❏ Salsa
- ❏ Soy sauce
- ❏ Vegetable cooking spray
- ❏ Worcestershire sauce
- ❏ Chili sauce

spices

- ❏ Chili powder
- ❏ Crab/shrimp boil
- ❏ Creole seasoning
- ❏ Dried minced onion
- ❏ Garlic salt and powder
- ❏ Greek seasoning
- ❏ Italian seasoning
- ❏ Lemon-pepper seasoning
- ❏ Mexican seasoning
- ❏ Pepper: black, ground red, dried crushed red
- ❏ Seasoned salt and pepper

pasta, rice, grains, nuts

- ❏ Pasta: couscous, macaroni, thin spaghetti, rotini
- ❏ Rice: boil-in-bag rice and rice mixes
- ❏ Pecans, chopped
- ❏ Quick-cooking oatmeal and grits

canned goods

- ❏ Broth and soups
- ❏ Veggies
- ❏ Pasta sauce
- ❏ Fruits
- ❏ Tomatoes, diced regular and Mexican-style, Cajun-style, Italian-style
- ❏ Tomato sauce
- ❏ Bell peppers, roasted
- ❏ Instant potato flakes

deli/bakery

- ❏ Roasted chicken
- ❏ Breads/rolls
- ❏ Sliced meats
- ❏ Salad bar items

produce

- ❏ Fruits, whole and jarred
- ❏ Garlic, cloves and jarred minced
- ❏ Potatoes: baking, round red
- ❏ Broccoli florets
- ❏ Cauliflower florets
- ❏ Onions: Spanish, green, red
- ❏ Peppers: green, red, yellow
- ❏ Salad greens, packages of premixed washed
- ❏ Spinach, package of washed leaves
- ❏ Vegetables, packages of single and mixed cut

READY SET GO!

New-Fashioned Banana
Pudding, page 47

streamlined
SOUTHERN
favorites

Benne Seed Chicken

Benne Seed Chicken

Benne seed is the Southern term for sesame seed.

PREP: 10 MIN., COOK: 40 MIN., OTHER: 2 HR.

make ahead

4 chicken leg-thigh quarters
    (about 2 pounds), separated
1 onion, quartered
2 garlic cloves
1 (1-inch) piece peeled fresh ginger
2 tablespoons sugar
2 teaspoons salt
2 teaspoons ground coriander
1 teaspoon dried crushed red pepper
3 tablespoons lemon juice
3 tablespoons soy sauce
2 tablespoons sesame oil
¼ to ½ cup benne (sesame) seeds

1. Place chicken legs and thighs in a shallow dish or large zip-top plastic freezer bag.

2. Process onion and next 9 ingredients in a blender or food processor until smooth, stopping to scrape down sides; pour over chicken. Cover or seal, and chill 2 to 8 hours.

3. Remove chicken from marinade, discarding marinade. Place chicken in a lightly greased shallow roasting pan. Sprinkle with benne seeds.

4. Bake at 375° for 20 minutes on each side or until done. **Makes** 4 servings.

Italian-Seasoned Fried Chicken

You can cut up a broiler fryer yourself, buy it precut, or take advantage of packaged chicken "parts." Buy all legs or thighs if dark meat is your preference, or all breasts if white meat is your choice.

PREP: 10 MIN., COOK: 25 MIN.

¾ cup Italian-seasoned breadcrumbs
½ cup grated Parmesan cheese
¼ cup finely chopped fresh parsley
¾ teaspoon dried oregano
1 large egg
½ cup milk
1 tablespoon all-purpose flour
1 (3- to 3½-pound) package chicken pieces
Vegetable oil

1. Stir together breadcrumbs and next 3 ingredients. Whisk together egg, milk, and flour. Dip chicken in egg mixture; dredge in breadcrumb mixture.
2. Pour oil to a depth of 1 inch in a large heavy skillet; heat oil to 350°. Fry chicken 20 to 25 minutes or until golden, turning occasionally. Drain on paper towels. **Makes** 4 servings.

how to cut up chicken

Cutting up your own chicken saves money, and some cooks even believe it tastes better that way. Here's a quick lesson on doing it right.
- Remove the legs by cutting at the joints with a sharp knife.
- Crack the back thigh joint, finding the point with your fingers. Cut straight through to remove the thigh; repeat on the other side. Use kitchen shears to trim extra skin and fat.
- Stretch wings and cut the joints, removing the wings.
- Cut down the back from the tail end to the neck. Clip along the ribs with shears. You'll now have a large breast section.
- Press your fingers on the neck end of the breast; the wishbone connects to these two muscles. You will feel a V-shaped breastbone. Cut straight down from the top of the breast to the cutting board, cutting between the ribs and wishbone from the rest of the breast. Your piece will be V-shaped. Be careful not to crack the bone.

Honey-Pecan Chicken Thighs

Chicken thighs are as versatile and convenient as chicken breasts but lower in price. If you can't find boneless thighs at the store, ask the butcher to remove the bones.

PREP: 20 MIN., COOK: 40 MIN., OTHER: 2 HR.

make
ahead

½ teaspoon salt
½ teaspoon ground black pepper
½ teaspoon ground red pepper
½ teaspoon dried thyme
8 skinned and boned chicken thighs
¾ cup honey, divided
¾ cup Dijon mustard, divided
2 garlic cloves, minced
1 cup finely chopped pecans
½ teaspoon curry powder
Garnish: flat-leaf parsley sprigs

1. Combine first 4 ingredients; sprinkle evenly over chicken in a shallow dish. Stir together ½ cup honey, ½ cup mustard, and garlic; pour over chicken. Cover and chill 2 to 8 hours.
2. Remove chicken from marinade; discard marinade.
3. Dredge chicken in pecans; place on a lightly greased rack in an aluminum foil-lined broiler pan.
4. Bake at 375° for 40 minutes or until chicken is done.
5. Stir together remaining honey, remaining mustard, and ½ teaspoon curry powder; serve sauce with chicken. Garnish, if desired. **Makes** 4 servings.

Simple Fried Chicken

Simple Fried Chicken

Chilling Simple Fried Chicken before frying adds crispiness to the coating.

PREP: 10 MIN., COOK: 45 MIN., OTHER: 1 HR.

3 cups all-purpose flour
2 teaspoons paprika
1½ teaspoons salt
3 large eggs
⅓ cup milk
2 tablespoons lemon juice
1 (4½-pound) whole chicken, cut up
Vegetable oil

1. Stir together flour, paprika, and salt in a shallow dish. Whisk together eggs, milk, and lemon juice in a bowl. Dredge chicken in flour mixture; dip in egg mixture. Chill 1 hour.

2. Pour oil to a depth of 2 inches into a 13- x 9-inch electric skillet; heat to 350°. Fry chicken 10 minutes on each side or until golden brown. Reduce heat to 300°; cover and cook 20 to 25 minutes or until done. Drain on paper towels. **Makes** 8 to 10 servings.

Crispy Oven-Fried Chicken

Less messy than the pan-fried version, this recipe gets extra flavor from Creole and Italian seasoning.

PREP: 20 MIN., COOK: 45 MIN., OTHER: 8 HR.

1 quart water
1 teaspoon salt
1 (3½-pound) package chicken pieces
½ cup nonfat buttermilk
3 cups crushed cornflakes cereal
2 to 3 teaspoons Creole seasoning
2 teaspoons dried Italian seasoning
½ teaspoon garlic powder
⅛ teaspoon freshly ground black pepper
⅛ teaspoon ground red pepper (optional)

1. Stir together 1 quart water and 1 teaspoon salt in a large bowl; add chicken. Cover and chill 8 hours.
2. Drain chicken; rinse with cold water, and pat dry. Place chicken in a shallow dish; pour buttermilk over chicken, turning to coat.
3. Combine crushed cereal, next 4 ingredients, and, if desired, ground red pepper in a large zip-top plastic freezer bag. Add chicken to bag, 2 pieces at a time; seal and shake to coat. Place chicken on a lightly greased 15- x 10-inch jelly-roll pan. Repeat with remaining chicken and cereal mixture.
4. Bake on lowest oven rack at 400° for 45 minutes or until done. (Do not turn chicken.) **Makes** 4 to 6 servings.

Garlic Fried Chicken Breasts

A quick soak in a salty milk mixture makes this chicken extra moist and flavorful. Stir up the breading and heat the oil while it soaks.

30 minutes or less
PREP: 10 MIN., COOK: 20 MIN.

4 small bone-in chicken breasts
1 tablespoon salt
1 teaspoon pepper
2 large eggs
1 cup milk
2 cups all-purpose flour
1 teaspoon garlic powder
1 teaspoon paprika
Vegetable oil

1. Sprinkle chicken with salt and pepper, and place in a shallow bowl. Whisk together eggs and milk; pour over chicken, turning pieces to coat. Let stand 5 minutes.
2. Combine flour, garlic powder, and paprika in a zip-top freezer bag. Drop 1 chicken breast at a time into bag; seal bag, and shake to coat.
3. Pour oil to a depth of 2 inches in a large, heavy skillet. Heat oil to 360°. Add chicken, and cook, uncovered, 20 minutes or until done, turning as needed. Drain. **Makes** 4 servings.

Pecan Chicken

Using just 3 ingredients to flavor this chicken makes a quick main dish. Pounding chicken breasts shortens the cooking time.

30 minutes or less
PREP: 12 MIN., COOK: 18 MIN.

4 skinned and boned chicken breasts
2 tablespoons honey
2 tablespoons Dijon mustard (we used Grey Poupon)
2 tablespoons finely chopped pecans

1. Place chicken between 2 sheets of heavy-duty plastic wrap, and flatten to ¼-inch thickness using a meat mallet or rolling pin.
2. Stir together honey and mustard; spread on both sides of chicken, and dredge in pecans. Arrange in a lightly greased 8-inch square baking dish.
3. Bake at 350° for 15 to 18 minutes or until done. **Makes** 4 servings.

Santa Fe Chicken and Dressing

Santa Fe Chicken and Dressing

PREP: 15 MIN., COOK: 40 MIN.

4 cups cubed country-style stuffing
2 cups chopped cooked chicken
1 (15½-ounce) can golden hominy, drained
1 (4.5-ounce) can chopped green chiles, drained
½ cup chopped red bell pepper
½ cup minced fresh cilantro
1 (10¾-ounce) can cream of mushroom soup
1 (8¾-ounce) can cream-style corn
1 cup sour cream
2 teaspoons ground cumin
1 cup (4 ounces) shredded Monterey Jack cheese
Tortilla chips (optional)
Salsa (optional)

1. Combine first 6 ingredients in a large bowl; add soup and next 3 ingredients, stirring well. Spread in a lightly greased 2-quart shallow baking dish.
2. Bake, covered, at 350° for 35 minutes or until thoroughly heated. Uncover and sprinkle evenly with cheese; bake 5 more minutes or until cheese melts. Serve with tortilla chips and salsa, if desired. **Makes** 4 to 6 servings.

King Ranch Chicken Casserole

Rediscovering the King Ranch Casserole brings back fond childhood memories. We've published several versions of this family favorite, and this one's the quickest yet. No sautéing is needed; just stir together the ingredients and pop in the oven.

PREP: 13 MIN., COOK: 32 MIN.

1 (10-ounce) package frozen
    seasoning blend
2 cups chopped cooked chicken
1 (10¾-ounce) can cream of chicken soup
1 (10¾-ounce) can cream of mushroom
    soup
1 (10-ounce) can diced tomatoes and green
    chiles
1 teaspoon chili powder
½ teaspoon garlic salt
12 (6-inch) corn tortillas
2 cups (8 ounces) shredded Cheddar cheese,
    divided

1. Stir together first 7 ingredients.
2. Tear tortillas into 1-inch pieces; layer one-third of tortilla pieces in a lightly greased 13- x 9-inch baking dish. Top with one-third of chicken mixture and ⅔ cup of cheese. Repeat layers twice.
3. Bake at 350° for 32 minutes or until casserole is thoroughly heated and bubbly. **Makes** 6 servings.
Note: Freeze casserole up to 1 month, if desired. Thaw in refrigerator overnight, and bake as directed.

Quick Chicken and Dumplings

30 minutes or less
PREP: 10 MIN., COOK: 20 MIN.

4 cups water
3 cups chopped cooked chicken
2 (10¾-ounce) cans cream of chicken soup
2 teaspoons chicken bouillon granules
1 teaspoon seasoned pepper
1 (7.5-ounce) can refrigerated buttermilk biscuits

1. Bring first 5 ingredients to a boil in a Dutch oven over medium-high heat, stirring often.
2. Separate biscuits in half, forming 2 rounds; cut each round in half. Drop biscuit pieces, 1 at a time, into boiling mixture; stir gently. Cover, reduce heat to low, and simmer, stirring occasionally, 15 to 20 minutes. (Recipe can be frozen up to 1 month, if desired.) **Makes** 4 to 6 servings.

Light Chicken and Dumplings: Use reduced-sodium, reduced-fat cream of chicken soup; reduced-fat biscuits; and chopped cooked chicken breasts.

Barbecue-Battered Chicken Strips

PREP: 20 MIN., COOK: 7 MIN. PER BATCH

3 pounds skinned and boned chicken breasts
3 cups all-purpose flour
1½ teaspoons seasoned salt
1½ teaspoons pepper
¾ teaspoons garlic powder
2 cups buttermilk
¾ cup honey-smoked barbecue sauce
2 large eggs
Vegetable oil
Honey-smoked barbecue sauce

1. Cut each chicken breast into 3- x 1-inch strips, and set aside.
2. Combine flour and next 3 ingredients in a large shallow dish.
3. Whisk together buttermilk, ¾ cup barbecue sauce, and eggs in a bowl. Dredge chicken pieces in flour mixture; dip in buttermilk mixture, and dredge again in flour mixture. (If flour gets gummy, just press into chicken pieces.)
4. Pour oil to a depth of 1½ inches in a deep skillet or Dutch oven; heat to 360°. Fry chicken, in batches, 5 to 7 minutes or until golden. Drain on wire racks over paper towels. Serve with extra sauce. **Makes** 6 to 8 servings or 16 appetizer servings.

Barbecue-Battered Pork Chops: Substitute 3 pounds boneless breakfast pork chops for chicken, and proceed as directed. Serve in biscuits.

Warm Barbecue Salad

Leftover barbecue or purchased 'cue from your favorite joint isn't just for buns anymore, and neither is the sauce.

PREP: 10 MIN., COOK: 35 MIN.

3 cups shredded cooked chicken (see note)
Barbecue Dressing, divided
1 cup frozen whole kernel corn, thawed
2 bacon slices, cooked and crumbled
6 cups torn green leaf lettuce (about 1 head)
4 plum tomatoes, chopped
⅓ large red onion, sliced
⅔ cup shredded mozzarella cheese

1. Stir together chicken and 1 cup Barbecue Dressing in a lightly greased 9-inch square pan.
2. Bake, covered, at 350° for 35 minutes or until warm.
3. Toss together corn and next 4 ingredients. Top with warm chicken mixture, and sprinkle with cheese. Serve immediately with remaining dressing. **Makes** 6 servings.
Note: 3 cups shredded barbecued pork may be substituted.

Barbecue Dressing:
PREP: 10 MIN., COOK: 20 MIN.

1 (18-ounce) bottle barbecue sauce
⅓ cup firmly packed light brown sugar
½ cup honey
⅓ cup ketchup
1 tablespoon butter or margarine
1 tablespoon Worcestershire sauce
½ teaspoon seasoned salt
1 teaspoon lemon pepper

1. Stir together all ingredients in a saucepan; bring to a boil. Reduce heat; simmer, stirring occasionally, 10 minutes. Store in refrigerator up to 3 months, if desired. **Makes** 3 cups.

Warm Barbecue Salad

Chicken-Sausage Gumbo

Gumbo is one of the crowning glories of Louisiana cuisine. This flavorful stew is named for the West African word for okra, although not all gumbos actually contain okra.

PREP: 20 MIN., COOK: 25 MIN.

½ pound smoked sausage, cut into ½-inch-thick
    slices (we used Conecuh Original Smoked
    Sausage)
1 to 3 tablespoons vegetable oil
5 tablespoons all-purpose flour
1 cup coarsely chopped onion
1 cup chopped celery
2 large garlic cloves, pressed
1 medium-size green bell pepper, chopped
2 cups chicken broth
1 (28-ounce) can diced tomatoes
1 to 2 teaspoons Creole seasoning
4 cups chopped cooked chicken
Hot cooked rice

1. Cook sausage over high heat in a Dutch oven, stirring often, 5 minutes. Remove sausage with a slotted spoon. Drain on paper towels.
2. Add enough oil to drippings in Dutch oven to equal 3 tablespoons, and whisk in flour; cook over medium-high heat, whisking constantly, 5 minutes. Add onion, celery, garlic, and green pepper; cook, stirring often, 5 minutes. Stir in broth, diced tomatoes, and Creole seasoning. Bring to a boil; cover, reduce heat, and simmer 5 minutes. Add sausage and chicken, and simmer, covered, 5 minutes. Serve over rice. **Makes** 4 to 6 servings.

Crispy Fried Catfish

Frying fillet strips instead of whole catfish greatly speeds up the process. Three minutes, and these golden nuggets are ready to eat. Serve with Colorful Coleslaw (page 35).

20 minutes or less
PREP: 10 MIN., COOK: 3 MIN. PER BATCH

1 cup all-purpose flour
1 tablespoon salt
2 teaspoons ground black pepper
2 teaspoons ground red pepper
2½ cups cornmeal mix
1 tablespoon garlic powder
2 tablespoons dried thyme
10 (6- to 8-ounce) farm-raised catfish fillets, cut
    into strips
1 cup buttermilk
Peanut oil

1. Combine first 4 ingredients in a shallow dish.
2. Combine cornmeal mix, garlic powder, and thyme in a zip-top freezer bag.
3. Dredge catfish strips in flour mixture, and dip in buttermilk, allowing excess to drip off. Place catfish strips in cornmeal mixture; seal bag, and shake gently to coat.
4. Pour oil to a depth of 1½ inches into a large cast-iron or other heavy skillet; heat to 360°. Fry catfish strips, in batches, 3 minutes or until golden. Drain on paper towels, and serve immediately. **Makes** 10 servings.

frying success

1. Select an oil with a high smoke point, such as peanut oil.
2. Use a deep-fat thermometer to maintain an accurate temperature. When the oil is hot enough, the cooking process seals the outside of the fish or meat to lock in flavor and moisture.
3. Fry in batches to prevent the oil temperature from dropping too low.

Shrimp Jambalaya

Shrimp Jambalaya

PREP: 25 MIN., COOK: 50 MIN.

1 pound unpeeled, medium-size fresh shrimp
3 tablespoons vegetable oil
3 tablespoons all-purpose flour
½ pound cooked ham, diced
1 medium onion, chopped
1 cup chopped celery
1 cup chopped green bell pepper
4 garlic cloves, minced
2 (14½-ounce) cans chicken broth
1 (14½-ounce) can Cajun-style stewed tomatoes,
    undrained and chopped
¼ cup chopped fresh parsley
1½ teaspoons Creole seasoning
½ teaspoon ground red pepper
2 cups uncooked long-grain rice

1. Peel shrimp, and devein, if desired. Set aside.
2. Stir together vegetable oil and flour in a Dutch oven; cook over medium-high heat, stirring constantly, 12 to 15 minutes or until roux is caramel-colored.
3. Add ham, onion, celery, bell pepper, and garlic cloves, and sauté 7 minutes or until vegetables are tender. Stir in chicken broth, stewed tomatoes, parsley, Creole seasoning, and red pepper; bring to a boil. Stir in rice.
4. Cover, reduce heat, and simmer 20 minutes or until rice is tender.
5. Stir in shrimp; cover and cook 5 more minutes or just until shrimp turn pink. **Makes** 6 servings.

Pineapple-Glazed Ham

Pineapple-Glazed Ham

Even though it technically doesn't require additional cooking, reheating a fully cooked ham maximizes the flavor.

PREP: 30 MIN., COOK: 3 HR., OTHER: 15 MIN.

make ahead

4 cups pineapple juice
1 (1-inch) piece fresh ginger, peeled and sliced
4 garlic cloves, pressed
1 (7- to 9-pound) bone-in smoked fully cooked ham
12 to 16 whole cloves
¼ cup Dijon mustard
1 cup firmly packed brown sugar
1 (20-ounce) can pineapple slices in juice, drained (optional)
10 maraschino cherries, halved (optional)

1. Stir together first 3 ingredients in a saucepan; bring to a boil. Reduce heat to medium low, and simmer 25 minutes or until liquid is reduced by half. Pour mixture through a wire-mesh strainer into a bowl, discarding solids. Set pineapple juice mixture aside.

2. Remove skin and excess fat from ham. Make ¼-inch-deep cuts in a diamond design, and insert cloves at 1-inch intervals. Place ham in an aluminum foil-lined roasting pan. Spread mustard evenly over ham.
3. Pat brown sugar on top of mustard. Pour pineapple juice mixture into pan.
4. Arrange pineapple slices and maraschino cherries evenly over ham, if desired; secure with wooden picks.
5. Bake at 325° for 1 hour. Remove ham from oven; shield with aluminum foil to prevent excess browning, and bake an additional 1 to 1½ hours or until a meat thermometer inserted into thickest portion registers 140°, basting every 30 minutes with pan juices. Let stand 15 minutes before slicing.
6. Remove from pan, reserving drippings. Cover ham, and chill, if desired. Chill reserved drippings.
7. Remove and discard fat from drippings. Bring drippings to a boil in a small saucepan. Serve warm with ham. **Makes** 14 to 16 servings.

Chicken-fried Steak 'n' Country Gravy

This all-time classic is quicker than you might think! Be sure to serve this Southern steak with mashed potatoes for soaking up the gravy.

30 minutes or less
PREP: 14 MIN., COOK: 16 MIN.

2¼ teaspoons salt, divided
1¾ teaspoons ground black pepper, divided
4 (4-ounce) cubed steaks
1 sleeve saltine crackers (about 38 crackers), crushed
1¼ cups all-purpose flour, divided
½ teaspoon ground red pepper
½ teaspoon baking powder
4¾ cups milk, divided
2 large eggs
1 cup peanut oil
Garnish: chopped fresh parsley

1. Sprinkle ¼ teaspoon salt and ¼ teaspoon black pepper evenly over steaks. Set aside.

2. Combine cracker crumbs, 1 cup flour, 1 teaspoon salt, ½ teaspoon black pepper, red pepper, and baking powder.

3. Whisk together ¾ cup milk and eggs. Dredge steaks in cracker mixture; dip in milk mixture, and dredge again in cracker mixture.

4. Pour oil into a 12-inch skillet; heat to 360°. (Do not use a nonstick skillet.) Fry steaks 2 to 3 minutes. Turn and fry 2 to 3 minutes or until golden. Remove steaks to a wire rack in a jellyroll pan. Keep steaks warm in a 225° oven. Carefully drain hot oil, reserving cooked bits and 1 tablespoon drippings in skillet.

5. Whisk together remaining ¼ cup flour, 1 teaspoon salt, 1 teaspoon black pepper, and 4 cups milk. Add to reserved drippings in skillet, and cook, whisking constantly, over medium-high heat 10 minutes or until gravy is thickened. Serve over warm steaks. Garnish, if desired. **Makes** 4 servings.

Chicken-fried Steak 'n'
Country Gravy

Hot Tomato Grits

Hot Tomato Grits

Everything cooks in the same saucepan, so there's minimal cleanup with this cheesy main dish or side dish.

PREP: 10 MIN., COOK: 25 MIN.

2 bacon slices, chopped
2 (14-ounce) cans chicken broth
½ teaspoon salt
1 cup uncooked quick-cooking grits
2 large tomatoes, peeled and chopped
2 tablespoons canned chopped green chiles
1 cup (4 ounces) shredded Cheddar cheese
Garnishes: chopped tomato, cooked and crumbled bacon, shredded Cheddar cheese

1. Cook bacon in a heavy saucepan until crisp, reserving bacon and drippings in pan. Gradually add broth and salt; bring to a boil.
2. Stir in grits, tomato, and chiles; return to a boil, stirring often. Reduce heat, and simmer, stirring often, 15 minutes.
3. Stir in 1 cup cheese. Garnish, if desired. **Makes** 6 servings.

Quick Double-Cheese Grits

Quick-cooking grits make this cheesy dish a 15-minute marvel. Grits can be chilled and reheated. When reheating, whisk a tablespoon or two of warm water into grits over medium heat, adding more water as necessary.

20 minutes or less
PREP: 10 MIN., COOK: 5 MIN.

make ahead

6 cups water
½ teaspoon salt
1½ cups uncooked quick-cooking grits
1 cup (4 ounces) shredded extra-sharp Cheddar cheese
1 cup (4 ounces) shredded Monterey Jack cheese
2 tablespoons butter or margarine
½ teaspoon pepper

1. Bring 6 cups water and salt to a boil in a large saucepan. Gradually stir in grits. Cook 4 to 5 minutes, stirring often, until thickened. Remove from heat. Add shredded cheeses, butter, and pepper, stirring until blended. Serve immediately. **Makes** 8 servings.

Creamy Grits

Cream cheese and half-and-half put the "cream" in this Southern favorite. Quick-cooking grits have the germ removed, which gives them a longer shelf life than regular. They're a great pantry staple.

20 minutes or less
PREP: 10 MIN., COOK: 10 MIN.

2 cups half-and-half or whipping cream
¼ teaspoon salt
⅛ teaspoon garlic powder
⅛ teaspoon pepper
½ cup uncooked quick-cooking grits
2 ounces cream cheese, cubed
¾ cup (3 ounces) shredded sharp Cheddar cheese
¼ teaspoon hot sauce

1. Bring first 4 ingredients to a boil in a Dutch oven; gradually stir in grits. Return to a boil; cover, reduce heat, and simmer, stirring occasionally, 5 to 7 minutes or until thickened.
2. Add cheeses and hot sauce, stirring until cheeses melt. Serve immediately. **Makes** 4 servings.

Grits and Greens

Grits and Greens

This Southern classic can actually trace its roots to the Native Americans who first threw maize and greens together. The inspired match has been inseparable ever since.

PREP: 5 MIN., COOK: 35 MIN.

1 (16-ounce) package fresh collard greens
4 cups chicken broth, divided
1 cup whipping cream
1 cup uncooked stone-ground or regular grits
¼ to ½ cup milk
¼ cup butter
1½ cups freshly grated Parmesan cheese
¼ teaspoon freshly ground pepper
2 cups cubed cooked ham

1. Combine collard greens and 1 cup chicken broth in a large skillet; bring to a boil. Cover, reduce heat, and simmer 5 minutes or until tender. Drain collard greens, and plunge into ice water to stop the cooking process. Drain well on paper towels; set aside.
2. Bring whipping cream and remaining 3 cups chicken broth to a boil in a large saucepan; gradually stir in grits. Return to a boil over medium heat; cover, reduce heat, and simmer, stirring often, 25 to 30 minutes. Gradually add milk, as necessary, for desired consistency.
3. Add butter, cheese, and pepper to grits, stirring until butter and cheese melt. Stir in greens and ham. Cook, stirring constantly, until thoroughly heated. **Makes** 6 servings.

Fried Green Tomatoes

30 minutes or less
PREP: 7 MIN., COOK: 18 MIN.

2 medium-size green tomatoes
1 tablespoon Dijon mustard
1 teaspoon sugar
½ teaspoon salt
¼ teaspoon paprika
⅛ teaspoon ground red pepper
1½ teaspoons Worcestershire sauce
½ cup yellow cornmeal
¼ cup hot bacon drippings

1. Cut green tomatoes into ¼-inch-thick slices; chill.
2. Combine 1 tablespoon Dijon mustard and next 5 ingredients; spread on both sides of tomato slices. Coat tomatoes with cornmeal.
3. Fry tomato slices, in batches, in hot drippings in a large skillet over medium heat 3 minutes on each side or until browned. Drain on paper towels. **Makes** 4 servings.

"Fried" Green Tomato BLTs

Oven-frying speeds up the cooking process and minimizes the cleanup compared to the traditional frying procedure.

20 minutes or less
PREP: 10 MIN., COOK: 6 MIN.

1 medium-size green tomato, cut into ¼-inch-thick
    slices
⅛ teaspoon hot sauce (optional)
1 egg white, lightly beaten
1½ tablespoons self-rising cornmeal
2 green leaf lettuce leaves
2 (1-ounce) slices mozzarella cheese
4 bacon slices, cooked and halved
4 (1-ounce) slices white sandwich bread, toasted

1. Sprinkle tomato slices with hot sauce, if desired; dip in egg white, and dredge in cornmeal.
2. Place slices in a single layer on a large baking sheet coated with cooking spray. Lightly coat slices with cooking spray. Broil 3 inches from heat 3 minutes on each side or until tender and golden.
3. Layer lettuce, cheese, bacon, and tomato slices on 2 slices of toast. Top with remaining 2 slices of toast. Serve immediately. **Makes** 2 servings.

Savory Stuffed Tomatoes

Use a small spoon to scoop out the pulp of these tomatoes. If your tomatoes are too rounded to stand upright on the jellyroll pan, place them in a muffin tin instead—the cups will cradle the tomatoes.

10 minutes or less
PREP: 6 MIN., COOK: 4 MIN.

1 (1.5-ounce) slice whole grain bread
4 medium tomatoes
¼ teaspoon salt
¼ teaspoon freshly ground black pepper
2 tablespoons chopped fresh basil
2 tablespoons chopped pitted kalamata olives
1 garlic clove, minced
2 teaspoons olive oil

1. Place bread in a food processor; pulse 10 times or until coarse crumbs measure ½ cup, and set aside.
2. Cut top off each tomato. Scoop out pulp, leaving shells intact. Discard tops and pulp.
3. Place tomatoes on a jellyroll pan lined with foil. Sprinkle tomatoes with salt and pepper.
4. Combine breadcrumbs, basil, olives, and garlic. Spoon crumb mixture evenly into tomato shells. Drizzle each with ½ teaspoon oil.
5. Broil 3 to 4 minutes or until thoroughly heated. **Makes** 4 servings.

Basil Okra 'n' Tomatoes

Basil adds an aromatic twist to this traditional side dish.

30 minutes or less
PREP: 5 MIN., COOK: 20 MIN.

4 bacon slices
1 (16-ounce) package frozen sliced okra, thawed
2 tablespoons all-purpose flour
1 large onion, chopped
2 tomatoes, chopped
2 tablespoons minced fresh basil
½ teaspoon salt
½ teaspoon pepper

1. Cook bacon in a large skillet over medium heat until crisp; remove bacon, and drain on paper towels, reserving 2 tablespoons drippings in skillet. Crumble bacon, and set aside.
2. Dredge okra in flour.
3. Sauté onion in reserved drippings until tender. Add okra; cook, stirring occasionally, 5 minutes or until lightly browned. Stir in tomato and basil; cook over low heat, stirring occasionally, 6 to 8 minutes. Stir in salt and pepper. Sprinkle with bacon. **Makes** 4 servings.

Okra Fritters

These golden puffs are a refreshing way to serve this Southern favorite.

30 minutes or less
PREP: 5 MIN., COOK: 25 MIN.

¾ cup yellow cornmeal
¾ cup all-purpose flour
4 large eggs
½ cup salsa
1 tablespoon seasoned salt
2 cups chopped fresh okra (about 1 pound)
1 large tomato, seeded and diced
½ green bell pepper, chopped
1 small onion, chopped
6 green onions, chopped
½ teaspoon salt
¼ teaspoon ground red pepper (optional)
Vegetable oil

1. Stir together first 5 ingredients in a large bowl; stir in okra, next 5 ingredients, and if desired, ground red pepper.
2. Pour oil to depth of 2 inches into a Dutch oven; heat to 375°. Drop batter by tablespoonfuls into hot oil, and fry, in batches, until golden, turning once. Drain on paper towels, and serve immediately. **Makes** 3 dozen.

all about okra

Slender, green, fuzzy, fingerlike okra pods contain numerous small, edible seeds. Brought to the South by African slaves, okra remains popular in Southern cuisine. It's an ingredient in many dishes, such as gumbo, and it can also be fried, steamed, or grilled as a side dish. Okra has a mild flavor, and when cooked in liquid, it gives off a viscous substance that thickens the liquid. Okra is at its peak during summer months, but it's also available frozen and canned. Store fresh okra in a plastic bag in the refrigerator up to 3 days.

Crunchy Fried Okra

Pick small, tender okra pods, and skip the traditional slicing step to speed up this time-honored favorite.

20 minutes or less

PREP: 6 MIN., COOK: 3 MIN. PER BATCH

1½ cups buttermilk
1 large egg
1½ sleeves saltine crackers, finely crushed
1½ cups all-purpose flour
1 teaspoon salt
1 pound small fresh okra
Peanut oil

1. Stir together buttermilk and egg. Combine cracker crumbs, flour, and salt. Dip okra pieces in buttermilk mixture; dredge in cracker crumb mixture.

2. Pour oil to a depth of 2 inches into a Dutch oven; heat to 375°. Fry okra, in batches, 3 minutes or until golden, turning once. Drain on paper towels. **Makes 4 to 6 servings.**

Crunchy Fried Okra

Okra Creole

This spicy okra concoction will have you coming back for more.

PREP: 15 MIN., COOK: 25 MIN.

3 bacon slices
1 (16-ounce) package frozen sliced okra
1 (14.5-ounce) can diced tomatoes
1 cup frozen onion seasoning blend
1 cup frozen whole kernel corn
½ cup water
1 teaspoon Creole seasoning
¼ teaspoon pepper
Hot cooked rice (optional)

1. Cook bacon in a Dutch oven until crisp; remove bacon, and drain on paper towels, reserving drippings in Dutch oven. Crumble bacon.
2. Cook okra and next 6 ingredients in hot drippings in Dutch oven over medium-high heat, stirring occasionally, 5 minutes. Reduce heat to low, cover, and simmer 15 minutes or until vegetables are tender. Top with crumbled bacon. Serve over rice, if desired. **Makes** 4 servings.

Saucy Green Beans

Purchase one of the flavored tomato sauces for a change of pace.

30 minutes or less
PREP: 10 MIN., COOK: 15 MIN.

1 pound fresh green beans, trimmed (see note)
1 small sweet onion, chopped
1 large garlic clove, minced
2 tablespoons olive oil
1 (8-ounce) can tomato sauce
1 tablespoon sugar
½ to ¾ teaspoon salt
½ teaspoon freshly ground pepper
1 tablespoon red wine vinegar

1. Cook green beans in boiling water to cover 5 to 10 minutes or to desired degree of doneness; drain and set aside.
2. Meanwhile, sauté onion and garlic in hot oil in a large skillet over medium-high heat 5 minutes or until onion is tender.
3. Add tomato sauce and sugar; cook, stirring often, 5 minutes. Add green beans, salt, pepper, and vinegar; cook 5 minutes. **Makes** 4 servings.
Note: Substitute 1 pound frozen whole green beans for fresh green beans, if desired. Cook according to package directions; drain well.

Corn Pudding

30 minutes or less
PREP: 10 MIN., COOK: 20 MIN.

2 cups milk
½ cup yellow cornmeal
1 (16-ounce) package frozen whole kernel corn, thawed
½ teaspoon salt
2 tablespoons whipping cream

1. Bring milk to a boil in a heavy saucepan; gradually add cornmeal, stirring until blended after each addition. Cook, stirring constantly, just until mixture begins to boil. Reduce heat, and cook, stirring constantly, until thickened.
2. Add corn, stirring until mixture is consistency of whipped potatoes. Stir in salt and whipping cream. **Makes** 6 servings.

Bacon 'n' Herb Butterbeans

Fry the bacon, and stir up the other seasonings while the butterbeans simmer;
you'll be able to toss everything together in a jiffy.

PREP: 8 MIN., COOK: 34 MIN.

1 (16-ounce) package frozen butterbeans
4 bacon slices
4 green onions, sliced
1 large garlic clove, minced
½ cup chopped fresh parsley
¾ teaspoon seasoned salt

1. Cook butterbeans according to package directions; set aside.

2. Cook bacon in a large skillet until crisp; remove bacon, and drain on paper towels, reserving drippings in skillet. Crumble bacon, and set aside.

3. Sauté green onions and garlic in hot drippings 2 minutes or until tender. Stir in butterbeans, parsley, and seasoned salt; cook 1 minute or until thoroughly heated. Sprinkle with bacon. **Makes** 4 servings.

Bacon 'n' Herb
Butterbeans

Quick Black-Eyed Peas 'n' Ham

Quick Black-Eyed Peas 'n' Ham

No Southerner is satisfied for long without black-eyed peas. Get your fill with this quick hoppin' John-style recipe.

30 minutes or less

PREP: 5 MIN., COOK: 20 MIN.

1 medium onion, chopped
2 tablespoons vegetable oil
2 (15-ounce) cans black-eyed peas, rinsed and
   drained
¾ cup chopped cooked ham
¼ cup teriyaki marinade and sauce (we used
   Kikkoman)
1 teaspoon salt-free Creole seasoning
1¼ cups water
Hot cooked rice
Toppings: chopped tomato, sliced green onions

1. Sauté chopped onion in hot oil in a medium sauce-pan over medium-high heat 3 minutes. Add peas and next 4 ingredients. Bring to a boil; reduce heat, and simmer, stirring occasionally, 15 minutes. Serve over rice with desired toppings. **Makes** 4 servings.
Note: When you begin cooking, put some water on to boil for boil-in-bag rice—it'll be ready when the peas are.

Black-Eyed Pea Cakes

Canned black-eyed peas and packaged hush puppy mix make this recipe a snap to prepare.

PREP: 20 MIN., COOK: 3 MIN. PER BATCH, OTHER: 1 HR.

1 small onion, chopped
1 tablespoon olive oil
2 (15.5-ounce) cans black-eyed peas, rinsed, drained, and divided
1 (8-ounce) container chive-and-onion cream cheese, softened
1 large egg
½ teaspoon salt
1 teaspoon hot sauce
1 (8-ounce) package hush puppy mix with onion
Olive oil
Toppings: sour cream, green tomato relish

1. Sauté onion in 1 tablespoon hot oil in a large skillet over medium-high heat until tender.
2. Process onion, 1 can of peas, and next 4 ingredients in a blender or food processor until mixture is smooth, stopping to scrape down sides. Stir in hush puppy mix, and gently fold in remaining can of peas.
3. Shape mixture by 2 tablespoonfuls into 3-inch patties, and place on a wax paper-lined baking sheet. Cover and chill 1 hour.
4. Cook patties, in batches, in 3 tablespoons hot oil (adding oil as needed) in a skillet over medium heat 1½ minutes on each side or until patties are golden. Drain on paper towels, and keep warm. Serve with desired toppings. **Makes** 30 patties.

Colorful Coleslaw

Serve this cool side with Crispy Fried Catfish (page 22).

10 minutes or less
PREP: 10 MIN.

1 (10-ounce) package finely shredded cabbage
4 green onions, chopped
1 medium-size green bell pepper, chopped
1 medium tomato, seeded and chopped
3 tablespoons mayonnaise
½ teaspoon salt

1. Stir together all ingredients. Cover and chill, if desired. **Makes** 6 servings.

Jalapeño Coleslaw

You can quickly snip the jalapeño peppers in a cup using kitchen shears.

10 minutes or less
PREP: 5 MIN.

⅓ cup sour cream
⅓ cup mayonnaise
¼ cup chopped pickled jalapeño peppers
2 tablespoons red wine vinegar
2 tablespoons vegetable oil
1 garlic clove, minced
¼ teaspoon salt
⅛ teaspoon black pepper
1 (16-ounce) package shredded coleslaw mix

1. Stir together first 8 ingredients in a large bowl; add coleslaw mix, tossing to coat. Cover and chill, if desired. **Makes** 4 to 6 servings.

Blackened Tomato Salad

Blackened Tomato Salad

The juice from the tomatoes creates the fantastic marinade for this salad.

PREP: 20 MIN., COOK: 8 MIN., OTHER: 1 HR.

make ahead

4 large tomatoes
1 tablespoon olive oil
3 tablespoons sliced fresh basil
¼ cup olive oil
1½ tablespoons red wine vinegar
½ teaspoon salt
¼ teaspoon freshly ground pepper
Garnish: sliced fresh basil leaves

1. Cut tomatoes into quarters; remove and discard seeds. Pat tomatoes dry, and brush sides evenly with 1 tablespoon olive oil.
2. Cook tomato quarters in a hot cast-iron skillet over high heat 1½ to 2 minutes on each side or until blackened. Remove from skillet, and cool, reserving juice from skillet.
3. Toss tomato with reserved juice, 3 tablespoons basil, and next 4 ingredients in a large bowl. Cover and let stand, stirring occasionally, 1 hour. Garnish, if desired. **Makes** 4 servings.

Fresh Mozzarella-Tomato-Basil Salad

PREP: 10 MIN., OTHER: 4 HR.

make ahead

½ pound fresh mozzarella cheese,
    drained
4 large red tomatoes, sliced
½ teaspoon salt
3 tablespoons extra virgin olive oil
Freshly ground pepper to taste
½ cup shredded or chopped fresh basil
6 iceberg lettuce leaves (optional)

1. Slice cheese into 12 (¼-inch) slices. Alternate tomato and cheese slices on a platter; sprinkle evenly with salt.
2. Drizzle with olive oil. Cover and chill at least 4 hours. Sprinkle with freshly ground pepper to taste and basil. Serve on lettuce leaves, if desired. **Makes** 6 to 8 servings.

Creole Potato Salad

Leaving the peel on the potatoes adds nutrients and color—and speeds up the prep time.

30 minutes or less
PREP: 18 MIN., COOK: 12 MIN.

make ahead

3 pounds red potatoes, cubed
½ cup mayonnaise
½ cup Creole mustard
1 tablespoon red wine vinegar
1¼ teaspoons garlic salt
1 teaspoon prepared horseradish
½ teaspoon dried thyme
¼ teaspoon ground red pepper
6 hard-cooked eggs, chopped
1 medium-size sweet onion, diced

1. Combine potato and water to cover in a saucepan; cook 12 minutes or until tender. Drain and cool slightly.
2. Stir together mayonnaise and next 6 ingredients in a large bowl; add potato, egg, and onion, tossing gently. Serve at room temperature or chilled. **Makes** 8 servings.

Potato Salad With Cucumbers and Tomatoes

An olive oil-basil vinaigrette adds a healthy twist to this Southern favorite.

PREP: 30 MIN., COOK: 30 MIN.

make
ahead

5 pounds potatoes
⅔ cup olive oil
½ cup red wine vinegar
1½ teaspoons salt
1 teaspoon pepper
¼ cup chopped fresh basil
1 cucumber, peeled, seeded, and chopped
2 pints grape or cherry tomatoes
1 large yellow tomato, diced
Garnish: fresh basil sprig

1. Cook potatoes in boiling salted water to cover 30 minutes or until tender; drain.
2. Cool potatoes slightly, and cut into 1-inch cubes.
3. Stir together oil and next 3 ingredients in a large bowl; stir in chopped basil.
4. Add potatoes, cucumber, and tomatoes, tossing to coat. Chill until ready to serve. Garnish, if desired. **Makes** 10 to 12 servings.

Potato Salad With Cucumbers and Tomatoes

Dilled Potato Salad

Dilled Potato Salad

There's no need to cook the peas for this salad. Just thaw them, and stir them in.

PREP: 15 MIN., COOK: 20 MIN., OTHER: 2 HR.

make ahead

2 pounds new potatoes, cut into wedges
1 (10-ounce) package frozen petite sweet green
    peas, thawed and drained
½ cup mayonnaise
½ cup plain yogurt
1 tablespoon Dijon mustard
1 teaspoon garlic salt
¼ teaspoon pepper
1 small sweet onion, chopped
3 tablespoons minced fresh dill

1. Combine potato and water to cover in a saucepan; cook 20 minutes or until tender. Drain and add peas.
2. Meanwhile, stir together mayonnaise and next 6 ingredients in a large bowl. Add potato mixture; toss gently to coat. Cover and chill at least 2 hours. **Makes** 8 servings.

Tomato-Basil Cream Soup

Tomato-Basil Cream Soup

PREP: 40 MIN.; COOK: 1 HR., 12 MIN.

make ahead

4 shallots, diced
2 garlic cloves, pressed
1 celery rib, chopped
½ pound leeks, chopped
2 tablespoons oil
2 (14½-ounce) cans Italian-style tomatoes, undrained and chopped
1 tablespoon dried basil
2 (14-ounce) cans chicken broth
¼ teaspoon salt
1 cup whipping cream
Garnishes: lemon slices, fresh basil sprigs

1. Cook first 4 ingredients in hot oil in a Dutch oven over low heat, stirring often, 10 to 12 minutes or until tender. (Do not brown.) Add tomatoes and dried basil; cook over medium heat, stirring occasionally, 10 minutes. Add broth and salt; bring to a boil. Reduce heat, and simmer, stirring occasionally, 1 hour. Cool.
2. Process mixture, in batches, in a food processor or blender until smooth, stopping to scrape down sides.
3. Heat in Dutch oven over medium heat. Stir in 1 cup whipping cream; cook, stirring constantly, until thoroughly heated. (Do not boil.) Garnish, if desired.
Makes 6½ cups.

Spicy Tortilla Soup

30 minutes or less
PREP: 5 MIN., COOK: 23 MIN.

½ cup chopped onion
1 garlic clove, minced
1 tablespoon vegetable oil
3 medium zucchini, sliced
4 cups chicken broth
1 (16-ounce) can stewed tomatoes, undrained
1 (15-ounce) can tomato sauce
1 (11-ounce) can sweet whole kernel corn, undrained
1 teaspoon ground cumin
½ teaspoon pepper
Tortilla chips
½ cup (2 ounces) shredded Monterey Jack or
    Cheddar cheese

1. Sauté onion and garlic in hot oil in a Dutch oven over medium heat until onion is tender. Add zucchini and next 6 ingredients; bring to a boil. Cover, reduce heat, and simmer 15 minutes.
2. Spoon soup into individual bowls. Top with tortilla chips and shredded cheese. **Makes** 2¼ quarts.

White Bean Soup

Ham gives this soup a smoky flavor. Using the canned kind keeps things simple.

20 minutes or less
PREP: 5 MIN., COOK: 15 MIN.

1 (16-ounce) can navy beans, undrained
1 (15.8-ounce) can great Northern beans, undrained
1 cup water
¼ cup chopped onion
½ cup preshredded carrot
¼ cup butter or margarine, melted
1 (5-ounce) can chunk ham, drained and flaked

1. Combine beans in a large saucepan; mash slightly with a potato masher. Stir in 1 cup water, and cook over low heat until thoroughly heated.
2. Meanwhile, sauté onion and carrot in butter in a saucepan over medium-high heat until onion is tender. Add sautéed vegetables and ham to bean mixture. Cook over low heat 10 minutes, stirring occasionally. **Makes** 1 quart.

Turnip Greens Stew

Frozen seasoning blend is a mixture of diced onion, red and green bell peppers, and celery. Substitute chopped fresh vegetables, if desired.

PREP: 10 MIN., COOK: 25 MIN.

make
ahead

2 cups chopped cooked ham
1 tablespoon vegetable oil
3 cups chicken broth
2 (16-ounce) packages frozen chopped turnip greens
1 (16-ounce) package frozen seasoning blend
    (we used McKenzie's Seasoning Blend)
1 teaspoon sugar
1 teaspoon seasoned pepper

1. Sauté chopped ham in hot oil in a Dutch oven over medium-high heat 5 minutes or until lightly browned. Add chicken broth and remaining ingredients; bring mixture to a boil. Cover, reduce heat to low, and simmer, stirring occasionally, 25 minutes. Cover and freeze leftovers up to 1 month, if desired. **Makes** 6 to 8 servings.

Collard Stew: Omit turnip greens. Sauté ham as directed. Add 1 (16-ounce) package frozen chopped collard greens, chicken broth, and remaining ingredients; bring to a boil. Cover, reduce heat to low, and simmer, stirring occasionally, 15 minutes. Add 1 (16-ounce) can black-eyed peas, drained; cook 10 minutes.

Chunky Beef Chili and
Old-Fashioned Skillet
Cornbread

Chunky Beef Chili

*This chili is great to keep on hand in the freezer for when you're late getting home. Just defrost it
in the microwave while you set the table.*

PREP: 7 MIN., COOK: 37 MIN.

make
ahead

2 pounds ground round
2 large onions, chopped
1 small green bell pepper, chopped
3 garlic cloves, minced
1 (16-ounce) can pinto beans
½ cup ketchup
1 (14½-ounce) can diced tomatoes
2 (8-ounce) cans tomato sauce
2½ tablespoons chili powder
1 teaspoon black pepper

1. Cook beef and next 3 ingredients in a Dutch oven
over medium heat, stirring until meat crumbles and
is no longer pink. Drain; pat dry with paper towels.
Wipe drippings from Dutch oven. Return meat mixture
to Dutch oven. Add beans, ketchup, and remaining
ingredients. Bring to a boil, reduce heat, and simmer,
uncovered, 25 minutes. Cover and freeze leftovers up to
3 months. **Makes** 10 cups.

Old-Fashioned Skillet Cornbread

Bacon drippings add extra flavor to this crispy, down-home cornbread.

30 minutes or less
PREP: 15 MIN., COOK: 15 MIN.

3 bacon slices
2 cups buttermilk
1 large egg
1¾ cups white cornmeal
1 teaspoon baking powder
1 teaspoon baking soda
1 teaspoon salt

1. Cook bacon in a 10-inch cast-iron skillet until crisp; remove bacon, and drain on paper towels, reserving drippings in skillet. Crumble bacon, and set aside.
2. Heat skillet in a 450° oven 3 minutes or until very hot.
3. Whisk together buttermilk and egg. Add cornmeal, stirring well.
4. Stir in bacon, baking powder, baking soda, and salt. Pour batter into hot skillet.
5. Bake at 450° for 15 minutes. **Makes** 8 servings.

Broccoli Cornbread Mini-Muffins

Mini-muffin pans speed up the cook time for these cheesy cornbread bites.

30 minutes or less
PREP: 10 MIN., COOK: 20 MIN.

1 (8½-ounce) package corn muffin mix
1 (10-ounce) package frozen chopped broccoli, thawed
1 cup (4 ounces) shredded Cheddar cheese
1 small onion, chopped
2 large eggs
½ cup butter or margarine, melted

1. Combine first 4 ingredients in a large bowl; make a well in center of mixture.
2. Stir together eggs and butter, blending well; add to broccoli mixture, stirring just until dry ingredients are moistened. Spoon into lightly greased mini-muffin pans, filling three-fourths full.
3. Bake at 325° for 15 to 20 minutes or until golden. Let stand 2 minutes before removing from pans. **Makes** 2 dozen.

Jalapeño Hush Puppies

If you like more spice in your hush puppies, simply mince the jalapeño pepper without seeding it—it'll save a little time too. If you have any puppies left over, pop them in a zip-top plastic freezer bag, and freeze for up to a month. Crisp them in a 400° oven until hot.

PREP: 15 MIN., COOK: 7 MIN. PER BATCH

make
ahead

1 cup self-rising flour
1 cup self-rising white cornmeal
½ teaspoon sugar
¼ teaspoon salt
1 small onion, grated
1 small jalapeño pepper, seeded and minced
1 cup buttermilk
1 large egg
Peanut oil

1. Combine first 4 ingredients; stir in onion and jalapeño pepper.
2. Whisk together buttermilk and egg; add to flour mixture.
3. Pour oil to a depth of 3 inches into a Dutch oven; heat to 375°. Drop batter by tablespoonfuls into oil; fry, in batches, 5 to 7 minutes or until golden. Drain on paper towels. **Makes** about 2½ dozen.

Blueberry-Pecan Cobbler

Blueberry-Pecan Cobbler

The pecans in this cobbler provide a surprise middle layer.

PREP: 10 MIN., COOK: 33 MIN.

3 pints fresh or frozen blueberries
1 cup sugar
⅓ cup all-purpose flour
¼ cup water
1½ tablespoons lemon juice
1 teaspoon vanilla extract
1 (15-ounce) package refrigerated piecrusts
½ cup chopped pecans, toasted
Vanilla ice cream

1. Bring first 6 ingredients to a boil in a saucepan over medium heat, stirring until sugar melts. Reduce heat to low; cook, stirring occasionally, 10 minutes.
2. Spoon half of blueberry mixture into a lightly greased 11- x 7-inch baking dish. Roll 1 piecrust to ⅛-inch thickness on a lightly floured surface; cut dough into an 11- x 7-inch rectangle. Place dough over blueberry mixture; sprinkle with pecans.
3. Bake at 475° for 10 minutes. Spoon remaining blueberry mixture over baked crust. Roll remaining piecrust to ⅛-inch thickness; cut into 1-inch strips. Arrange in lattice design over blueberry mixture.
4. Bake at 475° for 10 minutes or until golden. Serve with vanilla ice cream. **Makes** 4 servings.

Quick Peach Cobbler

A quick-to-make biscuit topping keeps this recipe easy. Try substituting apricots, cherries, or apples for the peaches, if you'd like.

PREP: 10 MIN., COOK: 25 MIN.

1½ teaspoons cornstarch
1 tablespoon cold water
1 (8.5-ounce) can sliced peaches, undrained
½ cup buttermilk baking mix (we used Pioneer)
2 teaspoons sugar
2 tablespoons milk
1 tablespoon vegetable oil
Vanilla ice cream

1. Dissolve cornstarch in 1 tablespoon cold water in a medium saucepan; add peaches, and cook over medium heat about 5 minutes or until mixture is thickened and bubbly. Pour into a 1-quart baking dish.
2. Combine baking mix and sugar; add milk and vegetable oil, stirring to form a soft dough. Drop dough by spoonfuls on top of peach mixture. Bake at 400° for 20 minutes or until golden brown. Serve hot with ice cream. **Makes** 2 servings.

Texas Star Pecan Pie

This decadent pie is sure to be a star on your favorite recipes list. A ready-made graham cracker crust rather than a traditional pastry crust is a refreshing twist. Serve it with vanilla ice cream and caramel sauce on top.

PREP: 10 MIN., COOK: 27 MIN.

make
ahead

4 egg whites
⅛ teaspoon salt
½ teaspoon vanilla extract
½ cup granulated sugar
¼ cup firmly packed brown sugar
1 cup chopped pecans
1 (9-inch) ready-made graham cracker crust

1. Beat egg whites in a small bowl at high speed with an electric mixer until foamy; add salt and vanilla, beating until soft peaks form.
2. Gradually add granulated sugar and brown sugar, 1 tablespoon at a time, beating until stiff peaks form. Stir in chopped pecans.
3. Spoon mixture into crust. Bake at 350° for 25 to 27 minutes or until pie is done. Cool on a wire rack. **Makes** 1 (9-inch) pie.

Coconut Cream Pie

Use a refrigerated or frozen piecrust to keep this recipe quick. It'll be ready in less than 20 minutes other than the stand and chill time.

PREP: 12 MIN., COOK: 6 MIN., OTHER: 1 HR.

¾ cup sugar, divided
¼ cup cornstarch
2 cups half-and-half
4 egg yolks
3 tablespoons butter
1 cup sweetened flaked coconut
2 teaspoons vanilla extract, divided
1 baked 9-inch pastry shell
1 cup whipping cream
Garnish: toasted coconut chips

1. Combine ½ cup sugar and cornstarch in a heavy saucepan; gradually whisk in half-and-half and egg yolks. Bring to a boil over medium heat, whisking constantly; boil 1 minute. Remove from heat. Stir in butter, coconut, and 1 teaspoon vanilla.
2. Place plastic wrap directly over custard mixture; cool to room temperature. Spoon custard mixture into pastry shell, and chill 30 minutes or until set.
3. Beat whipping cream at high speed with an electric mixer until foamy; gradually add remaining ¼ cup sugar and remaining 1 teaspoon vanilla, beating until soft peaks form. Spread or pipe whipped cream over pie. Garnish, if desired. Store in refrigerator. **Makes** 1 (9-inch) pie.

Honey-Pecan Pie Fingers

PREP: 10 MIN., COOK: 35 MIN.

1¼ cups all-purpose flour
1 cup sugar, divided
½ cup butter, softened
½ cup honey
3 tablespoons all-purpose flour
¼ teaspoon salt
2 eggs, lightly beaten
2 tablespoons butter, melted
1½ teaspoons vanilla extract
1 cup chopped pecans

1. Combine 1¼ cups flour and ⅓ cup sugar in a medium bowl; cut ½ cup softened butter into flour mixture with a pastry blender until mixture is crumbly. Press flour mixture firmly and evenly into an ungreased 9-inch square pan. Bake at 375° for 10 minutes or until edges of crust are lightly browned.
2. Combine remaining ⅔ cup sugar and remaining ingredients in a medium bowl; stir well. Pour evenly over prepared crust. Bake at 375° for 20 to 25 minutes, shielding with aluminum foil the last 5 minutes, if necessary. Cool on a wire rack. Cut into 1½- x 1-inch bars. **Makes** 4½ dozen.

Pecan Squares

Find toffee bits in the baking section of your supermarket.

PREP: 10 MIN., COOK: 25 MIN.

2 cups all-purpose flour
½ cup powdered sugar
1 cup butter or margarine, cut up
1 (14-ounce) can sweetened condensed milk
1 large egg
1 teaspoon vanilla extract
1 (7.5-ounce) package toffee bits (we used Heath Bits 'O Brickle)
1 cup chopped pecans

1. Combine flour and powdered sugar in a medium bowl. Cut in butter with a pastry blender until crumbly. Press mixture evenly into a lightly greased 13- x 9-inch pan.
2. Bake at 375° for 10 minutes. Combine sweetened condensed milk and remaining ingredients; pour over prepared crust. Bake at 375° for 15 minutes or until golden. Cool and cut into squares. **Makes** 3 dozen.

New-Fashioned Banana Pudding

Who knew you could make banana pudding just like Mom used to make? Half-and-half enriches instant pudding and makes it taste homemade. Sit down, and dip your spoon into this big bowl of comfort!

PREP: 20 MIN., COOK: 20 MIN.

2 cups half-and-half
1 cup milk
1 (5.1-ounce) package vanilla instant pudding mix
1 (12-ounce) package vanilla wafers
6 small ripe bananas
4 egg whites
⅓ cup sugar
½ teaspoon vanilla extract

1. Combine first 3 ingredients in a large bowl; beat at low speed with an electric mixer until blended. Beat at medium speed 2 minutes or until mixture is smooth and thickened.

2. Layer one-fourth of wafers in a 2½-quart baking dish. Slice 2 bananas, and layer over wafers. Pour one-third of pudding over bananas. Repeat layers twice, ending with pudding. Arrange remaining wafers around edge of baking dish.

3. Beat egg whites at high speed until foamy. Add ⅓ cup sugar, 1 tablespoon at a time, beating until stiff peaks form and sugar dissolves (2 to 4 minutes). Fold in vanilla extract.

4. Spread meringue over pudding, sealing to edge of dish. Bake at 325° for 20 minutes or until golden. **Makes** 8 servings.

New-Fashioned Banana Pudding

Chicken-Vegetable
Stir-fry, page 72

one-dish DINNERS

Veggie Scramble

Serve these veggie-filled eggs with whole grain toast.

20 minutes or less
PREP: 10 MIN., COOK: 10 MIN.

½ small red bell pepper
½ small green bell pepper
¼ small sweet onion
8 large eggs, lightly beaten
½ teaspoon freshly ground black pepper
¼ teaspoon salt
½ cup (2 ounces) shredded sharp Cheddar cheese

1. Chop bell peppers and onion. Cook in a large skillet coated with cooking spray over medium-high heat 5 minutes or until vegetables are tender.
2. Whisk together eggs, black pepper, and salt. Add mixture to vegetables in skillet, and cook, without stirring, until eggs begin to set on bottom. Draw a spatula across bottom of skillet to form large curds. Sprinkle with cheese, and continue cooking until eggs are thickened but still moist. (Do not stir constantly.) Remove from heat. Serve immediately. **Makes** 4 servings.

Green Eggs and Ham

Guacamole-stuffed eggs are topped with country ham in this storybook-inspired recipe.

20 minutes or less
PREP: 15 MIN., COOK: 5 MIN.

6 ounces thinly sliced country ham
12 large hard-cooked eggs
1 ripe avocado, peeled and mashed
2 tablespoons finely chopped onion
1 garlic clove, minced
2 tablespoons mayonnaise or salad dressing
1½ to 2 tablespoons fresh lime juice
1 teaspoon hot sauce
1 small tomato, peeled, seeded, and finely chopped

1. Cook ham in a nonstick skillet over medium heat 5 minutes or until lightly browned, turning once. Drain and finely chop.
2. Cut eggs in half lengthwise, and carefully remove yolks. Mash yolks with a fork; add avocado and next 5 ingredients, stirring well. Fold in tomato, and spoon into egg whites. Top with ham. **Makes** 2 dozen.

Ham 'n' Cheddar Omelets

Omelet aficionados like to have two omelet pans. The process is simple enough to cook two at a time, and your meal can be ready in half the time.

20 minutes or less
PREP: 8 MIN., COOK: 10 MIN.

6 large eggs, lightly beaten
3 green onions, chopped
¼ teaspoon salt
¼ teaspoon pepper
2 teaspoons butter, divided
½ cup chopped cooked ham, divided
½ cup (2 ounces) shredded sharp Cheddar cheese, divided

1. Combine first 4 ingredients in a medium bowl; stir with a wire whisk until blended.
2. Place an 8-inch omelet pan or nonstick skillet over medium heat until hot. Add 1 teaspoon butter, and rotate pan to coat bottom. Pour half of egg mixture into skillet. As mixture starts to cook, gently lift edges with a spatula, and tilt pan so uncooked portion flows underneath.
3. Sprinkle ¼ cup ham and ¼ cup cheese over half of omelet. Fold omelet in half, and transfer to a serving plate. Repeat procedure with remaining butter, egg mixture, ham, and cheese. **Makes** 2 servings.

omelet secrets

- Have all filling ingredients prepared before you begin cooking the omelet.
- When cooking omelets on the stovetop, use 2 or 3 eggs per omelet; any more and the omelet is difficult to handle.
- If an omelet gets a tear, add an attractive garnish to cover it up. But if it falls apart, chop it up and serve it as scrambled eggs.

Ham-and-Broccoli Omelet

Ham-and-Broccoli Omelet

Simplify your meal preparation by purchasing diced ham in the deli section of your supermarket.

PREP: 15 MIN., COOK: 35 MIN.

2 tablespoons butter
2 cups diced cooked ham
1 medium-size sweet onion, diced
2½ cups chopped fresh broccoli
1 teaspoon salt
¾ teaspoon freshly ground pepper
12 large eggs
½ cup sour cream
¼ teaspoon baking powder
6 plum tomatoes, seeded and chopped
1 (8-ounce) block Havarti cheese with jalapeños,
    shredded (see note)
½ cup chopped fresh basil (optional)

1. Melt butter in a 12-inch ovenproof skillet; add ham, onion, and broccoli. Sauté 5 minutes. Stir in salt and pepper.
2. Beat eggs, sour cream, and baking powder at medium speed with an electric mixer 2 to 3 minutes. Pour over ham mixture.
3. Bake at 350° for 15 minutes. Remove from oven, and sprinkle with tomatoes, cheese, and, if desired, basil. Bake 15 more minutes or until set. Serve immediately.
Makes 10 to 12 servings.
Note: 1 (8-ounce) package shredded sharp Cheddar cheese may be substituted for the Havarti.

Easy Crawfish Omelet

Easy Crawfish Omelet

Serve this dish with bloody Marys and hash browns for a New Orleans-style meal. Chopped cooked shrimp makes a fine substitute for crawfish if it's easier to find in your area.

20 minutes or less
PREP: 8 MIN., COOK: 9 MIN.

1 tablespoon chopped fresh chives
1 tablespoon water
¼ teaspoon hot sauce
5 large eggs
¼ cup cooked crawfish tail meat, chopped
1 tablespoon Creole seasoning
1 tablespoon sour cream
⅓ cup sliced mushrooms
¼ cup finely diced ham (1½ ounces)
1 tablespoon olive oil
¼ cup shredded Cheddar cheese
Garnish: chopped chives

1. Whisk together first 4 ingredients; set aside.
2. Combine crawfish, Creole seasoning, and sour cream.
3. Sauté mushrooms and ham in hot oil in a 10-inch nonstick skillet for 3 minutes. Pour egg mixture into pan; let egg mixture set slightly. Carefully lift edges of omelet with a spatula, and tilt pan so uncooked portion flows underneath. Cook 3 minutes; flip omelet. Spoon crawfish mixture onto half of omelet. Carefully loosen omelet with a spatula; fold in half. Gently slide omelet onto a plate; top with cheese. Cut omelet in half. Garnish, if desired. **Makes** 2 servings.

Breakfast Burritos

Have a Southwest-style dinner with this blend of potatoes, onions, and eggs wrapped in warm flour tortillas. Instead of frying bacon, look for precooked bacon at your grocery store.

20 minutes or less
PREP: 8 MIN., COOK: 12 MIN.

1 (10-ounce) baking potato
8 bacon slices
4 green onions, sliced
3 large eggs, lightly beaten
⅓ cup milk
¼ teaspoon salt
¼ teaspoon pepper
4 (7-inch) flour tortillas
Toppings: sour cream, picante sauce

1. Prick potato with a sharp knife. Microwave at HIGH 5 minutes; let stand 5 minutes. Peel and dice potato.
2. While potato cooks, cook bacon in a large skillet until crisp; drain bacon on paper towels, reserving drippings in skillet. Crumble bacon, and set aside.
3. Sauté potato in drippings over medium-high heat 3 minutes or until potato begins to brown. Remove from skillet, using a slotted spoon; drain on paper towels. Sauté green onions in drippings 1 minute.
4. Combine eggs and next 3 ingredients; pour over green onions. Cook over medium heat 2 minutes or until set, stirring gently. Stir in bacon and potato. Remove from heat.
5. Place tortillas in a zip-top freezer bag; do not seal. Microwave at HIGH 1 minute or until warm.
6. Working with 1 tortilla at a time, spoon one-fourth of egg mixture down center of tortilla. Fold bottom third of tortilla over filling; fold opposite sides over filling, leaving top open. Repeat procedure with remaining tortillas and egg mixture. Serve with desired toppings. **Makes** 4 servings.

Breakfast Pizza

Enjoy breakfast for supper with this savory egg-topped pizza. Quickly snip fresh basil in a small cup using kitchen shears.

30 minutes or less
PREP: 8 MIN., COOK: 20 MIN.

1 (16-ounce) prebaked Italian pizza crust
1 (8-ounce) package shredded Italian cheese blend, divided
8 bacon slices, cooked and crumbled
4 plum tomatoes, sliced
½ teaspoon freshly ground pepper
2 large eggs
½ cup milk
¼ cup chopped fresh basil

1. Place pizza crust on a pizza pan or jelly-roll pan. Sprinkle half of cheese over pizza crust; top with bacon, tomato, and pepper. Whisk together eggs, milk, and basil; pour into center of pizza (it will spread to edges). Sprinkle with remaining cheese.
2. Bake at 425° for 20 minutes or until egg mixture is set. **Makes** 4 to 6 servings.

Southwest Egg Casserole

This recipe received our highest rating. You can prepare it the night before and pop it in the oven when you're ready to eat. Let it stand at room temperature 30 minutes before baking.

PREP: 15 MIN., COOK: 55 MIN.

make ahead

1 pound mild ground pork sausage
1 small onion, chopped
½ green bell pepper, chopped
2 (10-ounce) cans diced tomatoes and green chiles
8 (10-inch) flour tortillas, torn into bite-size pieces
3 cups (12 ounces) shredded colby-Jack cheese blend
6 large eggs
2 cups milk
1 teaspoon salt
½ teaspoon pepper

1. Cook sausage in a large skillet over medium-high heat, stirring until it crumbles and is no longer pink. Drain and return to skillet. Add chopped onion and bell pepper to sausage in skillet; sauté over medium-high heat 5 minutes or until vegetables are tender. Stir in 2 cans tomatoes and green chiles; reduce heat, and simmer 10 minutes.
2. Layer half each of tortilla pieces, sausage mixture, and cheese in a lightly greased 13- x 9-inch baking dish. Repeat layers.
3. Whisk together eggs, milk, salt, and pepper; pour over layers in baking dish. Cover and chill up to 8 hours, if desired.
4. Bake, lightly covered with aluminum foil, at 350° for 30 minutes or until golden and bubbly. **Makes** 6 to 8 servings.

Traditional Eggs Benedict

Traditional Eggs Benedict

20 minutes or less
PREP: 12 MIN., COOK: 8 MIN.

8 (½-ounce) Canadian bacon slices
Vegetable cooking spray
2 English muffins, split and toasted
4 large eggs, poached
Hollandaise Sauce
Garnishes: paprika and coarsely ground pepper
Fresh fruit, fresh mint sprig (optional)

1. Cook bacon in a skillet coated with cooking spray over medium heat until thoroughly heated, turning once. Drain on paper towels.
2. Place 2 bacon slices on each muffin half. Top each with a poached egg, and drizzle evenly with Hollandaise Sauce; garnish, if desired. Serve immediately with fresh fruit and mint sprig, if desired. **Makes** 2 servings.

Hollandaise Sauce:
PREP: 10 MIN., COOK: 10 MIN.

4 egg yolks
2 tablespoons fresh lemon juice
1 cup butter, melted
¼ teaspoon salt

1. Whisk yolks in top of a double boiler; gradually whisk in lemon juice. Place over hot water. (Do not boil.) Add butter, ⅓ cup at a time, whisking until smooth; whisk in salt. Cook, whisking constantly, 10 minutes or until thickened and a thermometer registers 160°. **Makes** 1½ cups.

Creamy Ham Casserole

Creamy Ham Casserole

Keep supper simple with Creamy Ham Casserole, a green salad or vegetable side dish, and crusty bread.

PREP: 25 MIN., COOK: 45 MIN.

3 cups cauliflower florets (about 1 medium
  cauliflower)
4 tablespoons butter or margarine
⅓ cup all-purpose flour
1 cup milk
1 cup (4 ounces) shredded Cheddar cheese
½ cup sour cream
2 cups cubed cooked ham
1 (3-ounce) can sliced mushrooms, drained
1 cup soft breadcrumbs
1 tablespoon cold butter or margarine

1. Cook 3 cups cauliflower florets in boiling salted water to cover 10 to 12 minutes or until tender; drain and set aside.
2. Melt 4 tablespoons butter in a medium saucepan over medium-high heat. Whisk in ⅓ cup flour until smooth. Gradually add 1 cup milk, whisking constantly, until mixture begins to thicken. Add shredded Cheddar cheese and ½ cup sour cream, stirring until cheese melts. (Do not boil.)
3. Stir cauliflower, ham, and mushrooms into cheese sauce; pour into a 2-quart baking dish. Sprinkle breadcrumbs evenly over casserole. Cut 1 tablespoon butter into pieces, and sprinkle evenly over breadcrumbs.
4. Bake at 350° for 45 minutes or until golden and bubbly. **Makes** 6 servings.

Double-Stuffed Ham-and-Broccoli Potatoes

PREP: 25 MIN.; COOK: 1 HR., 30 MIN.

6 (10-ounce) baking potatoes (see note)
2 cups chopped cooked ham
1 (10-ounce) package frozen chopped broccoli,
    thawed and drained
1 (8-ounce) container soft chive-and-onion
    cream cheese
1 teaspoon garlic salt
½ teaspoon freshly ground black pepper
½ cup (2 ounces) shredded Cheddar
    cheese

1. Pierce potatoes with a fork, and bake at 450° for 1 hour or until tender. Let potatoes cool to touch.

2. Cut potatoes in half lengthwise, and scoop out pulp, leaving 8 (¼-inch-thick) shells intact; reserve remaining 4 shells for another use, if desired.

3. Stir together potato pulp, ham, and next 4 ingredients until blended. Spoon mixture evenly into 8 potato shells. Sprinkle with ½ cup shredded Cheddar cheese. Place stuffed potatoes on a baking sheet.

4. Bake at 350° for 25 to 30 minutes or until cheese is melted. **Makes** 8 servings.

Note: 1 (22-ounce) package frozen mashed potatoes may be substituted for baking potatoes. Prepare mashed potatoes according to package directions. Stir in ham and next 4 ingredients. Spoon into a lightly greased 11- x 7-inch baking dish; sprinkle with shredded Cheddar cheese. Bake as directed.

Double-Stuffed Ham-and-Broccoli Potatoes

Chunky Ham Pot Pie

PREP: 10 MIN.; COOK: 1 HR., 5 MIN.; OTHER: 10 MIN.

2 tablespoons butter or margarine
1 cup chopped onion
1 (10-ounce) package frozen cut broccoli or florets
1 pound new potatoes, coarsely chopped
1 (10¾-ounce) can cream of potato soup
1 (8-ounce) container sour cream
1 cup (4 ounces) shredded sharp Cheddar cheese
¾ cup milk
½ teaspoon garlic powder
½ teaspoon salt
¼ teaspoon pepper
2½ cups chopped cooked ham
½ (15-ounce) package refrigerated piecrusts

1. Melt 2 tablespoons butter in a large skillet over medium heat; add chopped onion. Cook, stirring often, 10 minutes or until onion is tender and begins to brown. Set aside.
2. Cook broccoli according to package directions; drain well, and set aside.
3. Cook chopped new potatoes in boiling water to cover 10 minutes or until barely tender; drain.
4. Combine cream of potato soup and next 6 ingredients in a large bowl, stirring well. Stir in onion, broccoli, new potatoes, and chopped ham. Spoon ham mixture into a lightly greased 3½-quart casserole dish. (Cover and chill 8 hours, if desired. Let stand at room temperature 30 minutes before baking.)
5. Unroll piecrust onto a lightly floured surface. Roll pastry to extend ¾ inch beyond edges of casserole. Place pastry over ham mixture. Seal edges, and crimp. Cut slits in pastry to allow steam to escape.
6. Bake, uncovered, at 400° for 45 minutes or until crust is golden. Let stand 10 minutes before serving. **Makes** 6 to 8 servings.
Note: You can divide this pot pie into 2 (2-quart) dishes. Bake one now, and freeze one for later. You will need the whole package of piecrusts for two casseroles. Top the casserole to be frozen with crust before freezing, but do not cut slits in top until ready to bake. Let frozen casserole stand at room temperature 30 minutes before baking.

Tortellini Carbonara

This one-dish meal uses only one pan, so cleanup is easy.

20 minutes or less
PREP: 5 MIN., COOK: 12 MIN.

1 (9-ounce) package refrigerated cheese-filled tortellini
4 bacon slices
1 garlic clove, minced
⅓ cup shredded Parmesan cheese
¼ cup whipping cream
1 tablespoon minced fresh parsley
¼ teaspoon freshly ground pepper

1. Cook tortellini in a Dutch oven according to package directions; drain tortellini, and set aside.
2. Cook bacon in same pan until crisp; remove bacon, and drain on paper towels, reserving 1½ tablespoons drippings in pan. Crumble bacon.
3. Cook garlic in reserved bacon drippings 30 seconds.
4. Return tortellini to pan. Add reserved bacon, Parmesan cheese, and remaining 3 ingredients to tortellini; toss gently. Serve immediately. **Makes** 2 servings.

tortellini tidbits

- Refrigerated pasta, such as tortellini, makes a nice choice for a quick meal because it cooks up superfast.
- As it cooks, pasta needs plenty of room to roam in rapidly boiling water. Using plenty of water and stirring two or three times during cooking keeps pasta from sticking or clumping.
- Taste-test a piece of pasta for doneness near the end of cooking. Pasta's ready when it's firm but tender, chewy not soggy.

Tortellini Carbonara

Beefy Noodle Casserole

Beefy Noodle Casserole

30 minutes or less

PREP: 7 MIN., COOK: 17 MIN.

4 ounces uncooked wide egg noodles
1 pound ground chuck
1 (14-ounce) jar pasta sauce
1 (8-ounce) package cream cheese, cubed
1 cup cottage cheese
½ cup sour cream
½ cup shredded Parmesan cheese
Garnish: chopped fresh parsley

1. Cook noodles according to package directions; drain. Place noodles in a lightly greased 11- x 7-inch baking dish. Set aside.

2. Meanwhile, cook beef in a large skillet, stirring until it crumbles and is no longer pink; drain. Stir in pasta sauce; set aside.

3. Place cream cheese in a 1-quart glass bowl; microwave at HIGH 1 minute or until softened. Stir in cottage cheese and sour cream. Spread mixture over noodles. Spoon beef mixture over cream cheese mixture. Sprinkle with Parmesan cheese. Cover tightly with heavy-duty plastic wrap; fold back a small corner to allow steam to escape. Microwave at HIGH 6 to 8 minutes or until mixture is thoroughly heated, giving dish a half-turn after 4 minutes. Garnish, if desired. **Makes** 4 servings.

Corn Chip Chili Pie

20 minutes or less
PREP: 4 MIN., COOK: 13 MIN.

1 pound ground chuck
1 medium onion, chopped
1 (16-ounce) can kidney beans, drained
1 (11-ounce) can sweet whole kernel corn, drained
1 (8-ounce) can tomato sauce
1 (2¼-ounce) can sliced ripe olives, drained
1 (1.25-ounce) package chili seasoning
1 cup (4 ounces) shredded sharp Cheddar cheese
1 cup coarsely crushed corn chips

1. Combine beef and onion in a 2½-quart baking dish. Cover with wax paper. Microwave at HIGH 5 to 6 minutes or until meat is no longer pink, stirring at 2-minute intervals to crumble meat; drain.
2. Stir in beans and next 4 ingredients. Cover and microwave at HIGH 4 to 5 minutes or until thoroughly heated, giving dish a half-turn after 2 minutes. Sprinkle with cheese and corn chips.
3. Microwave at MEDIUM HIGH (70% power), uncovered, 2 minutes or until cheese melts. **Makes** 6 servings.

Weeknight Pizza Casserole

PREP: 10 MIN., COOK: 35 MIN., OTHER: 5 MIN.

1 pound ground beef
1 (3.5-ounce) package sliced pepperoni
1 (2¼-ounce) can sliced ripe olives, drained
1 medium-size green bell pepper, chopped (optional)
1 (14-ounce) jar pizza sauce
1 (8-ounce) package shredded mozzarella cheese
¾ cup all-purpose baking mix
1 cup milk
2 large eggs, lightly beaten

1. Cook ground beef in a large skillet over medium-high heat, stirring until meat crumbles and is no longer pink; drain. Stir in pepperoni, olives, and, if desired, bell pepper. Spoon into a lightly greased 8-inch square baking dish. Top with sauce and cheese.
2. Combine baking mix, milk, and eggs, stirring until smooth. Pour over cheese, spreading evenly.
3. Bake, uncovered, at 400° for 30 to 35 minutes or until golden. Let stand 5 minutes before serving.
Makes 4 servings.

Deep-Dish Taco Squares

Use hot picante sauce to pack a punch in this scrumptious Tex-Mex creation.

PREP: 7 MIN., COOK: 34 MIN., OTHER: 5 MIN.

2 cups all-purpose baking mix
½ cup water
1 pound ground chuck
1 small green bell pepper, chopped
1 (8-ounce) jar picante sauce
⅓ cup mayonnaise
1 (8-ounce) container sour cream
1 cup (4 ounces) shredded sharp Cheddar cheese
Paprika
Picante sauce (optional)

1. Combine baking mix and ½ cup water in a medium bowl, stirring with a fork until blended. Press mixture into a lightly greased 11- x 7-inch baking dish. Bake at 375° for 9 minutes.
2. While crust bakes, cook beef and bell pepper in a large skillet over medium-high heat, stirring until meat crumbles and is no longer pink; drain. Stir in jar of picante sauce; spoon over crust.
3. Stir together mayonnaise, sour cream, and cheese; spoon over meat mixture, spreading to within ½ inch of edges. Sprinkle with paprika.
4. Bake, uncovered, at 375° for 25 minutes or until thoroughly heated. Let stand 5 minutes; cut into squares. Serve taco squares with additional picante sauce, if desired. **Makes** 4 servings.

Shepherd's Pie

Shepherd's Pie

PREP: 15 MIN., COOK: 40 MIN.

1 (22-ounce) package frozen mashed potatoes (we
 tested with Ore-Ida Frozen Mashed Potatoes)
1 pound ground beef
1 onion, chopped
½ cup frozen sliced carrots, thawed
2 tablespoons all-purpose flour
2 teaspoons salt, divided
½ teaspoon pepper, divided
1 cup beef broth
1 large egg, lightly beaten
½ cup (2 ounces) shredded Cheddar cheese

1. Prepare potatoes according to package directions; set aside.
2. Meanwhile, brown beef and onion in a large skillet over medium-high heat 5 to 6 minutes, stirring until beef crumbles and is no longer pink. Drain and return to skillet; add carrot. Stir in flour, 1 teaspoon salt, and ¼ teaspoon pepper. Add broth, and cook, stirring constantly, 3 minutes or until slightly thickened. Spoon beef mixture into a lightly greased 11- x 7-inch baking dish.
3. Stir together potatoes, egg, remaining 1 teaspoon salt, and remaining ¼ teaspoon pepper. Spread evenly over beef mixture.
4. Bake at 350° for 25 minutes. Sprinkle with cheese, and bake 5 more minutes. **Makes** 6 servings.

Easy Skillet Tacos

PREP: 10 MIN., COOK: 25 MIN., OTHER: 5 MIN.

1 pound ground beef
1 small onion, chopped
1 teaspoon olive oil
1 tablespoon chili powder
1½ teaspoons ground cumin
1 teaspoon salt
1 (15-ounce) can pinto beans, rinsed and drained
1 (8-ounce) can tomato sauce
¾ cup water
½ cup salsa
1½ cups (6 ounces) shredded Cheddar cheese
1 tablespoon chopped fresh cilantro
Taco shells or flour tortillas, warmed
Toppings: shredded lettuce, diced tomatoes, salsa,
 sour cream

1. Cook ground beef in a large skillet over medium-high heat, stirring until beef crumbles and is no longer pink. Drain well. Remove ground beef; wipe skillet with a paper towel.
2. Sauté onion in hot oil in same skillet over medium-high heat. Add chili powder, cumin, salt, and ground beef. Cook, stirring occasionally, 5 to 7 minutes. Stir in beans, tomato sauce, ¾ cup water, and salsa. Mash pinto beans in skillet with fork, leaving some beans whole. Bring to a boil; reduce heat, and simmer, uncovered, 8 to 10 minutes or until liquid is reduced.
3. Top evenly with cheese and cilantro. Cover, turn off heat, and let stand 5 minutes or until cheese melts. Serve with taco shells or tortillas and desired toppings. **Makes** 4 to 6 servings.

Taco Dinner Mac and Cheese

PREP: 15 MIN., COOK: 25 MIN.

8 ounces elbow macaroni
1 pound ground beef
1 (1.25-ounce) envelope reduced-sodium taco
 seasoning mix
¾ cup water
2 tablespoons butter
2 tablespoons all-purpose flour
2 cups milk
1 (8-ounce) block sharp Cheddar cheese, shredded
Toppings: chopped tomato, chopped avocado,
 sliced green onions, sour cream, salsa

1. Prepare pasta according to package directions. Drain and keep warm.
2. Brown ground beef in a nonstick skillet over medium-high heat until it crumbles and is no longer pink. Drain.
3. Return beef to skillet; stir in taco seasoning mix and ¾ cup water. Bring mixture to a boil, and cook, stirring occasionally, 7 minutes or until most of the liquid evaporates. Remove beef mixture from heat.
4. Melt butter in a large saucepan or Dutch oven over medium-low heat; whisk in flour until smooth. Cook, whisking constantly, 2 minutes. Gradually whisk in milk, and cook, whisking constantly, 5 minutes or until thickened. Remove from heat.
5. Stir in 1½ cups Cheddar cheese until melted. Stir in cooked pasta and beef mixture. Sprinkle with remaining ½ cup cheese. Serve immediately with desired toppings. **Makes** 4 servings.

Beef-and-Lime Rice Salad

Beef-and-Lime Rice Salad

Serve this salad right away, or chill and serve cold.

PREP: 15 MIN., COOK: 35 MIN.

make
ahead

1 pound lean ground beef
1 teaspoon salt, divided
3 cups water
½ teaspoon cumin
1½ cups uncooked long-grain rice
1 teaspoon grated lime rind
1 tablespoon fresh lime juice
Toppings: salsa, shredded Cheddar cheese, sour
    cream, chopped tomatoes, chopped green
    onions, avocado slices

1. Cook beef and ½ teaspoon salt in a 3-quart sauce-pan over medium-high heat, stirring until beef crumbles and is no longer pink. Drain and pat dry with paper towels. Wipe pan clean.
2. Add 3 cups water, ½ teaspoon cumin, and remaining ½ teaspoon salt to saucepan. Bring to a boil, and add rice; cover, reduce heat, and cook 20 to 25 minutes or until water is absorbed and rice is tender. Stir in cooked beef, 1 teaspoon lime rind, and 1 tablespoon lime juice. Serve salad with desired toppings. **Makes** 4 servings.

Beef-and-Bean Chimichangas

30 minutes or less
PREP: 10 MIN., COOK: 20 MIN.

1 pound ground chuck
1 medium onion, chopped
2 garlic cloves, pressed
¼ teaspoon salt
1 (16-ounce) can refried beans
½ cup tomato sauce
1 tablespoon chili powder
¾ teaspoon ground cumin
10 (10-inch) flour tortillas, warmed
Vegetable oil
Salsa Verde
2 cups (8 ounces) shredded Monterey Jack cheese

1. Cook first 4 ingredients in a large skillet until meat is browned, stirring until it crumbles. Drain; stir in refried beans and next 3 ingredients.
2. Place ⅓ cup meat mixture just below center of each tortilla. Fold bottom edge of tortilla over meat filling; fold in left and right sides. Roll up to form a rectangle, and secure with a wooden pick.
3. Pour oil to a depth of 2 inches into a Dutch oven, and heat to 375°. Fry chimichangas, in batches, 1½ minutes on each side or until golden brown. Drain on paper towels. Remove wooden picks.
4. Arrange chimichangas on a large ovenproof platter or baking sheet; top with Salsa Verde, and sprinkle evenly with Monterey Jack cheese.
5. Broil 5½ inches from heat 1 to 2 minutes or until cheese melts. Serve immediately. **Makes** 8 to 10 servings.

Salsa Verde:
PREP: 15 MIN.

5 Anaheim chile peppers, seeded
1 large jalapeño pepper, seeded
1 large onion, diced
1 small tomato, diced
2 garlic cloves, minced
¼ cup fresh cilantro leaves
¼ cup lime juice
¼ teaspoon salt
¼ teaspoon sugar
¼ teaspoon ground cumin

1. Combine all ingredients in a bowl; cover and chill until ready to serve. **Makes** 2 cups.

Tostadas

20 minutes or less
PREP: 5 MIN., COOK: 15 MIN.

1½ pounds lean ground beef
1 small onion, chopped
1 garlic clove, pressed
½ teaspoon salt
2 teaspoons chili powder
Vegetable oil
6 (8-inch) flour tortillas
1 (15-ounce) can kidney beans, rinsed and drained
1 large tomato, chopped
½ pound iceberg lettuce, shredded
1 large avocado, peeled and chopped
2 cups (8 ounces) shredded sharp Cheddar cheese
Toppings: sour cream, salsa

1. Cook first 5 ingredients in a large skillet over medium heat, stirring until beef crumbles and is no longer pink; drain and set aside.
2. Pour oil to a depth of ¼ inch into a heavy skillet. Fry tortillas, 1 at a time, in hot oil over high heat 20 seconds on each side or until crisp and golden brown. Drain on paper towels.
3. Layer beef mixture, beans, tomato, and next 3 ingredients on warm tortillas. Serve with desired toppings. **Makes** 6 servings.

Beef Lombardi

Beef Lombardi

PREP: 10 MIN.; COOK: 1 HR., 21 MIN.

1 pound lean ground beef
1 (14½-ounce) can diced tomatoes
1 (10-ounce) can diced tomatoes and green chiles
2 teaspoons sugar
2 teaspoons salt
¼ teaspoon pepper
1 (6-ounce) can tomato paste
1 bay leaf
1 (6-ounce) package medium egg noodles
6 green onions, chopped (about ½ cup)
1 cup sour cream
1 cup (4 ounces) shredded sharp Cheddar cheese
1 cup shredded Parmesan cheese
1 cup (4 ounces) shredded mozzarella cheese
Garnish: fresh parsley sprigs

1. Cook ground beef in a large skillet over medium heat 5 to 6 minutes, stirring until it crumbles and is no longer pink. Drain. Stir in both cans of tomatoes and next 3 ingredients; cook 5 minutes. Stir in tomato paste, and add bay leaf; cook 30 minutes. Discard bay leaf.
2. Meanwhile, cook egg noodles according to package directions, and drain. Stir together cooked egg noodles, chopped green onions, and 1 cup sour cream until blended.
3. Place noodle mixture in a lightly greased 13- x 9-inch baking dish. Top with beef mixture; sprinkle evenly with cheeses.
4. Bake, covered, at 350° for 35 minutes. Uncover and bake 5 more minutes. Garnish, if desired. **Makes** 6 servings.
Note: Freeze casserole up to 1 month, if desired. Thaw in refrigerator overnight. Bake as directed.

Light Beef Lombardi: Substitute low-fat or fat-free sour cream and 2% reduced-fat Cheddar cheese. Reduce amount of cheeses on top to ½ cup each.

Easy Beef Casserole

To make ahead, prepare the recipe except for topping with the seasoned potatoes. Cover and chill. Let stand at room temperature while the oven preheats. Top with potatoes; bake.

PREP: 20 MIN., COOK: 35 MIN.

1 pound ground beef
¼ teaspoon salt
½ (16-ounce) package frozen mixed vegetables
1 (10¾-ounce) can cream of chicken soup
1 cup (4 ounces) shredded Cheddar cheese
½ (32-ounce) package frozen seasoned potatoes (we tested with Ore-Ida)

1. Cook ground beef and salt in a large skillet over medium heat, stirring until meat crumbles and is no longer pink; drain well. Spoon ground beef into a lightly greased 2½-quart shallow baking dish.
2. Layer vegetables, soup, and cheese over ground beef. Top with potatoes.
3. Bake at 400° for 30 minutes or until potatoes are golden. **Makes** 4 to 6 servings.

Skillet Beef Burgundy Stew

PREP: 20 MIN., COOK: 40 MIN.

½ cup all-purpose flour
1 teaspoon salt
½ teaspoon pepper
2 pounds boneless sirloin steak, cut into 1-inch cubes
1 medium onion, coarsely chopped
3 tablespoons vegetable oil
6 medium carrots, cut into ½-inch-thick slices
1 (10½-ounce) can beef consommé, undiluted
1 (8-ounce) package fresh mushrooms, quartered
1½ cups dry red wine
1 pound small red potatoes, peeled and quartered
1 (1-ounce) envelope dry onion soup mix
1 teaspoon dried thyme

1. Combine first 3 ingredients. Dredge steak cubes in flour mixture.
2. Sauté steak and onion in hot oil in a Dutch oven 4 to 5 minutes or until steak is browned. Add carrots and remaining ingredients; bring to a boil. Cover, reduce heat, and simmer, stirring occasionally, 30 minutes or until meat and vegetables are tender. **Makes** 6 servings.

Beef With Ginger

Beef With Ginger

Add dried crushed red pepper, if desired, for a little more heat in this dish. Chilling the beef in the freezer for 5 minutes makes it easier to cut into very thin slices.

30 minutes or less
PREP: 24 MIN., COOK: 6 MIN.

Fluffy White Rice
1 pound sirloin steak, chilled
½ teaspoon pepper
¼ teaspoon salt
½ cup fat-free reduced-sodium beef broth
2 teaspoons cornstarch
2 tablespoons grated fresh ginger
2 teaspoons vegetable oil
½ teaspoon minced garlic
2 teaspoons lite soy sauce
6 green onions, cut diagonally into 1-inch
      pieces
½ teaspoon dried crushed red pepper (optional)
Garnish: sliced green onions

1. Prepare Fluffy White Rice as directed; keep warm.
2. Cut chilled steak diagonally across the grain into very thin slices. Sprinkle with pepper and salt; set aside.
3. Stir together beef broth and cornstarch in a small bowl until smooth; set cornstarch mixture aside.
4. Sauté ginger in hot oil in a large nonstick skillet over high heat 2 minutes or until slightly golden. Add garlic, and sauté 30 seconds. Add steak; cook 2 minutes, stirring constantly. Stir in soy sauce.
5. Stir cornstarch mixture; drizzle over beef mixture. Cook, stirring constantly, 1 minute or until thickened. Add 6 green onions, and, if desired, crushed red pepper; cook 1 minute. Serve immediately over Fluffy White Rice; garnish, if desired. **Makes** 4 servings.

Fluffy White Rice:
Rinsing the rice before cooking reduces its starchiness, making for a fluffy, not sticky, product. This recipe is also used in the Chicken-and-Snow Pea Stir-fry on page 73.

PREP: 5 MIN., COOK: 25 MIN., OTHER: 10 MIN.

1 cup uncooked long-grain rice
1½ cups water
1 teaspoon vegetable oil

1. Place rice in a large bowl. Rinse with water 3 or 4 times or until water is no longer cloudy; drain.
2. Bring rice, 1½ cups water, and oil to a boil in a heavy saucepan. Cover, reduce heat, and simmer 15 minutes or until rice is tender. Remove from heat, and let stand 10 minutes. Fluff with a fork. **Makes** 4 servings.

Steak Stir-fry

PREP: 20 MIN., COOK: 12 MIN.

¾ cup beef broth
¼ cup lite soy sauce
1 tablespoon cornstarch
1¼ pounds boneless top sirloin steak
¼ cup vegetable oil
1 garlic clove, minced
1 teaspoon ground ginger
½ teaspoon salt
½ teaspoon pepper
1 large green bell pepper, cut into strips
1 large red bell pepper, cut into strips
1 large onion, thinly sliced
1 (8-ounce) can sliced water chestnuts, drained
4 green onions, cut into 1-inch pieces
Hot cooked rice

1. Stir together first 3 ingredients in a small bowl; set aside.
2. Trim excess fat from steak. Slice diagonally across grain into thin strips.
3. Pour oil around top of preheated wok or skillet, coating sides; heat at medium-high 2 minutes. Add garlic and next 3 ingredients, and stir-fry 1 minute. Add steak to wok; stir-fry 2 minutes or until no longer pink. Remove steak from wok with a slotted spoon, and drain on paper towels.
4. Add pepper strips and onion to wok; stir-fry 5 minutes or until crisp-tender. Add steak, water chestnuts, green onions, and reserved beef broth mixture; stir-fry 2 minutes or until mixture is thickened. Serve over rice. **Makes** 4 servings.

Steak Stir-fry

Beef Salad With Cilantro

PREP: 20 MIN., COOK: 12 MIN., OTHER: 10 MIN.

1 pound boneless top sirloin steak
¾ teaspoon salt
½ small red onion, sliced (about ¼ cup)
3 green onions, chopped
¼ cup chopped fresh mint leaves
¼ cup chopped fresh cilantro
1 jalapeño pepper, seeded
¼ cup fresh lime juice
2 tablespoons fish sauce
1 tablespoon olive oil
1 tablespoon brown sugar
½ teaspoon red pepper flakes
1 medium head romaine lettuce,
    chopped
¼ cup chopped peanuts

1. Sprinkle steak evenly with salt.
2. Heat a large cast-iron grill skillet over medium-high heat until hot. Grill steak 4 to 6 minutes on each side or to desired degree of doneness. Remove from grill; cover lightly with aluminum foil, and let stand 10 minutes before slicing.
3. Combine red onion and next 9 ingredients in a large bowl, tossing to coat.
4. Slice steak diagonally across the grain into thin strips. Stir steak into onion mixture. Serve over romaine lettuce. Sprinkle with peanuts. **Makes** 4 servings.

Beef Salad With Cilantro

Steak-and-Spinach Salad With Hot Pan Dressing

Serve with your favorite crusty garlic bread.

PREP: 15 MIN., COOK: 20 MIN.

1 (1½-pound) boneless top sirloin steak
½ teaspoon salt
½ teaspoon freshly ground pepper
1 teaspoon butter, divided
1 teaspoon olive oil, divided
2 medium portobello mushroom caps, sliced
    (about 1½ cups)
2 teaspoons minced garlic
½ cup red wine
½ cup beef broth
¼ cup balsamic vinegar
1 (6-ounce) package fresh baby spinach
2 plum tomatoes, sliced
1 small red onion, thinly sliced
½ lemon
⅓ cup crumbled Roquefort cheese

1. Sprinkle steak evenly with ½ teaspoon salt and ½ teaspoon pepper.
2. Heat a large nonstick skillet over medium heat for 2 minutes. Melt ½ teaspoon butter with ½ teaspoon oil. Add steak, and cook until well browned on 1 side (about 6 minutes). Turn steak, and cook 3 to 5 minutes or to desired doneness. Remove steak from pan, and set aside.
3. Melt remaining ½ teaspoon butter with ½ teaspoon oil in skillet over medium heat. Sauté mushrooms and garlic 4 minutes. Stir in wine, broth, and balsamic vinegar, stirring to loosen particles from bottom of skillet. Bring to a boil; reduce heat, and cook 4 to 5 minutes.
4. Toss together spinach, tomatoes, onion, and hot mushroom mixture in pan; divide evenly among 4 plates. Squeeze lemon juice evenly over top.
5. Cut steak into ½-inch slices, and arrange over salads. Sprinkle cheese evenly over top. **Makes** 4 servings.

Roast Beef-Blue Cheese Salad

10 minutes or less
PREP: 10 MIN.

8 ounces thinly sliced roast beef
1 pint cherry tomatoes
1 (8.5-ounce) package mixed salad greens
¼ cup crumbled blue cheese or feta cheese
¼ cup olive oil vinaigrette
Parmesan Toasts

1. Arrange roast beef slices into 2 stacks; roll up stacks. Cut into 1-inch slices. Arrange beef and tomatoes over salad greens. Sprinkle with blue cheese, and drizzle with olive oil vinaigrette. Serve with Parmesan Toasts. **Makes** 4 servings.

Parmesan Toasts:

PREP: 10 MIN., COOK: 3 MIN.

4 Italian bread slices
1 tablespoon butter or margarine, melted
¼ cup freshly grated Parmesan cheese
¼ teaspoon freshly ground pepper

1. Brush each bread slice evenly with butter. Sprinkle evenly with cheese and pepper. Place on a baking sheet.
2. Broil 3½ inches from heat 3 minutes or until lightly browned. **Makes** 4 servings.

Chicken-Vegetable Stir-fry

Chicken-Vegetable Stir-fry

Put on a bag of boil-in-bag rice when you start the stir-fry, and the rice will be ready when the chicken's done.

20 minutes or less
PREP: 3 MIN., COOK: 15 MIN.

1 cup chicken broth
¼ cup lite soy sauce
1 to 2 tablespoons Asian garlic-chili sauce
2 tablespoons cornstarch
1 tablespoon grated fresh ginger
2 tablespoons dark sesame oil
1 pound chicken breast strips
1 (16-ounce) package frozen vegetable stir-fry blend
Hot cooked rice

1. Whisk together first 5 ingredients. Heat sesame oil in a large nonstick skillet or wok at medium-high heat 2 minutes. Add chicken, and stir-fry 7 minutes or until lightly browned. Add vegetables, and stir-fry 4 minutes. Add broth mixture, and stir-fry 2 minutes or until thickened. Serve over rice. **Makes** 4 servings.

Chicken-and-Snow Pea Stir-fry

Peanut oil—with good monounsaturated fat—is a heart-healthy choice for cooking Chicken-and-Snow Pea Stir-fry.

PREP: 5 MIN., COOK: 30 MIN.

Fluffy White Rice (see recipe on page 68)
¾ cup chicken broth
¼ cup soy sauce
1½ tablespoons cornstarch
2 skinned and boned chicken breasts, cut into
　　¼-inch-wide strips
1 tablespoon peanut or vegetable oil
4 celery ribs, sliced
¼ pound fresh snow peas, trimmed
4 large mushrooms, sliced
3 green onions, sliced
1 (2-ounce) package slivered almonds, toasted
Garnish: green onion strips

1. Prepare Fluffy White Rice as directed, and keep warm.
2. Stir together broth, soy sauce, and cornstarch.
3. Cook chicken in hot oil in a large skillet over medium-high heat, stirring constantly, 6 minutes or until almost done. Add celery and next 3 ingredients, and cook, stirring constantly, 3 to 4 minutes or until vegetables are crisp-tender and chicken is done. Stir in broth mixture. Bring to a boil, stirring constantly; boil, stirring constantly, 1 minute. Serve over Fluffy White Rice, and sprinkle with almonds. Garnish, if desired. **Makes** 4 servings.

Chicken-and-Snow Pea Stir-fry

Chicken With Fresh Herbs
and Vegetables

Chicken With Fresh Herbs and Vegetables

*Serve over rice or linguine for a one-dish meal. If you don't have fresh herbs, substitute
1 tablespoon dried basil and 1 teaspoon dried oregano.*

30 minutes or less
PREP: 9 MIN., COOK: 20 MIN.

¼ cup fine, dry breadcrumbs
6 tablespoons shredded Parmesan cheese, divided
4 skinned and boned chicken breasts
2 tablespoons olive oil
10 large mushrooms, quartered
1 large green bell pepper, thinly sliced
3 large tomatoes, coarsely chopped
1 large garlic clove, pressed
½ teaspoon salt
¼ cup chopped fresh basil
1 tablespoon chopped fresh oregano

1. Combine breadcrumbs and 4 tablespoons Parmesan cheese, and dredge chicken in mixture.
2. Cook chicken in hot oil in a large skillet over medium-high heat 4 minutes on each side or until browned. Remove chicken from skillet.
3. Add mushrooms and bell pepper to skillet; sauté 2 minutes. Add tomatoes, garlic, and salt; return chicken to skillet. Cover, reduce heat, and simmer 10 minutes. Stir in basil, oregano, and remaining 2 tablespoons Parmesan cheese. Serve immediately. **Makes** 4 servings.

Chicken-Vegetable Pilaf

PREP: 10 MIN., COOK: 40 MIN., OTHER: 5 MIN.

¼ cup butter or margarine, divided
1 (8-ounce) package sliced fresh mushrooms
2 celery ribs, sliced
2 cups uncooked long-grain rice
3 (10½-ounce) cans condensed chicken broth,
    undiluted
3 cups chopped cooked chicken
1½ cups shredded carrots (about 3 large carrots)
1 (4-ounce) jar diced pimiento, drained
1 (3.8-ounce) can sliced black olives, drained
½ teaspoon pepper
½ cup slivered almonds, toasted

1. Melt 2 tablespoons butter in a Dutch oven over
medium-high heat; add mushrooms and celery, and
sauté 4 to 5 minutes or until tender. Remove from pan,
and set aside. Wipe pan clean with a paper towel.
2. Melt remaining 2 tablespoons butter in Dutch oven;
add rice, and sauté 6 to 8 minutes or until lightly
browned.
3. Stir in mushroom mixture, broth, and next 5 ingredients; bring to a boil. Cover, reduce heat, and simmer
20 to 25 minutes or until liquid is absorbed. Remove
from heat, and let stand 5 minutes.
4. Sprinkle with toasted almonds. **Makes** 6 to 8 servings.

Sweet-and-Sour Chicken and Rice

*Skinned and boned chicken thighs contain a little more fat
than breast meat, but they're flavorful, nutritious, and moist.*

PREP: 15 MIN., COOK: 1 HR.

½ teaspoon salt
½ teaspoon pepper
2 pounds skinned and boned chicken thighs
Vegetable cooking spray
1 small onion, diced
1 medium-size red bell pepper, chopped
2 garlic cloves, minced
1 cup uncooked long-grain rice
1 cup sweet-and-sour dressing (we tested with
    Old Dutch Sweet & Sour Dressing)
1 cup low-sodium, fat-free chicken broth
2 green onions, chopped

1. Sprinkle salt and pepper evenly over chicken thighs.
Cook chicken in a Dutch oven coated with cooking
spray over medium-high heat 2 to 3 minutes on each
side or until browned. Remove chicken from pan, and
set aside.
2. Add onion, bell pepper, and garlic to Dutch oven
coated with cooking spray; sauté 5 minutes. Add rice;
sauté 2 minutes or until rice is opaque.
3. Stir in dressing and broth. Add chicken thighs; bring
to a boil. Cover, reduce heat, and simmer 45 minutes or until liquid is absorbed and chicken is done.
Sprinkle with green onions. **Makes** 8 servings.

Chicken Spaghetti

PREP: 15 MIN., COOK: 20 MIN.

1 (12-ounce) package spaghetti
1 medium onion, chopped
1 small green bell pepper, chopped
Vegetable cooking spray
1 (14-ounce) can chicken broth
1 (14¼-ounce) can Italian-style stewed tomatoes
1 (6-ounce) can Italian-style tomato paste
1 (16-ounce) package pasteurized processed cheese
    product, cubed
3 cups chopped cooked chicken

1. Prepare spaghetti according to package directions.
Drain and keep warm.
2. Sauté onion and bell pepper in a Dutch oven coated
with cooking spray over medium-high heat 3 to 4
minutes. Stir in broth, tomatoes, and tomato paste.
Bring to a boil; reduce heat, and simmer 10 minutes.
Stir in cheese; cook 1 minute or until melted. Stir in
pasta and chicken; cook 2 to 3 minutes or until thoroughly heated. **Makes** 6 to 8 servings.

Stuffed Peppers With
Chicken and Corn

Stuffed Peppers With Chicken and Corn

PREP: 19 MIN., COOK: 41 MIN.

4 large red bell peppers
1 (12-ounce) package frozen corn soufflé, thawed
    (we tested with Stouffer's Corn Soufflé)
3 cups chopped cooked chicken
1 cup fresh corn kernels (about 2 ears)
¾ cup soft breadcrumbs
1 (4.5-ounce) can chopped green chiles, drained
½ medium-size sweet onion, diced
1 tablespoon taco seasoning
2 cups (8 ounces) shredded Monterey Jack cheese
    with peppers, divided
Garnish: chopped fresh cilantro

1. Cut peppers in half lengthwise, leaving stems intact; remove seeds. Place cut sides down on a lightly greased baking sheet. Broil 6 inches from heat 4 to 5 minutes or until they begin to blister.
2. Combine corn soufflé and next 6 ingredients; stir in 1 cup cheese.
3. Turn peppers cut sides up; spoon corn mixture evenly into peppers.
4. Bake at 375° for 25 minutes. Top evenly with remaining 1 cup cheese; bake 5 to 10 more minutes or until cheese melts. Garnish, if desired. **Makes** 8 servings.

Chicken-and-Broccoli Casserole

PREP: 15 MIN., COOK: 40 MIN.

make ahead

½ cup butter, divided
4 skinned and boned chicken breasts, cut into
    1-inch pieces
1 (16-ounce) package fresh broccoli florets
¼ cup all-purpose flour
2 cups milk
½ cup (2 ounces) shredded Swiss cheese
½ cup finely shredded Parmesan cheese
1 teaspoon lemon juice
¼ teaspoon salt
2 tablespoons finely shredded Parmesan cheese

1. Melt ¼ cup butter in a large skillet over medium heat; add chicken, and sauté until done. Remove chicken from skillet, and set aside.
2. Cook broccoli in a steamer basket over boiling water 2 minutes or until crisp-tender. Remove from heat; drain well, and set aside.
3. Melt remaining ¼ cup butter in skillet over medium heat. Whisk in flour, and cook, whisking constantly, 1 minute. Gradually add milk, and cook, whisking constantly, until thickened and bubbly. Remove from heat, and stir in Swiss cheese, ½ cup Parmesan cheese, lemon juice, and salt.
4. Layer half of chicken, broccoli, and cheese sauce in a lightly greased 11- x 7-inch baking dish. Repeat layers once. Cover and chill casserole up to 8 hours, if desired. Remove from refrigerator, and let stand at room temperature 30 minutes before baking.
5. Bake, covered, at 350° for 20 minutes. Uncover and sprinkle with 2 tablespoons Parmesan cheese; bake 5 more minutes. **Makes** 4 servings.

Creamed Chicken in Biscuit Bowls

You can also serve this over toast points, split biscuits, cornbread, waffles, or puff pastry shells.

30 minutes or less
PREP: 10 MIN., COOK: 20 MIN.

2 tablespoons butter or margarine
½ cup finely chopped onion (about 1 small onion)
½ cup finely chopped celery
½ cup sliced fresh mushrooms
1 (10¾-ounce) can condensed cream of chicken
    soup
½ cup milk
¼ teaspoon dried tarragon
1 cup (4 ounces) shredded sharp Cheddar cheese
2½ cups chopped cooked chicken
½ (16-ounce) package frozen peas and carrots,
    thawed
1 (2-ounce) jar diced pimiento, drained
¼ teaspoon salt
½ teaspoon pepper
Biscuit Bowls
Garnish: parsley sprigs

1. Melt butter in a large skillet over medium-high heat; add onion, celery, and mushrooms, and sauté 2 to 3 minutes or until tender. Whisk in cream of chicken soup, ½ cup milk, and tarragon; cook over medium-low heat, stirring occasionally, 3 to 4 minutes. Add cheese, stirring constantly, until cheese melts. Stir in cooked chicken and next 4 ingredients.

2. Cook over low heat, stirring often, 10 minutes or until thoroughly heated. Spoon mixture evenly into Biscuit Bowls. Garnish, if desired. **Makes** 8 servings.

Chicken Pot Pie in Biscuit Bowls: Substitute 1 (10-ounce) thawed package frozen mixed vegetables for peas and carrots. Add ½ teaspoon dried thyme and ½ teaspoon poultry seasoning. Omit tarragon, sliced mushrooms, and pimiento. Proceed with recipe as directed. **Makes** 8 servings.

Biscuit Bowls:

PREP: 15 MIN., COOK: 14 MIN.

1 (16.3-ounce) can refrigerated jumbo flaky biscuits
Vegetable cooking spray

1. Roll each biscuit into a 5-inch circle.
2. Invert 8 (6-ounce) custard cups or ramekins, several inches apart, on a lightly greased baking sheet. Coat outside of cups with cooking spray. Mold flattened biscuits around outside of custard cups.
3. Bake at 350° for 14 minutes. Cool slightly, and remove biscuit bowls from cups. **Makes** 8 servings.
Note: Frozen biscuits may be substituted. Let thaw at room temperature for 30 minutes. Biscuits may be slightly sticky; lightly flour before rolling out. Bake at 350° for 16 to 18 minutes.

Chicken Tetrazzini

To make ahead: Cover and chill before baking. Let stand 30 minutes at room temperature before baking; uncover and bake 35 minutes or until thoroughly heated.

PREP: 35 MIN., COOK: 45 MIN.

make ahead

8 ounces spaghetti
3 tablespoons butter
1 medium onion, chopped
1 green bell pepper, chopped
1 garlic clove, pressed
3 tablespoons all-purpose flour
2 cups milk
3 cups chopped cooked chicken
1 cup (4 ounces) shredded Cheddar cheese, divided
1 (10¾-ounce) can cream of mushroom soup
¼ cup dry white wine or chicken broth
1 (4-ounce) can sliced mushrooms, drained
1 (2-ounce) jar diced pimiento, drained
2 tablespoons chopped fresh parsley
1 tablespoon salt
½ teaspoon pepper

1. Prepare spaghetti according to package directions. Drain.

2. Melt butter in a large skillet over medium heat; add onion, bell pepper, and garlic, and sauté until tender. Stir in flour; cook, stirring constantly, 1 minute. Gradually stir in milk; cook over medium heat, stirring constantly, until thickened and bubbly. Stir in spaghetti, chicken, ¾ cup Cheddar cheese, and next 7 ingredients. Spoon into 4 (2-cup) lightly greased oven-safe bowls.

3. Bake at 350° for 20 minutes; sprinkle with remaining ¼ cup Cheddar cheese, and bake 5 more minutes.

Makes 4 servings.

Note: Entire recipe may be baked as directed in a lightly greased 2-quart baking dish.

Chicken Tetrazzini

Pronto Chicken Pot Pie

PREP: 23 MIN., COOK: 53 MIN., OTHER: 10 MIN.

2 tablespoons butter
1 cup chopped sweet onion
1¼ cups chicken broth
1½ cups peeled, cubed sweet potato (about 1 small
   sweet potato)
1 (10¾-ounce) can cream of chicken soup
1 cup frozen petite green peas
1 tablespoon chopped fresh thyme
3 cups chopped cooked chicken
½ (15-ounce) package refrigerated piecrusts
1 large egg, beaten

1. Melt butter in a large saucepan over medium heat; add onion, and sauté 4 minutes or until tender. Add broth and sweet potato; bring to a boil. Cover; reduce heat, and simmer 15 minutes or until sweet potato is just tender. Stir in soup and next 2 ingredients. Cook 2 minutes or until mixture is bubbly. Fold in chicken.
2. Spoon chicken mixture into a lightly greased 9-inch (1¼-inch-deep) pie plate. Roll piecrust into a 12-inch circle; fit over chicken mixture in pie plate, cutting dough around edges to leave a 1-inch overhang. Fold edges under, and crimp. Cut several slits in top of crust for steam to escape. Brush crust with egg.
3. Bake at 400° for 30 minutes or until crust is golden brown. Let stand 10 minutes. **Makes** 4 to 6 servings.

Leslie's Favorite Chicken-and-Wild Rice Casserole

PREP: 30 MIN., COOK: 45 MIN.

make
ahead

2 (6.2-ounce) packages fast-cooking
    long-grain and wild rice mix
¼ cup butter
2 medium onions, chopped
4 celery ribs, chopped
2 (8-ounce) cans sliced water chestnuts, drained
5 cups chopped cooked chicken
4 cups (16 ounces) shredded Cheddar cheese, divided
2 (10¾-ounce) cans cream of mushroom soup
2 (8-ounce) containers sour cream
1 cup milk
½ teaspoon salt
½ teaspoon pepper
½ cup soft breadcrumbs (optional)

1. Prepare rice according to package directions. Set aside.
2. Melt butter in a large skillet over medium heat; add onions, celery, and water chestnuts. Sauté 10 minutes or until tender.
3. Stir in rice, chicken, 3 cups cheese, and next 5 ingredients; spoon mixture into a lightly greased 15- x 10-inch baking dish or a 4-quart baking dish. Top evenly with breadcrumbs, if desired.
4. Bake casserole at 350° for 30 minutes. Sprinkle with remaining 1 cup cheese, and bake 5 more minutes. **Makes** 6 to 8 servings.
Note: Casserole may be frozen up to 1 month. Let stand at room temperature 1 hour. Bake, covered, at 350° for 30 minutes. Uncover; bake 55 more minutes. Sprinkle with 1 cup cheese; bake 5 more minutes.

Cheesy Chicken Casserole

Place crackers in a zip-top plastic freezer bag, seal all but a small corner to allow air to escape, and crush with a rolling pin.

PREP: 15 MIN., COOK: 30 MIN., OTHER: 5 MIN.

4 cups shredded cooked chicken
1 (10¾-ounce) can chicken-and-mushroom soup
1 (8-ounce) container sour cream
¼ teaspoon pepper
1 (8-ounce) block sharp Cheddar cheese,
    shredded and divided
25 round buttery crackers, coarsely crushed

1. Stir together chicken, soup, sour cream, pepper, and 1½ cups cheese; spoon mixture into a lightly greased 2-quart baking dish.
2. Combine remaining ½ cup cheese and cracker crumbs; sprinkle evenly over top.
3. Bake casserole at 350° for 30 minutes or until bubbly. Let stand 5 minutes before serving. **Makes** 4 to 6 servings.

chopped cooked chicken

Lots of speedy recipes call for chopped cooked chicken. Turn to the chart on page 10 for quick ways to get the amount you need. It's also easy to keep chopped cooked chicken on hand in your freezer. Just freeze leftover chopped cooked chicken or turkey in 1- or 2-cup batches for up to 1 month to use as needed.

Heavenly Chicken
Lasagna

Heavenly Chicken Lasagna

PREP: 30 MIN.; COOK: 1 HR., 5 MIN; OTHER: 10 MIN.

 make ahead

1 tablespoon butter

½ large onion, chopped

1 (10½-ounce) can reduced-fat cream of chicken soup

1 (10-ounce) container refrigerated light Alfredo sauce (we tested with Buitoni Light Alfredo Sauce)

1 (7-ounce) jar diced pimiento, undrained

1 (6-ounce) jar sliced mushrooms, drained

⅓ cup dry white wine

½ teaspoon dried basil

1 (10-ounce) package frozen chopped spinach, thawed

1 (15-ounce) container ricotta cheese

½ cup grated Parmesan cheese

1 large egg, lightly beaten

9 ounces no-cook lasagna noodles

3 cups chopped cooked chicken

3 cups (12 ounces) shredded sharp Cheddar cheese, divided

1. Melt butter in a skillet over medium-high heat. Add onion, and sauté 5 minutes or until tender. Remove from heat; stir in soup and next 5 ingredients. Reserve 1½ cups sauce; set aside.

2. Drain spinach well, pressing between layers of paper towels. Stir together spinach and next 3 ingredients.

3. Place 3 lasagna noodles in a lightly greased 13- x 9-inch baking dish. Layer with half each of sauce, spinach mixture, and chicken. Sprinkle with 1 cup Cheddar cheese. Repeat layers once. Top with remaining 3 noodles and reserved 1½ cups sauce. Cover and chill up to 1 day ahead, if desired. Let stand at room temperature 30 minutes before baking.

4. Bake, covered, at 350° for 50 to 55 minutes. Sprinkle with remaining 1 cup Cheddar cheese, and bake 5 more minutes or until cheese is melted. Let stand 10 minutes before serving. **Makes** 8 to 10 servings.

Chicken Cannelloni With Roasted Red Bell Pepper Sauce

For easy freezing, prepare and stuff cannelloni shells. Wrap each unbaked shell tightly in wax paper, and freeze until ready to serve. Let thaw in the refrigerator. Unwrap and place in a baking dish; top with your favorite supermarket pasta sauce or our Roasted Red Bell Pepper Sauce, and bake as directed.

PREP: 30 MIN., COOK: 30 MIN.

 make ahead

1 (8-ounce) package cannelloni or manicotti shells
4 cups finely chopped cooked chicken
2 (8-ounce) containers chive-and-onion cream cheese
1 (10-ounce) package frozen chopped spinach, thawed and well drained
1 cup (4 ounces) shredded mozzarella cheese
½ cup Italian-seasoned breadcrumbs
¾ teaspoon garlic salt
1 teaspoon seasoned pepper
Roasted Red Bell Pepper Sauce
Garnish: chopped fresh basil or parsley

1. Cook pasta according to package directions; drain and set aside.
2. Stir together chicken and next 6 ingredients in a large bowl.
3. Cut 1 side of pasta shells lengthwise, opening each shell.

4. Spoon ½ cup chicken mixture into each shell, gently pressing cut sides together. Place shells, seam side down, in 2 lightly greased 11- x 7-inch baking dishes.
5. Pour Roasted Red Bell Pepper Sauce evenly over shells.
6. Bake, covered, at 350° for 25 to 30 minutes or until thoroughly heated. Garnish, if desired. **Makes** 6 to 8 servings.

Roasted Red Bell Pepper Sauce:
Savor this rich sauce over your favorite pasta or grilled meats.

PREP: 5 MIN.

2 (7-ounce) jars roasted red bell peppers, drained
1 (16-ounce) jar creamy Alfredo sauce (we tested with Bertolli Creamy Alfredo sauce)
1 (3-ounce) package shredded Parmesan cheese

1. Process all ingredients in a blender until smooth, stopping occasionally to scrape down sides. **Makes** 3½ cups.

Chicken Cannelloni With Roasted Red Bell Pepper Sauce

Chicken-and-Refried Bean Tacos

To save time, let folks assemble their own tacos.

30 minutes or less
PREP: 10 MIN., COOK: 15 MIN.

1 (16-ounce) can refried beans
¾ cup salsa, divided
1 (10.7-ounce) taco dinner kit
½ medium-size green bell pepper, chopped
1 teaspoon vegetable oil
2 cups shredded cooked chicken
½ cup water
8 (6-inch) flour tortillas
1 small tomato, chopped
1 cup (4 ounces) shredded Cheddar cheese

1. Microwave refried beans, ¼ cup salsa, and 1½ teaspoons taco seasoning mix from dinner kit in a microwave-safe bowl at HIGH 1½ minutes or until thoroughly heated, stirring once. Set aside.

2. Sauté bell pepper in hot oil in a heavy skillet over medium heat 5 minutes or until tender. Stir in chicken, remaining taco seasoning mix, remaining ½ cup salsa, and ½ cup water. Cook, stirring occasionally, 8 to 10 minutes or until thoroughly heated.

3. Heat taco shells and tortillas according to package directions.

4. Spread about 2 tablespoons refried bean mixture over 1 side of each flour tortilla, leaving a ½-inch border. Place 1 taco shell in center of each tortilla, and press sides of tortilla up and onto sides of taco shell. Fill taco shells evenly with chicken mixture, tomato, and cheese. Serve immediately. **Makes** 4 servings.

Chicken-and-Refried
Bean Tacos

Chicken Burritos

PREP: 25 MIN., COOK: 15 MIN.

3 cups chopped cooked chicken
1 (1¼-ounce) envelope taco seasoning mix
1 (16-ounce) can refried beans
6 (8-inch) flour tortillas
1 (8-ounce) package shredded sharp Cheddar cheese
3 plum tomatoes, diced
1 small onion, diced
Salsa verde or salsa

1. Place chicken and seasoning mix in a large zip-top plastic freezer bag; seal and shake to coat.
2. Spread refried beans evenly down center of flour tortillas. Top with chicken, shredded cheese, diced tomatoes, and diced onion; roll up. Wrap each burrito in foil.
3. Bake at 350° for 15 minutes. Serve with salsa verde. **Makes** 4 servings.

Creamy Poblano Chicken

PREP: 10 MIN., COOK: 25 MIN.

3 tablespoons butter or margarine
1 large sweet onion, chopped
2 poblano chile peppers, seeded and diced
3 garlic cloves, minced
8 skinned and boned chicken breasts, cut into bite-size pieces
1 teaspoon salt
½ teaspoon pepper
1 (10¾-ounce) can condensed cream of chicken soup
½ cup chicken broth
1 (8-ounce) container sour cream
1 (8-ounce) package shredded sharp Cheddar cheese

1. Melt butter in a Dutch oven over medium-high heat. Add onion, poblanos, and garlic; sauté 5 minutes. Add chicken, salt, and pepper; cook, stirring often, 8 to 10 minutes or until chicken is done. Stir in soup, broth, and sour cream. Add cheese; cook 7 to 8 minutes. **Makes** 6 to 8 servings.

Easy Enchilada Casserole

PREP: 15 MIN., COOK: 30 MIN.

1 medium onion, chopped
2 tablespoons vegetable oil
1 (19-ounce) can enchilada sauce
1 (15-ounce) can black beans, rinsed and drained
1 (14½-ounce) can diced tomatoes with green chiles
1 (8-ounce) can Mexican-style corn, drained
1 teaspoon fajita seasoning or chili powder
1 teaspoon ground cumin
1 (10-ounce) package 6-inch corn tortillas
3 cups chopped cooked chicken (see note)
3 cups (12 ounces) shredded Mexican four-cheese blend

1. Sauté onion in hot oil in a large skillet over medium-high heat until tender. Stir in enchilada sauce and next 5 ingredients. Reduce heat to low, and cook, stirring often, 5 minutes or until thoroughly heated.
2. Spoon one-third of sauce mixture in a lightly greased 13- x 9-inch baking dish. Layer with one-third of tortillas, half of chicken, and 1 cup cheese. Repeat layers with one-third each of sauce mixture and tortillas, remaining chicken, and 1 cup cheese. Top with remaining sauce mixture, tortillas, and 1 cup cheese.
3. Bake at 350° for 15 to 20 minutes or until golden and bubbly. **Makes** 8 servings.
Note: 2 pounds lean ground beef, cooked and drained, may be substituted.

Spicy Chicken Salad

Spicy Chicken Salad

PREP: 21 MIN., COOK: 16 MIN.

3 cups chopped tomato
¾ cup diced yellow bell pepper
¼ cup diced red onion
1 tablespoon sugar
3 tablespoons cider vinegar
½ teaspoon salt
¼ teaspoon pepper
5 tablespoons olive oil, divided
¼ cup lemon juice
¼ cup Dijon mustard
1 tablespoon honey
4 skinned and boned chicken breasts
3 tablespoons Spicy Seasoning
1 pound sugar snap peas, trimmed
8 cups torn romaine lettuce

1. Toss together first 7 ingredients in a bowl; cover tomato mixture, and chill.
2. Whisk together 3 tablespoons oil, lemon juice, mustard, and honey in a large bowl; cover and chill.
3. Rub chicken with Spicy Seasoning.
4. Cook chicken in remaining 2 tablespoons oil in a large heavy skillet over medium-high heat 7 minutes on each side or until done. Remove from skillet, and cool. Cut chicken into thin strips, and set aside.
5. Arrange sugar snap peas in a steamer basket over boiling water; cover and steam 2 minutes or until crisp-tender. Plunge into ice water to stop the cooking process, and drain. Toss peas and lettuce with mustard mixture. Top each serving evenly with tomato mixture and chicken strips. **Makes** 4 servings.

Spicy Seasoning:
Use this flavorful rub to season fish, poultry, and meats.

PREP: 5 MIN.

2½ tablespoons paprika
2 tablespoons garlic powder
1 tablespoon salt
1 tablespoon onion powder
1 tablespoon dried thyme
1 tablespoon ground red pepper
1 tablespoon ground black pepper

1. Stir together all ingredients. Store in an airtight container. **Makes** about ½ cup.

Greek Chicken Salad

Stuff leftovers in a pita pocket for a light lunch on the go!

20 minutes or less

PREP: 15 MIN.

3 cups cubed cooked chicken breast
    (about 3 breast halves)
2 medium cucumbers, peeled, halved, seeded, and
    sliced
1 (4-ounce) package crumbled feta cheese
1 (2¼-ounce) can sliced ripe olives, drained
¼ cup chopped fresh parsley
1 cup mayonnaise
½ cup plain yogurt
1 tablespoon dried oregano
3 garlic cloves, minced
Spinach or lettuce leaves

1. Combine first 5 ingredients in a large bowl. Combine mayonnaise and next 3 ingredients; stir mixture well. Stir mayonnaise mixture into chicken mixture, tossing gently to coat; cover and chill salad until ready to serve. Serve over spinach leaves. **Makes** 5 servings.

Southwestern Chicken Salad

This recipe makes great use of broken tortilla chips that often get left in the bottom of the bag. Enjoy them sprinkled over this main-dish salad.

PREP: 5 MIN., OTHER: 30 MIN.

3 cups chopped cooked chicken
1 (8-ounce) package shredded Mexican
    four-cheese blend
1 ripe avocado, diced
1 small tomato, chopped
1 (2¼-ounce) can sliced ripe olives, drained
1 (8-ounce) package shredded iceberg lettuce
1 (8-ounce) container sour cream
½ cup picante sauce
Tortilla chips, crumbled

1. Combine first 5 ingredients; cover and chill at least 30 minutes. Divide lettuce evenly among 8 salad plates. Spoon chicken mixture evenly over lettuce; top with sour cream, picante sauce, and crumbled tortilla chips. **Makes** 8 servings.

Chicken-Black Bean Salad

Chicken-Black Bean Salad

For a milder degree of heat, remove the seeds from the jalapeño peppers before chopping.

30 minutes or less

PREP: 30 MIN.

make
ahead

3 tablespoons olive oil
1 tablespoon lemon juice
3 garlic cloves, minced
2 jalapeño peppers, chopped
2 tablespoons chopped fresh oregano
1½ teaspoons ground cumin
½ teaspoon salt
½ teaspoon pepper
3 cups chopped cooked chicken
1 (15-ounce) can black beans, rinsed and drained
1 cup frozen whole kernel corn, thawed
1 large tomato, diced
3 tablespoons chopped fresh cilantro
6 taco salad shells
6 to 8 cups shredded lettuce
Garnish: fresh cilantro sprigs

1. Whisk together first 8 ingredients in a large bowl. Add chicken and next 4 ingredients, tossing to coat. Cover and chill, if desired.

2. Heat taco shells according to package directions. Fill shells with shredded lettuce; top evenly with chicken mixture. Garnish, if desired. **Makes** 6 servings.

Fruity Chicken Salad

It's best to chill dressing for at least an hour to let flavors fully blend.

20 minutes or less
PREP: 20 MIN.

make
ahead

¾ cup sugar
⅓ cup red wine vinegar
1 teaspoon salt
1 teaspoon dry mustard
1 teaspoon grated onion
1 cup vegetable oil
1 tablespoon poppy seeds (optional)
3 cups chopped cooked chicken
6 cups torn fresh spinach
1 quart strawberries, sliced
3 kiwifruit, peeled and sliced
1 cup sliced almonds, toasted

1. Process first 5 ingredients in a blender until smooth, stopping to scrape down sides.
2. Turn blender on high; add oil in a slow, steady stream. Pour mixture into a serving bowl, and stir in poppy seeds, if desired. Toss together chicken and dressing; chill until ready to serve.
3. Place spinach on individual serving plates; top with fruit, chicken mixture, and almonds. **Makes** 6 to 8 servings.

Fruity Chicken Salad

Fish and Vegetable Dinner

30 minutes or less
PREP: 10 MIN., COOK: 15 MIN.

4 (6-ounce) orange roughy fillets
½ teaspoon salt
¼ teaspoon black pepper
½ cup buttermilk dressing
2 cups broccoli florets
1 medium-size red bell pepper, seeded and cut into
    strips
1 small onion, cut into strips

1. Place fish in an 11- x 7-inch baking dish; sprinkle with salt and black pepper. Spread 2 tablespoons dressing over each fillet. Arrange broccoli, pepper strips, and onion evenly over fish.
2. Cover with heavy-duty plastic wrap; fold back a small corner to allow steam to escape. Microwave at HIGH 13 to 15 minutes or until fish flakes easily when tested with a fork, giving dish a half-turn after 7 minutes. **Makes** 4 servings.

Tuna-and-White Bean Salad

PREP: 20 MIN., OTHER: 2 HR.

make ahead

1 small sweet onion, diced
½ cup olive oil
¼ cup red wine vinegar
¼ cup chopped fresh parsley
2 tablespoons chopped fresh or 2 teaspoons
    dried basil
2 teaspoons sugar
1 teaspoon garlic salt
¾ teaspoon pepper
3 tablespoons lemon juice
2 (15½-ounce) cans white beans, rinsed and drained
1 (12-ounce) can solid white tuna in spring water,
    drained and broken into chunks
Lettuce leaves

1. Whisk together first 9 ingredients in a medium bowl; add beans and tuna, tossing gently. Cover and chill at least 2 hours. Serve on lettuce-lined plates. **Makes** 3 to 4 servings.

Crawfish Étouffée

This speedy version of the classic gets high flavor from a quick simmer with frozen seasoning blend.

PREP: 3 MIN., COOK: 33 MIN.

1 pound fresh or frozen peeled crawfish tails, thawed
½ teaspoon ground red pepper
¼ cup vegetable oil
¼ cup all-purpose flour
1 (10-ounce) package frozen seasoning blend, thawed
4 green onions, chopped
1 teaspoon salt
½ teaspoon black pepper
1 cup chicken broth
Hot cooked rice

1. Sprinkle crawfish with red pepper; set aside.
2. Cook oil and flour in a Dutch oven over medium-low heat, stirring constantly, 20 minutes or until roux is copper penny-colored.
3. Stir in seasoning blend and green onions; cook, stirring constantly, until vegetables are tender. Add crawfish tails, salt, black pepper, and broth; cook, uncovered, over low heat 10 minutes, stirring occasionally. Serve over rice. **Makes** 4½ cups.

Shrimp Destin

PREP: 25 MIN., COOK: 7 MIN.

2 pounds unpeeled, large raw shrimp
½ cup butter
⅓ cup chopped green onions
1 tablespoon minced garlic
¼ cup dry white wine
1 teaspoon lemon juice
⅛ teaspoon salt
¼ teaspoon coarsely ground pepper
1 tablespoon chopped fresh dill or 1 teaspoon
    dried dillweed
1 tablespoon chopped fresh parsley
2 (3¼-ounce) French rolls, split lengthwise and
    toasted (see note)
Garnish: fresh parsley sprigs

1. Peel shrimp; devein, if desired.

2. Melt butter in a large skillet over medium heat; sauté onions and garlic 2 minutes or until tender. Add shrimp, wine, and next 3 ingredients. Cook 5 minutes or until shrimp turn pink, stirring occasionally. Stir in dill and parsley.

3. Place toasted roll halves on 4 individual serving plates. Spoon 1 cup shrimp mixture over each roll, and serve immediately. Garnish, if desired. **Makes** 4 servings.

Note: You can serve Shrimp Destin over hot cooked rice instead of rolls, if desired.

Shrimp Destin

Shrimp and Grits

Shrimp and Grits

30 minutes or less
PREP: 15 MIN., COOK: 10 MIN.

2 pounds frozen, peeled, deveined large raw shrimp
2 teaspoons Cajun seasoning
1 teaspoon dried Italian seasoning
1 teaspoon paprika
¼ cup butter or margarine
2 garlic cloves, pressed
1 cup chicken broth, divided
2 teaspoons Worcestershire sauce
1 teaspoon hot sauce
2 teaspoons all-purpose flour
Hot cooked grits

1. Thaw shrimp according to package directions. Rinse and drain well.
2. Combine Cajun seasoning, Italian seasoning, and paprika in a large bowl; add shrimp, and toss to coat.
3. Melt butter in a large skillet over medium heat; add garlic, and sauté 1 minute. Add shrimp, ¾ cup broth, Worcestershire sauce, and hot sauce; cook 5 minutes or just until shrimp turn pink. Remove shrimp with a slotted spoon, reserving broth mixture in skillet.
4. Whisk together flour and remaining ¼ cup chicken broth until blended; whisk flour mixture into broth mixture in skillet, and cook, whisking constantly, 2 to 3 minutes or until thickened. Add shrimp, and cook 1 minute. Serve immediately over hot grits. **Makes** 4 servings.

Shrimp and Tortellini

It's faster to purchase peeled shrimp for this dish, but if you'd rather, purchase one pound in the shell.

20 minutes or less
PREP: 5 MIN., COOK: 7 MIN.

1 (9-ounce) package refrigerated cheese-filled
    tortellini
¾ pound peeled, medium-size raw shrimp
1 shallot, minced
2 tablespoons chopped fresh basil or 2 teaspoons
    dried basil
⅓ cup butter or margarine, melted
½ cup grated Parmesan cheese
Garnish: fresh basil sprigs

1. Cook tortellini according to package directions; drain.
2. Meanwhile, cook shrimp, shallot, and chopped basil in butter in a large skillet over medium-high heat, stirring constantly, 5 minutes or just until shrimp turn pink. Add tortellini and Parmesan cheese; toss gently. Garnish, if desired. **Makes** 4 servings.

Marinated Shrimp Salad

Buy 2½ pounds medium-size raw shrimp if starting with raw shrimp in the shell.

PREP: 12 MIN., OTHER: 3 HR.

make
ahead

1 cup bottled vinaigrette
1 bunch green onions, chopped
2 celery ribs, chopped
2 garlic cloves, minced
1¼ pounds cooked peeled, medium-size shrimp
8 cups mixed salad greens
Garnishes: lemon wedges, paprika

1. Combine vinaigrette, green onions, celery, and garlic in a large bowl. Add shrimp, tossing to coat; cover and chill 3 hours.
2. Arrange shrimp mixture on salad greens, and garnish, if desired. **Makes** 8 servings.

Shrimp Oriental

PREP: 40 MIN., COOK: 10 MIN.

2 pounds unpeeled, large raw shrimp
2 (8-ounce) cans pineapple chunks, undrained
½ cup sugar
2 tablespoons cornstarch
1 teaspoon salt
¼ cup rice wine vinegar
2 tablespoons chili sauce
⅓ cup ketchup
1 teaspoon soy sauce
1 green bell pepper, diced
1 red bell pepper, diced
Hot cooked rice (optional)

1. Peel shrimp, and devein, if desired. Set shrimp aside.
2. Drain pineapple, reserving juice. Stir together pineapple juice, sugar, and next 6 ingredients.
3. Cook pineapple juice mixture in a large skillet or wok over high heat, stirring constantly, 15 to 30 seconds or until thickened. Add diced bell peppers, and cook 3 to 4 minutes. Add pineapple chunks and shrimp. Cook, stirring often, 3 to 5 minutes or just until shrimp turn pink. Serve over hot cooked rice, if desired. **Makes** 4 servings.

Oven-Fried Catfish, page 106

HEALTHY
'n' quick

Vegetable Pasta

Vegetable Pasta

Ridged penne pasta makes a sturdy base for this chunky tomato-vegetable sauce, but you can substitute an equal amount of another favorite pasta if you'd like. A great time-saver, preseasoned canned tomatoes add excellent flavor to your homemade pasta sauce.

30 minutes or less
PREP: 8 MIN., COOK: 16 MIN.

8 ounces uncooked penne pasta
4 teaspoons olive oil, divided
2 medium zucchini, cut into ¼-inch-thick slices (about 3 cups)
1 medium onion, cut into ¼-inch-thick slices (about 1¼ cups)
2 garlic cloves, minced
2 (14½-ounce) cans Italian-style stewed tomatoes, undrained
¼ teaspoon salt
¼ teaspoon freshly ground pepper
½ cup chopped fresh basil
¼ cup freshly grated Parmesan cheese

1. Cook pasta according to package directions, omitting salt and fat; drain. Add 2 teaspoons olive oil; keep pasta warm.
2. Meanwhile, heat remaining olive oil in a large nonstick skillet over medium-high heat. Add zucchini, onion, and garlic to pan. Sauté 4 minutes or until lightly browned. Remove vegetables from skillet, and keep warm.
3. Add tomatoes, salt, and pepper to skillet. Cook over medium-high heat 12 minutes or until thickened, stirring occasionally. Stir in vegetables and basil. Serve over pasta; sprinkle with cheese. **Makes** 4 servings (serving size: 1 cup pasta, 1 cup vegetable mixture, and 1 tablespoon cheese).

Per serving: Calories 350 (18% from fat); Fat 7.1g (sat 1.7g, mono 3.9g, poly 0.9g); Protein 12.7g; Carb 61.6g; Fiber 6.6g; Chol 4mg; Iron 2.1mg; Sodium 933mg; Calc 143mg

Spinach-and-Cheese Calzones

To save time preparing this recipe, place frozen spinach in refrigerator overnight to thaw.

PREP: 19 MIN., COOK: 24 MIN.

1 (10-ounce) package frozen chopped spinach,
    thawed and well drained
½ cup chopped onion
½ (6-ounce) package Canadian-style bacon, chopped
1 tablespoon garlic powder
½ teaspoon salt
1 (15-ounce) container part-skim ricotta cheese
1¼ cups (5 ounces) shredded light pizza cheese
    blend
1 teaspoon dried Italian seasoning
2 (11-ounce) cans refrigerated crusty French loaf
1 (26-ounce) jar fat-free garlic-and-herb pasta sauce
    (we used Healthy Choice)

1. Sauté first 5 ingredients in a large nonstick skillet coated with cooking spray 6 minutes or until bacon is browned. Remove from heat. Combine ricotta cheese, pizza cheese blend, and Italian seasoning; stir into spinach mixture.
2. Unroll each bread loaf on a lightly floured surface, and cut each into 4 rectangles. Spoon a heaping ⅓ cup spinach mixture onto half of each rectangle. Fold dough over spinach filling, pressing edges to seal. Crimp edges with a fork dipped in flour.
3. Place calzones on baking sheets coated with cooking spray. Coat each calzone with cooking spray.
4. Bake at 400° for 18 minutes or until golden. Serve with pasta sauce. **Makes** 8 servings (serving size: 1 calzone and ¼ cup pasta sauce).

Per serving: Calories 378 (22% from fat); Fat 9.3g (sat 4.8g, mono 2.3g, poly 0.6g); Protein 23.6g; Carb 50.4g; Fiber 3.6g; Chol 28mg; Iron 3.6mg; Sodium 1,249mg; Calc 332mg

Vegetable-Cheese Melts

Nothing tastes better than homegrown vegetables from the garden. Give them a unique twist in this sandwich.

20 minutes or less
PREP: 10 MIN., COOK: 7 MIN.

1 teaspoon vegetable oil
1 small zucchini, cut into ¼-inch-thick slices
1 large red bell pepper, cut into ¼-inch strips
1 small onion, thinly sliced and separated into
    rings
¼ teaspoon ground cumin
2 tablespoons creamy mustard-mayonnaise blend
4 (1.1-ounce) rye bread slices, toasted
¼ cup (1 ounce) shredded colby-Jack cheese
    blend

1. Heat oil in a large nonstick skillet over medium-high heat. Add zucchini, bell pepper, and onion; cook 6 minutes or until tender. Stir in cumin.
2. Spread 1½ teaspoons mustard-mayonnaise blend on each of 4 toast slices. Place 2 slices, mustard side up, on a baking sheet. Arrange 1 cup vegetable mixture on top of each. Sprinkle evenly with cheese. Broil 3 inches from heat 40 seconds or until cheese melts. Top with remaining toast, mustard side down. Serve immediately. **Makes** 2 servings (serving size: 1 sandwich).

Per serving: Calories 292 (27% from fat); Fat 8.7g (sat 3.6g, mono 2.2g, poly 1.3g); Protein 10.2g; Carb 43.7g; Fiber 6.7g; Chol 13mg; Iron 2.6mg; Sodium 712mg; Calc 146mg

Mediterranean Ravioli

Frozen ravioli and commercial tomato sauce speed up preparation of this trendy one-dish meal.

20 minutes or less
PREP: 9 MIN., COOK: 11 MIN.

1 (14.5-ounce) package light cheese ravioli (we used Buitoni Light Four-Cheese Ravioli)
2 teaspoons olive oil
1 small eggplant, peeled and cut into 1-inch cubes
1 cup chopped onion
2 garlic cloves, minced
2 cups chunky tomato sauce (we used Classico Tomato and Basil)
3 tablespoons freshly grated Parmesan cheese

1. Cook ravioli according to package directions, omitting salt and fat. Rinse and drain; set aside.
2. Meanwhile, coat a large nonstick skillet with cooking spray. Add oil; place over medium-high heat until hot. Add eggplant, onion, and garlic; cook, stirring constantly, 5 minutes or until tender. Stir in tomato sauce, and cook 1 minute or until thoroughly heated.
3. Combine ravioli and eggplant mixture in a large bowl, and toss gently to coat. Sprinkle evenly with Parmesan cheese. **Makes** 6 servings (serving size: 1 cup).

Per serving: Calories 269 (20% from fat); Fat 6.2g (sat 2.3g, mono 1.3g, poly 0.2g); Protein 12.9g; Carb 42.2g; Fiber 5.3g; Chol 29mg; Iron 1.9mg; Sodium 613mg; Calc 178mg

Fettuccine Primavera

Enjoy the bounty of vegetables with each bite of this creamy pasta classic. We found that Knorr Alfredo sauce mix offered the most abundant creaminess. We made it extra creamy by adding Parmesan cheese.

30 minutes or less
PREP: 9 MIN., COOK: 14 MIN.

1 small onion, chopped
1 red bell pepper, cut into thin strips
1 cup fresh broccoli florets
1 cup sliced fresh mushrooms
8 ounces fresh sugar snap peas
1 (9-ounce) package refrigerated fettuccine
1 (1.6-ounce) package Alfredo sauce mix (we used Knorr)
1½ cups 1% low-fat milk
1 tablespoon butter
½ cup (2 ounces) shredded Parmesan cheese, divided
¼ teaspoon freshly ground pepper

1. Cook onion in a large nonstick skillet coated with cooking spray over medium heat, stirring constantly, 3 minutes or until tender. Add bell pepper strips, broccoli, and mushrooms. Cook, stirring constantly, until vegetables are crisp-tender. Stir in peas, and cook 2 minutes.
2. Meanwhile, prepare pasta according to package directions, omitting salt and fat. Rinse and drain; set aside.
3. Prepare sauce mix according to package directions, using 1% low-fat milk and 1 tablespoon butter. Stir in ¼ cup cheese.
4. Combine vegetables, pasta, and sauce, tossing gently.
5. Sprinkle remaining cheese over top of pasta. Sprinkle with pepper. Serve immediately. **Makes** 6 servings (serving size: 1 cup).

Per serving: Calories 266 (25% from fat); Fat 7g (sat 3.7g, mono 1.8g, poly 0.3g); Protein 12.7g; Carb 35.2g; Fiber 3.4g; Chol 16mg; Iron 0.8mg; Sodium 636mg; Calc 197mg

Macaroni and Cheese

Macaroni and Cheese

Mac 'n' cheese goes with virtually anything. Serve it with your favorite veggies for a meatless meal.

PREP: 10 MIN., COOK: 25 MIN.

1 (12-ounce) container 1% low-fat cottage cheese
1 (8-ounce) container light sour cream
4 cups cooked elbow macaroni (cooked without salt
    or fat)
2 cups (8 ounces) shredded 2% reduced-fat sharp
    Cheddar cheese
½ cup fat-free milk
1 green onion, chopped
½ teaspoon salt
½ teaspoon pepper
1 large egg
Butter-flavored cooking spray
¼ cup fine, dry breadcrumbs (commercial)
¼ teaspoon paprika

1. Process cottage cheese and sour cream in a blender until smooth, stopping to scrape down sides.
2. Combine cottage cheese mixture, macaroni, and next 6 ingredients; spoon into a 2-quart deep baking dish coated with butter-flavored cooking spray. Sprinkle with breadcrumbs and paprika; coat with cooking spray.
3. Cover and bake at 400° for 20 minutes. Uncover and bake 5 more minutes. **Makes** 8 servings.

Per serving: Calories 289 (35% from fat); Fat 10.8g (sat 6.7g, mono 0.4g, poly 0.2g); Protein 20g; Carb 24.9g; Fiber 0.3g; Chol 63mg; Iron 0.8mg; Sodium 697mg; Calc 306mg

Fresh Mozzarella and
Basil Pizza

Fresh Mozzarella and Basil Pizza

*This recipe makes a pizza for one person, but enough dough for six pizzas. If you don't have time to prepare
fresh dough, some pizza parlors and supermarkets sell pizza dough on request. Bake pizza on a pizza stone or
heavy baking sheet that withstands high baking temperatures. High heat makes the crust crisp.*

PREP: 30 MIN., COOK: 10 MIN., OTHER: 20 MIN.

make
ahead

1 (4-ounce) portion Pizza Dough
    (recipe on facing page)
½ teaspoon extra virgin olive oil
1 large plum tomato, thinly sliced
1 tablespoon sliced fresh basil
4 thin slices (2 ounces) fresh mozzarella cheese
1 (1-ounce) slice country ham or pancetta
    ham, cut into thin strips
¼ teaspoon freshly ground pepper

1. Preheat oven to 450°. Shape Pizza Dough ball into a
6- to 8-inch circle on a lightly floured surface. (Dough
doesn't need to be perfectly round.) Place dough on
a piece of parchment paper. Fold up edges of dough,
forming a 1-inch border. Brush oil over dough using a
pastry brush or your fingers.

2. Cover pizza dough circle loosely with plastic wrap,
and let rise in a warm place (85°), free from drafts,
15 to 20 minutes.

3. Heat pizza stone or heavy baking sheet 10 to 12
minutes in oven.

4. Remove and discard plastic wrap from dough.
Layer tomato and next 3 ingredients on pizza dough.
Sprinkle with pepper. Carefully transfer unbaked pizza
on parchment paper to hot pizza stone.

5. Bake at 450° for 10 minutes or until crust is golden.
Makes 1 pizza.

Note: If you use all this pizza dough and repeat directions above, you'll have 6 personal pan pizzas. Other-
wise you can divide dough into 3 larger portions and
make 3 large pizzas that bake at 450° for 16 minutes.
P.S. Double the toppings on each large pizza, too.

Per pizza: Calories 508 (38% from fat); Fat 21.4g (sat 10.2g, mono 5.4g, poly 1.2g);
Protein 23.4g; Carb 52.8g; Fiber 2.9g; Chol 60mg; Iron 4mg; Sodium 1,063mg; Calc 346mg

Pizza Dough:

The dough can be frozen up to 1 month. To freeze, wrap each portion in plastic wrap, and place in zip-top plastic freezer bags. Thaw in refrigerator overnight, or let stand at room temperature 4 hours.

PREP: 15 MIN.; OTHER: 1 HR., 37 MIN.

1 cup warm water (100° to 110°)
⅛ teaspoon sugar
1 (¼-ounce) envelope active dry yeast
3 to 3½ cups all-purpose flour
1½ teaspoons salt
1 tablespoon extra virgin olive oil
Vegetable cooking spray

1. Stir together 1 cup warm water and sugar in a 2-cup glass measuring cup. Sprinkle with yeast, and let stand 5 to 7 minutes or until mixture is bubbly; stir until blended.
2. Place 3 cups flour and salt in a food processor. With motor running, add yeast mixture and olive oil; process mixture until dough forms. (If dough is too sticky, add more flour, 2 tablespoons at a time.) Place dough in a large bowl coated with cooking spray; lightly coat dough with cooking spray. Cover with a clean cloth, and let rise in a warm place (85°), free from drafts, 1 hour or until doubled in bulk.
3. Punch dough down. Turn dough in bowl, and coat with cooking spray; cover with cloth, and let rise in a warm place, free from drafts, 30 minutes or until doubled in bulk. Cut dough into 6 equal portions, shaping each portion into a 3-inch ball. **Makes** 6 individual dough rounds.

Per dough round: Calories 253 (11% from fat); Fat 3g (sat 0.4g, mono 1.9g, poly 0.5g); Protein 6.9g; Carb 48.3g; Fiber 2g; Chol 0mg; Iron 3mg; Sodium 586mg; Calc 11mg

Broccoli-Ginger Stir-Fry

20 minutes or less
PREP: 6 MIN., COOK: 12 MIN.

6 ounces uncooked angel hair pasta
¾ cup vegetable broth
⅓ cup lite soy sauce
3 tablespoons dry white wine
1 tablespoon cornstarch
2 teaspoons minced fresh ginger
3 large garlic cloves, minced
1 teaspoon olive oil
1 (16-ounce) package broccoli stir-fry blend (we used Birds Eye)

1. Cook pasta according to package directions, omitting salt and fat. Drain pasta, and keep warm.
2. Meanwhile, stir together broth and next 5 ingredients; set aside.
3. Heat olive oil in a large nonstick skillet or wok at medium-high heat. Add vegetables; stir-fry 8 minutes.
4. Stir in broth mixture, and cook 2 minutes or until slightly thickened. Serve over pasta. **Makes** 4 servings.

Per serving: Calories 233 (9% from fat); Fat 2.4g (sat 0.3g, mono 0.9g, poly 0.4g); Protein 9.4g; Carb 42.7g; Fiber 3.4g; Chol 0mg; Iron 1mg; Sodium 1,028mg; Calc 31mg

Pork Dumplings

This recipe makes a bunch, so ask a friend to help you assemble the dumplings; then freeze some for later.

PREP: 2 HR., COOK: 25 MIN.

make ahead

1½ pounds lean boneless pork loin
    chops, cut into chunks
1 (12-ounce) package 50%-less-fat ground pork
    sausage
1½ teaspoons salt
15 water chestnuts, finely chopped
1 to 2 tablespoons minced fresh ginger
½ cup cornstarch
2 teaspoons lite soy sauce
½ cup low-sodium fat-free chicken broth
¼ cup sugar
1 teaspoon teriyaki sauce
1 teaspoon sesame oil
¼ cup chopped fresh parsley
4 green onions, diced
2 (16-ounce) packages won ton wrappers
Oyster sauce (optional)
Thai chili sauce (optional)
Ginger Dipping Sauce (optional)

1. Process pork loin in a food processor until finely chopped.
2. Combine pork loin, pork sausage, and next 11 ingredients.
3. Cut corners from won ton wrappers to form circles. Drop 1 teaspoon mixture onto middle of each skin. Gather up won ton sides, letting dough pleat naturally. Lightly squeeze the middle while tapping the bottom on a flat surface so it will stand upright.
4. Arrange dumplings in a bamboo steam basket over boiling water. Cover and steam 20 to 25 minutes. Serve with sauces, if desired. **Makes** 116 dumplings.
Note: To freeze, arrange dumplings on a baking sheet; freeze 2 hours. Place in zip-top plastic freezer bags; label and freeze for up to 3 months. To cook dumplings from frozen state, steam 22 to 25 minutes.

Per dumpling: Calories 40 (18% from fat); Fat 0.8g (sat 0.2g, mono 0.3g, poly 0.2g); Protein 2.5g; Carb 6g; Fiber 0.2g; Chol 6mg; Iron 0.4mg; Sodium 101mg; Calc 7mg

Ginger Dipping Sauce:

PREP: 10 MIN., COOK: 1 MIN.

1 garlic clove, minced
1 tablespoon minced fresh ginger
1 teaspoon dark sesame oil
2 tablespoons lite soy sauce
1 tablespoon rice wine vinegar
2 teaspoons teriyaki sauce
1 green onion, minced

1. Sauté garlic and ginger in hot oil 1 minute; remove from heat. Whisk in soy sauce and remaining ingredients. **Makes** ⅓ cup.

Per tablespoon: Calories 17 (48% from fat); Fat 0.9g (sat 0.1g, mono 0.4g, poly 0.4g); Protein 0.7g; Carb 1.4g; Fiber 0.1g; Chol 0mg; Iron 0.1mg; Sodium 335mg; Calc 4mg

Pork-and-Pepper Skillet

Sautéed peppers look pretty with this pork. Garlic mashed potatoes round out the meal nicely.

20 minutes or less
PREP: 7 MIN., COOK: 10 MIN.

8 (2-ounce) wafer-thin boneless center-cut pork loin
    chops
¼ teaspoon dried thyme
¼ teaspoon salt
½ teaspoon pepper
1 teaspoon olive oil
1 small onion, cut into thin strips
2 red bell peppers, cut into thin strips
1 garlic clove, minced
1 tablespoon red wine vinegar

1. Rub both sides of pork with thyme, salt, and pepper. Heat oil in a large nonstick skillet over medium-high heat; add pork. Cook 2 minutes on each side. Remove pork from skillet.
2. Sauté onion, bell pepper, and garlic in same skillet 4 minutes or until crisp-tender. Return pork to skillet, and cook 2 minutes. Drizzle with vinegar. **Makes** 4 servings.

Per serving: Calories 224 (49% from fat); Fat 12.2g (sat 4.3g, mono 5.9g, poly 1.1g); Protein 22.1g; Carb 6.8g; Fiber 1.7g; Chol 59mg; Iron 1.2mg; Sodium 578mg; Calc 28.6mg

Pork-and-Pepper Skillet

Marinated London Broil

Marinated London Broil

*For the juiciest flavor, pull this hearty cut of beef off the grill just before it reaches desired doneness.
It will continue to cook as it stands.*

PREP: 5 MIN.; COOK: 30 MIN.; OTHER: 24 HR., 10 MIN.

make
ahead

1 (12-ounce) can cola soft drink
1 (10-ounce) bottle teriyaki sauce
1 (2½- to 3-pound) London broil

1. Combine cola and teriyaki sauce in a shallow dish
or large zip-top plastic freezer bag; add London broil.
Cover or seal, and chill 24 hours, turning occasionally.

2. Remove London broil from marinade, discarding
marinade.

3. Grill, covered with grill lid, over medium heat (300°
to 350°) 12 to 15 minutes on each side or to desired
degree of doneness. Let stand 10 minutes, and cut
diagonally across the grain into thin slices. **Makes** 8
servings.

Per serving: Calories 228 (35% from fat); Fat 8.8g (sat 3.6g, mono 3.5g, poly 0.3g);
Protein 30.7g; Carb 6.1g; Fiber 0g; Chol 48mg; Iron 2.2mg; Sodium 923mg; Calc 27mg

Grilled Flank Steak With Molasses Barbecue Glaze

Flank steak provides an excellent source of iron in this sweet 'n' tangy grilled dinner.

PREP: 3 MIN., COOK: 12 MIN., OTHER: 2 HR.

½ cup molasses
¼ cup coarse-grained mustard
1 tablespoon olive oil
1 (1½-pound) flank steak
6 (8-inch) flour tortillas
1 cup shredded lettuce
1 large tomato, chopped
¾ cup (3 ounces) shredded reduced-fat Cheddar
    cheese
½ cup light sour cream

1. Whisk together first 3 ingredients.
2. Place steak in a shallow dish or large zip-top plastic freezer bag. Reserve ¼ cup molasses mixture; pour remaining molasses mixture over steak. Cover or seal, and chill 2 hours, turning occasionally. Remove meat from marinade, discarding marinade.
3. Grill, covered with grill lid, over medium-high heat (350° to 400°) 6 minutes on each side or to desired degree of doneness, brushing often with reserved marinade. Cut steak diagonally across the grain into very thin strips. Serve steak with tortillas and remaining ingredients. **Makes** 6 servings.

Per serving: Calories 283 (30% from fat); Fat 9.4g (sat 3g, mono 3.9g, poly 1.3g); Protein 9.5g; Carb 40.7g; Fiber 1.4g; Chol 14mg; Iron 2.8mg; Sodium 376mg; Calc 181mg

make-ahead grill tip

Marinate lean meats such as flank steak, pork tenderloin, and chicken, or rub them with spice rubs. Then freeze the meat in zip-top plastic freezer bags. When thawed, meats will be perfectly seasoned and ready to go on the grill.

Zucchini-Beef Spaghetti

Use any leftover fresh zucchini as a garnish. Just chop or shred what you have left, and sprinkle on top of the meat mixture.

PREP: 13 MIN., COOK: 20 MIN.

1 pound extra-lean ground beef
1 (8-ounce) package sliced fresh mushrooms
2 cups thinly sliced zucchini
1 cup chopped onion
½ teaspoon salt
¼ teaspoon dried crushed red pepper
4 garlic cloves, minced
2½ cups pasta sauce
6 cups hot cooked spaghetti (cooked without salt
    or fat)
2 tablespoons grated Parmesan cheese

1. Brown ground beef in a large nonstick skillet coated with cooking spray, stirring until it crumbles and is no longer pink. Add mushrooms and next 5 ingredients to beef in skillet. Sauté 5 minutes, stirring often. Stir in pasta sauce. Bring to a boil; cover, reduce heat, and simmer 5 minutes or to desired consistency. Serve over hot cooked spaghetti; top with cheese. **Makes** 6 servings.

Per serving: Calories 406 (21% from fat); Fat 9.4g (sat 3.2g, mono 3.2g, poly 0.8g); Protein 26.8g; Carb 53.7g; Fiber 5.8g; Chol 29mg; Iron 5mg; Sodium 612mg; Calc 126mg

Deviled Chicken Breasts

30 minutes or less
PREP: 8 MIN., COOK: 22 MIN.

2 tablespoons Italian-seasoned breadcrumbs
4 (4-ounce) skinned and boned chicken breasts
1 tablespoon olive oil
½ cup dry white wine
½ teaspoon dried savory, crushed
¼ teaspoon salt
¼ teaspoon coarsely ground pepper
1 (4-ounce) jar whole mushrooms, drained
1 tablespoon lemon juice
1 tablespoon honey mustard

1. Place breadcrumbs in a large zip-top plastic freezer bag; add chicken. Seal bag; shake until well coated.
2. Heat oil in a nonstick skillet over medium heat. Add chicken; cook 3 minutes on each side or until browned. Add wine and next 4 ingredients; cover, reduce heat, and simmer 15 minutes or until chicken is done.
3. Remove chicken and mushrooms with a slotted spoon; place on a serving platter. Add lemon juice and mustard to skillet; stir. Cook 1 minute or until heated; serve with chicken. **Makes** 4 servings (serving size: 1 chicken breast and 1 tablespoon sauce).

Per serving: Calories 191 (27% from fat); Fat 5.7g (sat 1g, mono 3.1g, poly 1g); Protein 27.4g; Carb 6.1g; Fiber 0.5g; Chol 66mg; Iron 1.2mg; Sodium 404mg; Calc 24mg

Oven-Fried Catfish

You can use 1 teaspoon seasoned salt instead of the four seasonings, if desired. Serve with Baked Hush Puppies (page 113) and store-bought slaw.

30 minutes or less
PREP: 8 MIN., COOK: 21 MIN.

2 cups cornflakes cereal
¾ teaspoon celery salt
¼ teaspoon onion powder
⅛ teaspoon ground red pepper
Dash of black pepper
4 (6-ounce) catfish fillets, halved
Vegetable cooking spray

1. Place cereal in a zip-top plastic freezer bag. Seal and crush to measure ¾ cup crumbs, using a meat mallet or rolling pin. Combine crumbs, salt, and next 3 ingredients in a shallow dish. Coat both sides of fish with cooking spray. Dredge fish in crumb mixture, pressing gently to coat. Arrange fish in a single layer on a baking sheet coated with cooking spray. Coat tops of fish with cooking spray.
2. Bake at 400° for 21 minutes or until fish flakes with a fork. **Makes** 4 servings.

Per serving: Calories 211 (22% from fat); Fat 4.9g (sat 1.2g, mono 1.5g, poly 1.5g); Protein 28.9g; Carb 11g; Fiber 0.3g; Chol 99mg; Iron 0.9mg; Sodium 471mg; Calc 28mg

Oven-Fried Catfish and
Baked Hush Puppies (page 113)

Grilled Tuna Sandwiches

30 minutes or less
PREP: 10 MIN., COOK: 16 MIN.

1 (1-inch-thick) tuna steak (about ¾ pound)
2 tablespoons olive oil, divided
½ teaspoon salt
½ teaspoon pepper
8 slices sourdough bread
¼ teaspoon ground red pepper (optional)
¼ cup finely chopped green onions
¼ cup mayonnaise
2 tablespoons fresh lime juice
2 teaspoons prepared horseradish
1 large tomato, thinly sliced
1 ripe avocado, sliced

1. Rub tuna with 1 tablespoon olive oil, and sprinkle salt and pepper evenly on both sides of tuna.
2. Grill, covered with grill lid, over medium-high heat (350° to 400°) 6 to 7 minutes on each side or to desired degree of doneness.
3. Brush bread slices with remaining 1 tablespoon olive oil, and grill 1 minute on each side or until golden.
4. Flake tuna; combine with ground red pepper, if desired, and next 4 ingredients. Spread tuna mixture evenly on 1 side of each of 4 grilled bread slices; top with tomato and avocado slices. Cover with remaining 4 bread slices. **Makes** 4 servings.

Per serving: Calories 623 (42% from fat); Fat 29g (sat 4.5g, mono 14g, poly 8.5g); Protein 29.9g; Carb 61.5g; Fiber 7.3g; Chol 42mg; Iron 4mg; Sodium 1,038mg; Calc 109mg

Pesto-Crusted Orange Roughy

20 minutes or less
PREP: 5 MIN., COOK: 15 MIN.

2 tablespoons pesto
½ cup fine, dry breadcrumbs
¼ teaspoon pepper
4 (4-ounce) orange roughy fillets
Vegetable cooking spray

1. Combine pesto, breadcrumbs, and pepper in a shallow dish. Dredge fillets in breadcrumb mixture; place in an 11- x 7-inch baking dish coated with cooking spray. Coat fillets with cooking spray. Bake at 400° for 15 minutes or until fish flakes with a fork. **Makes** 4 servings.

Per serving: Calories 172 (25% from fat); Fat 4.7g (sat 1.1g, mono 2.9g, poly 0.4g); Protein 20.2g; Carb 11.2g; Fiber 0.9g; Chol 25mg; Iron 1mg; Sodium 529mg; Calc 105mg

Sautéed Shrimp and Linguine

30 minutes or less
PREP: 10 MIN., COOK: 14 MIN.

8 ounces uncooked linguine
1 tablespoon dark sesame oil
1 small onion, chopped
2 garlic cloves, minced
6 plum tomatoes, coarsely chopped
1 (2¼-ounce) can sliced ripe olives, drained
¼ cup lemon juice
1½ teaspoons dried Italian seasoning
½ teaspoon salt
½ teaspoon freshly ground pepper
1½ pounds peeled, medium-size fresh shrimp
2 ounces crumbled feta cheese

1. Cook pasta according to package directions, omitting salt and fat. Drain.
2. Meanwhile, heat oil in a large nonstick skillet over medium-high heat. Add onion and garlic, and sauté 3 minutes or until tender. Add tomato and next 5 ingredients; cook 6 minutes, stirring constantly. Add shrimp; cook 5 minutes or just until shrimp turn pink, stirring occasionally. Serve over pasta; sprinkle with cheese. **Makes** 6 servings (serving size: 1 cup shrimp mixture and ⅔ cup pasta).

Per serving: Calories 378 (21% from fat); Fat 8.7g (sat 2.6g, mono 2.5g, poly 2.2g); Protein 38.3g; Carb 36.1g; Fiber 2.8g; Chol 238mg; Iron 6mg; Sodium 618mg; Calc 162mg

Grilled Balsamic-Glazed
Peaches

Grilled Balsamic-Glazed Peaches

Freestone peaches are the best choice for this recipe because the pits can be easily removed.

PREP: 15 MIN., COOK: 14 MIN., OTHER: 10 MIN.

½ cup balsamic vinegar
3 tablespoons light brown sugar
1 teaspoon cracked pepper
⅛ teaspoon salt
6 firm, ripe peaches, halved
¼ cup vegetable oil

1. Combine first 4 ingredients in a saucepan. Bring to a boil; reduce heat, and simmer 2 to 3 minutes.
2. Remove pits from peaches; do not peel. Place peaches in a shallow dish. Pour vinegar mixture over peaches, tossing to coat. Let stand 10 minutes.

3. Remove peaches from vinegar mixture, reserving 2 tablespoons. Set remaining vinegar mixture aside.
4. Whisk together reserved 2 tablespoons vinegar mixture with oil, blending well. Set vinaigrette aside.
5. Place peach halves, cut sides down, on a lightly greased grill rack. Grill, covered with grill lid, over medium heat (300° to 350°) 5 minutes on each side or until firm and golden, basting with remaining vinegar mixture. Serve with vinaigrette. **Makes** 6 servings.

Per serving: Calories 165 (53% from fat); Fat 9.7g (sat 1g, mono 4.1g, poly 4.1g);
Protein 0.9g; Carb 21.1g; Fiber 1.6g; Chol 0mg; Iron 0.6mg; Sodium 54mg; Calc 14mg

Garlic-and-Herb Cheese Grits

10 minutes or less
PREP: 3 MIN., COOK: 7 MIN.

4 cups low-sodium, fat-free chicken broth
1 cup quick-cooking grits, uncooked
¼ teaspoon freshly ground pepper
1 (5-ounce) package light garlic-and-herb spreadable
    cheese

1. Bring chicken broth to a boil in a medium saucepan over high heat; gradually stir in grits. Cook, stirring constantly, 5 to 7 minutes or until thickened.
2. Remove from heat; stir in pepper and cheese. Serve immediately. **Makes** 5 cups (serving size: 1 cup).

Per serving: Calories 128 (37% from fat); Fat 5.3g (sat 3.8g, mono 0.1g, poly 0.2g); Protein 7.6g; Carb 26.9g; Fiber 0.5g; Chol 25mg; Iron 1.3mg; Sodium 644mg; Calc 4mg

Hummus

Use ½ cup of this creamy bean spread inside a pita to make a sandwich. Or serve it as a dip with pita chips or vegetables.

10 minutes or less
PREP: 10 MIN.

1 (19-ounce) can chickpeas (garbanzo
    beans), rinsed and drained
¼ cup tahini
1 tablespoon chopped fresh parsley
1 garlic clove
⅓ cup fresh lemon juice
1½ teaspoons ground cumin
¼ teaspoon ground red pepper
1 shallot, quartered
1 tablespoon lite soy sauce

1. Process all ingredients in a food processor until smooth, stopping to scrape down sides. **Makes** 1¾ cups (serving size: ¼ cup).

Per serving: Calories 137 (39% from fat); Fat 5.9g (sat 0.8g, mono 2g, poly 2.6g); Protein 6g; Carb 16.9g; Fiber 4.3g; Chol 0mg; Iron 2mg; Sodium 8mg; Calc 41mg

Southwestern Tabbouleh Salad

This nutrient-packed salad has both great texture and flavor. Add some whole wheat pita bread on the side.

PREP: 40 MIN., OTHER: 30 MIN.

1 cup uncooked bulgur wheat
1 cup boiling water
2 tomatoes, chopped
4 green onions, chopped
1 (15½-ounce) can black beans, rinsed and drained
¼ cup chopped fresh cilantro
½ teaspoon grated lime rind
¼ cup fresh lime juice
2 tablespoons olive oil
½ teaspoon ground cumin
½ teaspoon ground red pepper
1 (8¾-ounce) can no-salt-added corn kernels, drained
¼ teaspoon salt
Garnish: fresh parsley

1. Place bulgur in a large bowl, and add 1 cup boiling water. Cover and let stand 30 minutes. Add tomato and next 10 ingredients to bulgur. Toss gently. Cover and chill up to 8 hours. Garnish, if desired. **Makes** 8 cups.

Per cup: Calories 157 (23% from fat); Fat 4g (sat 0.6g, mono 2.8g, poly 0.6g); Protein 4g; Carb 28g; Fiber 6.7g; Chol 0mg; Iron 1.3mg; Sodium 226mg; Calc 24mg

Roasted Garlic-Potato Soup

20 minutes or less
PREP: 10 MIN., COOK: 3 MIN.

2 cups fat-free milk
1½ cups water
½ (7.6-ounce) package roasted garlic instant mashed
    potatoes
1 cup (4 ounces) shredded 2% reduced-fat sharp
    Cheddar cheese, divided
¼ teaspoon freshly ground pepper

1. Combine milk and 1½ cups water in a large saucepan; bring to a boil. Remove from heat; add potatoes, and whisk until well blended. Add ¾ cup cheese, stirring until cheese melts. Spoon evenly into 4 bowls; sprinkle evenly with remaining ¼ cup cheese and pepper. **Makes** 4 servings (serving size: 1 cup).

Per serving: Calories 146 (40% from fat); Fat 6.5g (sat 3.9g, mono 0.1g, poly 0g); Protein 12.7g; Carb 11g; Fiber 0.2g; Chol 20mg; Iron 0.2mg; Sodium 299mg; Calc 354mg

Southwestern Tabbouleh Salad

Best-Ever Buttermilk Biscuits

Toast leftover biscuits for breakfast—and don't forget the honey!

20 minutes or less
PREP: 8 MIN., COOK: 10 MIN.

make
ahead

1 cup all-purpose flour
1½ teaspoons baking powder
½ teaspoon baking soda
¼ teaspoon salt
2 tablespoons chilled butter or margarine, cut into
    small pieces
½ cup low-fat buttermilk
Honey (optional)

1. Lightly spoon flour into a dry measuring cup; level with a knife.

2. Combine flour and next 3 ingredients in a bowl; cut in butter with a pastry blender or 2 knives until mixture is crumbly. Add buttermilk; stir just until dry ingredients are moistened.

3. Turn dough out onto a lightly floured surface; knead 4 or 5 times. Roll dough to ½-inch thickness; cut with a 2½-inch biscuit cutter. Place on a lightly greased baking sheet. Bake at 450° for 10 minutes or until golden. Serve warm with honey, if desired. **Makes** 7 servings (serving size: 1 biscuit).

Per serving: Calories 102 (32% from fat); Fat 3.6g (sat 2.2g, mono 1g, poly 0.2g); Protein 2.5g; Carb 14.8g; Fiber 0.5g; Chol 10mg; Iron 0.9mg; Sodium 298mg; Calc 79mg

Best-Ever Buttermilk
Biscuits

Parmesan Corn Muffins

30 minutes or less
PREP: 10 MIN., COOK: 15 MIN.

make
ahead

2 cups white cornmeal mix
¾ cup all-purpose flour
½ cup grated Parmesan cheese
¼ teaspoon ground red pepper
2½ cups fat-free buttermilk
½ cup egg substitute
2 tablespoons vegetable oil

1. Combine first 4 ingredients in a large bowl; make a
well in center of mixture.
2. Stir together buttermilk, egg substitute, and oil; add
to dry ingredients, stirring just until moistened. Spoon
into muffin pans coated with cooking spray, filling
two-thirds full.
3. Bake at 425° for 15 minutes or until golden. Remove
from pans immediately, and cool on wire racks. **Makes**
17 muffins (serving size: 1 muffin).

Per serving: Calories 118 (29% from fat); Fat 3.7g (sat 1g, mono 1.5g, poly 0.9g); Protein 5g;
Carb 16g; Fiber 1g; Chol 5mg; Iron 1.2mg; Sodium 284mg; Calc 138mg

Baked Hush Puppies

*Serve these crisp "puppies" with Oven-Fried Catfish
(page 106).*

PREP: 11 MIN., COOK: 13 MIN. PER BATCH

2 cups self-rising cornmeal mix
⅛ teaspoon ground red pepper
2 large eggs, lightly beaten
¾ cup 1% low-fat milk
¼ cup vegetable oil
½ cup finely chopped onion

1. Combine cornmeal mix and red pepper in a large
bowl; make a well in center of mixture.
2. Combine eggs and next 3 ingredients in a large
bowl; stir well. Add egg mixture to cornmeal mixture,
stirring just until dry ingredients are moistened. Spoon
about 1 tablespoon batter into miniature (1¾-inch)
muffin pans coated with cooking spray.
3. Bake at 425° for 13 minutes or until golden. Remove
from pans, and serve immediately. **Makes** about 3 dozen
(serving size: 1 hush puppy).

Per serving: Calories 69 (30% from fat); Fat 2.4g (sat 0.3g, mono 1.2g, poly 0.7g);
Protein 1.6g; Carb 10.7g; Fiber 0g; Chol 12mg; Iron 0.9mg; Sodium 229mg; Calc 19mg

Jalapeño Cornbread

PREP: 11 MIN., COOK: 21 MIN.

1 tablespoon vegetable oil
1 cup self-rising yellow cornmeal
2 teaspoons baking powder
2 large eggs
3 tablespoons nonfat sour cream
1 (8¾-ounce) can cream-style corn
¼ cup sliced pickled jalapeño pepper, chopped

1. Heat oil in an 8-inch cast-iron skillet in a 450° oven
5 minutes or until hot.
2. Combine cornmeal and baking powder in a large
bowl; make a well in the center of mixture. Combine
eggs and next 3 ingredients; add to cornmeal mixture,
stirring just until dry ingredients are moistened.
3. Remove pan from oven. Stir hot oil into batter. Pour
batter into hot skillet. Bake at 450° for 21 minutes or
until golden. Remove from pan immediately. Cut into
wedges. **Makes** 8 servings.

Per serving: Calories 137 (26% from fat); Fat 3.9g (sat 0.6g, mono 1.5g, poly 0.7g);
Protein 3.7g; Carb 21.6g; Fiber 1.6g; Chol 54mg; Iron 1.2mg; Sodium 526mg; Calc 102mg

Blueberry Sherbet

Blueberry Sherbet

All you need to make this easy and flavorful dessert is just 5 ingredients, a pan, your freezer, and a blender.

PREP: 15 MIN., OTHER: 8 HR.

make ahead

2 cups fresh or frozen blueberries, thawed
1 cup fat-free buttermilk
½ cup sugar
1 tablespoon fresh lemon juice
½ teaspoon vanilla extract
Garnish: fresh mint sprig

1. Process first 5 ingredients in a blender until smooth. Pour into a 9-inch square pan; cover and freeze 4 hours or until firm.
2. Process frozen mixture, in batches, in a blender until smooth. Cover and freeze 4 hours or until frozen. Garnish, if desired. **Makes** 3 cups.

Per ½ cup: Calories 110 (4% from fat); Fat 0.5g (sat 0.2g, mono 0.1g, poly 0.1g); Protein 1.7g; Carb 26g; Fiber 1.3g; Chol 1mg; Iron 0.1mg; Sodium 46mg; Calc 51mg

Blueberry Cheesecake

At less than half the calories and one-third the fat of a classic cheesecake, this recipe is a keeper.

PREP: 20 MIN.; COOK: 1 HR., 15 MIN.; OTHER: 9 HR.

make ahead

1 cup graham cracker crumbs
3 tablespoons butter, melted
1 tablespoon sugar
2 (8-ounce) packages ⅓-less-fat cream cheese, softened
1 (8-ounce) package fat-free cream cheese, softened
1 cup sugar
3 tablespoons all-purpose flour
½ teaspoon salt
2 large eggs
2 egg whites
1 (8-ounce) container light sour cream
1 teaspoon vanilla extract
1 tablespoon grated lemon rind
1½ cups fresh or frozen blueberries
1 cup fat-free frozen whipped topping, thawed
¼ cup light sour cream

1. Combine first 3 ingredients in a small bowl. Press mixture on bottom and 1½ inches up sides of a 9-inch springform pan coated with cooking spray.
2. Bake at 350° for 5 minutes. Remove from oven; set aside.
3. Beat cream cheese at medium speed with an electric mixer until smooth.
4. Combine 1 cup sugar, flour, and salt. Add to cream cheese, beating until blended. Add eggs, 1 at a time, beating well after each addition. Add egg whites, beating until blended.
5. Add 8-ounce container sour cream, vanilla, and lemon rind, beating just until blended. Gently stir in blueberries. Pour mixture into prepared pan.
6. Bake at 300° for 1 hour and 10 minutes or until center of cheesecake is firm. Turn off oven, and let cheesecake stand in oven, with oven door partially open, 30 minutes.
7. Remove cheesecake from oven; cool in pan on a wire rack 30 minutes. Cover cheesecake, and chill 8 hours. Gently run a knife around edges of pan to release sides.
8. Stir together whipped topping and ¼ cup sour cream. Spread over cheesecake. **Makes** 12 servings.

Per serving: Calories 315 (45% from fat); Fat 15.6g (sat 9.5g, mono 1.5g, poly 0.5g); Protein 10.2g; Carb 33.4g; Fiber 0.8g; Chol 83mg; Iron 0.6mg; Sodium 469mg; Calc 110mg

storing berries

Store blueberries in airtight containers in the refrigerator up to five days. Remember not to wash the berries until you're ready to eat them or use them in a recipe. If you're lucky enough to have more than you can eat in five days, freeze the rest. Place unwashed berries in a single layer on a baking sheet. Place the baking sheet in the freezer. Once they're frozen, transfer the berries into airtight containers, and store them in the freezer up to five months.

Pears With Raspberry
Sherbet

Pears With Raspberry Sherbet

20 minutes or less

PREP: 15 MIN.

5 tablespoons fat-free chocolate sundae syrup, divided (we used Smucker's)
1 (29-ounce) can pear halves in extra light syrup, drained
1¼ cups raspberry sherbet
1¼ cups fresh raspberries
Garnish: fresh mint sprigs

1. Drizzle 2 tablespoons chocolate syrup evenly over 5 dessert plates. Place pear halves on chocolate syrup, using a slotted spoon. Top each serving with ¼ cup sherbet; drizzle evenly with remaining chocolate syrup. Sprinkle raspberries over pear halves. Garnish, if desired. Serve immediately. **Makes** 5 servings (serving size: 1 pear half, ¼ cup sherbet, 1 tablespoon chocolate syrup, and ¼ cup raspberries.)

Per serving: Calories 175 (3% from fat); Fat 0.7g (sat 0.3g, mono 0g, poly 0.1g); Protein 1.8g; Carb 41.8g; Fiber 4g; Chol 3mg; Iron 0.5mg; Sodium 72mg; Calc 47mg

Sautéed Pineapple

Brown sugar adds a sweetness to this pineapple you won't be able to resist.

10 minutes or less

PREP: 3 MIN., COOK: 7 MIN.

2 (20-ounce) cans pineapple chunks in juice
1 tablespoon reduced-calorie margarine
2 tablespoons brown sugar
1 tablespoon rum or ½ teaspoon rum extract
½ teaspoon ground cinnamon

1. Drain pineapple chunks, reserving ¼ cup juice.
2. Melt margarine in a large nonstick skillet over medium heat; add pineapple chunks, reserved juice, brown sugar, rum, and cinnamon. Bring to a boil; reduce heat, and simmer 5 minutes, stirring frequently. Serve warm. **Makes** 6 servings.

Per serving: Calories 91 (9% from fat); Fat 0.9g (sat 0.2g, mono 0.4g, poly 0.3g); Protein 0g; Carb 18.9g; Fiber 1g; Chol 0mg; Iron 0.4mg; Sodium 33mg; Calc 5mg

Oatmeal-Raisin Cookies

With their crispy edges and chewy middle, no one will guess that these quick little gems are healthy.

PREP: 8 MIN., COOK: 12 MIN. PER BATCH

make
ahead

¼ cup margarine, softened
½ cup granulated sugar
½ cup firmly packed brown sugar
½ cup egg substitute
2 teaspoons vanilla extract
¾ cup all-purpose flour
¼ teaspoon baking soda
⅛ teaspoon salt
1½ cups quick-cooking oats, uncooked
½ cup raisins

1. Beat margarine at medium speed with an electric mixer. Gradually add sugars, beating well. Add egg substitute and vanilla; mix well.
2. Combine flour and next 3 ingredients. Gradually add to margarine mixture, mixing well. Stir in raisins.
3. Drop dough by 2 teaspoonfuls onto baking sheets coated with cooking spray. Bake at 350° for 10 to 12 minutes or until lightly browned. Remove to wire racks to cool. **Makes** 3 dozen (serving size: 1 cookie).

Per serving: Calories 64 (21% from fat); Fat 1.5g (sat 0.3g, mono 0.7g, poly 0.5g); Protein 1.2g; Carb 11.8g; Fiber 0.5g; Chol 0mg; Iron 0.4mg; Sodium 40mg; Calc 7mg

Grilled Pork Chops With Pistachio Pesto
and Parmesan Cheese Grits, page 124

quickies from the GRILL

Peppered Rib-eye Steaks

To save time, work on the side dishes while the steaks chill in the refrigerator.

PREP: 6 MIN., COOK: 16 MIN., OTHER: 1 HR.

make
ahead

3 teaspoons dried thyme
3 teaspoons garlic powder
2 teaspoons freshly ground black pepper
1½ teaspoons salt
1½ teaspoons ground red pepper
1½ teaspoons lemon pepper
1½ teaspoons dried parsley flakes
6 (1½-inch-thick) rib-eye steaks
3 tablespoons olive oil

1. Combine first 7 ingredients. Brush steaks with oil; rub with pepper mixture. Cover and chill 1 to 24 hours.

2. Grill, covered with grill lid, over medium-high heat (350° to 400°) 6 to 8 minutes on each side or to desired degree of doneness. **Makes** 6 servings.

Peppered Rib-eye Steak, Cheesy Green Onion-and-Bacon Mashed Potatoes (page 336), Fresh Mozzarella-Tomato-Basil Salad (page 37), and Marinated Grilled Squash (page 147)

Grilled Gorgonzola Rib-eye Steaks

Coarsely grained kosher salt adds nice texture to the seasoning blend slathered on these steaks. You can prepare this recipe without kosher salt by substituting 1 teaspoon regular salt in place of 1½ teaspoons kosher salt.

30 minutes or less
PREP: 5 MIN., COOK: 19 MIN.

1 tablespoon minced garlic
1 tablespoon minced shallot
2 tablespoons olive oil
1½ teaspoons kosher salt
½ teaspoon ground white pepper
4 (8-ounce) rib-eye steaks
4 ounces Gorgonzola cheese
¼ cup fine, dry breadcrumbs (commercial)
8 large green onions

1. Combine first 5 ingredients; stir well. Brush about two-thirds of mixture evenly over both sides of steaks. Grill, covered with grill lid, over medium-high heat (350° to 400°) 6 to 8 minutes on each side or to desired degree of doneness.
2. Remove steaks from grill, and place on a rack in a broiler pan. Crumble cheese evenly over steaks; sprinkle breadcrumbs evenly over cheese. Place green onions around steaks on rack. Brush remaining garlic mixture over green onions. Broil 5½ inches from heat 3 minutes or until cheese is lightly browned. **Makes** 4 servings.

Asian Grilled Flank Steak

Score steak diagonally across the grain at ¾-inch intervals to encourage the marinade to seep in.

PREP: 10 MIN., COOK: 20 MIN., OTHER: 8 HR.

make ahead

1½ pounds flank steak
¼ cup soy sauce
¼ cup vegetable oil
2 tablespoons cider vinegar
2 tablespoons honey
½ teaspoon ground ginger
¼ teaspoon garlic powder

1. Score steak diagonally across grain at ¾-inch intervals. Place steak in a large zip-top plastic freezer bag or shallow dish. Combine soy sauce and remaining

5 ingredients. Pour ½ cup marinade over steak; seal or cover, and marinate in refrigerator 8 to 24 hours, turning occasionally. Cover and chill remaining marinade.
2. Remove steak from marinade, discarding marinade in bag or dish. Grill steak, without grill lid, over medium-high heat (350° to 400°) 8 to 10 minutes on each side or to desired degree of doneness, basting with reserved marinade during last 5 minutes. To serve, slice diagonally across grain. **Makes** 4 servings.

Peppered Flank Steaks

No fresh thyme? No problem. Almost any herb works well with this tangy pepper-based seasoning.

PREP: 13 MIN., COOK: 16 MIN., OTHER: 8 HR.

make ahead

¾ cup olive oil
⅓ cup red wine vinegar
¼ cup Dijon mustard
2 green onions, chopped
4 garlic cloves, minced
1½ tablespoons coarsely ground pepper
1 tablespoon minced fresh thyme
1 teaspoon salt
2 (1½-pound) flank steaks

1. Combine first 8 ingredients in a large zip-top plastic freezer bag. Add steaks; seal bag securely.
2. Marinate in refrigerator 8 to 24 hours, turning occasionally.
3. Remove steaks from marinade, discarding marinade. Grill, covered with grill lid, over medium-high heat (350° to 400°) 8 minutes on each side or to desired degree of doneness.
4. Slice steaks diagonally across the grain into thin slices. **Makes** 8 to 10 servings.

Steak Salad
Niçoise

Steak Salad Niçoise

PREP: 10 MIN.; COOK: 25 MIN.; OTHER: 1 HR., 5 MIN.

1 (16-ounce) bottle vinaigrette
2 tablespoons Dijon mustard
2 teaspoons anchovy paste (optional)
1½ pounds flank steak
4 medium-size new potatoes, cut into
    ¼-inch-thick slices
¼ pound small green beans, trimmed
4 plum tomatoes, each cut into 4 wedges
16 kalamata or ripe black olives
2 hard-cooked eggs, quartered
    (optional)
6 cups gourmet salad greens

1. Whisk together vinaigrette, mustard, and, if desired, anchovy paste.

2. Pour ½ cup vinaigrette mixture into a shallow dish or zip-top plastic freezer bag, and add flank steak. Cover or seal, and chill 1 hour, turning occasionally. Reserve remaining vinaigrette mixture.
3. Cook potatoes in boiling water to cover in a large saucepan 10 minutes; add green beans, and cook 5 minutes or until beans are crisp-tender. Drain and rinse with cold water to stop the cooking process.
4. Remove flank steak from marinade; discard marinade.
5. Grill steak, covered with grill lid, over medium-high heat (350° to 400°) 5 minutes on each side or to desired degree of doneness. Remove from grill, and let stand 5 minutes. Cut steak diagonally across the grain into ¼-inch-thick slices.
6. Arrange steak, green beans, potatoes, tomatoes, olives, and, if desired, eggs on salad greens. Serve with reserved vinaigrette mixture. **Makes** 4 servings.

Texas Grilled Sirloin and Serrano Chile Salsa

PREP: 15 MIN., COOK: 16 MIN., OTHER: 1 HR.

1 pound lean boneless top sirloin steak, trimmed
¼ cup lime juice
2 tablespoons chopped fresh or 2 teaspoons
    dried oregano
1 tablespoon chopped fresh or 2 teaspoons
    dried cilantro
1 teaspoon pepper
1 garlic clove, pressed
½ teaspoon salt
Serrano Chile Salsa
Garnishes: fresh cilantro sprigs, lime slices

1. Combine steak and next 5 ingredients in a large zip-top plastic freezer bag; seal and shake well. Chill 1 hour, turning occasionally.
2. Remove steak from marinade, discarding marinade. Sprinkle steak evenly with salt. Grill steak, covered with grill lid, over medium-high heat (350° to 400°) 7 to 8 minutes on each side or to desired degree of doneness. Cut diagonally across the grain into thin slices. Serve with Serrano Chile Salsa. Garnish, if desired. **Makes** 4 servings.

Serrano Chile Salsa:

PREP: 15 MIN., OTHER: 1 HR.

6 serrano chile peppers, diced
1 pound plum tomatoes, diced
¼ cup orange juice
2 tablespoons diced red onion
2 tablespoons diced yellow or red bell pepper
2 tablespoons minced fresh cilantro
1 tablespoon rice vinegar
½ teaspoon salt
½ teaspoon sugar

1. Combine serrano chile peppers and remaining ingredients; cover and chill 1 hour. **Makes** 2 cups.

Italian Grilled Steak

This recipe uses thinly pounded steaks that don't require a lot of time on the grill. Serve with salad and garlic bread.

PREP: 10 MIN., COOK: 12 MIN., OTHER: 2 HR.

4 (1-inch-thick) chuck-eye steaks
½ teaspoon salt
¼ teaspoon pepper
½ cup olive oil
¼ cup balsamic vinegar
2 garlic cloves, chopped
1 teaspoon chopped fresh thyme

1. Place chuck-eye steaks between 2 sheets of heavy-duty plastic wrap; flatten to a ½-inch thickness using a meat mallet or rolling pin.
2. Sprinkle chuck-eye steaks evenly with salt and pepper.
3. Combine oil and next 3 ingredients in a large shallow dish or zip-top plastic freezer bag; add steaks. Cover or seal; chill 1 to 2 hours.
4. Remove steaks from marinade, discarding marinade.
5. Grill steaks, covered with grill lid, over medium-high heat (350° to 400°) 6 minutes on each side or until done. **Makes** 4 servings.

Grilled Pork Chops With Pistachio Pesto and Parmesan Cheese Grits

30 minutes or less
PREP: 2 MIN., COOK: 20 MIN.

4 (1-inch-thick) center-cut bone-in pork chops (we
    tested with Berkshire)
½ teaspoon kosher salt
¼ teaspoon freshly ground black pepper
Parmesan Cheese Grits
Pistachio Pesto with Sun-dried Tomatoes

1. Sprinkle pork chops with salt and pepper. Grill pork
chops, covered with grill lid, over medium-high heat
(350° to 400°) 8 to 10 minutes on each side or until done.
2. Serve chops over Parmesan Cheese Grits, and top each
serving with 2 tablespoons Pistachio Pesto with Sun-
dried Tomatoes. **Makes** 4 servings.

Parmesan Cheese Grits:
PREP: 3 MIN., COOK: 10 MIN.

1 (14-ounce) can chicken broth
1½ cups milk
¾ cup uncooked quick-cooking grits
1 cup freshly grated Parmesan cheese
1 teaspoon freshly ground pepper

1. Bring chicken broth and milk just to a boil in a large
saucepan. Slowly stir in grits. Cover and reduce heat
to medium-low. Cook 6 to 7 minutes, stirring occasionally, or until mixture is thickened. Add cheese and
pepper, stirring until cheese is melted. **Makes** 3½ cups.

Pistachio Pesto with Sun-dried Tomatoes:
PREP: 6 MIN.

½ cup refrigerated pesto sauce
½ cup shelled pistachio nuts, chopped
⅓ cup drained and julienne-cut sun-dried tomatoes
    packed in oil, chopped
3 tablespoons extra virgin olive oil

1. Combine all ingredients, stirring well. Store leftovers
in refrigerator and spread on bread before toasting, or
toss with hot pasta. **Makes** 1¼ cups.

**Grilled Pork Chop With Pistachio Pesto
and Parmesan Cheese Grits**

Blue Cheese-Stuffed Chop

Blue Cheese-Stuffed Chops

Ask your butcher to cut pockets in the loin chops for you—it will save time and keep the recipe easy. Serve these cheesy chops with a crisp green salad topped with grilled red peppers for a splash of color. Simply cut bell peppers in half, remove seeds, and flatten peppers with the palm of your hand. Grill 8 minutes on each side along with the chops, and they will all be ready at the same time.

PREP: 13 MIN., COOK: 19 MIN.

½ cup crumbled blue cheese
2 green onions, thinly sliced
4 (1-inch-thick) bone-in pork loin chops, trimmed
    and cut with pockets
1 tablespoon all-purpose flour
¼ cup sour cream
½ teaspoon chicken bouillon granules
⅛ teaspoon pepper
¾ cup milk
Crumbled blue cheese (optional)
Cracked pepper (optional)

1. Toss together ½ cup crumbled blue cheese and green onions in a small bowl. Stuff mixture into pockets of chops; secure openings with wooden picks. Grill, covered with grill lid, over medium-high heat (350° to 400°) 8 minutes on each side or until done. Remove wooden picks. Set aside, and keep warm.

2. Combine flour and next 3 ingredients in a small saucepan, whisking until smooth. Gradually whisk in milk. Bring to a boil over medium heat, stirring constantly; reduce heat, and simmer 3 minutes, whisking constantly, until mixture is thickened and bubbly. Serve chops with sauce; top with crumbled blue cheese and cracked pepper, if desired. **Makes** 4 servings.

Pork Medallions in
Mustard Sauce

Pork Medallions in Mustard Sauce

This dish pairs nicely with Carrot-Sweet Potato Puree (page 329) and green beans.

PREP: 15 MIN., COOK: 25 MIN., OTHER: 8 HR.

make
ahead

2 tablespoons vegetable oil
2 tablespoons coarse-grained mustard
½ teaspoon salt
½ teaspoon coarsely ground pepper
1½ pounds pork tenderloin
1 teaspoon pepper
Mustard Sauce

1. Stir together first 4 ingredients. Rub mixture over pork, and place in a large zip-top plastic freezer bag. Seal and chill 8 hours; rub pork evenly with 1 teaspoon pepper.

2. Grill, covered with grill lid, over medium-high heat (350° to 400°) for 10 minutes; turn meat, and grill 15 more minutes or until a meat thermometer inserted in thickest portion of tenderloin registers 155°. Slice pork, and serve with Mustard Sauce. **Makes** 4 servings.

Mustard Sauce:
This sauce may also be served with chicken or fish.

PREP: 5 MIN., COOK: 20 MIN.

1¾ cups whipping cream
¼ cup coarse-grained mustard
¼ teaspoon salt
⅛ teaspoon ground white pepper

1. Cook whipping cream in a heavy saucepan over medium heat until reduced to 1¼ cups (about 20 minutes). Do not boil. Stir in remaining ingredients, and cook 1 more minute. Store in an airtight container in refrigerator up to 3 days. **Makes** 1¼ cups.

Molasses Pork Tenderloin With Red Wine Sauce

PREP: 10 MIN.; COOK: 20 MIN.; OTHER: 8 HR., 10 MIN.

 make ahead

¾ cup lite soy sauce
1 cup molasses
3 tablespoons fresh lemon juice
3 tablespoons olive oil
2 tablespoons minced fresh ginger
1 large garlic clove, minced
1 (2- to 2½-pound) package pork tenderloins
Red Wine Sauce

1. Combine first 6 ingredients in a shallow dish or zip-top plastic freezer bag; add tenderloins. Cover or seal, and chill 8 hours. Remove tenderloins from marinade, discarding marinade.
2. Grill tenderloins, covered with grill lid, over medium-high heat (350° to 400°) 20 minutes or until a meat thermometer inserted in thickest portion registers 155°, turning occasionally. Let stand 10 minutes before slicing. Serve with Red Wine Sauce. **Makes** 6 to 8 servings.
Note: Pork tenderloins may be pan-seared in a hot skillet to brown and then baked at 375° for 15 to 20 minutes.

Red Wine Sauce:

PREP: 10 MIN., COOK: 12 MIN.

½ small sweet onion, minced
2 tablespoons butter
½ cup dry red wine
1 (14-ounce) can beef broth
¼ cup water
2 tablespoons cornstarch
¼ teaspoon salt

1. Sauté onion in butter in a large saucepan over medium-high heat 3 minutes or until browned. Add wine; cook 3 minutes. Add broth; bring to a boil, and cook 5 minutes.
2. Stir together ¼ cup water, 2 tablespoons cornstarch, and ¼ teaspoon salt; add to broth mixture, stirring constantly, 1 minute or until mixture thickens to desired consistency. Remove from heat, and serve over pork tenderloins. **Makes** 1¼ cups.

Grilled Pork Cosmopolitan Salad

This tasty recipe is based on the ever-cool and colorful Cosmopolitan cocktail.

PREP: 15 MIN., COOK: 25 MIN., OTHER: 25 MIN.

¼ cup jellied cranberry sauce
¼ cup orange marmalade
⅓ cup orange juice
¼ cup fresh lime juice (about 3 limes)
¼ cup peanut oil
2¼ teaspoons salt, divided
2 tablespoons vodka
1 tablespoon minced or grated fresh ginger
2 (1-pound) packages pork tenderloins
2 teaspoons lemon pepper
½ teaspoon ground red pepper
2 (10-ounce) packages European blend salad greens
½ cup dried cranberries
1 (11-ounce) can mandarin oranges, drained

1. Whisk together cranberry sauce and marmalade in a small saucepan over low heat until melted. Remove from heat. Whisk in orange juice, lime juice, and oil. Reserve ½ cup of cranberry mixture, and add ¼ teaspoon salt; set aside. Pour remaining cranberry mixture into a shallow dish or zip-top plastic freezer bag; add vodka, ginger, and pork, turning to coat all sides. Cover or seal, and chill 15 minutes, turning occasionally. Remove pork from marinade, discarding marinade.
2. Stir together lemon pepper, ground red pepper, and remaining 2 teaspoons salt; sprinkle evenly over pork.
3. Grill, covered with grill lid, over medium-high heat (350° to 400°) 10 minutes on each side or until a meat thermometer inserted in thickest portion registers 155°. Remove from grill, and cover with aluminum foil. Let stand 10 minutes. Cut pork diagonally into ¼-inch-thick slices.
4. Toss together salad greens, cranberries, oranges, and reserved ½ cup cranberry mixture; serve with pork. **Makes** 6 to 8 servings.

Garlic-Lime Chicken

Garlic-Lime Chicken

A short soak in a zingy marinade infuses this grilled chicken with flavor. Layer this zesty chicken atop black beans and prepared yellow saffron rice mix, such as Mahatma.

PREP: 3 MIN., COOK: 12 MIN., OTHER: 20 MIN.

½ cup lite soy sauce
¼ cup fresh lime juice
1 tablespoon Worcestershire sauce
½ teaspoon dry mustard
½ teaspoon coarsely ground pepper
2 garlic cloves, minced
4 skinned and boned chicken breasts
Garnish: lime wedges

1. Combine first 6 ingredients in a large zip-top plastic freezer bag; add chicken. Seal bag; marinate in refrigerator 20 minutes, turning bag once.
2. Remove chicken from marinade, discarding marinade. Coat grill rack with cooking spray; place rack on grill over medium-high heat (350° to 400°). Place chicken on rack, and grill, covered with grill lid, 6 minutes on each side or until done. Garnish, if desired. **Makes** 4 servings.

poultry pointers

- Store poultry well-wrapped in plastic wrap in the coldest part of your refrigerator up to 2 days.
- Don't store raw chicken next to food you plan on eating raw such as lettuce.
- Always rinse chicken before cooking, and use a clean knife and a cutting board that you can sanitize.
- Wash your hands, knife, and cutting board with hot, soapy water immediately after use to prevent cross-contamination with other foods.

Teriyaki Grilled Chicken Thighs

PREP: 10 MIN., COOK: 20 MIN., OTHER: 8 HR.

make ahead

8 large chicken thighs, skinned, if desired
    (about 2 pounds)
½ cup soy sauce
5 green onions, chopped
¼ cup lime juice
2 tablespoons dark brown sugar
1 tablespoon honey
1 teaspoon dried crushed red pepper
1 garlic clove, pressed

1. Place chicken in an 11- x 7-inch baking dish. Combine soy sauce and next 6 ingredients; pour over chicken. Cover and marinate in refrigerator 8 hours, turning occasionally.
2. Drain chicken, reserving marinade. Bring reserved marinade to a boil in a small saucepan; remove from heat, and reserve for basting.
3. Cook chicken, without grill lid, over medium heat (300° to 350°) 10 minutes on each side or until done, basting often with reserved marinade. **Makes** 4 servings.

Grilled Chicken With Sweet Soy
Slaw and Dipping Sauce

Grilled Chicken With Sweet Soy Slaw and Dipping Sauce

The dipping sauce will keep in the refrigerator, covered, for several weeks. Warm sauce over medium-low heat on the cooktop before serving. You can use sauce as a marinade for steaks or shrimp, too.

PREP: 5 MIN., COOK: 26 MIN., OTHER: 10 MIN.

make
ahead

2 cups soy sauce
2 tablespoons canola oil
8 pieces crystallized ginger
2 garlic cloves, minced
3 cups sugar
6 skinned and boned chicken breasts
2 (12-ounce) packages broccoli slaw
¼ cup green onions, chopped
1 tablespoons sesame seeds, toasted
Salt and pepper to taste

1. Combine first 4 ingredients in a small saucepan over medium heat. Stir in sugar. Cook, stirring occasionally, for 10 minutes or until sugar dissolves. Remove from heat. (Mixture will thicken.) Reserve 1½ cups soy mixture, and set aside.

2. Brush both sides of chicken evenly with remaining soy mixture; cover and let stand 10 minutes.

3. Grill, covered with grill lid, over medium-high heat (350° to 400°) 6 to 8 minutes on each side or until done.

4. Toss together broccoli slaw, green onions, sesame seeds, and ½ cup reserved soy mixture; top with grilled chicken. Season with salt and pepper to taste. Serve with remaining 1 cup reserved soy mixture. **Makes** 6 servings.

Grilled Salmon With Sweet Soy Slaw and Dipping Sauce: Substitute 6 (4-ounce) salmon fillets for chicken, and grill 4 to 6 minutes on each side or until fish flakes with a fork.

Sesame-Ginger Chicken

Stir together just four tangy and sweet ingredients to baste on grilled Sesame-Ginger Chicken.
Use kitchen shears to cut the green onion garnish.

30 minutes or less
PREP: 10 MIN., COOK: 12 MIN.

1 tablespoon sesame seeds, toasted
2 tablespoons soy sauce
2 tablespoons honey
2 teaspoons grated fresh ginger
Vegetable cooking spray
4 skinned and boned chicken breasts
Mixed salad greens
Garnish: sliced green onions

1. Stir together toasted sesame seeds and next 3 ingredients.
2. Coat cooking grate with cooking spray; place on grill over medium-high heat (350° to 400°). Place chicken on grate; grill 6 minutes on each side or until done, basting often with sauce mixture. Serve over salad greens. Garnish, if desired. **Makes** 4 servings.
Note: Soy sauce mixture may also be basted on pork.

Sesame-Ginger Chicken

Honey Barbecue Chicken

Honey Barbecue Chicken

make ahead

PREP: 5 MIN.; COOK: 1 HR., 10 MIN.

Vegetable cooking spray
6 bone-in chicken breasts
8 chicken drumsticks
2 teaspoons salt
1 teaspoon pepper
Honey Barbecue Sauce

1. Coat cold cooking grate with cooking spray, and place on grill over medium-high heat (350° to 400°). Sprinkle chicken evenly with salt and pepper. Place on food grate.

2. Grill, covered with grill lid, 5 to 10 minutes on each side. Reduce heat to low (under 300°); grill, covered, 40 to 50 minutes for breasts and 30 to 40 minutes for drumsticks or until done. Brush chicken with 1 cup Honey Barbecue Sauce during last 10 minutes of grilling. Serve with remaining 1 cup sauce. **Makes** 8 to 10 servings.

Honey Barbecue Sauce:
This sauce can be made up to a week in advance.

PREP: 15 MIN., COOK: 10 MIN.

¼ cup butter
1 medium onion, diced (about 1 cup)
1 cup ketchup
⅓ cup water
¼ cup honey
2 tablespoons lemon juice
1 tablespoon Worcestershire sauce
¼ teaspoon ground black pepper

1. Melt butter in small saucepan over medium heat; add onion, and sauté 4 to 5 minutes or until tender. Stir in ketchup and remaining ingredients; bring to a boil. Reduce heat, and simmer, uncovered, 5 minutes. Store leftover sauce in an airtight container in refrigerator up to 1 week. **Makes** about 2 cups.

Grilled Southwestern Chicken With Pineapple Salsa

Serve with yellow rice garnished with chopped fresh cilantro.

20 minutes or less
PREP: 10 MIN., COOK: 8 MIN.

make ahead

4 skinned and boned chicken breasts
2 tablespoons olive oil
1 tablespoon chili powder
2 teaspoons garlic salt
2 teaspoons paprika
Pineapple Salsa

1. Place chicken between 2 sheets of heavy-duty plastic wrap; flatten to a ½-inch thickness using a meat mallet or rolling pin. Rub evenly with olive oil, and sprinkle evenly with chili powder, garlic salt, and paprika.
2. Grill chicken, covered with grill lid, over medium-high heat (350° to 400°) 4 minutes on each side or until done. Serve with Pineapple Salsa. **Makes** 4 servings.

Pineapple Salsa:

PREP: 10 MIN., COOK: 4 MIN.

¼ cup diced red bell pepper
3 tablespoons light brown sugar
2 tablespoons chopped fresh cilantro
2 tablespoons orange juice
2 tablespoons fresh lime juice
1 tablespoon chopped chipotle pepper in adobo
        sauce
1 tablespoon butter
1 (15-ounce) can sliced pineapple, drained

1. Stir together first 6 ingredients.
2. Melt butter in a skillet over medium-high heat; add pineapple slices, and cook 2 minutes on each side or until golden brown. Coarsely chop; combine with bell pepper mixture. Store in an airtight container in the refrigerator up to 1 week. **Makes** 2 cups.

Grilled Chicken With Lemon-Yogurt Coleslaw

30 minutes or less
PREP: 14 MIN., COOK: 16 MIN.

4 skinned and boned chicken breasts
½ teaspoon garlic salt
1 teaspoon lemon pepper seasoning
½ cup plain yogurt
1 tablespoon sugar
2 tablespoons lemon juice
½ cup crumbled feta cheese
2 tablespoons minced fresh chives
1 (10-ounce) package finely shredded cabbage

1. Sprinkle chicken with garlic salt and lemon pepper.
2. Grill chicken breasts, covered with grill lid, over medium-high heat (350° to 400°) 7 to 8 minutes on each side or until done. Cool slightly, and cut into thin strips.
3. Whisk together yogurt and next 4 ingredients, and toss with cabbage. Serve chicken strips over coleslaw. **Makes** 4 servings.

Tuna Steaks With Green Peppercorn Sauce

Green peppercorns bottled in brine create a pleasant pepper flavor for this grilled fish. Look for them in the condiment section of the grocery store. If you can't find bottled green peppercorns, substitute 3 tablespoons drained capers plus ¼ teaspoon freshly ground pepper instead.

20 minutes or less
PREP: 3 MIN., COOK: 10 MIN.

3 tablespoons butter or margarine, melted
1 tablespoon chopped garlic
1 tablespoon lemon juice
6 (8-ounce) tuna steaks
¼ cup Dijon mustard
¼ cup dry red wine
3 tablespoons green peppercorns in brine, drained
2 tablespoons low-sodium teriyaki sauce
1 tablespoon butter or margarine

1. Combine first 3 ingredients in a small bowl. Brush mixture evenly over both sides of tuna steaks. Grill steaks, covered with grill lid, over medium-high heat (350° to 400°) about 5 minutes on each side or until fish flakes with a fork.
2. Meanwhile, combine mustard and remaining 4 ingredients in a small saucepan, stirring well; cook over medium heat until butter melts and sauce is thoroughly heated. To serve, spoon sauce over tuna steaks. **Makes** 6 servings.

Pacific Rim Tuna Steaks

You can make the ginger marinade for these tuna steaks ahead and store it in the refrigerator up to a week.

PREP: 7 MIN., COOK: 12 MIN., OTHER: 15 MIN.

¼ cup soy sauce
¼ cup fresh lime juice
1 tablespoon dried crushed red pepper
2 tablespoons sweet rice wine
2 tablespoons dark sesame oil
1 tablespoon grated fresh ginger
1 garlic clove, minced
6 (4-ounce) tuna steaks (1 inch thick)
Garnish: fresh cilantro sprigs

1. Combine first 7 ingredients in a large zip-top plastic freezer bag; add fish. Seal bag, and chill 15 minutes, turning occasionally.
2. Remove fish from marinade, reserving marinade. Grill, covered with grill lid, over medium heat (300° to 350°) 5 to 6 minutes on each side or until fish flakes with a fork, basting twice with reserved marinade. Remove fish to a serving platter. Garnish, if desired. **Makes** 6 servings.

Swordfish Steaks With Basil Butter

Basil gives an herb-accented punch to this mild-flavored fish. Team leftover butter with any fish, shellfish, or veggies within three days.

PREP: 5 MIN., COOK: 16 MIN., OTHER: 8 HR.

½ cup butter, softened
¼ cup loosely packed fresh basil leaves
¼ cup Dijon mustard
1½ teaspoons capers
8 (8-ounce) swordfish steaks (about 1 inch thick)
½ teaspoon salt
¼ teaspoon freshly ground pepper
Garnishes: basil sprigs, lemon wedges

1. Process first 4 ingredients in a blender or food processor until blended, stopping to scrape down sides. Cover and chill 8 to 24 hours.
2. Sprinkle steaks with salt and pepper. Grill steaks, covered with grill lid, over medium-high heat (350° to 400°) about 8 minutes on each side or until fish flakes with a fork.
3. Serve with basil butter. Garnish, if desired. **Makes** 8 servings.

Swordfish Steak With
Basil Butter

Honey-Macadamia Mahimahi

Mahimahi and macadamia nuts blend deliciously because they both hail from the tropics. If you need a substitute for the mahimahi, any firm white fish will do. To toast the macadamias, toss them in a dry skillet over medium heat for a few minutes. When you detect their aroma, they're done.

20 minutes or less
PREP: 9 MIN., COOK: 11 MIN.

2 (8-ounce) mahimahi fillets
½ teaspoon vegetable oil
¼ teaspoon salt
⅛ teaspoon pepper
3 tablespoons honey, divided
¼ cup macadamia nuts, finely chopped
    and toasted

1. Rub fillets with oil; sprinkle both sides evenly with salt and pepper. Brush 1 side of fillets with 1½ tablespoons honey; place fillets in a lightly greased grill basket, brushed side up.
2. Grill, covered with grill lid, over medium-high heat (350° to 400°) 7 minutes; turn basket. Baste fillets with remaining 1½ tablespoons honey, and sprinkle with nuts. Grill, covered, 3 to 4 more minutes or until fish flakes with a fork. Serve immediately. **Makes** 2 servings.

Grilled Trout

Lemon slices are stuffed into each trout during grilling, and lemon juice is cooked in the sauce, lending a citrus flavor to the fish and the sauce drizzled over each fillet.

30 minutes or less
PREP: 10 MIN., COOK: 12 MIN.

3 (1-pound) whole trout, dressed (heads and
    fins removed)
3 tablespoons butter or margarine, melted
2 medium lemons, thinly sliced
3 tablespoons butter or margarine
2 tablespoons fresh lemon juice
¼ teaspoon pepper

1. Brush cavity of each fish evenly with 3 tablespoons melted butter; stuff each fish evenly with lemon slices.
2. Place fish in a lightly greased grill basket. Place grill basket on food rack, and grill, covered with grill lid, over medium-high heat (350° to 400°) about 3 to 4 minutes on each side or until fish flakes with a fork.
3. Melt 3 tablespoons butter in a small saucepan over medium heat; cook 3 minutes or until golden. Stir in lemon juice and pepper.
4. Separate each trout into 2 fillets; discard lemon slices. Place trout, skin side down, on a serving platter. Drizzle butter sauce evenly over fillets. **Makes** 6 servings.

flavors of fish

Do you like mild-flavored fish or those with robust flavors? Here's a guide to help you select or substitute fish according to your taste preferences.

- Mild fish such as catfish, cod, flounder, grouper, orange roughy, and tilapia readily accept the flavor of seasonings and sauces.
- Medium-flavored fish such as tuna, farm-raised salmon, swordfish, and mahimahi have a fishier taste compared to the mild group.
- Wild salmon, mackerel, and kingfish are the most full-flavored fish.
- Shellfish such as blue crabs, shrimp, scallops, and lobster are mild in flavor.
- King and Dungeness crabs, oysters, mussels, and clams are medium-flavored shellfish.

Grilled Salmon With Nectarine-Onion Relish

Sweet-and-spicy Nectarine-Onion Relish tops lightly seasoned grilled salmon.

20 minutes or less
PREP: 5 MIN., COOK: 10 MIN.

make
ahead

4 (6-ounce) salmon fillets
½ teaspoon freshly ground pepper
⅛ teaspoon salt
Nectarine-Onion Relish
Garnish: halved jalapeño pepper

1. Sprinkle salmon fillets evenly with pepper and salt.
2. Grill fillets, covered with grill lid, over medium-high heat (350° to 400°) 5 minutes on each side or until fish flakes with a fork. Serve immediately with relish. Garnish, if desired. **Makes** 4 servings.

Nectarine-Onion Relish:
Save the leftovers to top grilled chicken and other meats.

PREP: 20 MIN., OTHER: 2 HR.

3 medium nectarines, coarsely chopped
1 red bell pepper, coarsely chopped
1 red onion, coarsely chopped
¼ cup thinly sliced fresh basil
¼ cup white wine vinegar
½ teaspoon grated orange rind
¼ cup fresh orange juice
2 tablespoons seeded and minced jalapeño pepper
2 tablespoons fresh lime juice
2 teaspoons sugar
2 garlic cloves, minced
⅛ teaspoon salt

1. Stir together chopped nectarines and remaining ingredients in a medium bowl; chill 2 hours. **Makes** 8 cups.

Fish Skewers

Use any combination of these fish fillets for tasty kabobs. Double the recipe for a larger crowd.

PREP: 22 MIN., COOK: 8 MIN., OTHER: 30 MIN.

1 (8-ounce) tuna fillet
1 (8-ounce) grouper fillet
1 (8-ounce) salmon fillet, skinned
4 metal or wooden skewers
1 (8-ounce) bottle olive oil-and-vinegar dressing
¼ cup chopped fresh flat-leaf parsley
1 tablespoon fresh rosemary, chopped
1 tablespoon pink peppercorns
2 tablespoons lemon juice

1. Cut each fish fillet into 1½-inch-thick pieces.
2. Thread fish pieces 2 inches apart evenly onto skewers. Place kabobs in a shallow dish.
3. Stir together olive oil-and-vinegar dressing and next 4 ingredients; pour over fish. Chill 30 minutes.
4. Remove fish from marinade, discarding marinade.
5. Grill, covered with grill lid, over high heat (400° to 500°) 4 minutes on each side or until fish reaches desired degree of doneness. **Makes** 2 to 3 servings.
Note: If using wooden skewers, soak in water 30 minutes beforehand to prevent burning.

Shrimp Skewers With Cilantro Salsa

Fresh tomato, onion, and cilantro in this salsa give a boost to simple grilled shrimp.

PREP: 15 MIN., COOK: 8 MIN., OTHER: 15 MIN.

1½ pounds peeled, large raw shrimp (2 pounds if purchased unpeeled)
8½ tablespoons fresh lime juice, divided
3 tablespoons olive oil, divided
3 medium tomatoes, seeded and diced
1 medium onion, diced
1 jalapeño pepper, minced
1 garlic clove, minced
¼ cup chopped fresh cilantro
¾ teaspoon salt, divided
¼ teaspoon black pepper

1. Lightly grease 8-inch metal skewers. Thread shrimp onto skewers; place in a shallow dish.
2. Combine 6 tablespoons lime juice and 2 tablespoons olive oil; pour over shrimp. Cover and chill 15 minutes.
3. Meanwhile, combine remaining 2½ tablespoons lime juice, 1 tablespoon olive oil, tomato, onion, jalapeño, garlic, cilantro, and ½ teaspoon salt in a medium bowl. Cover and chill salsa.
4. Remove shrimp skewers from marinade, reserving marinade.
5. Grill shrimp, covered with grill lid, over medium-high heat (350° to 400°) 3 to 4 minutes on each side or just until shrimp turn pink, brushing with reserved marinade. Sprinkle with remaining ¼ teaspoon salt and ¼ teaspoon black pepper. Serve shrimp immediately with salsa. **Makes** 4 to 5 servings.

Shrimp Skewers With
Cilantro Salsa

Greek Feta Burger

Greek Feta Burgers

These are delicious with oven-roasted potatoes. Sprinkle the potatoes with Greek seasoning for a complementary flavor.

20 minutes or less
PREP: 10 MIN., COOK: 10 MIN.

make ahead

1 pound ground chuck
1 (4-ounce) package crumbled feta cheese
1 garlic clove, minced
¼ cup chopped fresh mint
1 teaspoon salt
½ teaspoon pepper
1 teaspoon chopped fresh or crushed dried rosemary
Fresh spinach leaves
4 hamburger buns with onions
2 plum tomatoes, chopped
1 small onion, diced
Cucumber-Dill Sauce

1. Combine first 7 ingredients; shape into 4 patties.
2. Grill patties, covered with grill lid, over medium-high heat (350° to 400°) 5 minutes on each side or until done. Place patties on spinach-lined hamburger buns. Top with tomatoes, onion, and Cucumber-Dill Sauce. **Makes** 4 servings.

Cucumber-Dill Sauce:
PREP: 5 MIN.

¼ cup peeled, seeded, and diced cucumber
¼ cup sour cream
½ teaspoon chopped fresh dill
1 garlic clove, minced

1. Stir together all ingredients. Cover and chill up to 2 days. **Makes** ½ cup.

Turkey Cheeseburgers

These patties can be shaped ahead, wrapped in plastic wrap, and stored in zip-top plastic freezer bags in the freezer up to three months. Dark turkey meat mixed with turkey breast makes these burgers tender and juicy.

PREP: 20 MIN., COOK: 12 MIN., OTHER: 30 MIN.

make ahead

1 pound ground turkey breast
1 pound ground turkey (dark meat)
1 large egg, lightly beaten
10 saltine crackers, finely crushed
3 to 4 green onions, sliced (about ½ cup)
2 teaspoons salt
1 teaspoon fresh or dried rosemary
¾ teaspoon pepper
½ teaspoon garlic powder
8 mozzarella cheese slices
Lemon Mayonnaise
8 onion buns, split
Lettuce leaves
Tomato slices

1. Combine first 9 ingredients until blended. Shape mixture into 8 patties. Cover and chill 30 minutes or until firm.

2. Grill turkey patties, covered with grill lid, over medium-high heat (350° to 400°) 5 to 6 minutes on each side or until done. Top each patty with 1 cheese slice during last minute of grilling.

3. Spread Lemon Mayonnaise evenly on cut sides of buns. Top bun bottoms, mayonnaise sides up, with lettuce, turkey patties, and tomato slices. Cover with bun tops, mayonnaise sides down. **Makes** 8 servings.

Lemon Mayonnaise:

PREP: 5 MIN.

1 cup light or regular mayonnaise
½ teaspoon grated lemon rind
1 tablespoon fresh lemon juice
¼ teaspoon pepper

1. Stir together all ingredients. Cover and chill up to 2 days. **Makes** about 1 cup.

Turkey Cheeseburger

Stuffed Southwestern
Burger

Stuffed Southwestern Burgers

PREP: 30 MIN., COOK: 10 MIN.

1 avocado
3 plum tomatoes, chopped
1 garlic clove, pressed
2 teaspoons lemon juice
1½ teaspoons salt, divided
1½ teaspoons pepper, divided
2 pounds lean ground beef
1 small onion, finely chopped
2 teaspoons chili powder
1 (8-ounce) block Monterey Jack cheese with
    peppers, cubed
6 large sesame seed buns, toasted
Toppings: leaf lettuce, tomato slices, red onion slices

1. Mash avocado with a fork; stir in chopped tomatoes, garlic, lemon juice, ½ teaspoon salt, and ½ teaspoon pepper. Set aside.

2. Combine ground beef, onion, remaining 1 teaspoon salt, remaining 1 teaspoon pepper, and chili powder; shape into 12 thin patties.

3. Top 6 patties with cheese cubes; cover with remaining patties, pressing edges to seal.

4. Grill patties, covered with grill lid, over medium-high heat (350° to 400°) 5 minutes on each side or until done. Serve on buns with desired toppings and avocado mixture. **Makes** 6 servings.

Mozzarella-Basil Burgers

30 minutes or less
PREP: 15 MIN., COOK: 10 MIN.

½ cup mayonnaise
1 garlic clove, pressed
2 pounds lean ground beef
½ cup Italian-seasoned breadcrumbs
2 large eggs, lightly beaten
3 tablespoons ketchup
1 (6-ounce) package mozzarella cheese slices
8 hamburger buns, split
24 large fresh basil leaves
Toppings: tomato slices, red onion slices

1. Stir together ½ cup mayonnaise and garlic; set aside.
2. Combine ground beef and next 3 ingredients. Shape into 8 patties.
3. Grill patties, covered with grill lid, over medium-high heat (350° to 400°) 5 minutes on each side or until done. Top each patty with a cheese slice.
4. Place buns, cut sides down, on grill rack, and grill until lightly browned. Spread mayonnaise mixture on cut sides of buns; top each bottom half with 3 basil leaves, beef patty, desired toppings, and top halves of buns. **Makes** 8 servings.

Grilled Portobello Burgers

PREP: 14 MIN., COOK: 6 MIN., OTHER: 20 MIN.

6 large portobello mushroom caps
½ cup teriyaki sauce (we used Kikkoman)
6 (1-ounce) slices mozzarella cheese
¼ cup mayonnaise
6 sourdough buns, split

1. Combine mushroom caps and teriyaki sauce in a zip-top plastic bag, turning to coat; seal and let stand 20 minutes. Drain mushrooms, discarding marinade.
2. Grill mushrooms, covered with grill lid, over medium-high heat (350° to 400°) 2 minutes on each side. Top with cheese, and grill 2 minutes.
3. Spread mayonnaise on cut sides of buns. Grill buns, cut sides down, 1 minute or until toasted. Place mushrooms in buns, and serve immediately. **Makes** 6 servings.

Jalapeño Cheeseburgers

30 minutes or less
PREP: 15 MIN., COOK: 10 MIN.

2 pounds ground chuck
½ teaspoon salt
½ teaspoon pepper
1 (3-ounce) package cream cheese, softened
1 tablespoon grated onion
1 to 2 jalapeño peppers, seeded and minced
6 sandwich buns
Toppings: lettuce leaves, red onion slices,
    tomato slices

1. Combine first 3 ingredients; shape into 12 thin patties.
2. Stir together cream cheese, onion, and jalapeño peppers; spoon evenly in center of 6 patties. (Do not spread to edges.) Top with remaining patties, pressing edges to seal.
3. Grill patties, covered with grill lid, over medium-high heat (350° to 400°) 5 minutes on each side or until done. Serve on buns with desired toppings. **Makes** 6 servings.

Grilled Vegetable Sandwiches

Focaccia comes in all shapes and sizes and can be found in the bakery section of the grocery store. If the exact dimensions can't be found, use the closest in size possible.

PREP: 18 MIN., COOK: 18 MIN., OTHER: 10 MIN.

¼ cup soy sauce
¼ cup lemon juice
1 tablespoon honey
½ teaspoon ground red pepper
2 small zucchini, cut diagonally into ½-inch-thick
    slices
1 medium-size red onion, cut into ¼-inch-thick slices
2 red bell peppers, cut into 1-inch-wide strips
1 (12- x 7-inch) focaccia (Italian flatbread)
2 (4-ounce) packages garlic-and-herb-flavored
    goat cheese

1. Stir together first 4 ingredients in a large bowl; add vegetables, tossing gently to coat. Let mixture stand at room temperature 10 minutes, stirring occasionally.
2. Remove vegetables with a slotted spoon, reserving marinade, and place in a large lightly greased grill basket. Cut focaccia in half horizontally.
3. Place grill basket on grill rack. Grill, covered with grill lid, over medium-high heat (350° to 400°) 8 minutes on each side or until vegetables are tender. Set aside. Place focaccia halves, cut sides down, on grill rack. Grill, without grill lid, 2 minutes or until toasted.
4. Toss grilled vegetables in reserved marinade. Spread goat cheese evenly over cut sides of focaccia; spoon grilled vegetable mixture evenly on bottom half of focaccia. Top with remaining focaccia half. Cut sandwich into 4 wedges; serve immediately. **Makes** 4 servings.

Grilled Tomatoes

A quick sizzle on the grill heats these Italian-inspired tomatoes just enough to serve alongside a deserving grilled entrée. Leftovers make a great addition to pasta salad.

10 minutes or less
PREP: 5 MIN., COOK: 4 MIN.

4 large tomatoes, cut in half crosswise
2 tablespoons olive oil
2 garlic cloves, minced
¼ cup chopped fresh basil
½ teaspoon salt
½ teaspoon pepper

1. Brush cut sides of tomato halves with oil, and sprinkle evenly with garlic and remaining ingredients.
2. Grill, covered with grill lid, over medium-high heat (350° to 400°) about 2 minutes on each side. Serve immediately. **Makes** 8 servings.

great grilled veggies

- Be sure to select vegetables that take well to grilling, such as zucchini, squash, peppers, tomatoes, onions, corn, and mushrooms.
- Clean and trim the vegetables before you grill them. Thick slices work best.
- Marinate the vegetables or brush them with oil for best results.
- Put small vegetable pieces in a grill basket or on skewers. Place larger vegetables directly on the grill.
- Vegetables are done when the skin begins to blister and the interior is tender.

Grilled Red Onions

Grilled Red Onions

Insert skewers through onion slices to hold them together. Soak wooden skewers
in water 30 minutes beforehand to prevent burning.

PREP: 20 MIN., COOK: 10 MIN., OTHER: 8 HR.

make
ahead

12 (8-inch) wooden skewers
3 medium-size red or sweet onions
1½ cups dry white wine
¼ cup butter or margarine
1 teaspoon chopped fresh thyme
⅛ teaspoon pepper
Garnish: fresh thyme

1. Insert 4 wooden skewers (1 at a time) through each onion about ½ inch apart to create horizontal segments.

Cut onions into slices between skewers. (Leave skewers in place to hold onion slices together during marinating and cooking.)
2. Place onion slices in a shallow container; add wine. Cover and chill 8 hours, turning occasionally. Drain.
3. Melt butter in a small saucepan; stir in chopped thyme and pepper. Brush onion slices with butter mixture, reserving some for basting.
4. Grill onions, covered with grill lid, over medium-high heat (350° to 400°) 10 minutes, turning and basting often with reserved butter mixture. Serve on a platter. Garnish, if desired. **Makes** 6 servings.

sides   145

Grilled Corn With
Jalapeño-Lime Butter

Grilled Corn With Jalapeño-Lime Butter

Minced jalapeño mixed into butter adds a twinge of spice to this corn. Use any leftover butter for steamed vegetables within five days.

30 minutes or less
PREP: 7 MIN., COOK: 20 MIN.

½ cup butter, softened
2 jalapeño peppers, seeded and minced
2 tablespoons grated lime rind
1 teaspoon fresh lime juice
6 ears fresh corn
1 tablespoon olive oil
2 teaspoons kosher salt
1 teaspoon freshly ground black pepper

1. Combine first 4 ingredients, and shape into a 6-inch log; wrap in wax paper, and chill while grilling corn.
2. Rub corn with olive oil; sprinkle evenly with salt and black pepper.
3. Grill corn, covered with grill lid, over high heat (400° to 500°), turning often, 15 to 20 minutes or until tender. Serve with flavored butter. **Makes** 6 servings.

Grilled Okra and Tomatoes

This recipe pairs two Southern foods with a favorite style of Southern cooking. Toss the veggies on the grill the last 10 minutes that your entrée grills.

20 minutes or less
PREP: 8 MIN., COOK: 10 MIN.

6 large tomatoes (about 3 pounds)
2 pounds small fresh okra
2 tablespoons olive oil
¾ teaspoon salt
¼ teaspoon freshly ground pepper

1. Toss tomatoes and okra with oil. Place okra in a grill wok or basket.
2. Grill okra, covered with grill lid, over medium heat (300° to 350°) 3 minutes, stirring or turning occasionally. Place tomatoes on grill rack beside wok; grill tomatoes and okra 5 to 7 minutes, turning tomatoes and okra occasionally.
3. Peel tomatoes, if desired, and cut into large chunks; toss gently with okra, salt, and ground pepper. Arrange on a platter, and serve immediately. **Makes** 8 servings.

Marinated Grilled Squash

PREP: 15 MIN., COOK: 20 MIN., OTHER: 1 HR.
(pictured on page 120)

3 medium-size yellow squash, sliced diagonally
3 medium-size zucchini, sliced diagonally
⅓ cup olive oil
1 tablespoon lemon juice
1 garlic clove, pressed
½ teaspoon dried marjoram
¼ teaspoon salt
¼ teaspoon pepper

1. Place yellow squash and zucchini in a zip-top plastic freezer bag.
2. Whisk together oil and next 5 ingredients. Pour over vegetables. Seal and chill 1 hour. Remove vegetables from marinade, reserving marinade.
3. Grill, covered with grill lid, over medium-high heat (350° to 400°) 20 minutes or until crisp-tender, turning and brushing occasionally with reserved marinade. **Makes** 6 servings.

Caramelized
French Onion Soup,
page 170

SLOW-COOKER
favorites

Savory Pot Roast

Savory Pot Roast

PREP: 20 MIN.; COOK: 7 HR., 15 MIN.

make
ahead

1 (3-pound) beef sirloin tip roast,
    cut in half
2 tablespoons vegetable oil
1 medium onion, chopped
2 garlic cloves, minced
1 cup brewed coffee
¾ cup water, divided
1 beef bouillon cube
1 teaspoon salt
2 teaspoons dried basil
½ teaspoon coarsely ground pepper
All-purpose flour

1. Brown roast on all sides in hot oil in a large skillet over medium-high heat 5 minutes on each side. Place roast in a 4½-quart slow cooker.
2. Add onion and garlic to skillet, and sauté 2 minutes or until tender. Stir in 1 cup coffee, ½ cup water, bouillon cube, and next 3 ingredients until blended. Transfer to slow cooker.
3. Cover and cook on LOW 6 to 7 hours or until tender. Transfer roast to a serving platter; measure drippings, and return to slow cooker. For every cup of drippings, add 1 tablespoon flour to the remaining ¼ cup water. Whisk flour and water until blended. Whisk flour mixture into drippings. Cook, uncovered, on HIGH 5 minutes or until gravy thickens, whisking frequently. Serve gravy with roast. **Makes** 6 to 8 servings.

Zippy Barbecue Pot Roast

Grill some Texas toast to serve with this roast and gravy.

PREP: 23 MIN., COOK: 6 HR. (HIGH) OR 1 HR. (HIGH)
AND 8 HR. (LOW)

make ahead

1½ teaspoons garlic salt
½ teaspoon pepper
1 (4- to 5-pound) boneless chuck roast, trimmed
2 tablespoons vegetable oil
1 (12-ounce) can cola soft drink
1 (12-ounce) bottle chili sauce
2 tablespoons Worcestershire sauce
2 tablespoons hot sauce
3 tablespoons cornstarch
¼ cup water

1. Combine garlic salt and pepper; rub over roast. Brown roast on all sides in hot oil in a large skillet. Transfer roast to a 4-quart slow cooker. Cut roast in half to ensure even cooking. Combine cola and next 3 ingredients; pour over roast. Cover and cook on HIGH 5 to 6 hours or on HIGH 1 hour and then LOW 7 to 8 hours. Remove roast, reserving juices in slow cooker; keep roast warm.
2. Combine cornstarch and ¼ cup water, stirring well; stir into juices in slow cooker. Cook, uncovered, on HIGH 15 minutes or until thickened, stirring occasionally. Serve gravy over roast. **Makes** 10 to 12 servings.

Chuck Roast Barbecue

Spoon leftovers into serving-size freezer containers, and freeze up to 3 months.

PREP: 25 MIN.; COOK: 6 HR., 10 MIN.

make ahead

2 medium onions, chopped
1 (2- to 2½-pound) boneless chuck roast, trimmed
¾ cup cola soft drink
¼ cup Worcestershire sauce
1 tablespoon cider vinegar
2 garlic cloves, minced
½ cup spicy barbecue sauce
6 hamburger buns

1. Place onion in a 4-quart slow cooker. Cut roast in half to ensure even cooking. Place roast on top of onion. Combine cola and next 3 ingredients; reserve ½ cup cola mixture. Pour remaining cola mixture over roast and onion.
2. Cover and cook on HIGH 6 hours or until roast is very tender. Remove meat and onion to a platter, using a slotted spoon. Discard juices.
3. Add reserved cola mixture and barbecue sauce to slow cooker; stir well, and cook, uncovered, on HIGH 10 minutes.
4. Meanwhile, shred meat with 2 forks; return meat and onion to slow cooker until sauce is heated, stirring occasionally. Spoon barbecue onto buns. **Makes** 6 servings.

Sauerbraten

The tang of white vinegar is softened by the spicy sweetness of crumbled gingersnaps in this classic German dish. Serve the tender marinated beef and sauce over spaetzle (tiny noodles or dumplings) for authenticity.

PREP: 27 MIN.; COOK: 9 HR., 12 MIN.; OTHER: 24 HR.

make ahead

1 (3-pound) rump roast
1½ cups sliced onion
1 cup water
1 cup white vinegar
2 tablespoons salt
2 tablespoons sugar
1 lemon, sliced
10 whole cloves
6 peppercorns
3 bay leaves
15 crisp gingersnaps, crumbled (we used Nabisco)

1. Trim fat from roast; cut roast in half crosswise. Place roast halves in a deep glass bowl. Combine onion and next 8 ingredients; stir well. Pour mixture over meat; cover and marinate in refrigerator 24 to 36 hours, turning meat occasionally.
2. Remove roast from marinade, reserving 1½ cups marinade. Discard remaining marinade. Place roast in a 6-quart slow cooker; pour reserved 1½ cups marinade over meat. Cover and cook on HIGH 1 hour; reduce to LOW, and cook 7 to 8 hours or until roast is tender.
3. Remove roast from slow cooker; set aside, and keep warm. Increase to HIGH. Pour cooking liquid through a sieve into a bowl; discard solids. Return liquid to slow cooker. Add gingersnaps; cover and cook 12 minutes. Serve with roast. **Makes** 6 servings.

Company
Pot Roast

Company Pot Roast

PREP: 25 MIN.; COOK: 10 HR., 10 MIN.

make
ahead

1 (2-pound) boneless chuck roast,
    trimmed
1½ tablespoons freshly ground pepper
1 tablespoon vegetable oil
14 small red potatoes, quartered (about 2 pounds)
3 small onions, quartered
1 (16-ounce) package baby carrots
2 (10½-ounce) cans French onion soup
1 (2.8-ounce) tube dried tomato paste
¼ cup all-purpose flour
½ cup water

1. Rub both sides of roast with pepper. Brown roast on all sides in hot oil in a large nonstick skillet over medium-high heat. Place roast in a 6-quart slow cooker.

2. Arrange vegetables around roast. Combine soup and tomato paste in a small bowl, stirring with a wire whisk; pour evenly over roast and vegetables.

3. Cover and cook on HIGH 1 hour. Reduce to LOW, and cook 9 more hours or until roast and vegetables are tender. Remove roast and vegetables to a platter; cover and keep warm.

4. Pour drippings into a large skillet. Combine flour and water in a small bowl, whisking until smooth; gradually add to drippings in skillet. Bring to a boil; cook, stirring constantly, 10 minutes or until gravy is slightly thickened and bubbly. Serve gravy with roast and vegetables. **Makes** 8 servings.

Slow-cooker Chunky Beef Chili

PREP: 25 MIN.; COOK: 4 HR.

make
ahead

3 pounds boneless chuck roast, cut into
    ½-inch pieces
6 teaspoons vegetable oil
1 onion, chopped
1 tablespoon chili powder
1 (6-ounce) can tomato paste
1 (32-ounce) container beef broth
2 (8-ounce) cans tomato sauce
2 teaspoons minced garlic
1 teaspoon salt
1 teaspoon ground oregano
1 teaspoon ground cumin
½ teaspoon ground black pepper
¼ teaspoon ground red pepper
Toppings: crackers, sour cream, shredded cheese,
    chopped onion

1. Brown chuck roast pieces, in 4 batches, using 1½ teaspoons hot oil per batch, in a large Dutch oven over medium-high heat. Add chopped onion, and sauté 5 minutes or until onion is tender. Stir in 1 tablespoon chili powder; cook, stirring constantly, 1 minute. Stir in tomato paste, and cook 3 minutes. Stir in beef broth, stirring to loosen particles from bottom of Dutch oven; stir in tomato sauce, minced garlic, and next 5 ingredients.
2. Carefully transfer meat mixture into a 6-quart slow cooker. Cover and cook on LOW 4 hours or until chuck roast is tender. Serve chili with desired toppings. **Makes** 7 cups.

Slow-cooker
Chunky Beef Chili

Roast Beef With Horseradish Sauce

Serve with sautéed onions and peppers and Swiss cheese on hoagie rolls for a delicious sandwich.

PREP: 15 MIN., COOK: 4 HR. (HIGH) OR 10 HR. (LOW), OTHER: 15 MIN.

1 teaspoon Creole seasoning
½ teaspoon dried marjoram
¼ teaspoon dried thyme
¼ teaspoon pepper
1 (2¾-pound) eye of round roast, trimmed
3 garlic cloves, cut into 12 pieces
Horseradish Sauce

1. Combine Creole seasoning and next 3 ingredients in a small bowl; rub mixture over entire surface of roast.
2. Cut 12 (1-inch) slits in roast; stuff each slit with 1 piece of garlic. Place in a 4½-quart slow cooker.
3. Cover and cook on HIGH 3½ to 4 hours or on LOW 8 to 10 hours. Let stand 15 minutes; cut roast diagonally across the grain into thin slices. Serve with Horseradish Sauce. **Makes** 8 servings.

Horseradish Sauce:

PREP: 5 MIN.

1 (8-ounce) carton reduced-fat sour cream
½ cup light mayonnaise
1 to 2 tablespoons prepared horseradish
1 garlic clove, pressed

1. Combine all ingredients; cover and chill until ready to serve. **Makes** 1½ cups.

Peppery Flank Barbecue

PREP: 5 MIN., COOK: 7 HR.

2 (1¼-pound) flank steaks, cut in half crosswise
1¼ teaspoons pepper
1 cup chopped onion
2 tablespoons molasses
1 (28-ounce) bottle original-flavored barbecue sauce (we used Kraft Original)

1. Rub steak evenly with pepper. Place steak in a 4-quart slow cooker; top with onion, molasses, and barbecue sauce. Turn steak to coat.

2. Cover and cook on HIGH 1 hour; reduce to LOW, and cook 6 hours. Remove steak, reserving sauce in slow cooker.
3. Shred steak with 2 forks. Return shredded steak to slow cooker; stir well to coat with sauce. **Makes** 8 servings.

Beef Burgundy

Thaw your onions in the refrigerator overnight to make your prep in the kitchen even shorter.

PREP: 14 MIN., COOK: 6 HR.

1 (2-pound) boneless top round steak, trimmed and cut into 1½-inch cubes
⅓ cup all-purpose flour
1 (10½-ounce) can condensed beef broth, undiluted
½ cup dry red wine
2 garlic cloves, minced
2 tablespoons tomato paste
½ teaspoon dried thyme
½ teaspoon salt
¼ teaspoon pepper
2 (16-ounce) packages frozen small whole onions, thawed and drained
1 (8-ounce) package sliced fresh mushrooms
Hot cooked medium egg noodles

1. Place a lightly greased nonstick skillet over high heat until hot. Add steak; sauté 2 minutes. Reduce heat to medium-high; cook steak 5 more minutes or until browned. Drain.
2. Meanwhile, whisk together flour and next 7 ingredients in a 3½-quart slow cooker, stirring until smooth. Add steak, onions, and mushrooms, stirring well. Cover and cook on HIGH 1 hour; reduce to LOW, and cook 5 hours or until meat is tender. Serve over noodles. **Makes** 6 servings.

Slow-cooker Fajitas

Serve this dish at your next gathering. Buy enough steak for your party when it's on sale at the grocery store.
If you're serving a crowd, cook and freeze 1 recipe each day, or borrow a few slow cookers from your neighbors.

PREP: 12 MIN., COOK: 5 HR. (HIGH) OR 10 HR. (LOW)

make
ahead

1½ pounds flank steak, cut into 4 to 6 pieces
1 medium onion, chopped
1 green bell pepper, sliced
1 jalapeño pepper, seeded and chopped
2 garlic cloves, pressed
1 tablespoon chopped fresh cilantro
1 teaspoon chili powder
1 teaspoon ground cumin
1 teaspoon ground coriander
¾ to 1 teaspoon salt
1 (10-ounce) can diced tomatoes and green chiles,
    drained
Flour tortillas
Toppings: shredded Cheddar cheese, sour cream,
    salsa
Garnish: cilantro sprigs

1. Place steak in a 5-quart slow cooker; top with onion and next 9 ingredients.
2. Cover and cook on HIGH 5 hours or on LOW 10 hours. Remove meat, and shred with 2 forks. Serve with tortillas and desired toppings. Garnish, if desired. **Makes** 4 to 6 servings.
Note: To freeze after cooking: Before shredding meat, reserve at least 1 cup of drippings, if desired, and shred with 2 forks. Place shredded meat and drippings in a large zip-top plastic freezer bag. Seal and freeze up to 1 month. Thaw in refrigerator, and thoroughly heat before serving.

Slow-cooker Fajitas

Country Steak With Gravy

Country Steak With Gravy

Serve with hot cooked rice or mashed potatoes.

PREP: 5 MIN., COOK: 7 HR.

1 (1½-pound) boneless top round steak
　　(½ inch thick), trimmed
1 (12-ounce) jar beef gravy (we used Heinz)
2 tablespoons tomato paste
½ teaspoon salt
½ teaspoon garlic powder
½ teaspoon pepper
½ teaspoon dried thyme

1. Cut steak into 6 equal pieces; place in a lightly greased 4-quart slow cooker. Combine gravy and remaining ingredients; pour over steak. Cover and cook on HIGH 1 hour; reduce to LOW and cook 5½ to 6 hours or until meat is tender. **Makes** 6 servings.

Beefy Pasta Sauce

A little red wine fools you into thinking this spaghetti sauce is homemade.

PREP: 11 MIN., COOK: 7 HR.

1½ pounds ground round
1 cup chopped onion
2 (26-ounce) jars onion and roasted garlic pasta
　　sauce
¼ cup dry red wine
½ teaspoon dried Italian seasoning
½ teaspoon salt
1 (8-ounce) package sliced fresh mushrooms
Hot cooked pasta

1. Cook ground beef and onion in a large skillet, stirring until beef crumbles and is no longer pink. Drain well. Place beef mixture in a 5-quart slow cooker. Add pasta sauce and next 4 ingredients to slow cooker. Cover and cook on LOW 7 hours. Serve over hot cooked pasta. **Makes** 9 cups.

Peppered Beef Brisket in Beer

Beer adds an earthy essence to this tender brisket.

PREP: 15 MIN., COOK: 6 HR. (HIGH) OR 1 HR. (HIGH)
AND 9 HR. (LOW)

1 large onion, sliced and separated into rings
1 (4-pound) beef brisket, trimmed
¾ teaspoon pepper
¾ cup beer
½ cup chili sauce
3 tablespoons brown sugar
2 garlic cloves, crushed
3 tablespoons all-purpose flour
3 tablespoons water

1. Place onion rings in a 4-quart slow cooker. Cut brisket in half to ensure even cooking. Sprinkle brisket with pepper. Place over onion rings in slow cooker. Combine beer and next 3 ingredients; pour over brisket. Cover and cook on HIGH 4 to 6 hours or on HIGH 1 hour and then LOW 7 to 9 hours.
2. Remove brisket to a serving platter, reserving juices in slow cooker. Combine flour and water, stirring well; slowly whisk into juices in slow cooker. Cook, uncovered, on HIGH 5 minutes or until thickened, stirring often. Serve sauce over brisket. **Makes** 10 servings.

Caribbean-Style Pork

Cumin seeds and peanut butter create a sweetly spiced sauce for this tender pork.

PREP: 30 MIN., COOK: 7 HR.

make
ahead

2 pounds boneless pork chops
1 tablespoon olive oil, divided
2 cups chopped red bell pepper
1 bunch green onions, cut into 1-inch pieces
2 tablespoons hoisin sauce
2 tablespoons soy sauce
1 tablespoon fresh lime juice
2 tablespoons creamy peanut butter
1 teaspoon cumin seeds, crushed
1 teaspoon dried crushed red pepper
1 teaspoon bottled minced garlic

1. Cut pork into 1-inch pieces. Heat 1½ teaspoons oil in a large nonstick skillet over medium-high heat. Add half of pork; sauté 10 minutes or until browned. Remove from skillet with a slotted spoon, and drain on paper towels. Repeat procedure with remaining oil and pork.

2. Place pork, bell pepper, and green onions in a 4-quart slow cooker coated with cooking spray; stir well.

3. Add hoisin sauce and remaining ingredients to slow cooker; stir well.

4. Cover and cook on HIGH 1 hour. Reduce to LOW, and cook 5 to 6 hours. **Makes** 6 servings.

Apple Cider Pork and Vegetables

PREP: 15 MIN., COOK: 8 HR.

make ahead

4 small sweet potatoes, peeled and
     cut into ½-inch slices
1 (7-ounce) package dried mixed fruit
1 medium onion, thinly sliced
1 bay leaf
¾ teaspoon salt
½ teaspoon pepper
½ teaspoon dried rosemary, crushed
1½ pounds lean boneless pork, cut into 1-inch pieces
½ cup all-purpose flour
2 tablespoons vegetable oil
1 cup apple cider

1. Place first 7 ingredients in a 5-quart slow cooker.
2. Dredge pork in flour; brown in hot oil in a skillet over medium-high heat. Remove pork, reserving drippings in skillet. Place pork in slow cooker. Stir apple cider into reserved drippings; pour over pork.
3. Cook, covered, on LOW 6 to 8 hours. Discard bay leaf. **Makes** 4 servings.

Pork Chops and Gravy

The slow cooker simmers these chops nice and tender. Serve pork chops with mashed potatoes and gravy. Try Ore-Ida frozen mashed potatoes to save time.

PREP: 20 MIN.; COOK: 5 HR., 10 MIN.

make ahead

6 (6-ounce) bone-in center-cut pork
     loin chops (about ½ inch thick)
1 tablespoon vegetable oil
1 (14-ounce) can chicken broth
1½ teaspoons dry mustard
½ teaspoon salt
¼ teaspoon garlic powder
⅔ cup all-purpose flour
Freshly ground pepper (optional)

1. Trim fat from chops. Brown chops, in batches, in hot oil in a large nonstick skillet over medium-high heat. Place chops in a 4½-quart slow cooker.
2. Combine broth, mustard, salt, and garlic powder; stir well. Pour broth mixture over pork chops in slow cooker. Cover with lid; cook on HIGH 1 hour. Reduce to LOW; cook 4 hours or until pork chops are tender.

Remove pork chops from slow cooker, reserving cooking liquid. Set chops aside, and keep warm. Increase to HIGH.
3. Place flour in a small bowl. Gradually add 1 cup cooking liquid to flour, stirring with a wire whisk until well blended. Stir flour mixture into cooking liquid in slow cooker. Cook, uncovered, 10 minutes or until thickened, stirring occasionally. Spoon gravy over chops; sprinkle with pepper, if desired. **Makes** 6 servings.

Spiced Pork

PREP: 20 MIN., COOK: 5 HR. (HIGH) OR 10 HR. (LOW)

make ahead

1 (2-pound) boneless pork loin roast,
     trimmed and cut into 2-inch pieces
2 (14.5-ounce) cans diced tomatoes, undrained
1 large onion, chopped
⅓ cup raisins
2 tablespoons tomato paste
2 tablespoons cider vinegar
1 tablespoon chopped pickled jalapeño peppers
1 teaspoon beef bouillon granules
½ teaspoon salt
¼ teaspoon freshly ground pepper
¼ teaspoon ground cinnamon
⅛ teaspoon ground cloves
Hot cooked rice (optional)

1. Place pork in a 4½-quart slow cooker. Add tomatoes and next 10 ingredients, stirring well.
2. Cover and cook on HIGH 4 to 5 hours or on LOW 8 to 10 hours.
3. Remove pork from slow cooker using a slotted spoon; cool slightly, and shred using 2 forks. Return to slow cooker; cook until thoroughly heated. Serve over hot cooked rice, if desired. **Makes** 8 servings.

Easy Spanish Pork Dip
Sandwiches

Easy Spanish Pork Dip Sandwiches

Find mojo criollo on the Hispanic foods aisle of your grocery store.

PREP: 20 MIN., COOK: 6 HR.

make
ahead

3 tablespoons garlic pepper
2 teaspoons salt
1 (4- to 5-pound) boneless pork shoulder roast, cut
   in half
¼ cup vegetable oil
¾ cup mojo criollo Spanish marinating sauce (we
   used La Lechonera)
2 (0.87-ounce) envelopes pork gravy mix
2 cups water
¼ cup white vinegar
2 bay leaves
1 medium-size sweet onion, thinly sliced
8 mini French rolls

1. Sprinkle garlic pepper and salt evenly over roast.

Cook roast in hot oil in a large skillet 2 minutes on each side or until lightly browned. Place in a 6-quart slow cooker, fat sides up.

2. Combine Spanish marinating sauce and next 3 ingredients; pour over roast in slow cooker. Add bay leaves; top with sliced onion.

3. Cover and cook on HIGH 1 hour. Reduce heat to LOW, and cook 4 to 5 hours or until meat is tender and shreds easily. Discard bay leaves.

4. Remove pork to a large bowl, reserving liquid and onion slices in slow cooker; shred pork with 2 forks. Add 1 cup reserved liquid to shredded pork to moisten.

5. Slice mini French rolls in half. Place shredded pork and onion slices on bottom bread slices; top with remaining bread slices.

6. Spoon remaining reserved liquid into individual bowls for dipping. **Makes** 8 sandwiches.

Spicy-Sweet Ribs and Beans

Slow cookers don't brown food, so we broil these ribs for extra flavor before adding them to the pot.

PREP: 30 MIN., COOK: 6 HR. (HIGH) OR
10 HR. (LOW)

2 (16-ounce) cans pinto beans, drained
4 pounds country-style pork ribs, trimmed
1 teaspoon garlic powder
½ teaspoon salt
½ teaspoon pepper
1 medium onion, chopped
1 (10.5-ounce) jar red jalapeño jelly
1 (18-ounce) bottle hickory-flavored barbecue sauce
      (we used Kraft Thick 'n Spicy Hickory Smoke)
1 teaspoon green hot sauce (we used Tabasco)

1. Place beans in a 5-quart slow cooker; set aside.
2. Cut ribs apart; sprinkle with garlic powder, salt, and pepper. Place ribs on a broiling pan.
3. Broil 5½ inches from heat 18 to 20 minutes or until browned, turning once. Add ribs to slow cooker, and sprinkle with onion.
4. Meanwhile, combine jelly, barbecue sauce, and hot sauce in a saucepan; cook over low heat until jelly melts. Pour over ribs; stir gently.
5. Cover and cook on HIGH 5 to 6 hours or on LOW 9 to 10 hours. Remove ribs. Drain bean mixture, reserving sauce. Skim fat from sauce. Arrange ribs over bean mixture; serve with sauce. **Makes** 8 servings.

Hearty Baked Beans

Double your pleasure and ease with 2 slow cookers and one of our barbecue beefs on page 151 to accompany these beans.

PREP: 30 MIN., COOK: 3 HR. (HIGH) OR 6 HR. (LOW)

3 bacon slices, chopped
1 large onion, chopped
2 garlic cloves, minced
3 (16-ounce) cans pinto beans, drained
⅓ cup firmly packed brown sugar
⅓ cup molasses
⅓ cup ketchup
2½ tablespoons prepared mustard
½ medium-size green bell pepper, chopped

1. Cook bacon slices in a large skillet until crisp; remove bacon, reserving drippings in skillet.
2. Sauté onion and garlic in reserved drippings until tender.
3. Combine bacon, onion mixture, beans, and remaining ingredients in a slow cooker.
4. Cover and cook on HIGH 2½ to 3 hours or on LOW 5 to 6 hours. **Makes** 6 to 8 servings.

Pinto Beans With Ham

Just like many moms used to make! Some may remember this recipe served with a little more liquid; others remember it as less saucy.

PREP: 6 MIN., COOK: 10 HR., OTHER: 8 HR.

1 (16-ounce) package dried pinto beans
5½ cups water
1 large onion, chopped
1 (8-ounce) package diced cooked ham (we used
      Cumberland Gap)
1 tablespoon chili powder
2 teaspoons salt
1 teaspoon pepper
¼ teaspoon dried oregano
¼ teaspoon ground cumin
2 garlic cloves, minced

1. Sort and wash beans; place in a 3½- to 5-quart slow cooker. Cover with water 2 inches above beans; soak at least 8 hours. Drain; add 5½ cups water and remaining ingredients.
2. Cover and cook on LOW 10 hours or until beans are tender. Serve with French bread or cornbread. **Makes** 8 servings.

Lamb Meatballs With Chutney Sauce

Serve these juicy meatballs and sweet sauce over couscous.

PREP: 25 MIN., COOK: 3 HR.

1½ pounds ground lean boneless
    leg of lamb
½ cup fine, dry breadcrumbs (commercial)
2 green onions, finely chopped
3 tablespoons minced seeded pickled jalapeño
    peppers
½ teaspoon salt
1 large egg
2 garlic cloves, minced
½ cup mango chutney
¼ cup tomato paste
3 tablespoons soy sauce
2 tablespoons pickled jalapeño pepper liquid

1. Combine ground lamb and next 6 ingredients in a bowl; stir well. Shape into 42 (1-inch) meatballs. Place meatballs in a 3½- to 4-quart slow cooker.
2. Combine chutney and next 3 ingredients in a bowl; stir well. Pour over meatballs. Cover and cook on HIGH 1 hour; reduce to LOW, and cook 2 hours or until done. **Makes** 6 servings.

Saucy Drumsticks and Thighs

After simmering in a well-seasoned sauce, this chicken is fall-off-the-bone tender. Serve this saucy chicken over rice or egg noodles.

PREP: 5 MIN., COOK: 6 HR.

6 chicken drumsticks (about 1½ pounds),
    skinned
6 chicken thighs (about 1½ pounds), skinned
1 (14½-ounce) can diced tomatoes with roasted
    garlic, undrained
1 (6-ounce) can tomato paste
¼ cup dried onion flakes
2 teaspoons chicken bouillon granules
1 teaspoon dried Italian seasoning
½ teaspoon garlic powder
½ teaspoon dried crushed red pepper

1. Place chicken in a 4-quart slow cooker. Combine tomatoes and remaining ingredients; stir well. Pour over chicken. Cover and cook on HIGH 1 hour; reduce to LOW, and cook 4 to 5 hours or until chicken is tender. **Makes** 6 servings.

Provençale Chicken Supper

PREP: 10 MIN., COOK: 6 HR.

4 (6-ounce) skinned, bone-in
    chicken breasts
2 teaspoons dried basil
¼ teaspoon salt, divided
¼ teaspoon black pepper, divided
1 cup diced yellow bell pepper
1 (16-ounce) can navy beans, rinsed and drained
1 (14½-ounce) can pasta-style chunky tomatoes,
    undrained

1. Place chicken in a 4½-quart slow cooker; sprinkle with dried basil, ⅛ teaspoon salt, and ⅛ teaspoon black pepper.
2. Combine remaining ⅛ teaspoon salt, remaining ⅛ teaspoon black pepper, bell pepper, beans, and tomatoes in a bowl; stir well. Spoon over chicken. Cover and cook on HIGH 1 hour; reduce to LOW, and cook 5 hours.
3. To serve, place 1 chicken breast into each of 4 shallow bowls; top each with bean mixture. **Makes** 4 servings.

Provençale Chicken Supper

Chicken-and-Wild Rice Hot Dish

Chicken-and-Wild Rice Hot Dish

With an earthy blend of wild rice, mushrooms, and walnuts, this is a great casserole to serve the family on a cool autumn evening.

PREP: 15 MIN., COOK: 4 HR.

make ahead

4 skinned and boned chicken breasts
    (about 2 pounds)
1 cup chopped onion
1 cup chopped celery
5 garlic cloves, pressed
2 (6-ounce) packages uncooked long-grain and wild
    rice mix (we tested with Uncle Ben's)
2 (14-ounce) cans chicken broth with roasted garlic
2 (10¾-ounce) cans cream of mushroom soup
1 (8-ounce) package sliced fresh mushrooms
1 (8-ounce) can sliced water chestnuts, drained
1 cup chopped walnuts, toasted
2 tablespoons butter

1. Brown chicken in a lightly greased large nonstick skillet over medium-high heat; remove from pan, and cut into ½-inch pieces. Add onion, celery, and garlic to pan; sauté 3 to 4 minutes or until tender.
2. Combine rice mix and remaining 6 ingredients in a 5-quart slow cooker. Stir in chicken and vegetables.
3. Cover and cook on LOW 4 hours or until rice is tender and liquid is absorbed. **Makes** 6 servings.

Braised Chicken Thighs With Rosemary and Potatoes

PREP: 20 MIN., COOK: 5 HR.

8 chicken thighs (about 2½ pounds)
¾ teaspoon salt, divided
½ teaspoon pepper, divided
1 tablespoon vegetable oil
1 medium onion, halved lengthwise and sliced
2 large baking potatoes (about 1½ pounds), peeled and sliced
⅔ cup chicken broth
1½ teaspoons dried rosemary
4 garlic cloves, minced

1. Sprinkle chicken evenly with ¼ teaspoon salt and ¼ teaspoon pepper. Heat oil in a large nonstick skillet over medium-high heat; add chicken, and cook 3 to 4 minutes on each side or until browned.
2. Place onion in a 4-quart slow cooker; top with potato. Arrange chicken on top of potato.
3. Combine remaining ½ teaspoon salt, ¼ teaspoon pepper, broth, rosemary, and garlic in a small bowl; pour over chicken. Cover and cook on HIGH 1 hour; reduce to LOW, and cook 4 hours or until chicken is done and vegetables are tender. **Makes** 4 servings.

Chicken Pepper Pot

PREP: 5 MIN., COOK: 8 HR.

2 (16-ounce) packages frozen pepper stir-fry, thawed
4 (6-ounce) skinned chicken breasts
1 (11-ounce) can tomato bisque
1 tablespoon white wine Worcestershire sauce
½ teaspoon garlic powder
¼ teaspoon coarsely ground pepper

1. Place all ingredients in a 4- or 5-quart slow cooker; stir well. Cover and cook on HIGH 1 hour; reduce to LOW, and cook 6 to 7 hours. **Makes** 4 servings.

Chicken Barbecue

Cola soft drink adds sweetness to this tangy barbecue mixture.

PREP: 20 MIN., COOK: 4 HR. (HIGH) OR 9 HR. (LOW)

3 pounds skinned and boned chicken breasts, cut into 2-inch pieces
1 (18-ounce) bottle barbecue sauce
½ cup cola soft drink (not diet) (we used Coca-Cola)
1 medium onion, chopped
2 tablespoons lemon juice
2 teaspoons Worcestershire sauce
Hamburger buns (optional)

1. Place chicken in a 4½-quart slow cooker. Add barbecue sauce and next 4 ingredients, stirring well.
2. Cover and cook on HIGH 4 hours or on LOW 9 hours. Remove chicken from slow cooker; cool slightly, and shred using 2 forks. Return to slow cooker; cook until thoroughly heated. Serve with hamburger buns, if desired. **Makes** 8 servings.

slow cooking: the heat is on

- It generally takes twice as long to cook food on the low heat setting as the high heat setting.
- Resist the urge to lift the lid; each time the cover is removed, it can take up to 30 minutes to regain lost heat and steam.

Apricot-Glazed Turkey and Sweet Potatoes

PREP: 5 MIN., COOK: 8 HR.

6 cups (1-inch) cubed peeled sweet
　　potato (about 1¾ pounds)
1 cup apricot preserves, divided
1 teaspoon salt, divided
2 bay leaves
2 (¾-pound) turkey tenderloins

1. Place sweet potato, ½ cup preserves, and ½ teaspoon
salt in a 4½- to 5-quart slow cooker; toss well. Add
bay leaves. Arrange tenderloins over sweet potato,
and sprinkle with remaining ½ teaspoon salt. Spread
remaining ½ cup preserves over tenderloins.
2. Cover and cook on HIGH 1 hour; reduce to LOW,
and cook 7 hours or until turkey and sweet potato are
tender. Remove turkey from slow cooker, and slice.
Discard bay leaves. Serve turkey with sweet potato and
cooking liquid. **Makes** 6 servings.

Thai Coconut Shrimp and Rice

*Friends will hardly believe this shrimp and fresh snow pea
sensation cooked in your slow cooker. If you want to buy the
shrimp in the shell instead of peeled, purchase 2 pounds.*

PREP: 17 MIN.; COOK: 4 HR., 50 MIN.

2 red bell peppers, cut into strips
1 (32-ounce) container chicken broth
1½ cups uncooked converted rice (we used Uncle
　　Ben's)
1 tablespoon garlic-chili sauce
1 (14-ounce) can coconut milk
10 (⅛-inch-thick) slices peeled fresh ginger
5 garlic cloves, minced
1½ pounds peeled, medium-size raw shrimp
2 cups fresh sugar snap peas, trimmed
½ cup (1-inch) sliced green onion tops
⅓ cup fresh lime juice

1. Place first 7 ingredients in a 5-quart slow cooker;
stir well. Cover and cook on LOW 4 hours.
2. Increase to HIGH. Add shrimp and remaining
3 ingredients; cover and cook 50 minutes or just until
shrimp turn pink. Spoon into bowls. **Makes** 8 servings.

Thai Coconut Shrimp and Rice

Enchilada Casserole

Enchilada Casserole

You control the spice in this Tex-Mex favorite with the type of salsa and enchilada sauce you use.

PREP: 10 MIN.; COOK: 5 HR., 30 MIN.

3 tablespoons chopped green chiles,
　　divided
¾ cup chunky salsa
¼ cup chopped fresh cilantro
1 (15.5-ounce) can black beans, rinsed and drained
1 (11-ounce) can yellow corn with red and green bell
　　peppers
1 (10-ounce) can enchilada sauce
1 (8½-ounce) package corn muffin mix
2 large eggs, lightly beaten
2 tablespoons chopped roasted red bell peppers
1½ cups (6 ounces) shredded Monterey Jack cheese
Sour cream (optional)
Garnish: chopped fresh cilantro

1. Stir together 2 tablespoons green chiles and next 5 ingredients in a 3½-quart slow cooker. Cover and cook on LOW 4 hours.

2. Stir together remaining 1 tablespoon green chiles, muffin mix, eggs, and roasted red bell peppers. Spoon batter evenly over bean mixture in slow cooker. Cover and cook on LOW 1 hour and 20 minutes or until cornbread is done.

3. Sprinkle cheese over cornbread. Cover and cook 5 to 10 minutes or until cheese melts. Serve with sour cream, if desired. Garnish, if desired. **Makes** 6 servings.

Eggplant and Artichoke Parmigiana

PREP: 20 MIN., COOK: 6 HR.

1 (25-ounce) jar roasted garlic pasta sauce
　　with Merlot wine (we used Sutter Home)
½ teaspoon freshly ground pepper
1 (1-pound) eggplant, cut into ¼-inch-thick slices
1 (9-ounce) package frozen artichoke hearts, thawed
　　and drained
1 cup (4 ounces) shredded part-skim mozzarella
　　cheese
2 tablespoons chopped fresh parsley
1 tablespoon chopped fresh oregano
Hot cooked spaghetti
¼ cup finely shredded fresh Parmesan cheese

1. Combine pasta sauce and pepper; stir well. Spoon ½ cup pasta sauce into a 4-quart slow cooker. Arrange half of eggplant slices over sauce; top with half of artichoke hearts, and sprinkle with half of mozzarella cheese. Spoon ½ cup pasta sauce over mozzarella cheese.

2. Repeat layers with remaining eggplant, artichoke hearts, and mozzarella cheese. Top with remaining pasta sauce; sprinkle with parsley and oregano.

3. Cover and cook on LOW 5 to 6 hours or until eggplant is tender. Serve over hot cooked spaghetti; sprinkle with Parmesan. **Makes** 4 servings.

Caramelized French Onion Soup

Caramelized French Onion Soup

Large sweet onions are slow-cooked until golden brown, adding rich flavor to Caramelized French Onion Soup.

PREP: 10 MIN.; COOK: 2 HR., 35 MIN.

make ahead

Caramelized Onions
1 (10.5-ounce) can beef consommé, undiluted
1 (10.5-ounce) can condensed beef broth, undiluted
2 cups water
½ teaspoon dried thyme
¼ cup dry white wine
3 cups large croutons
1 cup (4 ounces) shredded Swiss cheese
Coarsely ground pepper

1. Combine Caramelized Onions and next 4 ingredients in a 3½-quart slow cooker.
2. Cover and cook on HIGH 2½ hours or until thoroughly heated. Stir in wine.
3. Ladle soup into 6 ovenproof bowls; top evenly with croutons and cheese. Place bowls on a jelly-roll pan.

4. Broil 3 inches from heat 5 minutes or until cheese melts. Sprinkle with pepper. Serve immediately. **Makes** 6 servings.

Caramelized Onions:

PREP: 5 MIN., COOK: 8 HR.

2 extra-large sweet onions (about 3 pounds)
1 (10.5-ounce) can condensed chicken or beef broth, undiluted
¼ cup butter

1. Cut onions in half; cut each half into ½-inch-thick slices.
2. Combine onion slices, broth, and butter in a 3½-quart slow cooker. Cover and cook on HIGH 8 hours or until golden brown and very soft. Store in an airtight container, and chill up to 2 weeks, or, if desired, freeze up to 2 months. **Makes** 2 cups.

Black Bean Soup

Sturdy black beans provide the base for this traditional Mexican soup. We prefer Bush brand because the beans hold their shape best.

PREP: 10 MIN., COOK: 6 HR.

2 (15-ounce) cans black beans, rinsed
    and drained
2 (4.5-ounce) cans chopped green chiles
1 (14½-ounce) can Mexican-style stewed tomatoes,
    undrained
1 (14½-ounce) can diced tomatoes, undrained
1 (11-ounce) can sweet whole kernel corn, drained
4 green onions, sliced
2 to 3 tablespoons chili powder
1 teaspoon ground cumin
½ teaspoon dried minced garlic

1. Combine all ingredients in a 5-quart slow cooker.
2. Cover and cook on HIGH 5 to 6 hours. **Makes** 8 cups.

Spicy Vegetable Soup

For a not-so-spicy vegetable soup, use the mild variety of canned tomatoes and green chiles instead of the regular.

PREP: 5 MIN., COOK: 8 HR.

2 (16-ounce) packages frozen vegetable
    soup mix
2 (14.5-ounce) cans diced tomatoes with basil, garlic,
    and oregano, undrained
1 (10-ounce) can diced tomatoes and green chiles
1 (14.5-ounce) can beef broth
1 large onion, chopped
¾ teaspoon salt

1. Place all ingredients in a 4-quart slow cooker; stir well. Cover and cook on LOW 8 hours or until vegetables are tender. **Makes** 8 servings.

Homestyle Potato Soup

PREP: 5 MIN.; COOK: 5 HR., 30 MIN.

1 (14-ounce) can chicken broth
1 (1-pound, 4-ounce) package refrigerated diced
    potatoes with onion
4 green onions, coarsely chopped
3 tablespoons butter or margarine, cut into small
    pieces
¾ teaspoon salt
½ teaspoon freshly ground pepper
3 garlic cloves, minced
¼ cup all-purpose flour
1½ cups milk
½ cup (2 ounces) shredded sharp Cheddar cheese

1. Place first 7 ingredients in a 4-quart slow cooker; stir well. Cover and cook on LOW 5 hours or until vegetables are tender. Increase to HIGH.
2. Place flour in a bowl; gradually add milk, stirring with a wire whisk until smooth. Stir into soup. Cover and cook 30 minutes or until thickened, stirring twice. Ladle into bowls; sprinkle evenly with cheese. **Makes** 5½ cups.

Caramel Pie

Caramel Pie

Wake up to pie? Indeed! This pie filling cooks 9 hours, so it's a great candidate to cook while you sleep. If you'd like to make this pie with a twist, slice a couple of bananas, and top the crust with the slices before pouring the caramel on top.

PREP: 4 MIN., COOK: 9 HR., OTHER: 2 HR.

1 (14-ounce) can sweetened condensed
    milk
1 (9-inch) ready-made graham cracker crust
1 (8-ounce) container frozen whipped topping,
    thawed
2 (1.4-ounce) chocolate-covered toffee candy bars,
    coarsely chopped (we used Skor)

1. Pour milk into a 2-cup glass measuring cup; cover with aluminum foil.
2. Place measuring cup in a 3½-quart slow cooker; carefully pour hot water in slow cooker to reach the level of milk in measuring cup. Cover and cook on LOW 9 hours.
3. Pour caramelized milk into crust; cool completely. Spread whipped topping over pie; sprinkle with chopped candy bars. Cover and chill 2 hours or until ready to serve. **Makes** 1 (9-inch) pie.

slow-cooker cleanup

- Always allow the cooker insert to cool completely before washing it. Cold water poured over a hot insert can cause cracking.
- Never immerse a slow cooker into water. Simply unplug it, and wipe it with a cloth.
- A new product that simplifies slow-cooker cleanup is a clear, heavy-duty plastic liner made to fit 3- to 6½-quart oval and round slow cookers. It's as simple as fitting the plastic liner inside your slow cooker before adding the recipe ingredients. When you're finished cooking, simply serve the meal directly from the cooker. Once the cooker has cooled, just toss the plastic liner along with the mess.

Apple Grunt

This old-fashioned fruit dessert is topped with slightly sweet biscuit dough. Reduced-fat baking mix works equally well in this classic dessert.

PREP: 20 MIN., COOK: 6 HR.

5 medium-size Golden Delicious apples
    (about 2 pounds), peeled and cut into
    ½-inch wedges
½ cup sugar
⅓ cup all-purpose flour
¼ teaspoon apple pie spice
2 cups all-purpose baking mix (we used Bisquick)
¾ cup milk
3 tablespoons sugar
3 tablespoons butter or margarine, melted
3 cups vanilla ice cream

1. Place apple, ½ cup sugar, flour, and apple pie spice in a 4-quart slow cooker; stir well.
2. Combine baking mix, milk, 3 tablespoons sugar, and butter in a bowl; stir just until moist. Spoon dough over apple mixture.
3. Cover and cook on LOW 6 hours. Divide mixture evenly between 9 dessert dishes; top each serving with ice cream. Serve warm. **Makes** 9 servings.

Avocado-Corn Salsa, page 182

quick
NIBBLES

Coffee-Kissed Pecan Brie

Coffee-Kissed Pecan Brie

Pecans lend a nice texture contrast to the soft creamy Brie. Serve this hot from the oven so the cheese is smooth and gooey.

20 minutes or less
PREP: 10 MIN., COOK: 5 MIN.

1 (13.2-ounce) Brie round
½ cup chopped pecans, toasted
2 tablespoons coffee-flavored liqueur
1½ tablespoons brown sugar
Apple slices or gingersnaps

1. Trim rind from top of cheese, cutting to within ½ inch of edge. Place in a small baking dish.
2. Combine pecans, liqueur, and brown sugar; spread over top of cheese.
3. Bake at 350° for 3 to 5 minutes or just until soft. Serve immediately with apple slices or gingersnaps.
Makes 8 appetizer servings.

Warmed Cranberry Brie

This almost-effortless appetizer is ready in just minutes.

20 minutes or less
PREP: 15 MIN., COOK: 5 MIN.

1 (15-ounce) Brie round
1 (16-ounce) can whole-berry cranberry sauce
¼ cup firmly packed brown sugar
2 tablespoons spiced rum (see note)
½ teaspoon ground nutmeg
¼ cup chopped pecans, toasted
Apple and pear slices

1. Trim rind from top of Brie, leaving a ⅓-inch border. Place on a baking sheet.
2. Stir together cranberry sauce and next 3 ingredients; spread mixture evenly over top of Brie. Sprinkle with pecans.
3. Bake at 500° for 5 minutes. Serve with apple and pear slices. **Makes** 8 appetizer servings.
Note: 2 tablespoons orange juice may be substituted for spiced rum.

Garlic-and-Dill Feta Cheese Spread

PREP: 10 MIN., OTHER: 8 HR.

make ahead

1 (8-ounce) package cream cheese, softened
1 (4-ounce) package crumbled feta cheese
¼ cup mayonnaise
1 garlic clove, minced
1 tablespoon chopped fresh dill or ½ teaspoon dried dillweed
½ teaspoon seasoned pepper
¼ teaspoon salt
Cucumber slices (optional)

1. Process first 7 ingredients in a food processor until smooth, stopping to scrape down sides. Cover and chill 8 hours. Serve with cucumber slices, if desired.
Makes about 1 cup.
Note: Spread may be frozen in an airtight container up to 1 month. Thaw in refrigerator at least 24 hours. Stir before serving.

(clockwise from top) Tapenade, Herbed
Feta Spread, Cucumber-Yogurt Spread,
and Béarnaise Mayonnaise

Tapenade

Try this classic olive spread with grilled fish or vegetables on sliced focaccia.

10 minutes or less

PREP: 10 MIN.

make
ahead

1 (6-ounce) jar pitted kalamata olives, drained
1 anchovy fillet, rinsed
2 garlic cloves, chopped
1 small shallot, chopped
1 teaspoon capers
¼ cup olive oil
1 tablespoon lemon juice
1 tablespoon chopped fresh parsley
Garnishes: olives, lemon slice, chopped fresh parsley

1. Process first 5 ingredients in a food processor until smooth. With processor running, pour oil through food chute, stopping to scrape down sides. Stir in lemon juice and 1 tablespoon chopped parsley. Garnish, if desired. **Makes** 1 cup.

Herbed Feta Spread

10 minutes or less
PREP: 10 MIN.

1 (8-ounce) package feta cheese,
    softened
1 (8-ounce) package cream cheese, softened
3 tablespoons chopped fresh basil
3 tablespoons chopped fresh chives
2 tablespoons olive oil
2 tablespoons balsamic vinegar
⅓ cup pine nuts, toasted
Garnish: fresh basil sprigs
Toasted pita chips or baguette slices

1. Stir together first 6 ingredients until smooth. Cover and chill up to 1 week. Stir in pine nuts just before serving. Garnish, if desired. Serve with toasted pita chips or baguette slices. **Makes** 2½ cups.

Cucumber-Yogurt Spread

Serve this refreshing spread on soft rolls with grilled chicken, sliced turkey, or fresh tomato slices.

PREP: 15 MIN., OTHER: 24 HR.

1 (16-ounce) container plain nonfat
    yogurt
2 small cucumbers, peeled, seeded, and finely
    chopped
2 garlic cloves, pressed
6 small mint leaves, minced
¼ teaspoon salt
¼ teaspoon pepper
Garnishes: cucumber slices, fresh mint sprigs

1. Line a mesh strainer with a paper coffee filter. Spoon yogurt into filter, and place strainer over a bowl. Cover and chill at least 24 hours.
2. Spoon yogurt into a bowl, discarding liquid (yogurt will have a very thick consistency). Stir in chopped cucumber and next 4 ingredients. Cover and chill up to 3 days. Garnish, if desired. **Makes** 2 cups.

Béarnaise Mayonnaise

Substitute this for regular mayonnaise on sandwiches.

20 minutes or less
PREP: 15 MIN., COOK: 5 MIN.

⅓ cup dry white wine
1 tablespoon white wine vinegar
2 shallots, minced
1 cup mayonnaise
2 tablespoons chopped fresh tarragon
1 teaspoon grated lemon rind
⅛ teaspoon pepper
Garnish: fresh tarragon sprig

1. Cook first 3 ingredients over medium-high heat 5 minutes or until liquid is reduced to 1 tablespoon. Remove from heat, and cool.
2. Stir together mayonnaise and next 3 ingredients; stir in wine reduction. Cover and chill up to 1 week. Garnish, if desired. **Makes** 1 cup.

Tomato-Basil Mayonnaise: Stir together 1 cup mayonnaise, 2 tablespoons tomato paste, and 2 tablespoons chopped basil until blended.

Gremolata Mayonnaise: Stir together 1 cup mayonnaise, 2 tablespoons chopped fresh parsley, 2 tablespoons grated lemon rind, and 1 garlic clove, pressed.

Pesto-Goat Cheese Spread

PREP: 15 MIN., OTHER: 2 HR.

1 (11-ounce) log goat cheese
1 (8-ounce) package cream cheese, softened
2 cups loosely packed fresh basil leaves
½ cup pine nuts, toasted
3 garlic cloves
2 tablespoons balsamic vinegar
Toasted pita chips or baguette slices

1. Process first 6 ingredients in a food processor until smooth. Cover and chill 2 hours before serving. Store in an airtight container in refrigerator up to 1 week, or freeze in an airtight container up to 4 months. Serve with toasted pita chips or baguette slices. **Makes** 3 cups.

Cherry-Cheese
Ring

Cherry-Cheese Ring

The cheese mixture may be prepared up to 2 days ahead and stored in an airtight container in the refrigerator.

PREP: 20 MIN., OTHER: 8 HR.

make
ahead

1 (1-pound) block sharp Cheddar cheese,
    shredded
1 cup mayonnaise
½ cup chopped onion
¼ teaspoon salt
¼ teaspoon pepper
¼ to ½ teaspoon ground red pepper
1 cup chopped pecans, toasted
1 (12-ounce) jar cherry or strawberry preserves
Crackers or bread rounds

1. Beat first 6 ingredients at medium speed with an electric mixer until blended; stir in pecans. Spoon into a lightly greased 5-cup ring mold. Cover and chill 8 hours. Invert mold onto a serving platter, and place a warm damp cloth on ring mold; gently lift mold from cheese mixture.

2. Spoon preserves in center of cheese mixture, and serve immediately with crackers or bread rounds.
Makes 12 to 16 appetizer servings.

Cheddar-Chili Cheesecake

PREP: 25 MIN.; COOK: 1 HR., OTHER: 30 MIN.

¼ cup fine, dry breadcrumbs
¼ cup (1 ounce) shredded sharp Cheddar cheese
3 (8-ounce) packages cream cheese, softened
12 thin slices cooked ham, diced and divided
1 (10-ounce) block sharp Cheddar cheese, shredded
5 green onions, chopped
3 large eggs
2 small jalapeño peppers, minced
1 garlic clove, minced
1 cup sour cream
2 tablespoons milk
Crackers

1. Stir together breadcrumbs and ¼ cup shredded cheese; sprinkle on bottom of a buttered 9-inch springform pan. Set aside.
2. Beat cream cheese at medium speed with an electric mixer; add half of ham, shredded cheese, and next 6 ingredients, beating at low speed until well blended. Pour half of cream cheese mixture into prepared pan; top with remaining ham. Pour remaining half of cream cheese mixture over ham.
3. Bake at 325° for 1 hour or until center is set. Let stand 30 minutes. Gently run a knife around the edge of cheesecake, and release sides. Serve slightly warm or at room temperature with crackers. **Makes** 6 to 8 appetizer servings.

Mexican Cheese Spread

Serve this creamy spread with stone-ground wheat crackers or bagel chips.

20 minutes or less
PREP: 13 MIN.

make ahead

2 cups (8 ounces) shredded sharp Cheddar cheese
½ cup sour cream
¼ cup butter or margarine, softened
2 green onions, chopped
1 (2-ounce) jar diced pimiento, drained
2 tablespoons chopped green chiles

1. Combine first 3 ingredients in a mixing bowl; beat at medium speed with an electric mixer until blended.
2. Stir in green onions, pimiento, and chiles. Cover and chill cheese spread, if desired. **Makes** 2 cups.

Five-Minute Salsa

You control the consistency of this salsa by how long you process the ingredients.

10 minutes or less
PREP: 5 MIN.

1 (14½-ounce) can stewed tomatoes, undrained
1 (10-ounce) can diced tomatoes and green chiles, undrained
¼ teaspoon garlic powder
½ teaspoon pepper

1. Combine all ingredients in a blender; process 15 seconds or until smooth. Transfer mixture to a bowl; cover and chill, if desired. Serve with tortilla chips. **Makes** 2¾ cups.

Black Bean Salsa

This tangy salsa is made for Open-Faced Southwestern Chicken Sandwiches (page 269), but it's also great served with chips as an appetizer. Prepare this salsa a day ahead to allow the flavors to mingle.

20 minutes or less
PREP: 15 MIN.

1 plum tomato
1 avocado
⅓ cup chopped red onion
1 (15-ounce) can black beans, rinsed and drained
1½ tablespoons chopped fresh cilantro
1 tablespoon olive oil
2 tablespoons lime juice
⅛ teaspoon dried crushed red pepper
⅛ teaspoon salt

1. Dice tomato. Peel, seed, and dice avocado. Combine tomato, avocado, onion, beans, and cilantro in a bowl.
2. Whisk together oil and remaining 3 ingredients. Toss with bean mixture. Cover and chill, if desired. **Makes** about 3 cups.

Avocado-Corn Salsa

If you prefer canned corn, substitute 2 (15.25-ounce) cans sweet whole kernel corn for the frozen kind.

PREP: 12 MIN., OTHER: 2 HR.

2½ cups frozen whole kernel corn, thawed
1 medium tomato, chopped
1 jalapeño pepper, seeded and chopped
¼ cup chopped bell pepper
¼ cup chopped red onion
¼ cup chopped fresh cilantro
¼ cup white wine vinegar
2 tablespoons lime juice
½ teaspoon salt
3 small avocados, peeled and chopped

1. Combine all ingredients except avocado. Gently stir in avocado. Cover and chill at least 2 hours. Serve with tortilla chips or grilled fish or chicken. **Makes** about 6 cups.

Carolina Caviar

This isn't a real caviar, but rather a salsa made from black-eyed peas that, for Southerners, rivals the flavor of the ritzier roe. It marinates in Italian dressing, so spoon the spicy blend into a serving bowl using a slotted spoon.

PREP: 20 MIN., OTHER: 8 HR.

2 (15.8-ounce) cans black-eyed peas, rinsed and drained
1 (16-ounce) bottle Italian dressing
1 (11-ounce) can white shoepeg corn, drained
1 large firm tomato, chopped
1 green bell pepper, chopped
1 small onion, chopped
1 cup chopped fresh parsley
4 green onions, chopped
1 tablespoon chopped fresh cilantro
2 garlic cloves, minced

1. Stir together all ingredients in a large bowl. Cover and chill 8 to 24 hours. Spoon mixture into a serving bowl, using a slotted spoon. Serve with tortilla chips. **Makes** 8 cups.

Avocado-Corn Salsa

Texas Caviar

Texas Caviar

20 minutes or less
PREP: 20 MIN.

make
ahead

2 (15½-ounce) cans black-eyed peas
    with jalapeño peppers, rinsed and drained
1 (10-ounce) can diced tomato and green chiles
2 avocados, diced
1 small green bell pepper, diced
½ red onion, diced
¾ cup zesty Italian dressing
1 tablespoon fresh lime juice
¼ teaspoon salt
Corn chips

1. Stir together black-eyed peas and next 7 ingredients. Cover and chill, if desired. Serve with corn chips. **Makes** 6 cups.

Layered Nacho Dip

This quick version of the classic is the perfect meatless appetizer. With plentiful veggies, sour cream, and cheese, it's sure to please any crowd. This dip can be made ahead and chilled up to 4 hours.

20 minutes or less
PREP: 15 MIN.

make ahead

1 (16-ounce) can refried beans
2 teaspoons taco seasoning mix
1 (6-ounce) container refrigerated avocado dip or
    1 cup guacamole
1 (8-ounce) container sour cream
1 (4½-ounce) can chopped black olives, drained
2 large tomatoes, diced
1 small onion, diced
1 (4-ounce) can chopped green chiles
1½ cups (6 ounces) shredded Monterey Jack cheese

1. Stir together beans and seasoning mix; spread mixture in an 11- x 7-inch baking dish. Spread avocado dip and sour cream evenly over bean mixture. Sprinkle with olives and next 4 ingredients. Serve with corn or tortilla chips. **Makes** 8 cups.

Pizza Dip

Cut the cook time in half by microwaving this dip instead of baking it. It's done in 6 minutes on HIGH.

30 minutes or less
PREP: 12 MIN., COOK: 12 MIN.

1 (8-ounce) package cream cheese, softened
1 (14-ounce) jar pizza sauce
½ cup chopped green bell pepper
½ cup chopped pepperoni
1 (2¼-ounce) can sliced ripe olives, drained
1 (8-ounce) package shredded mozzarella cheese
2 green onions, chopped

1. Spread cream cheese in bottom of a 9-inch pieplate; spread pizza sauce over cream cheese. Sprinkle bell pepper, pepperoni, and olives over sauce. Top with mozzarella cheese.
2. Bake at 350° for 10 to 12 minutes or until cheese melts. Sprinkle with green onions. Serve warm with corn chips. **Makes** 8 to 10 servings.

Meaty Cheese Dip

You'll be amazed at the flavor from these 4 ingredients. The hot sausage and salsa keep things lively. Want a spicier dip? Substitute 1 (32-ounce) loaf Mexican pasteurized prepared cheese product for the regular cheese.

20 minutes or less
PREP: 3 MIN., COOK: 12 MIN.

1 pound ground chuck
½ pound ground hot pork sausage
1 (32-ounce) loaf pasteurized prepared cheese
    product, cubed
1 (8-ounce) jar medium salsa

1. Cook ground chuck and sausage in a large skillet, stirring until meat crumbles and is no longer pink; drain.
2. Add cheese and salsa; cook over low heat, stirring constantly, until cheese melts. Serve warm with large corn chips. **Makes** 6 cups.

Florentine Artichoke
Dip

Florentine Artichoke Dip

PREP: 10 MIN., COOK: 25 MIN.

1 (10-ounce) package frozen chopped spinach,
    thawed
2 (6-ounce) jars marinated artichoke hearts
3 garlic cloves, minced
½ cup light mayonnaise
1½ (8-ounce) packages cream cheese, softened
2 tablespoons lemon juice
1 teaspoon hot sauce
¼ cup fine, dry breadcrumbs
1 cup grated Parmesan cheese
Crackers or breadsticks

1. Drain spinach well; press between paper towels. Drain and chop artichoke hearts.
2. Combine spinach, artichoke hearts, garlic, and next 4 ingredients, stirring well. Spoon into a lightly greased 11- x 7-inch baking dish; sprinkle evenly with breadcrumbs and Parmesan cheese.
3. Bake at 375° for 25 minutes, and serve with crackers or breadsticks. **Makes** 4 cups.

Quick Fiesta Dip

PREP: 8 MIN., COOK: 2 MIN., OTHER: 5 MIN.

1 (9-ounce) package frozen corn niblets
1 (12-ounce) jar thick-and-chunky mild salsa
1 cup (4 ounces) shredded Colby or Cheddar cheese
Tortilla chips or corn chips

1. Cook corn according to package directions; drain.
2. Pour salsa into a 9-inch glass pieplate; stir in corn. Cover with plastic wrap; fold back a small section of wrap to allow steam to escape. Microwave at HIGH 2 minutes or until bubbly. Sprinkle cheese over salsa; cover with plastic wrap. Let stand 5 minutes or until cheese is melted. Serve with chips. **Makes** 1½ cups.

Swiss-Onion Dip

This dip offers a bit of punch, thanks to coarse grained mustard. Melba rounds make the perfect match for this savory dip.

30 minutes or less

PREP: 5 MIN., COOK: 25 MIN.

1 (10-ounce) package frozen chopped onion, thawed
3 cups (12 ounces) shredded Swiss cheese
1 cup mayonnaise
1 tablespoon coarse grained Dijon mustard
¼ teaspoon salt
⅛ teaspoon pepper

1. Press onion between layers of paper towels to remove excess moisture. Combine onion, cheese, and remaining ingredients; spoon mixture into an ungreased 1-quart baking dish.
2. Bake at 325° for 25 minutes or until lightly browned and bubbly. Serve warm. **Makes** 4 cups.

Vidalia Onion Dip

French baguette slices serve as sturdy dippers for this cheesy appetizer.

30 minutes or less

PREP: 8 MIN., COOK: 18 MIN.

2 tablespoons butter or margarine
3 large Vidalia onions, coarsely chopped
2 cups (8 ounces) shredded Swiss cheese
2 cups mayonnaise
¼ cup dry white wine
2 garlic cloves, minced
½ teaspoon hot sauce
1 (8-ounce) can sliced water chestnuts, drained and
    chopped (optional)

1. Melt butter in a large skillet over medium-high heat; add onion. Sauté 10 minutes or until tender.
2. Combine cheese and next 4 ingredients in a bowl; add water chestnuts, if desired. Stir in onion. Spoon mixture into a lightly greased shallow 2-quart baking dish. Microwave at MEDIUM HIGH (70% power) 8 minutes. **Makes** 6 cups.

Black-eyed Pea
Hummus

Black-eyed Pea Hummus

You can find tahini (ground sesame seeds) near the peanut butter in most large supermarkets.

PREP: 10 MIN., OTHER: 1 HR.

make
ahead

1 (15-ounce) can black-eyed peas,
    rinsed and drained
2 tablespoons tahini
2 tablespoons olive oil
¼ cup fresh lemon juice
2 garlic cloves
½ teaspoon salt
¼ teaspoon ground cumin
½ teaspoon freshly ground black pepper
⅛ teaspoon ground red pepper
3 tablespoons water
Olive oil
Garnish: fresh parsley
Pita chips

1. Process first 9 ingredients in a food processor until blended, stopping to scrape down sides. Gradually add 3 tablespoons water for desired consistency. Cover and chill 1 hour. Drizzle with olive oil, and garnish, if desired. Serve with pita chips. **Makes** 2 cups.

Traditional Hummus: Substitute 1 (15-ounce) can chickpeas, rinsed and drained, for black-eyed peas. Proceed with recipe as directed.

Quick Creamy Vegetable Dip

Serve with raw vegetables or as a topping for chili or baked potatoes.

PREP: 10 MIN., OTHER: 2 HR.

make ahead

½ cup mayonnaise
½ cup sour cream
1 (2-ounce) jar diced pimiento, drained
¼ cup chopped onion
¼ cup diced green bell pepper
½ teaspoon garlic salt
⅛ teaspoon black pepper
⅛ teaspoon hot sauce

1. Stir together all ingredients. Cover and chill 2 hours. **Makes** about 1½ cups.

Bacon-Blue Cheese Dip

To shave a couple of minutes off this recipe, use precooked bacon slices instead of cooking your own.

20 minutes or less
PREP: 20 MIN.

½ cup sour cream
1 (4-ounce) package crumbled blue cheese
1 (3-ounce) package cream cheese, softened
⅛ teaspoon hot sauce
2 tablespoons diced onion
4 bacon slices, cooked and crumbled

1. Process first 5 ingredients in a blender or food processor until smooth, stopping to scrape down sides. Stir in half of bacon. Place dip in a serving bowl. Sprinkle with remaining bacon. Serve with crackers, raw vegetables, or potato chips. **Makes** 1½ cups.

Cinco de Mayo Bean Dip

20 minutes or less
PREP: 10 MIN., COOK: 5 MIN.

1 (16-ounce) can refried beans
1 (8-ounce) package shredded Mexican four-cheese blend, divided
1 cup chunky salsa
1 (4½-ounce) can chopped black olives, drained
3 green onions, sliced
¼ teaspoon salt
¼ teaspoon garlic powder
Chopped fresh cilantro

1. Combine beans, 1 cup cheese, and next 5 ingredients. Spoon into a 9-inch pieplate. Top with remaining 1 cup cheese. Cover tightly with heavy-duty plastic wrap; fold back a small edge to allow steam to escape.
2. Microwave at HIGH 4 to 5 minutes or until cheese melts, stirring after 3 minutes. Sprinkle with chopped fresh cilantro. Serve with tortilla chips or corn chips. **Makes** 4¾ cups.

Curry Dip

Curry Dip

PREP: 10 MIN., OTHER: 4 HR.

1 cup nonfat or regular sour cream
½ cup fat-free or regular mayonnaise
2 tablespoons minced fresh parsley
1 teaspoon minced fresh chives
2 tablespoons grated onion
2 tablespoons lemon juice
1 teaspoon curry powder
2 teaspoons prepared mustard
½ teaspoon paprika
½ teaspoon dried tarragon
Assorted fresh vegetables

1. Stir together first 10 ingredients. Cover and chill at least 4 hours. Serve with assorted fresh vegetables. **Makes** 1½ cups.

Sweet 'n' Savory Snack Mix

This is the perfect after-school or in-the-car traveling snack mix.

20 minutes or less

PREP: 5 MIN., COOK: 12 MIN.

3 cups crispy corn or rice cereal squares
1 cup small pretzels
1 (6-ounce) can roasted almonds
8 ounces salted peanuts
⅓ cup firmly packed light brown sugar
1½ tablespoons Worcestershire sauce
Butter-flavored cooking spray
1 cup bear-shaped graham crackers
½ cup raisins

1. Combine first 4 ingredients in a large bowl. Stir together brown sugar and Worcestershire sauce until blended; pour over cereal mixture. Coat a 15- x 10-inch jelly-roll pan with butter-flavored cooking spray; spread cereal mixture in a single layer in pan, stirring to coat.
2. Bake at 325° for 12 minutes, stirring every 5 minutes. Stir in graham crackers and raisins. Cool completely. Store snack mix in an airtight container at room temperature. **Makes** 8 cups.

Mexicali Snack Mix

30 minutes or less

PREP: 7 MIN., COOK: 20 MIN.

1½ cups bite-size crispy wheat cereal squares
1½ cups roasted salted peanuts
1 cup salted sunflower seed kernels
1 cup nutlike toasted-corn snacks (we used CornNuts)
¼ cup butter or margarine, melted
2 teaspoons chili powder
¼ teaspoon ground cumin
¼ teaspoon dried crushed red pepper
⅛ teaspoon garlic powder

1. Combine first 4 ingredients; spread evenly in an ungreased 15- x 10-inch jelly-roll pan. Drizzle butter evenly over cereal mixture; stir well.
2. Combine chili powder and remaining ingredients; sprinkle evenly over cereal mixture, and stir gently.
3. Bake, uncovered, at 350° for 20 minutes, stirring after 10 minutes. Cool completely. Store in an airtight container at room temperature. **Makes** 5 cups.

snack mix secrets

Snack mixes generally stay fresh and crunchy up to 5 days in an airtight container at room temperature. It's important to bake a snack mix in an even layer so that all ingredients bake evenly and get crisp. Let mix cool completely before packaging.

Starry Snack Mix

Starry Snack Mix

Package this mix in cellophane bags for portable treats or party favors.

10 minutes or less

PREP: 5 MIN.

2 (8-ounce) packages crispy cereal squares snack mix
1 (15-ounce) package raisins
1 (12-ounce) jar honey-roasted peanuts
1 (11-ounce) package fish-shaped Cheddar cheese
    crackers

1. Combine all ingredients. Store in an airtight container at room temperature. **Makes** 18 cups.
Note: For testing purposes only, we used Chex Mix Bold Party Blend for crispy cereal squares snack mix.

Snack Crackers

20 minutes or less

PREP: 5 MIN., COOK: 15 MIN.

make
ahead

½ cup vegetable oil
1 (1-ounce) envelope Ranch dressing mix
1 (10-ounce) package oyster crackers
½ (10-ounce) package bite-size Cheddar cheese
    crackers (2 cups)

1. Whisk together oil and dressing mix in a large bowl; add crackers, tossing to coat. Spread mixture in a single layer on a lightly greased baking sheet.
2. Bake at 350° for 15 minutes, stirring after 7 minutes. Let cool in a single layer on wax paper. Store in an airtight container at room temperature. **Makes** 6 cups.

Snack Crackers

Balsamic Marinated
Olives

Spiced Pecans

Balsamic Marinated Olives

This make-ahead recipe can be easily halved for a smaller crowd. One cup of commercial balsamic vinaigrette is a great substitute for the olive oil and vinegar in this recipe.

PREP: 5 MIN.; OTHER: 8 HR., 30 MIN.

2 (6-ounce) jars ripe olives, drained
2 (6-ounce) jars kalamata olives, drained
2 (7½-ounce) jars pimiento-stuffed olives, drained
½ cup olive oil
½ cup balsamic vinegar
1 tablespoon dried Italian seasoning

1. Combine all ingredients; cover and chill at least 8 hours. Let stand 30 minutes at room temperature before serving. Serve with a slotted spoon. Store in refrigerator up to 2 weeks. **Makes** 6 cups.

Spiced Pecans

These sweet-hot nibbles are addictive. This recipe can be conveniently doubled for gift giving.

20 minutes or less
PREP: 3 MIN., COOK: 12 MIN.

2 cups pecan halves
¼ cup sugar
4 tablespoons butter, melted
2 teaspoons salt
½ teaspoon ground red pepper
4 teaspoons Worcestershire sauce

1. Stir together all ingredients; spread in a lightly greased 13- x 9-inch pan.
2. Bake at 350° for 10 to 12 minutes or until lightly toasted, stirring once. **Makes** 2 cups.

Lemon-Garlic Olives

PREP: 15 MIN., OTHER: 8 HR.

1 (21-ounce) jar pimiento-stuffed olives
8 sprigs fresh oregano
6 garlic cloves, pressed
4 lemon slices
20 black peppercorns
6 tablespoons lemon juice

1. Drain olives, reserving liquid.
2. Layer half each of olives, oregano, garlic, lemon slices, and peppercorns in a 1-quart jar; repeat layers.
3. Pour 6 tablespoons lemon juice into jar; add just enough of reserved olive liquid to fill. Replace lid, and chill at least 8 hours. Store in refrigerator up to 2 weeks.
Makes about 32 appetizer servings.

Citrusy Pecans

These sweet, spicy nuts are great by the handful, or you can also chop them and add to salads and spreads. Be sure to store the pecans in an airtight container or a sealed zip-top plastic freezer bag to prevent them from becoming sticky.

PREP: 15 MIN., COOK: 25 MIN.

1 egg white
2 cups pecan halves
½ cup firmly packed light brown sugar
2 teaspoons grated orange rind
2 tablespoons fresh orange juice
½ teaspoon salt
¼ teaspoon ground cinnamon
Vegetable cooking spray

1. Whisk egg white in a medium bowl until frothy; toss with pecans.
2. Stir together ½ cup brown sugar and next 4 ingredients in a large bowl. Add pecans, and toss. Drain well. Place pecans in a single layer on an aluminum foil-lined baking sheet coated with cooking spray.
3. Bake at 325°, stirring occasionally, for 20 to 25 minutes. **Makes** 2 cups.

Green Chile Pimiento Cheese
Tea Sandwiches

Green Chile Pimiento Cheese

20 minutes or less
PREP: 15 MIN.

make
ahead

2 (8-ounce) blocks extra-sharp Cheddar
    cheese, shredded
1 (8-ounce) block Monterey Jack cheese with
    peppers, shredded
1 cup mayonnaise
1 (4.5-ounce) can chopped green chiles
1 (4-ounce) jar diced pimiento, drained
¼ small sweet onion, minced
2 teaspoons Worcestershire sauce

1. Stir together all ingredients in a large bowl. **Makes**
about 6 cups.

Green Chile Pimiento Cheese Tea Sandwiches:
Spread ½ cup cheese mixture on each of 6 to 8 bread
slices; top with 6 to 8 bread slices. Trim crusts, and
cut sandwiches diagonally into quarters or lengthwise into thirds. Reserve remaining cheese mixture
for other uses.

Basic Deviled Eggs

30 minutes or less
PREP: 25 MIN.

make
ahead

6 large, hard-cooked eggs, peeled
2 tablespoons mayonnaise
1½ tablespoons sweet pickle relish
1 teaspoon prepared mustard
⅛ teaspoon salt
Dash of pepper

1. Slice eggs in half lengthwise, and carefully remove
yolks. Mash yolks with mayonnaise. Stir in relish,
mustard, salt, and pepper. Spoon yolk mixture into egg
whites. **Makes** 6 servings.

Stuffed Cherry Tomatoes

20 minutes or less
PREP: 18 MIN.

1 pint cherry tomatoes
½ (8-ounce) package cream cheese softened
    (see note)
1½ to 2 tablespoons whipping cream
1 tablespoon chopped fresh chives
⅛ teaspoon salt
⅛ teaspoon ground white pepper

1. Cut top off each tomato; scoop out pulp, leaving
shells intact. Discard pulp. Invert tomato shells onto
paper towels to drain.
2. Combine cream cheese and remaining 4 ingredients
in a small mixing bowl; beat at medium speed with an
electric mixer until creamy, adding enough whipping
cream to make a slightly soft mixture. Spoon filling
into tomato shells. **Makes** about 1½ dozen.
Note: Quickly soften 1 (8-ounce) package of cream
cheese by removing the foil wrapping and placing the
cheese on a microwave-safe plate. Then microwave at
MEDIUM (50% power) 1 minute or just until softened.

Smoky Green Chile Cheddar Cheese With Avocado-Mango Salsa

Smoky Green Chile Cheddar Cheese With Avocado-Mango Salsa

PREP: 40 MIN., OTHER: 8 HR.

make
ahead

2 (8-ounce) packages cream cheese,
    softened
2 (8-ounce) blocks Monterey Jack cheese with
    peppers, shredded
1 (16-ounce) block smoked Cheddar cheese,
    shredded (see note)
6 green onions, minced
2 (4.5-ounce) cans chopped green chiles,
    drained
1 (1¼-ounce) envelope taco seasoning mix
Avocado-Mango Salsa
Crackers or tortilla chips

1. Combine first 6 ingredients in a large bowl. Divide mixture into 2 equal portions. Shape each into a 6-inch round. Cover and chill 8 hours, or freeze up to 1 month; thaw in the refrigerator 8 hours.
2. Place cheese rounds on serving plates; top evenly with Avocado-Mango Salsa. Serve with crackers or tortilla chips. **Makes** 18 servings.

Note: Smoked Cheddar cheese may be found in the deli section of your grocery store. Cheese mixture may be divided into 4 portions and pressed into 4 lightly greased ramekins, if desired. Freeze and thaw as directed. Invert cheese mixture onto serving plates.

Avocado-Mango Salsa:

PREP: 20 MIN., OTHER: 8 HR.

¼ cup hot jalapeño jelly
¼ cup fresh lime juice
2 large mangoes, peeled and diced (see note)
2 large avocados, diced
1 large red bell pepper, diced
¼ cup chopped fresh cilantro

1. Whisk together jelly and lime juice in a large bowl. Stir in mangoes and remaining ingredients until blended. Cover and chill 8 hours. **Makes** about 5 cups.
Note: 1 (26-ounce) jar refrigerated mango pieces, drained, may be substituted.

Marinated Cheese, Olives, and Peppers

PREP: 15 MIN., OTHER: 1 HR.

make
ahead

1½ pounds cubed firm cheeses (such as
　　　Cheddar, Gouda, Havarti, or Monterey Jack)
2 cups olives
1 (7-ounce) jar roasted red bell peppers
Cheese Marinade

1. Combine cheeses, olives, and peppers in a large
zip-top plastic freezer bag or decorative airtight
container. Pour Cheese Marinade over mixture, and
chill at least 1 hour or up to 2 days. **Makes** 6 to
8 appetizer servings.

Cheese Marinade:

PREP: 10 MIN.

1½ cups olive oil
1 cup white balsamic vinegar
¼ cup fresh thyme leaves
2 tablespoons chopped fresh rosemary
1 teaspoon salt
½ teaspoon pepper

1. Whisk together all ingredients. Pour into an airtight
jar or decorative container. Store in refrigerator up to
1 week. **Makes** about 3 cups.

Marinated Cheese,
Olives, and Peppers

Bacon-Cheese Rounds

Bacon-Cheese Rounds

30 minutes or less

PREP: 15 MIN., COOK: 10 MIN.

1 cup (4 ounces) shredded Swiss cheese
8 bacon slices, cooked and crumbled (see note)
¼ cup mayonnaise
1 teaspoon grated onion
½ teaspoon celery salt
8 white bread slices
Garnish: chopped fresh chives

1. Stir together first 5 ingredients.
2. Cut each bread slice into 2 (2¼-inch) rounds.
Spread 1 heaping tablespoon cheese mixture on each
round. Place on a lightly greased baking sheet.
3. Bake at 325° for 10 minutes. Garnish, if desired.
Makes 8 appetizers.
Note: 1 (2.5-ounce) package fully cooked bacon pieces
may be substituted.

Bacon Biscuit Cups

PREP: 10 MIN., COOK: 22 MIN.

2 (3-ounce) packages cream cheese, softened
1 large egg
2 tablespoons milk
½ cup (2 ounces) shredded Swiss cheese
1 green onion, chopped
1 (10-ounce) can refrigerated flaky biscuits (we used Pillsbury)
5 fully cooked bacon slices, chopped (we used Oscar Mayer Ready to Serve Bacon)
Sliced green onions

1. Place cream cheese and egg in a mixing bowl. Beat at medium speed with an electric mixer; add milk, beating until smooth. Stir in Swiss cheese and chopped green onion.
2. Separate biscuits into 10 portions. Pat each portion into a 5-inch circle; press onto bottom and up sides of greased muffin cups, forming a ¼-inch edge. Sprinkle evenly with bacon; spoon cream cheese mixture into cups over bacon.
3. Bake at 375° for 22 minutes or until set. Sprinkle evenly with sliced green onions, lightly pressing into filling. Remove immediately from pan, and serve warm. **Makes** 10 biscuit cups.

Blue Cheese Crisps

These nutty snacks are sure to entice taste buds with the flavor combination of blue cheese and pecans.

20 minutes or less
PREP: 8 MIN., COOK: 8 MIN.

½ cup butter or margarine, softened
1 (4-ounce) package crumbled blue cheese, softened
½ cup chopped pecans or walnuts
1 (12-ounce) French baguette, cut into ½-inch slices

1. Stir together butter and blue cheese until blended; stir in pecans. Set aside.
2. Place baguette slices in a single layer on baking sheets.
3. Bake at 350° for 3 minutes. Turn slices, and spread evenly with blue cheese mixture. Bake 5 more minutes. Serve immediately. **Makes** 28 appetizers.

Spicy Jack Cheese Crisps

PREP: 20 MIN., COOK: 10 MIN. PER BATCH, OTHER: 8 HR.

make ahead

½ cup butter, softened
2 (8-ounce) blocks Monterey Jack cheese with peppers, shredded
2 cups all-purpose flour
96 pecan halves

1. Beat softened butter and Monterey Jack cheese at medium speed with an electric mixer until blended; add flour, beating until blended.
2. Divide dough into 3 equal portions; shape each portion into a 6-inch log. Cover and chill at least 8 hours.
3. Cut each log into 32 (⅛-inch) slices, and place on ungreased baking sheets. Gently press 1 pecan half into center of each wafer.
4. Bake, in batches, at 350° for 8 to 10 minutes. Remove crisps to wire racks to cool. Store in an airtight container. **Makes** 8 dozen.

Savory Tomato-Bacon Biscuits

A little red pepper pumps up the flavor in these Parmesan biscuits. They're yummy alone or made into these little sandwiches.

30 minutes or less
PREP: 20 MIN., COOK: 10 MIN.

2 cups all-purpose baking mix (we used Bisquick)
⅓ cup grated Parmesan cheese
1 tablespoon sugar
1 teaspoon dried Italian seasoning
¼ teaspoon ground red pepper
⅔ cup mayonnaise, divided
¼ cup milk
4 large plum tomatoes, each cut into 8 slices
10 bacon slices, cooked and crumbled

1. Combine first 5 ingredients in a medium bowl; stir in ⅓ cup mayonnaise and milk with a fork until moistened. Turn dough out onto a lightly floured surface, and knead 5 or 6 times.
2. Pat or roll dough to ¼-inch thickness; cut with a 1¾-inch round cutter, and place on a lightly greased baking sheet.
3. Bake at 425° for 8 to 10 minutes or until golden brown. Cool slightly.
4. Spread each biscuit evenly with half of remaining ⅓ cup mayonnaise; top with a tomato slice. Spread tomato slices with remaining mayonnaise; sprinkle with bacon. **Makes** 32 appetizer servings.

Tomato Crostini

Try these light and airy wedges as a simple savory appetizer.

20 minutes or less
PREP: 20 MIN.

¼ cup goat cheese
¼ cup cream cheese, softened
1 (6-inch) prebaked Italian pizza crust
5 plum tomatoes, chopped
1 tablespoon chopped fresh herbs (parsley, thyme, basil, or rosemary)

1. Stir together goat cheese and cream cheese; spread on pizza crust. Cut into wedges; top evenly with tomato and herbs. **Makes** 4 servings.

Easy Egg Salad Crostini

PREP: 20 MIN., COOK: 12 MIN., OTHER: 35 MIN.

make
ahead

1 (20-ounce) French bread baguette, thinly sliced
3 tablespoons melted butter
1 garlic clove, pressed
8 large hard-cooked eggs, grated
½ cup mayonnaise
½ teaspoon sugar
¼ teaspoon salt
¼ teaspoon freshly ground pepper

1. Arrange baguette slices on a baking sheet. Stir together butter and garlic; brush evenly on tops of baguette slices.
2. Bake at 350° for 10 to 12 minutes. Let stand 20 minutes.
3. Meanwhile, combine grated hard-cooked eggs and next 4 ingredients in a large bowl. Cover and chill at least 15 minutes or up to 2 days.
4. Spoon egg mixture evenly on toasted baguette slices. **Makes** about 3 dozen.

Thai Green Apple
Pork Lettuce Wraps

Thai Green Apple Pork Lettuce Wraps

PREP: 20 MIN., COOK: 15 MIN.

make
ahead

½ cup chopped Granny Smith apple
1 tablespoon lemon juice
3 garlic cloves, minced
1 jalapeño pepper, seeded and minced
¼ cup diced red onion
3 green onions, sliced
1 tablespoon vegetable oil
1 pound ground pork
¼ cup chunky peanut butter
2 tablespoons fish sauce
1¼ tablespoons sugar
¼ teaspoon salt
Iceberg or Bibb lettuce leaves

1. Toss chopped apple with lemon juice. Set aside.
2. Sauté garlic, minced jalapeño, ¼ cup diced red onion, and sliced green onions in hot oil in a large skillet 2 to 3 minutes or until vegetables are tender. Add pork to skillet, and cook, stirring constantly, 4 to 5 minutes or until pork is no longer pink. Stir in chunky peanut butter, fish sauce, sugar, and salt; cook, stirring often, until mixture is thoroughly heated.
3. Drain apple mixture, and stir into pork mixture. Serve in lettuce leaves. **Makes** 6 appetizer servings.

Quick Fiesta Quesadillas

30 minutes or less
PREP: 19 MIN., COOK: 6 MIN.

1½ cups diced cooked ham
3 plum tomatoes, seeded and chopped
1 cup crumbled goat cheese
½ medium-size red onion, diced
¼ cup chopped fresh cilantro
¼ cup lime juice
¼ cup (2 ounces) cream cheese, softened
1 (4.5-ounce) can chopped green chiles, drained
6 (8-inch) flour tortillas
Vegetable cooking spray

1. Combine first 8 ingredients. Spread 1 side of each tortilla with about ½ cup ham mixture; fold tortillas in half.
2. Cook tortillas, in batches, in a nonstick skillet coated with cooking spray over medium-high heat 1 minute on each side or until golden brown. Serve immediately. **Makes** 6 servings.

Santa Fe Chicken Quesadillas

If you have 2 skillets handy, heat both at the same time so the quesadillas will be hot off the griddle twice as fast.

20 minutes or less
PREP: 10 MIN., COOK: 8 MIN.

½ cup salsa
1 cup chopped cooked chicken
2 tablespoons chopped fresh cilantro
1 teaspoon ground cumin
1 (4-ounce) can chopped green chiles, drained
4 (7-inch) flour tortillas
1 cup (4 ounces) shredded sharp Cheddar cheese
Butter-flavored cooking spray
Salsa

1. Combine ½ cup salsa, chicken, and next 3 ingredients. Spoon mixture evenly onto half of each tortilla. Sprinkle evenly with cheese.
2. Coat a nonstick skillet with butter-flavored cooking spray; place over medium-high heat until hot. Add 1 tortilla; cook 1 minute. Fold in half; cook 30 seconds. Turn; cook other side 30 seconds. Repeat with remaining tortillas. Cut each into 4 wedges. Serve with salsa. **Makes** 16 appetizers.

Barbecue Quesadillas

30 minutes or less
PREP: 10 MIN., COOK: 12 MIN.

½ pound shredded barbecued pork
8 (6-inch) flour tortillas
1 cup shredded Mexican four-cheese blend or
    Monterey Jack cheese with peppers
Salsa
Guacamole

1. Divide pork evenly among tortillas; sprinkle each with 2 tablespoons cheese. Fold tortillas in half.
2. Cook quesadillas in a large nonstick skillet over medium heat 3 minutes on each side or until tortillas are crisp and cheese melts. Serve with salsa and guacamole. **Makes** 8 appetizer or 4 main-dish servings.

Santa Fe Chicken Quesadillas

Sesame Chicken Strips

Sesame Chicken Strips

30 minutes or less

PREP: 10 MIN., COOK: 15 MIN.

2 cups mayonnaise, divided
2 teaspoons dried minced onion
2 teaspoons dry mustard
1 cup crushed round buttery crackers (about
    20 crackers)
½ cup sesame seeds
1¾ pounds chicken breast tenders
2 tablespoons honey
2 teaspoons prepared mustard

1. Stir together 1 cup mayonnaise, minced onion, and dry mustard in a small bowl. Combine crushed crackers and sesame seeds in a separate bowl.
2. Dip chicken into mayonnaise mixture, and dredge in cracker mixture. Repeat procedure once. Place on a lightly greased rack on an aluminum foil-lined baking sheet.
3. Bake at 425° for 15 minutes or until chicken is done.
4. Stir together remaining 1 cup mayonnaise, honey, and mustard. Serve honey sauce with chicken. **Makes** 8 appetizer servings.

Sweet-and-Spicy Chicken Wings

To save prep time, purchase chicken drummettes or a bag of frozen wings that are already separated.

PREP: 10 MIN., COOK: 34 MIN., OTHER: 5 MIN.

1 (15-ounce) can tomato sauce
2 tablespoons butter
½ cup honey
¼ cup chipotle-flavored hot sauce
1 tablespoon grated lime rind
3 tablespoons fresh lime juice
¼ teaspoon ground red pepper
4 to 5 pounds chicken wings
1 tablespoon salt
1 teaspoon pepper
1 cup all-purpose flour
Peanut or vegetable oil

1. Heat tomato sauce and butter in a small saucepan over medium heat, stirring until butter melts. Stir in honey and next 4 ingredients; bring to a boil. Reduce heat; simmer, stirring often, 5 minutes. Set aside.
2. Cut off wing tips; discard. Cut wings in half at joint, if desired. Sprinkle wings evenly with salt and pepper; dredge lightly in flour, shaking off excess.
3. Pour oil to a depth of 1½ inches into a large, deep skillet or Dutch oven; heat oil to 375°. Fry wings, in 3 batches, 8 minutes per batch or until golden and crispy. Remove wings from oil using a slotted spoon; drain on layers of paper towels. (Allow oil to return to 375° before adding next batch of wings.)
4. Place wings in a large bowl. Drizzle with tomato sauce mixture, tossing to coat. Let stand 5 minutes before serving. **Makes** 4 to 6 appetizer servings.

Sweet-and-Spicy
Chicken Wings

Chicken Won Tons With
Hoisin-Peanut Dipping Sauce

Chicken Won Tons With Hoisin-Peanut Dipping Sauce

*You can stir up the chicken mixture and fill the won ton wrappers while the frying oil heats. The dipping sauce that
follows is great with these crispy won tons, but if you'd prefer, use one of the many bottled Asian sauces on the market.*

PREP: 25 MIN., COOK: 1½ MIN. PER BATCH

Peanut oil
1 cup chopped cooked chicken
1 cup finely shredded cabbage (prepackaged)
4 green onions, finely chopped
2 tablespoons finely chopped fresh cilantro
1 tablespoon hoisin sauce
2 teaspoons light brown sugar
1 teaspoon sesame oil
24 won ton wrappers
Hoisin-Peanut Dipping Sauce (recipe on facing page)

1. Pour peanut oil to a depth of 3 inches into a large
Dutch oven; heat to 375° (about 25 minutes).
2. While oil heats, combine chicken and next 6 ingredients in a medium bowl. Spoon 1 heaping teaspoon-
ful of meat mixture in center of each won ton wrapper;
moisten edges with water.
3. Carefully bring 2 opposite points of wrapper to
center over filling; pinch points gently to seal. Bring
remaining opposite points to center, and pinch gently
to seal.
4. Fry won tons, in batches, 1½ minutes or until golden,
turning once. Drain well on paper towels. Serve won
tons with Hoisin-Peanut Dipping Sauce. **Makes**
2 dozen.

Hoisin-Peanut Dipping Sauce:

PREP: 3 MIN., COOK: 3 MIN.

½ cup chicken broth
2 tablespoons hoisin sauce
2 tablespoons sesame oil
2 tablespoons soy sauce
1 tablespoon creamy peanut butter
1 teaspoon cornstarch

1. Combine all ingredients in a small saucepan; bring to a boil. Cook, stirring constantly, 1 minute. Serve with Chicken Won Tons or other Asian dippers. **Makes** ¾ cup.

Cocktail Meatballs

These tangy meatballs, covered with sauerkraut, cranberry sauce, and chili sauce, are delicious served alone or on sandwich rolls with melted Swiss.

PREP: 20 MIN., COOK: 25 MIN.

2 pounds lean ground beef
1 cup fine, dry breadcrumbs
1 (1.4-ounce) envelope onion soup and recipe mix
3 large eggs
1 (14.5-ounce) can sauerkraut, drained
1 (16-ounce) can whole-berry cranberry sauce
1 (12-ounce) bottle chili sauce
½ cup water
1 cup firmly packed light brown sugar

1. Combine ground beef, breadcrumbs, onion soup mix, and eggs in a large bowl; stir until blended. Shape into 1-inch meatballs. Place meatballs in a greased 13- x 9-inch baking dish.
2. Stir together sauerkraut and remaining 4 ingredients. Spoon over meatballs.
3. Bake, uncovered, at 450° for 25 minutes. **Makes** 12 appetizer servings.

Bourbon Meatballs

Packaged meatballs and purchased barbecue sauce make whipping up a big batch of this party food a snap.

30 minutes or less

PREP: 5 MIN., COOK: 19 MIN.

1 (32-ounce) package frozen cooked Italian-style meatballs (about 60 meatballs)
2 cups barbecue sauce (we used KC Masterpiece Original)
1 cup bourbon
1 cup honey
¾ cup prepared mustard
1 teaspoon Worcestershire sauce

1. Partially open package of meatballs; place package in a large microwave-safe bowl. Microwave at HIGH 3 to 4 minutes or until meatballs are thawed.
2. Meanwhile, combine barbecue sauce and remaining ingredients in a Dutch oven. Bring to a boil over medium heat.
3. As soon as meatballs are thawed, add them to sauce, and simmer, stirring occasionally, 15 minutes or until heated. **Makes** 12 to 14 appetizer servings.

Speedy Scampi, page 227

presto
PIZZA 'n'
PASTA

Pepperoni Pizza Pinwheels

Pepperoni Pizza Pinwheels

Kids love to dip these cheesy pizza bites into spaghetti sauce.

30 minutes or less
PREP: 8 MIN., COOK: 16 MIN.

1 (13.8-ounce) can refrigerated pizza crust dough
1 cup (4 ounces) shredded pizza cheese blend
½ cup grated Parmesan cheese
1 (3.5-ounce) package sliced pepperoni, chopped
½ cup spaghetti sauce, heated

1. Unroll pizza crust on a cutting board; roll crust into a 12- x 9-inch rectangle. Sprinkle with cheeses and pepperoni.
2. Roll up, starting with long side; moisten edge with water, and pinch seam to seal. Cut into 1-inch-wide slices, and place 1 inch apart in a lightly greased 15- x 10-inch jelly-roll pan; flatten pinwheels slightly.
3. Bake at 400° for 13 to 16 minutes or until golden. Serve immediately with warm spaghetti sauce. **Makes** 12 servings.

Pizza Rollups

These deli ham and fruit-filled sandwiches travel well for short distances, picnics, and camping.

20 minutes or less
PREP: 10 MIN., COOK: 10 MIN.

1 medium tomato, diced
5 (1-ounce) cooked ham slices, diced
1 small green bell pepper, diced
1 (8-ounce) can pineapple tidbits, drained
1/4 cup almonds, chopped
4 (8-inch) flour tortillas
1/4 cup pizza sauce
1 cup (4 ounces) shredded mozzarella cheese

1. Stir together first 5 ingredients.
2. Brush tortillas evenly with pizza sauce. Spread one-fourth of tomato mixture down center of each tortilla; sprinkle evenly with cheese. Roll up, and place, seam side down, in a lightly greased 13- x 9-inch pan.
3. Bake at 350° for 10 minutes. **Makes** 4 rollups.

Chicken-and-Three-Cheese French Bread Pizzas

If you have leftover cooked chicken on hand, substitute 1½ cups chopped cooked chicken for the canned variety.

20 minutes or less
PREP: 10 MIN., COOK: 10 MIN.

1/2 cup butter or margarine, softened
1/2 cup (2 ounces) shredded Cheddar cheese
1/3 cup freshly grated Parmesan cheese
1 garlic clove, pressed
1/4 teaspoon dried Italian seasoning
1 (16-ounce) sliced French bread loaf
1 (10-ounce) can white chicken, drained and flaked
1 cup (4 ounces) shredded mozzarella cheese
1/4 cup chopped red bell pepper
3 green onions, chopped

1. Combine first 5 ingredients in a small bowl; spread evenly over bread slices. Top with chicken; sprinkle with mozzarella cheese, bell pepper, and green onions.
2. Bake at 350° for 10 minutes or until cheese melts. **Makes** 6 servings.

Mediterranean Garlic Pizza

Be careful not to burn the garlic in this recipe, or it will taste bitter.

30 minutes or less
PREP: 5 MIN., COOK: 19 MIN.

1 (13.8-ounce) can refrigerated pizza crust dough
6 tablespoons dried tomato spread or dried tomato paste (we used California Sun Dry)
4 garlic cloves, thinly sliced
3/4 cup crumbled feta cheese with garlic and herbs
1/4 cup sliced ripe olives, coarsely chopped

1. Unroll pizza crust on baking sheet coated with cooking spray; pat dough into a 12- x 9-inch rectangle. Spread dried tomato spread evenly over dough, leaving a 1/2-inch border.
2. Coat a small nonstick skillet with cooking spray; place over medium heat until hot. Add garlic; sauté 5 minutes or until browned. Sprinkle garlic, feta, and olives evenly over tomato spread. Bake pizza at 450° for 12 to 14 minutes or until crust is lightly browned. **Makes** 4 servings.

Grilled Portobello Pizzas

Grilled portobellos lend a smoky, meaty flavor to this vegetarian delight. They should be tender and nicely browned.

20 minutes or less
PREP: 3 MIN., COOK: 8 MIN.

1 cup roasted garlic pasta sauce
½ cup chopped fresh basil, divided
8 large portobello mushroom caps
1 (8-ounce) bottle Italian dressing
1 cup (4 ounces) shredded Italian three-cheese
    blend

1. Stir together pasta sauce and ¼ cup basil. Set aside.
2. Combine half of mushroom caps and half of Italian dressing in each of 2 large zip-top plastic freezer bags, turning to coat. Seal and let stand 2 to 3 minutes. Remove mushrooms from marinade, discarding marinade.
3. Place mushrooms, stem side up, on a grill rack coated with cooking spray. Grill, covered with grill lid, over medium-high heat (350° to 400°) 3 minutes on each side. Turn mushrooms, stem side up, and spoon sauce mixture evenly into each. Grill 2 more minutes or until thoroughly heated. Sprinkle evenly with shredded cheese and remaining basil; serve immediately. **Makes** 8 servings.

Pesto-Tomato Pizza

It's easy to transfer the pizza to the oven rack. Just use a large flat baking sheet as a giant spatula.

30 minutes or less
PREP: 15 MIN., COOK: 10 MIN.

2 tablespoons pesto
1 (12-ounce) prebaked Italian pizza crust
¾ pound plum tomatoes, sliced
2 large garlic cloves, thinly sliced
½ cup (2 ounces) shredded mozzarella cheese
⅓ cup shredded Parmesan cheese
1 teaspoon coarsely ground pepper
2 tablespoons shredded fresh basil

1. Spread pesto evenly over bread shell; arrange tomatoes and garlic slices over pesto. Top with cheeses, and sprinkle with pepper.
2. Bake directly on oven rack at 450° for 10 minutes or until cheese melts. Remove from oven; sprinkle with basil. Serve immediately. **Makes** 4 servings.

Veggie Sausage Pizzas

30 minutes or less
PREP: 12 MIN., COOK: 15 MIN.

8 (1-inch-thick) French bread slices
1 sweet onion, sliced
1 medium-size green bell pepper, sliced
1 cup tomato-and-basil pasta sauce
1 cup (4 ounces) shredded mozzarella cheese
1 (8-ounce) package meatless breakfast patties,
    thawed and crumbled
½ cup shredded Parmesan cheese

1. Bake bread slices on a baking sheet at 425° for 5 minutes. Set aside.
2. Meanwhile, sauté sliced onion and bell pepper in a large nonstick skillet coated with cooking spray over medium-high heat 5 minutes.
3. Spread pasta sauce evenly on 1 side of each bread slice. Top evenly with mozzarella cheese, onion mixture, crumbled patties, and Parmesan cheese.
4. Bake at 425° for 8 to 10 minutes or until thoroughly heated. **Makes** 4 servings.

Roasted Vegetable Pizza

Roasted Vegetable Pizza

PREP: 18 MIN., COOK: 42 MIN.

1 small sweet onion, cut into thin wedges
1 tablespoon chopped fresh or 1 teaspoon dried
    thyme
2 tablespoons balsamic vinegar
1 teaspoon olive oil
¼ teaspoon salt
4 small red potatoes, each cut into 8 wedges
4 garlic cloves, thinly sliced
1 small yellow squash, thinly sliced
1 small red bell pepper, cut into 2-inch pieces
1 (13.8-ounce) can refrigerated pizza crust dough
1¼ cups (5 ounces) shredded sharp provolone cheese

1. Toss together onion, thyme, and next 7 ingredients; spoon into a 13- x 9-inch baking dish.
2. Bake vegetable mixture at 500° for 25 minutes, stirring once.
3. Unroll pizza dough on a lightly greased baking sheet; fold edges of dough to form an 11-inch circle.
4. Bake at 425° for 7 minutes; set aside.
5. Sprinkle half of shredded provolone cheese over prepared crust. Top with roasted vegetable mixture, and sprinkle evenly with remaining half of shredded cheese.
6. Bake at 425° for 10 minutes or until crust is lightly browned and cheese is melted. Serve immediately.
Makes 6 servings.

Roasted Chicken-and-White Bean Pizzas

Roasted Chicken-and-White Bean Pizzas

30 minutes or less

PREP: 20 MIN., COOK: 10 MIN.

1 (16-ounce) can great Northern beans, drained
1 teaspoon lemon juice
⅛ teaspoon garlic powder
⅛ teaspoon pepper
1 cup chopped roasted chicken
¼ teaspoon dried rosemary, crushed
3 (7-inch) prebaked pizza crusts (we used Mama Mary's Gourmet)
1 cup shredded fresh spinach
¾ cup (3 ounces) shredded sharp provolone cheese

1. Process great Northern beans and next 3 ingredients in a blender or food processor until smooth, stopping to scrape down sides.
2. Toss together chopped chicken and rosemary.
3. Spread ⅓ cup bean mixture evenly over each pizza crust, and top evenly with chicken mixture, shredded spinach, and shredded cheese.
4. Bake directly on oven rack at 450° for 10 minutes or until crusts are golden. Serve immediately. **Makes** 6 servings.

Quick 'n' Easy Chicken Barbecue Pizza

PREP: 10 MIN., COOK: 34 MIN.

1 small onion, chopped
½ red bell pepper, chopped
½ teaspoon salt
¼ teaspoon pepper
1 teaspoon olive oil
1 (13.8-ounce) can refrigerated pizza crust dough
½ cup hickory-smoked barbecue sauce
2 (6-ounce) packages grilled boneless, skinless
    chicken breast strips
2 cups (8 ounces) shredded Monterey Jack cheese
    with peppers
Garnish: finely chopped fresh parsley
Hickory-smoked barbecue sauce

1. Sauté first 4 ingredients in hot oil in a large skillet over medium-high heat 8 to 10 minutes or until vegetables are tender. Drain well.
2. Unroll pizza crust dough; press or pat into a lightly greased 13- x 9-inch pan.
3. Bake crust at 400° for 12 to 14 minutes. Spread ½ cup barbecue sauce evenly over top of pizza crust in pan. Arrange chicken strips evenly over barbecue sauce; top with onion mixture, and sprinkle evenly with cheese.
4. Bake at 400° for 8 to 10 minutes or until cheese melts. Garnish, if desired. Serve with extra sauce.
Makes 6 servings.

Quick 'n' Easy Chicken
Barbecue Pizza

Bistro Grilled Chicken Pizza

Use long-handled grilling tongs and a spatula to turn the dough with ease.

30 minutes or less
PREP: 15 MIN., COOK: 10 MIN.

1 (13.8-ounce) can refrigerated pizza crust dough
1 teaspoon olive oil
¾ cup pizza sauce
4 plum tomatoes, sliced
2 cups chopped cooked chicken
1 (4-ounce) package tomato-and-basil feta cheese
1 cup (4 ounces) shredded mozzarella cheese
2 tablespoons chopped fresh basil

1. Unroll dough, and place on a lightly greased 18- x 12-inch sheet of heavy-duty aluminum foil. Starting at center, press out dough to form a 13- x 9-inch rectangle. Brush dough evenly with olive oil.
2. Invert dough onto grill cooking grate; peel off foil. Grill, covered with grill lid, over medium heat (300° to 350°) 2 to 3 minutes or until bottom of dough is golden brown. Turn dough over, and grill, covered, 1 to 2 minutes or until bottom is set. Carefully remove crust from grill to an aluminum foil-lined baking sheet.
3. Microwave pizza sauce in a small microwave-safe bowl at HIGH 30 seconds or until warm, stirring once. Spread sauce evenly over crust; top with tomatoes and chicken. Sprinkle evenly with cheeses and basil. Return pizza to cooking grate (pizza should slide off easily).
4. Grill, covered, 3 to 5 more minutes or until crust is done and cheese is melted. **Makes** 6 servings.

Hamburger-Mushroom Pizza

This family favorite is sure to become a weeknight staple.

30 minutes or less
PREP: 15 MIN., COOK: 10 MIN.

6 ounces lean ground beef
1 (16-ounce) unsliced Italian bread loaf
½ cup pizza sauce
8 (⅛-inch-thick) onion slices, separated into rings
1 cup sliced fresh mushrooms
1 teaspoon dried Italian seasoning
½ teaspoon garlic powder
¼ teaspoon dried crushed red pepper
1½ cups (6 ounces) shredded pizza cheese blend

1. Cook ground beef in a large nonstick skillet over medium-high heat, stirring until it crumbles and is no longer pink. Drain and pat dry with paper towels, and set aside.
2. Cut bread in half horizontally. Place both halves, cut side up, on a baking sheet. Spread evenly with pizza sauce, and top with onion slices, mushrooms, and ground beef.
3. Stir together Italian seasoning, garlic powder, and red pepper; sprinkle over pizzas. Top evenly with shredded cheese.
4. Bake at 425° for 10 minutes or until cheese melts. Serve immediately. **Makes** 6 servings.

Cheeseburger Pizza

Cheeseburger Pizza

This fun twist on the traditional cheeseburger lends excitement to the dinner doldrums.

20 minutes or less

PREP: 4 MIN., COOK: 16 MIN.

1 pound ground beef
1 medium onion, chopped (about 1 cup)
2 garlic cloves, pressed
1 tablespoon Worcestershire sauce
2 tablespoons ketchup
2 tablespoons prepared mustard
1 (10-ounce) package prebaked Italian pizza crust
1 (8-ounce) package shredded pizza cheese blend, divided
Toppings: shredded lettuce, pickle slices, chopped tomato

1. Cook first 3 ingredients in a large skillet over medium heat 6 to 8 minutes, stirring until beef crumbles and is no longer pink; drain mixture well. Stir in Worcestershire sauce.

2. Combine ketchup and mustard; spread over pizza crust. Sprinkle with 1 cup cheese. Top with beef mixture and remaining cheese.

3. Bake at 450° for 8 minutes. Sprinkle with desired toppings. **Makes** 4 servings.

Bacon Penne Alfredo

Bacon Penne Alfredo

Mushrooms and garlic cooked in bacon drippings make this pasta dish irresistible. If you don't want to cook your own bacon, use precooked bacon, and substitute 2 tablespoons olive oil for the bacon drippings.

30 minutes or less
PREP: 8 MIN., COOK: 20 MIN.

16 ounces uncooked penne
1 (16-ounce) package sliced bacon
1 (8-ounce) package sliced fresh mushrooms
2 garlic cloves, minced
1 cup grated Parmesan cheese
2 cups whipping cream
½ teaspoon pepper
½ cup sliced green onions

1. Cook pasta according to package directions, including salt. Meanwhile, cook bacon in a large skillet until crisp; remove bacon, and drain on paper towels, reserving 2 tablespoons drippings in skillet. Crumble bacon.
2. Sauté mushrooms and garlic in hot drippings 3 minutes or until tender. Stir in pasta, Parmesan cheese, whipping cream, and pepper. Reduce heat to medium-low; simmer, uncovered, until sauce is thickened, stirring often. Stir in crumbled bacon and sliced green onions; serve immediately. **Makes** 4 to 6 servings.

Ziti With Sausage and Broccoli

20 minutes or less
PREP: 4 MIN., COOK: 15 MIN.

1 pound Italian sausage
8 ounces uncooked ziti
2 cups broccoli florets
2 garlic cloves, crushed
½ teaspoon dried crushed red pepper
1 teaspoon olive oil
2 (14½-ounce) cans diced tomatoes, undrained
½ cup freshly grated Romano or Parmesan cheese

1. Cut sausage diagonally into ½-inch-thick slices. Cook sausage in a large nonstick skillet over medium-high heat until browned; remove sausage, and set aside. Wipe skillet with paper towels.
2. Meanwhile, cook pasta according to package directions, adding broccoli during last 5 minutes of cooking time. Drain.
3. Cook garlic and red pepper in oil in skillet, stirring constantly, until lightly browned; add tomatoes, and cook until thoroughly heated. Remove from heat; keep warm.
4. Toss pasta and broccoli gently with sausage, tomato mixture, and cheese. Serve immediately. **Makes** 3 servings.

Creamy Tomato-Sausage Sauce With Shells

A hint of rosemary gives these creamy shells an herb essence, while a bit of red pepper adds a touch of heat. Penne pasta substitutes well in this dish for shells. The sauce is thick and chunky and needs a firm pasta to stand up to it.

20 minutes or less
PREP: 3 MIN., COOK: 17 MIN.

8 ounces uncooked medium pasta shells
1 tablespoon olive oil
1 pound mild bulk Italian sausage
2 (14½-ounce) cans diced tomatoes with green
    pepper, celery, and onions, undrained (we used
    Hunt's)
1 teaspoon chopped fresh rosemary
½ teaspoon salt
¼ teaspoon freshly ground black pepper
¼ teaspoon dried crushed red pepper
¾ cup heavy whipping cream
½ cup grated Parmesan cheese

1. Cook pasta according to package directions, including salt. Drain and keep warm.
2. Meanwhile, heat oil in a large nonstick skillet. Cook sausage, stirring often, over medium-high heat 8 minutes or until sausage is no longer pink.
3. Stir in tomatoes, rosemary, salt, black pepper, and crushed red pepper; cook, uncovered, over medium-high heat 6 minutes.
4. Add whipping cream; cook, stirring often, 3 minutes or until mixture begins to thicken. Pour sauce over pasta; add cheese, and toss well. **Makes** 4 servings.

Spinach-Stuffed Shells
PREP: 20 MIN., COOK: 30 MIN.

make ahead

18 uncooked jumbo shells
2 (10-ounce) packages frozen chopped spinach,
    thawed
1 pound lean ground beef
¼ teaspoon ground nutmeg
½ teaspoon salt, divided
½ teaspoon pepper, divided
1 (16-ounce) jar marinara sauce
1 (16-ounce) container 1% low-fat cottage cheese
1 large egg
¼ cup grated Parmesan cheese

1. Cook pasta shells according to package directions, and drain. Set aside.
2. Drain spinach well, pressing firmly between layers of paper towels. Set aside.
3. Cook ground beef in a large skillet, stirring until it crumbles and is no longer pink. Drain and pat dry with paper towels. Wipe pan drippings from skillet with a paper towel. Return beef to skillet, and stir in ground nutmeg, ¼ teaspoon salt, ¼ teaspoon pepper, and marinara sauce. Set aside.
4. Stir together spinach, cottage cheese, egg, Parmesan cheese, remaining ¼ teaspoon salt, and remaining ¼ teaspoon pepper. Spoon evenly into shells.
5. Spread half of marinara sauce mixture in a lightly greased 13- x 9-inch baking dish. Arrange stuffed shells over sauce; pour remaining sauce over shells.
6. Bake, covered, at 350° for 30 minutes.
Note: Stuffed shells and sauce may be frozen up to 1 month before baking. To bake, thaw in refrigerator overnight. Let stand at room temperature 30 minutes. Bake as directed. **Makes** 6 servings.

One-Skillet Spaghetti

Want to make this easy one-dish an adventure for kids? Use wagon wheel pasta instead of spaghetti noodles.

30 minutes or less
PREP: 5 MIN., COOK: 23 MIN.

1 pound ground chuck
1 small onion, chopped
2 (14-ounce) cans beef broth
1 (6-ounce) can tomato paste
¾ teaspoon garlic salt
1 teaspoon dried Italian seasoning
¼ teaspoon pepper
7 ounces uncooked spaghetti, broken into 3-inch
    pieces
Grated Parmesan cheese

1. Cook ground chuck and onion in a large skillet over medium-high heat, stirring until meat crumbles and is no longer pink; drain. Return to skillet. Stir in broth and next 4 ingredients. Bring to a boil; add pasta. Reduce heat, and simmer, uncovered, 15 minutes or until pasta is tender, stirring often. Sprinkle with cheese. **Makes** 4 servings.

Easy Spaghetti

Easy Spaghetti

Prefer a spaghetti sauce that has simmered all day? Try this one in a slow cooker. Cook ground beef and onion as directed. Add remaining ingredients except spaghetti; spoon into a slow cooker. Cook on LOW 6 to 7 hours or on HIGH 3 to 4 hours.

PREP: 20 MIN., COOK: 20 MIN.

make ahead

8 to 12 ounces uncooked spaghetti
1 pound ground beef
1 small onion, chopped
2 (14½-ounce) cans Italian-style diced tomatoes, undrained
2 (6-ounce) cans tomato paste
2 teaspoons dried Italian seasoning
1 teaspoon sugar
Garnish: fresh basil sprigs

1. Cook pasta according to package directions; keep warm.

2. Cook ground beef and onion in a large skillet, stirring until beef crumbles and is no longer pink; drain. Return to skillet. Stir in diced tomatoes and next 3 ingredients. Cook, stirring occasionally, over medium heat, about 20 minutes. Serve over hot cooked pasta. Garnish, if desired. **Makes** 4 to 6 servings.

Chicken Cacciatore

Chicken Cacciatore

Polenta is a traditional companion for this hunter-style stewed chicken. We think the stewed chicken is good over spaghetti, too.

PREP: 20 MIN.; COOK: 1 HR., 5 MIN.

¼ cup all-purpose flour
1 teaspoon salt
1 teaspoon pepper
2½ to 3 pounds assorted chicken pieces, skinned
¼ cup olive oil
1 large onion, chopped
3 garlic cloves, minced
½ cup dry red wine or white wine
1 (8-ounce) package sliced fresh mushrooms
1 (14.5-ounce) can whole tomatoes, undrained and
    quartered
1 (6-ounce) can tomato paste
3 bay leaves
1 teaspoon dried thyme
1 teaspoon dried oregano
¾ teaspoon salt
¼ teaspoon pepper
1 (2.25-ounce) can sliced ripe olives
2 medium-size green peppers, cut into strips
Hot cooked spaghetti or polenta

1. Combine first 3 ingredients in a shallow dish; dredge chicken in flour mixture. Brown chicken, in batches, in hot oil in a 12-inch skillet over medium-high heat. Remove chicken, reserving drippings; drain chicken on paper towels.
2. Cook onion and garlic in drippings in skillet over medium heat 5 minutes. Add wine, and cook over medium-high heat until wine evaporates. Stir in mushrooms and next 9 ingredients; add chicken to skillet. Bring to a boil; cover, reduce heat, and simmer 40 minutes or until chicken is tender. Discard bay leaves. Serve with hot cooked spaghetti or polenta. **Makes** 6 servings.

Cheesy Chicken Penne

The combination of sour cream and melted cheese makes this pasta creation incredibly saucy. Substitute 2 (8-ounce) loaves pasteurized prepared cheese product with peppers for regular prepared cheese product, if you desire a spicy version of this dish.

20 minutes or less
PREP: 10 MIN., COOK: 10 MIN.

8 ounces uncooked penne
1 (16-ounce) package pasteurized prepared cheese
    product, cubed
1 (8-ounce) container sour cream
½ cup milk
2½ cups prepackaged chopped cooked chicken

1. Cook pasta according to package directions, including salt; drain.
2. Meanwhile, cook cubed cheese, sour cream, and milk over medium-low heat, stirring constantly, 5 minutes or until cheese melts. Stir in pasta and chicken, and cook until thoroughly heated. **Makes** 4 to 6 servings.

Fettuccine With Pesto Chicken

20 minutes or less
PREP: 5 MIN., COOK: 11 MIN.

8 ounces uncooked fettuccine
1 pound chicken breast strips or 4 skinned and
    boned chicken breasts, cut into thin strips
1 red bell pepper, cut into thin strips
1 (7.5-ounce) jar pesto sauce
¼ teaspoon salt

1. Cook pasta according to package directions, including salt. Drain well, and keep pasta warm.
2. Meanwhile, cook chicken in a large nonstick skillet over medium-high heat, stirring constantly, 5 minutes or until done. Remove chicken from skillet, and keep warm.
3. Add bell pepper strips to skillet, and cook over medium heat 3 minutes or until crisp-tender, stirring occasionally. Add pesto sauce and chicken to skillet; cook over medium heat 3 minutes. Add pasta, tossing gently. Sprinkle with salt, and serve immediately. **Makes** 4 servings.

Cajun Chicken Pasta

PREP: 15 MIN., COOK: 20 MIN.

12 ounces uncooked linguine
2 pounds chicken breast strips
1 tablespoon Cajun seasoning
1¼ teaspoons salt, divided
¼ cup butter
1 small red bell pepper, thinly sliced (see note)
1 small green bell pepper, thinly sliced (see note)
1 (8-ounce) package fresh mushrooms
2 green onions (white and light green parts only),
    sliced (see note)
1½ cups half-and-half
¼ teaspoon lemon pepper
¼ teaspoon dried basil
¼ teaspoon garlic powder
Garnish: chopped green onions

1. Prepare pasta according to package directions.
2. Sprinkle chicken with Cajun seasoning and 1 teaspoon salt. Melt ¼ cup butter in a large nonstick skillet over medium-high heat; add chicken, and sauté 5 to 6 minutes or until done. Remove chicken.
3. Add bell peppers, mushrooms, and green onions to skillet, and sauté 9 to 10 minutes or until vegetables are tender and liquid evaporates.
4. Return chicken to skillet; stir in half-and-half, next 3 ingredients, and remaining ¼ teaspoon salt. Cook, stirring often, over medium-low heat 3 to 4 minutes or until thoroughly heated. Add pasta; toss to coat. Garnish, if desired; serve immediately. **Makes** 4 servings.
Note: Substitute ½ (16-ounce) bag frozen sliced green, red, and yellow bell peppers and onion, if desired. For testing purposes only, we used Birds Eye Pepper Stir-Fry.

Speedy Scampi

Speedy Scampi

Have your supermarket's seafood section peel and devein the shrimp for you. If you peel and devein them yourself, purchase 2⅓ pounds in the shell.

20 minutes or less
PREP: 10 MIN., COOK: 10 MIN.

12 ounces uncooked angel hair pasta
⅓ cup butter or margarine
1¾ pounds peeled and deveined large raw shrimp
2 green onions, sliced
4 large garlic cloves, minced
1 tablespoon grated lemon rind
½ cup fresh lemon juice
½ teaspoon salt
½ cup chopped fresh parsley
½ teaspoon hot sauce

1. Cook pasta according to package directions, including salt. Drain and keep pasta warm.
2. Meanwhile, melt butter in a large skillet over medium-high heat; add shrimp, and cook, stirring constantly, 5 minutes or just until shrimp turn pink. Stir in green onions and next 6 ingredients. Cook mixture 1 minute or until bubbly. Serve over hot cooked pasta. **Makes** 4 servings.

Shrimp and Feta Vermicelli

A side salad and crusty bread are all you need to round out this meal.

20 minutes or less
PREP: 5 MIN., COOK: 12 MIN.

8 ounces uncooked vermicelli
2 tablespoons olive oil
1 (14½-ounce) can diced tomatoes, undrained
¼ cup dry white wine
1¼ teaspoons dried Italian seasoning
½ teaspoon minced garlic
¼ teaspoon salt
¼ teaspoon black pepper
¼ teaspoon dried crushed red pepper
¾ pound peeled, medium-size raw shrimp
1 (4-ounce) package crumbled feta cheese

1. Cook pasta according to package directions, including salt; drain and keep warm.
2. Meanwhile, heat oil in a large skillet over medium heat. Add tomatoes and next 6 ingredients; bring to a boil. Reduce heat, and simmer, uncovered, 7 minutes, stirring occasionally. Add shrimp, and simmer 3 minutes or just until shrimp turn pink. Serve over pasta, and top with feta cheese. **Makes** 3 servings.

Saucy Scallop Fettuccine

20 minutes or less
PREP: 5 MIN., COOK: 10 MIN.

8 ounces uncooked fettuccine
1½ pounds bay scallops
2 tablespoons olive oil
½ cup whipping cream
2 tablespoons chopped fresh parsley
1 garlic clove, minced
½ teaspoon salt
¾ cup shredded Parmesan cheese
Freshly ground pepper

1. Cook fettuccine according to package directions, including salt; drain.
2. Meanwhile, sauté scallops in hot oil in a large skillet over medium-high heat 2 minutes. Drain scallops, reserving liquid. Return scallops and ½ cup liquid to skillet. Add cream and next 3 ingredients. Bring to a boil; remove from heat. Stir in fettuccine and cheese. Spoon into a large serving bowl; sprinkle with pepper. Serve immediately. **Makes** 4 servings.

Spicy Vegetables With Penne

Spicy Vegetables With Penne

PREP: 30 MIN., COOK: 15 MIN., OTHER: 30 MIN.

½ cup dried tomatoes
½ cup boiling water
12 ounces uncooked penne pasta
2 medium-size sweet onions, chopped
2 small zucchini, chopped
1 medium-size green bell pepper, chopped
1 medium-size red bell pepper, chopped
1 cup sliced fresh mushrooms
2 garlic cloves, minced
2 tablespoons olive oil
1 (24-ounce) jar hot-and-spicy pasta sauce (we tested
    with Newman's Own Fra Diavolo Sauce)
½ cup chopped fresh basil
½ teaspoon salt

1. Stir together dried tomatoes and ½ cup boiling water in a bowl; let stand 30 minutes. Drain, chop, and set aside.
2. Cook pasta according to package directions.
3. Sauté onions and next 5 ingredients in hot oil in a large skillet over medium-high heat 6 to 8 minutes or until vegetables are tender. Stir in chopped tomatoes.
4. Stir in pasta sauce; bring to a boil. Reduce heat to medium; stir in basil and salt, and simmer, stirring occasionally, 5 minutes. Serve over pasta. **Makes** 6 servings.

Ziti With Mozzarella and Tomato

Balsamic-laced tomatoes and vinaigrette give this pasta its zip.

20 minutes or less
PREP: 4 MIN., COOK: 10 MIN.

12 ounces uncooked ziti
2 (14½-ounce) cans diced tomatoes with balsamic
    vinegar, basil, and olive oil (we used Hunt's)
½ cup chopped black olives
⅓ cup diced red onion
¼ cup balsamic vinaigrette (we used Kraft)
1 (8-ounce) block mozzarella cheese, diced
½ cup grated Parmesan cheese
½ teaspoon pepper

1. Cook pasta according to package directions, including salt; drain.
2. Meanwhile, combine tomatoes and next 3 ingredients.
3. Add pasta, cheeses, and pepper; toss gently. Serve immediately. **Makes** 5 servings.

Artichoke Pasta

20 minutes or less
PREP: 5 MIN., COOK: 10 MIN.

12 ounces uncooked angel hair pasta
11 large garlic cloves, minced (about ⅓ cup)
¼ cup olive oil
2 (6-ounce) jars marinated quartered artichoke
    hearts, undrained
2 (3-ounce) packages shredded Parmesan and
    Romano cheese blend
½ cup chopped fresh basil

1. Cook pasta according to package directions, including salt; drain well, and return pasta to pan.
2. Meanwhile, cook garlic in olive oil in a large skillet over medium-high heat, stirring constantly, 1 minute or until tender. Add artichoke hearts, and cook 1 minute or until thoroughly heated. Pour artichoke mixture over warm pasta; add cheese, and toss well. Sprinkle with basil, and serve immediately. **Makes** 8 servings.

Fettuccine With Cream, Basil, and Romano

Crumbled bacon, freshly grated Romano cheese, and fresh basil mingle in the hot cooked fettuccine, creating a meal-in-one dish for two.

30 minutes or less
PREP: 10 MIN., COOK: 16 MIN.

8 ounces uncooked fettuccine
4 bacon slices
4 green onions, chopped (about ⅓ cup)
½ cup whipping cream
½ cup freshly grated Romano cheese
⅓ cup chopped fresh basil
Freshly ground pepper
Freshly grated Romano cheese

1. Cook fettuccine according to package directions, including salt. Drain and place in a large bowl.
2. Meanwhile, cook bacon in a large skillet until crisp; remove bacon, and drain on paper towels, reserving drippings in skillet. Crumble bacon, and set aside. Add green onions to drippings, and cook, stirring constantly, 1 minute.
3. Add cream; bring to a boil. Reduce heat, and simmer, uncovered, 1 minute or until slightly thickened. Stir in ½ cup Romano cheese and basil.
4. Pour sauce over pasta; add crumbled bacon, and toss well. Sprinkle pasta with pepper and additional Romano cheese. **Makes** 2 servings.

Thai Noodles

Thai Noodles

This spicy Asian noodle dish gets a wonderful kick from bottled peanut sauce. Create a fun Friday night dinner by serving these noodles in Asian-style take-out boxes—they also make cleanup a snap.

20 minutes or less
PREP: 8 MIN., COOK: 10 MIN.

8 ounces uncooked angel hair pasta
¾ cup Bangkok Padang peanut sauce (we used
    House of Tsang)
½ cup chopped unsalted dry-roasted peanuts, divided
¼ cup chopped fresh cilantro
½ cup shredded carrot
⅓ cup sliced green onions
3 tablespoons sesame seeds, toasted

1. Cook pasta according to package directions, including salt. Drain well, and return to pan. Add peanut sauce and ¼ cup chopped peanuts, tossing well.
2. Divide pasta evenly among 4 take-out boxes. Top each serving evenly with remaining peanuts, cilantro, carrot, green onions, and sesame seeds. Serve immediately. **Makes** 4 servings.

Blue Cheese Noodles

Blue cheese aficionados adore this dish. It has an entire package of the tangy cheese.

20 minutes or less
PREP: 5 MIN., COOK: 12 MIN.

12 ounces uncooked fettuccine
½ teaspoon canola oil
1 tablespoon chicken bouillon granules
½ cup butter or margarine
6 green onions, sliced
1 (4-ounce) package crumbled blue cheese
1 (8-ounce) container sour cream
1 teaspoon seasoned pepper
¼ teaspoon garlic powder

1. Cook fettuccine according to package directions, adding oil and bouillon granules to water. Drain and keep warm.
2. Meanwhile, melt butter in a large skillet; add green onions, and sauté until tender. Add cheese; reduce heat, and cook, stirring constantly, 5 minutes or until melted. Remove from heat; stir in sour cream, pepper, and garlic powder. Add fettuccine, tossing to coat; serve immediately. **Makes** 6 servings.

Alfredo Sauce

Alfredo Sauce

The heat from the cooked pasta will melt the cheese in this creamy recipe.

10 minutes or less
PREP: 10 MIN.

1 (3-ounce) package refrigerated finely shredded
    Parmesan cheese
½ cup butter or margarine, melted
½ cup whipping cream
2 tablespoons chopped fresh parsley
¼ teaspoon ground white pepper
Hot cooked linguine

1. Combine first 5 ingredients in a bowl; toss with hot cooked pasta. **Makes** 6 servings.

Tomato-Jalapeño Vermicelli

This recipe offers maximum heat from the jalapeño peppers when you don't seed them.

20 minutes or less
PREP: 10 MIN., COOK: 10 MIN.

7 ounces uncooked vermicelli
6 garlic cloves, crushed
2 tablespoons olive oil
4 jalapeño peppers, seeded and minced
8 plum tomatoes, chopped
½ cup shredded fresh basil
Freshly grated Parmesan cheese
½ teaspoon salt
Garnish: fresh basil leaves

1. Cook pasta according to package directions, including salt; drain.
2. Meanwhile, cook garlic in hot oil in a large skillet over medium-high heat, stirring constantly, until golden. Add minced pepper, and cook 1 minute. Add tomato; cook 3 minutes or until thoroughly heated, stirring occasionally. Stir in shredded basil. Serve over hot cooked pasta, and sprinkle with cheese and salt. Garnish, if desired. **Makes** 4 servings.

One-Pot Pasta Dinner

A packaged soup mix is the jump start ingredient for this herbed pasta recipe.

30 minutes or less
PREP: 8 MIN., COOK: 15 MIN.

4 cups water
2 cups uncooked rotini or tortellini
2 tablespoons dried minced onion
2 tablespoons dried crushed red pepper
½ teaspoon salt
1 (2.4-ounce) package tomato with basil soup mix
    (we used Knorr)
1 teaspoon dried oregano
1 teaspoon dried minced garlic
½ cup grated Parmesan cheese
¼ teaspoon ground red pepper

1. Bring 4 cups water to a boil in a Dutch oven. Add pasta and next 3 ingredients; cook 10 minutes or until tender. Add soup mix, oregano, and garlic; cook 5 minutes. Stir in cheese and red pepper. Serve immediately. **Makes** 2 servings.

Vermicelli With Chunky Vegetable Sauce

Vermicelli With Chunky Vegetable Sauce

If desired, stir in 1 pound cooked ground beef or 2 cups chopped cooked chicken when you add the pasta sauce.

PREP: 20 MIN., COOK: 27 MIN.

1 (16-ounce) package vermicelli
1 red bell pepper, diced
1 medium onion, diced
1 (8-ounce) package sliced fresh mushrooms
1 tablespoon olive oil
2 small zucchini, diced
4 garlic cloves, minced
1 teaspoon salt, divided
½ teaspoon freshly ground pepper, divided
1 (26-ounce) jar tomato-and-basil pasta sauce
Freshly grated Parmesan cheese (optional)

1. Prepare pasta according to package directions; drain and keep warm.

2. Sauté bell pepper, onion, and mushrooms in hot oil in a large nonstick skillet over medium-high heat 8 minutes; stir in zucchini, garlic, ¼ teaspoon salt, and ¼ teaspoon pepper. Cook, stirring occasionally, 4 minutes or until zucchini is tender.

3. Stir in pasta sauce, remaining ¾ teaspoon salt, and remaining ¼ teaspoon pepper; bring to a boil, stirring occasionally. Reduce heat, cover, and simmer 10 to 15 minutes. Serve over pasta. Sprinkle with cheese, if desired. **Makes** 6 servings.

Cheese Tortellini in Jalapeño Tomato Sauce

20 minutes or less

PREP: 2 MIN., COOK: 10 MIN.

1 (9-ounce) package refrigerated cheese-filled tortellini
1 (15-ounce) can chunky Italian-style tomato sauce (we used Hunt's)
1 jalapeño pepper, seeded and finely chopped
½ cup freshly grated Parmesan cheese

1. Cook pasta according to package directions; drain.
2. Meanwhile, combine tomato sauce and chopped pepper in a saucepan; cook over medium heat until thoroughly heated, stirring occasionally. Spoon over pasta; sprinkle with cheese. **Makes** 4 servings.

Veggie Mac-and-Cheese

PREP: 41 MIN., COOK: 39 MIN.

make ahead

8 ounces uncooked elbow macaroni
1 cup chopped fresh broccoli
1 cup diced yellow squash
½ cup diced carrot
1 small red onion, diced
2 garlic cloves, minced
2 teaspoons olive oil
1 (7-ounce) jar roasted red bell peppers, drained and diced
1 (16-ounce) container ricotta cheese
1 (12-ounce) can evaporated milk
1 tablespoon Dijon mustard
1 teaspoon salt
1 teaspoon freshly ground pepper
2 large eggs, lightly beaten
3 plum tomatoes, sliced
⅓ cup Italian-seasoned breadcrumbs
½ cup (2 ounces) shredded Romano cheese

1. Cook macaroni in a Dutch oven according to package directions; drain.
2. Sauté broccoli and next 4 ingredients in hot oil in Dutch oven over medium heat 3 to 4 minutes or until tender. Remove from heat; add macaroni, bell peppers, and next 5 ingredients, stirring until blended. Stir in beaten eggs.

3. Pour mixture into a lightly greased 13- x 9-inch baking dish. (If desired, cover and chill 8 hours, or freeze up to 1 month; thaw in refrigerator overnight. Let stand at room temperature 30 minutes before baking.) Top with tomato slices; sprinkle with Italian-seasoned breadcrumbs and Romano cheese.
4. Bake, covered, at 350° for 15 minutes; uncover and bake 20 more minutes or until golden. Serve warm.
Makes 6 to 8 servings.

Spinach-and-Onion Couscous

30 minutes or less

PREP: 5 MIN., COOK: 12 MIN., OTHER: 5 MIN.

1 medium onion, chopped
1 garlic clove, pressed
2 tablespoons olive oil
1 (14-ounce) can chicken broth
1 (10-ounce) package frozen chopped spinach
10 ounces uncooked couscous (about 1½ cups)
¾ cup freshly grated Parmesan cheese
2 tablespoons lemon juice
½ teaspoon salt
½ teaspoon freshly ground pepper
½ cup chopped pecans, toasted

1. Sauté onion and garlic in hot oil in a large saucepan until tender. Add broth and spinach; cook, stirring occasionally, until spinach thaws. Bring to a boil, stirring occasionally. Stir in couscous; cover, remove from heat, and let stand 5 minutes or until liquid is absorbed.
2. Stir in cheese and remaining ingredients. Serve couscous immediately. **Makes** 6 to 8 servings.

Garden Pasta Toss

Garden Pasta Toss

To save time, use presliced carrots from the produce section of your local supermarket.

PREP: 6 MIN., COOK: 15 MIN., OTHER: 8 HR.

make ahead

3 quarts water
2 teaspoons salt
8 ounces uncooked bow tie pasta
1 cup prepackaged broccoli florets
2 small carrots, cut into ¼-inch-thick slices
1 (14-ounce) can quartered artichoke hearts, drained
1 cup grape or cherry tomatoes, halved
4 green onions, sliced
½ teaspoon dried Italian seasoning
½ cup three-cheese Italian dressing (we used Ken's Steak House)
Shredded Parmesan cheese

1. Combine water and salt in a Dutch oven; bring to a boil. Add pasta; cook 9 minutes. Add broccoli and carrot; cook 1 minute. Drain. Rinse with cold water to stop the cooking process; drain.

2. Combine pasta mixture, artichoke hearts, tomatoes, green onions, and seasoning in a large bowl. Add dressing, tossing gently to coat. Cover and chill 8 hours. Sprinkle with cheese before serving. **Makes** 8 servings.

Pasta-Veggie Salad

Check the times on the pasta packages, and add the tortellini along with the final cooking of the fettuccine—it will cook in the same pot and be done at the same time.

20 minutes or less
PREP: 5 MIN., COOK: 15 MIN.

2 cups fresh snow pea pods, trimmed
2 cups broccoli florets
3 ounces uncooked fettuccine
1 (9-ounce) package refrigerated cheese-filled
    tortellini
1 pint cherry tomatoes
2 cups sliced fresh mushrooms
1 (7.5-ounce) can pitted ripe olives, drained
2 tablespoons freshly grated Parmesan cheese
1 to 1½ cups bottled Italian dressing
Garnish: freshly grated Parmesan cheese

1. Bring a large Dutch oven of water to a boil. Place snow peas in a wire mesh basket, and plunge into boiling water to cover 1 minute; remove and plunge peas immediately into cold water to stop the cooking process. Repeat procedure with broccoli, reserving boiling water.
2. Cook fettuccine and tortellini according to package directions in boiling water; drain and set aside.
3. Combine snow peas, broccoli, cherry tomatoes, mushrooms, and olives in a large bowl; add pastas and 2 tablespoons cheese, tossing to combine. Add desired amount of dressing, and toss well. Cover and chill, if desired. Garnish, if desired. **Makes** 8 to 10 servings.

Greek Pasta Salad

This bountiful salad offers a showy presentation at any gathering. If time is not an issue, fresh green beans make a wonderful substitute for frozen. You can cook them while the pasta cooks.

PREP: 15 MIN., COOK: 10 MIN., OTHER: 30 MIN.

make ahead

8 ounces uncooked rotini
2 tablespoons olive oil
1 head romaine lettuce, torn into bite-size pieces
½ (16-ounce) package frozen cut green beans,
    thawed
1 cup chopped celery (about 2 ribs)
2 tablespoons finely chopped red onion
1 (4-ounce) package crumbled feta cheese
⅓ cup pitted kalamata olives, chopped
2 large tomatoes, cut into wedges
¾ cup Greek dressing (we used Ken's Steak House
    with feta cheese, black olives, and olive oil)

1. Cook pasta according to package directions, including salt; drain. Toss together pasta and oil; cover and chill 30 minutes.
2. Layer lettuce, pasta, beans, and celery on a serving platter. Sprinkle with red onion, cheese, and olives. Arrange tomato wedges around salad; drizzle with dressing. **Makes** 4 servings.

Cheese Tortellini Pasta Salad

Substitute whole bite-size grape tomatoes for cherry tomatoes to save chopping.

20 minutes or less
PREP: 4 MIN., COOK: 12 MIN.

1 (20-ounce) package refrigerated
    cheese-filled tortellini
¼ cup balsamic vinegar
6 dried tomatoes in oil
1½ tablespoons chopped fresh rosemary
1 tablespoon sugar
¼ teaspoon salt
¼ teaspoon pepper
½ cup olive oil
1 pint cherry tomatoes, halved
3 tablespoons minced red onion

1. Cook pasta according to package directions, including salt; drain.
2. Meanwhile, process vinegar and next 5 ingredients in a food processor until smooth, stopping to scrape down sides. With processor running, pour oil in a slow, steady stream through food chute.
3. Combine tortellini, tomato halves, and onion in a large bowl. Drizzle dressing over pasta mixture; toss gently. Serve immediately, or cover and chill. **Makes** 4 to 6 servings.

Ham-and-Pasta Salad

20 minutes or less
PREP: 20 MIN.

8 ounces penne pasta, cooked
1½ cups diced ham
1 cup Ranch dressing
4 green onions, sliced
2 tablespoons chopped fresh parsley
2 tablespoons chopped fresh basil
1 garlic clove, minced
¼ teaspoon freshly ground black pepper

1. Toss together cooked pasta and remaining ingredients. Serve immediately. **Makes** 4 servings.

Peanut-Noodle Salad

This recipe can be easily halved for a side dish. Serve chilled or at room temperature. You can find soba noodles on the ethnic foods aisle at the grocery store.

30 minutes or less
PREP: 25 MIN.

2 large cucumbers
¾ cup lite soy sauce
½ cup coconut milk
½ cup rice wine vinegar
½ cup chunky peanut butter
4 garlic cloves, minced
1 teaspoon sesame oil
½ to 1 teaspoon dried crushed red pepper
½ teaspoon salt
1 (16-ounce) package soba noodles or angel hair
    pasta, cooked
1 (10-ounce) package shredded carrots
6 green onions, cut into 1½-inch pieces

1. Peel cucumbers; cut in half lengthwise, discarding seeds. Cut cucumber halves into crescent-shaped slices.
2. Whisk together soy sauce and next 7 ingredients in a large bowl; add sliced cucumbers, pasta, carrots, and green onions, tossing to coat. Cover and chill 8 hours, if desired. **Makes** 6 to 8 servings.

Peanut-Noodle
Salad

Hoisin Chicken-and-Pasta Salad

PREP: 30 MIN., COOK: 20 MIN.

16 ounces uncooked penne pasta
½ cup vegetable oil, divided
1 garlic clove, pressed
4 skinned and boned chicken breasts
½ cup chicken broth
½ cup Hoisin Mixture (recipe on facing page)
2 celery ribs, sliced
2 green onions, sliced
1 small cucumber, peeled, seeded, and sliced
½ small red bell pepper, cut into thin strips
¾ teaspoon salt
¾ teaspoon pepper
Mixed salad greens
2 teaspoons toasted sesame seeds

1. Prepare pasta according to package directions. Drain. Return to Dutch oven, and toss with 3 tablespoons oil.
2. Heat remaining 5 tablespoons oil in a large skillet over medium heat; add garlic, and sauté 1 minute. Add chicken, and cook 4 minutes on each side or until done. Remove chicken from skillet. Stir in chicken broth; bring to a boil. Reduce heat, and simmer 10 minutes or until reduced to ⅓ cup; remove from heat, and stir in Hoisin Mixture. Toss with pasta.
3. Cut chicken into ½-inch cubes. Add chicken, celery, and next 5 ingredients to pasta mixture; toss well. Spoon over salad greens; sprinkle with sesame seeds. Serve immediately. **Makes** 6 servings.

Hoisin Chicken-and-Pasta Salad

Hoisin Mixture:

This mixture also adds great flavor to stir-fry vegetables.

PREP: 5 MIN.

1 (7.25-ounce) jar hoisin sauce (see note)
1½ tablespoons sugar
2 tablespoons pale dry sherry
1½ tablespoons rice vinegar

1. Stir together all ingredients until sugar dissolves. Store in refrigerator up to 3 months. **Makes** 1¼ cups.
Note: Hoisin sauce may be found on the ethnic foods aisle of the grocery store.

Zesty Chicken-Pasta Salad

PREP: 20 MIN., CHILL: 1 HR.

make
ahead

8 ounces uncooked elbow macaroni
1 (12-ounce) bottle peppercorn-Ranch dressing
2½ cups chopped cooked chicken
1 (9-ounce) package frozen sweet peas, thawed
1 (2¼-ounce) can sliced ripe black olives, drained
1 pint cherry tomatoes, halved
Salt to taste

1. Cook macaroni according to package directions; drain and rinse with cold water.
2. Stir together cooked macaroni and remaining ingredients; cover and chill at least 1 hour. **Makes** 4 servings.

Chicken and Bow Tie Pasta Salad

PREP: 10 MIN., COOK: 30 MIN.

1 quart salted water
4 skinned and boned chicken breasts, cut into bite-size pieces
8 ounces uncooked bow tie pasta
1 cup chicken broth
1 celery rib, chopped (about ½ cup)
1 small onion, chopped (about ½ cup)
1 (10¾-ounce) can cream of mushroom soup or cream of chicken soup
1 (8-ounce) package pasteurized prepared cheese product, cubed

1. Bring 1 quart salted water to a gentle boil in a Dutch oven. Add chicken, and cook 12 minutes or until done. Remove chicken from water with a slotted spoon; set aside.
2. Return water to a boil; add pasta, and cook 10 minutes or until tender. Drain and keep warm.
3. Heat ¼ cup broth over medium-high heat in a Dutch oven; add celery and onion, and cook 5 minutes or until tender. Stir in chicken, soup, cheese, and remaining ¾ cup chicken broth, stirring until cheese is melted. Toss with warm pasta; serve immediately. **Makes** 4 servings.

Golden-Baked Mini
Reubens, page 259

everyday
SOUPS 'n'
SANDWICHES

Chicken Noodle Soup

Chicken Noodle Soup

PREP: 15 MIN., COOK: 25 MIN.

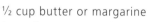

make ahead

½ cup butter or margarine
2 medium carrots, chopped
2 medium parsnips, chopped
1 medium-size sweet onion, diced
1 large celery rib, chopped
4 skinned and boned chicken breasts, cut
    into 1-inch pieces
¼ cup all-purpose flour
¼ teaspoon pepper
5 cups chicken broth
4 ounces uncooked wide egg noodles
2 tablespoons chopped fresh parsley

1. Melt butter in a large Dutch oven over medium-high heat. Add carrots and next 3 ingredients, and sauté 5 minutes. Add chicken, and sauté 5 minutes. Add flour and pepper, stirring until blended. Cook 1 minute, stirring constantly. Add broth; bring to a boil over medium-high heat, stirring constantly.

2. Add noodles; return to a boil. Reduce heat, and simmer, stirring occasionally, 10 minutes. Stir in parsley. (To freeze, let soup cool slightly, and spoon into freezerproof containers or zip-top plastic freezer bags. Cover or seal, and freeze up to 1 month. Thaw overnight in the refrigerator, and reheat.) **Makes** 9 cups.

Fiesta Turkey Soup With Green Chile Biscuits

Preheat the oven when you begin preparing the soup. Once the soup is simmering, start the biscuits.

PREP: 15 MIN., COOK: 30 MIN.

1 medium onion, diced
1 teaspoon vegetable oil
1 garlic clove, minced
3 cups chopped cooked turkey or chicken
1 (15-ounce) can chili beans
3½ cups chicken or turkey broth
1 (11-ounce) can yellow corn with red and green bell peppers, drained
1 (10-ounce) can diced tomatoes and green chiles
½ teaspoon chili powder
½ teaspoon ground cumin
⅛ teaspoon salt
⅛ teaspoon pepper
Toppings: sour cream, shredded Mexican four-cheese blend
Green Chile Biscuits

1. Sauté onion in hot oil in a large Dutch oven over medium heat 7 minutes or until tender. Add garlic, and sauté 1 minute. Stir in chopped turkey and next 8 ingredients. Bring to a boil, stirring occasionally; reduce heat, and simmer 15 minutes. Serve with desired toppings and Green Chile Biscuits. **Makes** 8 servings.

Green Chile Biscuits:

PREP: 5 MIN., COOK: 12 MIN.

2 cups all-purpose baking mix
1 cup (4 ounces) shredded Mexican four-cheese blend
1 (4.5-ounce) can chopped green chiles, drained
⅔ cup milk

1. Stir together baking mix and remaining ingredients until a soft dough forms. Turn dough out onto a lightly floured surface; knead 3 or 4 times.
2. Pat or roll dough to a ½-inch thickness; cut biscuits with a 2½-inch round cutter, and place on an ungreased baking sheet.
3. Bake at 450° for 10 to 12 minutes or until biscuits are golden brown. **Makes** 1 dozen.
Note: For testing purposes only, we used Bisquick All-Purpose Baking Mix.

Fiesta Turkey Soup With Green Chile Biscuits

Chunky Italian
Soup

Chunky Italian Soup

PREP: 20 MIN., COOK: 45 MIN.

make ahead

1 pound lean ground beef or beef tips
1 medium onion, chopped
2 (14½-ounce) cans Italian-style tomatoes
1 (10¾-ounce) can tomato soup, undiluted
4 cups water
2 garlic cloves, minced
2 teaspoons dried basil
2 teaspoons dried oregano
1 teaspoon salt
½ teaspoon pepper
1 tablespoon chili powder (optional)
1 (16-ounce) can kidney beans, drained
1 (16-ounce) can Italian green beans, drained
1 carrot, chopped
1 zucchini, chopped
8 ounces rotini pasta, cooked
Freshly grated Parmesan cheese (optional)

1. Cook beef and onion in a Dutch oven over medium heat, stirring until beef crumbles and is no longer pink; drain. Return mixture to pan.
2. Stir in tomatoes, next 7 ingredients, and, if desired, chili powder; bring to a boil. Reduce heat; simmer, stirring occasionally, 30 minutes. Stir in kidney beans and next 3 ingredients; simmer, stirring occasionally, 15 minutes. Stir in pasta. (To freeze, let soup cool slightly, and spoon into freezerproof containers or zip-top plastic freezer bags. Cover or seal, and freeze up to 1 month. Thaw overnight in the refrigerator, and reheat.) Sprinkle soup with cheese, if desired. **Makes** 10 cups.

Company Beef Stew

PREP: 20 MIN.; COOK: 2 HR., 10 MIN.; OTHER: 1 HR.

make ahead

1 (3-pound) boneless chuck roast, cut
    into 1-inch cubes
1 large onion, sliced
1 garlic clove, minced
1 tablespoon dried parsley flakes
1 bay leaf
½ teaspoon salt
½ teaspoon pepper
½ teaspoon dried thyme
1 cup dry red wine
2 tablespoons olive oil
4 bacon slices, cut crosswise into ¼-inch pieces
3 tablespoons all-purpose flour
1½ cups beef broth
½ pound baby carrots
1 (16-ounce) package frozen pearl onions, thawed
2 tablespoons butter or margarine
1 (8-ounce) package fresh mushrooms

1. Combine first 8 ingredients in a shallow dish or zip-top plastic freezer bag. Combine wine and oil; pour over meat mixture. Cover or seal; chill 1 hour. Drain well, reserving marinade.
2. Cook bacon in an ovenproof Dutch oven until crisp; remove bacon, reserving drippings in Dutch oven. Drain bacon on paper towels. (If desired, place bacon in a zip-top plastic freezer bag; seal and freeze up to 1 month. Thaw in refrigerator overnight.)
3. Brown meat mixture in reserved bacon drippings. Drain and return to Dutch oven. Sprinkle evenly with flour; cook, stirring constantly, 1 to 2 minutes. Add reserved marinade and beef broth; bring to a boil.
4. Bake, covered, at 300° for 1 hour and 30 minutes or until tender. Add carrots and onions; bake 30 more minutes.
5. Melt butter in a large skillet. Add mushrooms; sauté over medium-high heat until tender, and add to meat mixture. (To freeze, let soup cool slightly, and spoon into freezerproof containers or zip-top plastic freezer bags. Cover or seal, and freeze up to 1 month. Thaw overnight in the refrigerator, and reheat.)
6. Cook over medium heat in a Dutch oven, stirring occasionally, until thoroughly heated. Discard bay leaf. Sprinkle with bacon. **Makes** 6 cups.

Taco Soup

Taco Soup

Supper's on the table in 30 minutes with this Tex-Mex temptation. You probably have all the ingredients on hand. Using extra lean ground beef eliminates the extra fat and the draining step.

30 minutes or less
PREP: 11 MIN., COOK: 18 MIN.

1 pound ground chuck
2 cups water
½ cup diced green bell pepper
1 (16-ounce) jar medium picante sauce
1 (16-ounce) can pinto beans, undrained
1 (15-ounce) can tomato sauce
1 (11-ounce) can yellow corn with red and green bell peppers, undrained
1 (14½-ounce) can stewed tomatoes, undrained
Tortilla chips

1. Cook meat in a Dutch oven, stirring until it crumbles and is no longer pink; drain. Return meat to Dutch oven. Add 2 cups water and next 6 ingredients; bring to a boil. Reduce heat, and simmer, uncovered, 12 minutes, stirring occasionally. Serve soup with tortilla chips. **Makes** 12 cups.

Meatball Stew

Prepared meatballs from the freezer section of your supermarket make quick work of this stew.

30 minutes or less
PREP: 5 MIN., COOK: 20 MIN.

2 potatoes, cut into ½-inch cubes
1 small onion, chopped
1 (10½-ounce) can beef broth, undiluted
2 (15-ounce) cans tomato sauce
1¼ cups water
½ teaspoon dried Italian seasoning
¼ teaspoon pepper
1 (10-ounce) package frozen mixed vegetables
3 dozen frozen meatballs

1. Bring first 8 ingredients to a boil in a large saucepan. Cover, reduce heat, and simmer 10 minutes. Stir in meatballs; cover and simmer 5 to 10 minutes or until vegetables are tender and meatballs are thoroughly heated. **Makes** 8 cups.

Sausage, Spinach, and Bean Soup

30 minutes or less
PREP: 5 MIN., COOK: 20 MIN.

1 (8-ounce) package ground Italian sausage
1 teaspoon olive oil
5 garlic cloves, minced
½ teaspoon dried crushed red pepper
2 (10-ounce) packages fresh spinach, torn
2 (15-ounce) cans cannellini beans, undrained
3 cups chicken broth
¼ cup butter
½ cup freshly shredded Parmesan cheese
2 plum tomatoes, diced
2 tablespoons chopped fresh parsley
¼ teaspoon salt
¼ teaspoon pepper

1. Brown Italian sausage in hot oil in a Dutch oven over medium-high heat 10 minutes, stirring until it crumbles and is no longer pink. Add minced garlic and crushed red pepper, and sauté 2 minutes. Add spinach, and sauté 2 minutes or until wilted.
2. Stir in cannellini beans, and cook 1 minute. Add 3 cups chicken broth, and bring to a boil. Add ¼ cup butter, shredded Parmesan cheese, diced tomatoes, and 1 tablespoon chopped parsley; cook until thoroughly heated. Stir in salt and pepper. (To freeze, let soup cool slightly, and spoon into freezerproof containers or zip-top plastic freezer bags. Cover or seal, and freeze up to 1 month. Thaw overnight in the refrigerator, and reheat.) Sprinkle warm soup evenly with remaining 1 tablespoon chopped parsley. **Makes** about 10 cups.

Potato Soup With Ham

Down-home goodness comes in this bowl of warm potatoes in a cream base.

30 minutes or less
PREP: 11 MIN., COOK: 15 MIN.

4 bacon slices
1 small onion, chopped
2 cups half-and-half
1 (14-ounce) can chicken broth
1 (1-pound, 4-ounce) package refrigerated mashed potatoes (we used Simply Potatoes)
1 (12-ounce) package diced cooked ham (we used Hormel)
1 tablespoon chopped fresh thyme
¼ teaspoon pepper
1 cup (4 ounces) shredded sharp Cheddar cheese

1. Cook bacon in a Dutch oven until crisp; remove bacon, and drain on paper towels, reserving 1 tablespoon drippings in pan. Crumble bacon, and set aside.
2. Sauté onion in reserved drippings over medium heat until tender. Stir in half-and-half and next 6 ingredients, and bring to a boil. Reduce heat, and simmer 5 minutes. Top each serving evenly with bacon. **Makes** 7 cups.

Cream of Reuben Soup

PREP: 15 MIN., COOK: 30 MIN.

make ahead

6 cups chicken broth
¾ pound cooked corned beef, chopped
1 (10-ounce) can chopped sauerkraut, drained
1 large carrot, grated
1 small onion, chopped
1 garlic clove, minced
½ teaspoon dried thyme
¼ teaspoon ground white pepper
¼ teaspoon dried tarragon
1 bay leaf
3 tablespoons cornstarch
⅓ cup cold water
2 cups (8 ounces) shredded Swiss cheese
1 cup whipping cream
Rye bread cubes, toasted

1. Bring 6 cups chicken broth and next 9 ingredients to a boil in a Dutch oven over medium heat; reduce heat, and simmer 25 minutes. Remove and discard bay leaf.
2. Stir together 3 tablespoons cornstarch and ⅓ cup cold water, and stir into soup mixture. Bring to a boil over medium-high heat; boil, stirring constantly, 1 minute. Remove soup mixture from heat. (To freeze, let soup cool slightly, and spoon into freezerproof containers or zip-top plastic freezer bags. Cover or seal, and freeze up to 1 month. Thaw overnight in the refrigerator and reheat.)
3. Add 2 cups shredded Swiss cheese and 1 cup whipping cream, stirring until cheese melts. Top each serving with toasted rye bread cubes. **Makes** 12 cups.

So-Quick Seafood Chowder

Flounder or any other lean white fish works well in this chowder.

30 minutes or less
PREP: 15 MIN., COOK: 13 MIN.

½ (28-ounce) package frozen hash browns with onions and peppers (we used Ore Ida Potatoes O'Brien)
1 cup water
12 ounces fresh or frozen orange roughy fillets, thawed
1 (10¾-ounce) can cream of potato soup, undiluted
1 (12-ounce) can evaporated milk
¼ cup bacon bits (we used Hormel Real Bacon Bits)
2 teaspoons chopped fresh dill or ¾ teaspoon dried dillweed
¼ teaspoon salt
¼ teaspoon pepper
1 (4-ounce) jar diced pimiento, drained
Garnish: chopped fresh dill

1. Bring hash browns and 1 cup water to a boil in a large saucepan; reduce heat, cover, and simmer 5 minutes or until tender.
2. Meanwhile, cut fish fillets into 1-inch pieces; set aside.
3. Stir potato soup and next 5 ingredients into hash browns; return to a boil. Add fish and pimiento; cover, reduce heat, and simmer 3 minutes or until fish flakes with a fork. Garnish, if desired. Serve immediately. **Makes** 8 cups.

So-Quick Seafood
Chowder

Quick Shrimp Chowder

We've streamlined this favorite dish by using canned soup as the base.

PREP: 15 MIN., COOK: 20 MIN.

2 tablespoons butter
1 medium onion, chopped
2 (10¾-ounce) cans cream of potato soup
3½ cups milk
¼ teaspoon ground red pepper
1½ pounds unpeeled, medium-size raw shrimp, peeled (see note)
1 cup (4 ounces) shredded Monterey Jack cheese
Oyster crackers (optional)

1. Melt butter in a Dutch oven over medium heat; add onion, and sauté 8 minutes or until tender. Stir in cream of potato soup, milk, and pepper; bring to a boil. Add shrimp; reduce heat, and simmer, stirring often, 5 minutes or just until shrimp turn pink. Stir in Monterey Jack cheese until melted. Serve immediately. Serve with oyster crackers, if desired. **Makes** 12 cups. **Note:** 1½ pounds frozen shrimp, thawed; 1½ pounds peeled crawfish tails; or 3 cups chopped cooked chicken may be substituted.

Blue Satin Soup

This rich soup highlights the sharp flavor of blue cheese.

30 minutes or less
PREP: 5 MIN., COOK: 20 MIN.

2 tablespoons butter or margarine
¼ cup minced green onions
¼ cup minced celery
¼ cup all-purpose flour
1 (14-ounce) can chicken broth
1 cup half-and-half
1 cup milk
1 (4-ounce) package crumbled blue cheese
¼ cup dry sherry (optional)

1. Melt butter in a large saucepan over medium heat; add green onions and celery, and sauté until tender. Reduce heat to low; stir in flour. Cook, stirring constantly, 1 minute. Gradually stir in broth. Cook over medium heat, stirring constantly, 2 minutes. Add half-and-half, milk, and cheese; cook, stirring constantly, until mixture is thickened.
2. Stir in sherry, if desired. **Makes** 5 cups.

Herbed Cheese Soup

Goat cheese gives this soup a tangy bite, but feel free to substitute your favorite mild cheese to tone down the flavor.

20 minutes or less
PREP: 2 MIN., COOK: 18 MIN.

¼ cup butter or margarine
3 tablespoons all-purpose flour
1 tablespoon chopped fresh chives
1½ teaspoons paprika
½ teaspoon dry mustard
¼ teaspoon salt
2 cups chicken broth
2 cups half-and-half
8 ounces goat cheese, crumbled (see note)
1 garlic clove, minced
1 teaspoon dried basil
Garnish: chopped fresh chives

1. Melt butter in a large saucepan over medium-high heat. Whisk in flour and next 4 ingredients. Cook, whisking constantly, 3 minutes. Gradually whisk in broth and half-and-half; cook over medium heat, whisking constantly, until mixture is smooth and bubbly.
2. Add cheese, garlic, and basil; reduce heat, and simmer, whisking constantly, 10 minutes. Ladle soup into serving bowls. Garnish, if desired. **Makes** 4¾ cups. **Note:** Substitute 1 (8-ounce) package cream cheese, cubed, for the crumbled goat cheese, if desired.

Herbed Cheese Soup

Roasted Garlic-and-Basil Tomato Soup

PREP: 20 MIN., COOK: 25 MIN.

make
ahead

6 large garlic cloves, slightly flattened
2 (3-ounce) packages shallots, peeled and halved
2 tablespoons olive oil
2 (14½-ounce) cans Italian-style stewed tomatoes
1 teaspoon hot sauce
1 teaspoon balsamic vinegar
¼ teaspoon salt
¼ teaspoon freshly ground black pepper
Pinch of ground red pepper
3 cups chicken broth
3 tablespoons minced fresh basil
Basil Pesto Toast (optional)

1. Place garlic and shallots in an 8-inch square pan lined with aluminum foil; drizzle with oil.
2. Bake at 450° for 15 minutes, stirring twice; cool slightly.

3. Process garlic, shallots, tomatoes, and next 5 ingredients in a blender or food processor until smooth, stopping to scrape down sides.
4. Cook tomato mixture and broth in a medium saucepan over medium heat 5 minutes or until thoroughly heated. (To freeze, let soup cool, and spoon into freezerproof containers or zip-top plastic freezer bags. Cover or seal, and freeze up to 1 month. Thaw overnight in the refrigerator, and reheat.) Stir in basil; serve immediately with Basil Pesto Toast, if desired. **Makes** 7 cups.

Basil Pesto Toast: Lightly toast 1 French baguette in oven; cut warm bread into thin slices. Spread basil pesto evenly over 1 side of bread slices. Sprinkle with crumbled tomato-basil feta cheese. Broil bread slices, 3 inches from heat, 1 to 2 minutes or until lightly browned.

Roasted Garlic-and-Basil
Tomato Soup

Tomato-Basil
Bisque

Tomato-Basil Bisque

*This soup tastes as if fresh tomatoes have simmered all day—you'd
never guess the recipe's base is simply canned soup.*

20 minutes or less
PREP: 5 MIN., COOK: 8 MIN.

2 (10¾-ounce) cans tomato soup, undiluted
1 (14½-ounce) can diced tomatoes with basil, garlic,
    and oregano
2½ cups buttermilk
2 tablespoons chopped fresh basil
¼ teaspoon freshly ground pepper
Garnish: shredded fresh basil

1. Cook first 5 ingredients in a 3-quart saucepan over
medium heat, stirring often, 6 to 8 minutes or until
thoroughly heated. Garnish, if desired; serve immediately, or serve chilled. **Makes** about 7 cups.

Instant Gazpacho

20 minutes or less
PREP: 15 MIN.

make
ahead

5 green onions, sliced
1 small red or green bell pepper, diced
1 small cucumber, diced
2 plum tomatoes, diced
1 cup Bloody Mary mix
¼ teaspoon salt
¼ teaspoon pepper
⅓ cup sour cream
½ teaspoon prepared horseradish
⅓ cup croutons

1. Stir together first 7 ingredients. Chill 1 hour, if desired.
2. Stir together sour cream and horseradish; chill, if desired.
3. Ladle soup into bowls; sprinkle each serving with croutons, and dollop with sour cream mixture. **Makes** 2⅓ cups.

Black Bean Soup

Serve this simple and spicy comfort dish with fresh cornbread or tortilla chips.

PREP: 10 MIN., COOK: 30 MIN.

1 small onion, chopped
2 tablespoons olive oil
2 garlic cloves, chopped
3 cups chicken broth
3 (15-ounce) cans black beans, rinsed and drained
1 (10-ounce) can diced tomatoes and green chiles
1 pound shredded barbecued beef
2 tablespoons red wine vinegar
Toppings: sour cream, shredded Monterey Jack
       cheese, chopped fresh cilantro

1. Sauté onion in hot oil in a Dutch oven over medium heat 5 minutes or until tender; stir in garlic, and sauté 1 minute. Stir in chicken broth, beans, and tomatoes and green chiles; reduce heat, and simmer, stirring often, 15 minutes.
2. Process 1 cup bean mixture in a food processor until smooth. Return bean puree to Dutch oven; add beef, and simmer 10 minutes. Stir in vinegar. Serve with desired toppings. **Makes** 8 cups.

vegetable and bean soup secrets

• These hearty soups have many benefits. They can be cooked ahead and easily reheated. They're made from pantry ingredients, dried peas and beans, and often leftovers. And they provide plenty of protein and other nutrients, depending on the vegetables included.
• When you add vegetables to soup, remember that they don't all cook in the same amount of time. First, add the thickest vegetables that take the longest to cook. Then add remaining vegetables as the recipe directs. Be careful to cut like vegetables the same size so they'll cook evenly. Add frozen vegetables after fresh (no need to thaw them). Add canned vegetables last, and cook just until heated.

Quick Bean Soup

Quick Bean Soup

30 minutes or less
PREP: 15 MIN., COOK: 15 MIN.

1 large onion, chopped
1 small green bell pepper, chopped
2 teaspoons vegetable oil
1 (15-ounce) can kidney beans, rinsed and drained
1 (15-ounce) can pinto beans, rinsed and drained
1 (15-ounce) can black beans, rinsed and drained
2 (14½-ounce) cans no-salt-added stewed tomatoes, undrained
1 (14½-ounce) can fat-free chicken broth
1 cup picante sauce
1 teaspoon ground cumin

1. Sauté onion and bell pepper in hot oil in a large saucepan until tender. Add kidney beans and remaining ingredients; bring to a boil. Cover, reduce heat, and simmer 10 minutes. **Makes** 10 cups.

Golden-Baked
Mini Reubens

Golden-Baked Mini Reubens

These tangy little sandwiches are full of kraut and corned beef—perfect pickups for game-day fun!

30 minutes or less
PREP: 20 MIN., COOK: 10 MIN.

make ahead

½ cup Thousand Island dressing
1 (16-ounce) loaf party rye bread
1 (6-ounce) package Swiss cheese slices, halved
12 ounces thinly sliced corned beef
1 (14.5-ounce) can shredded sauerkraut, well drained
Butter-flavored cooking spray

1. Spread dressing evenly on 1 side of each bread slice; top half of slices evenly with half of cheese, corned beef, sauerkraut, and remaining cheese. Top with remaining bread slices.
2. Coat a baking sheet with butter-flavored cooking spray; arrange sandwiches on baking sheet. Coat the bottom of a second baking sheet with cooking spray; place, coated side down, on sandwiches to provide pressure while cooking.
3. Bake at 375° for 8 to 10 minutes or until bread is golden and cheese melts. **Makes** 20 sandwiches.
Note: To make ahead, place unbaked sandwiches on baking sheets, and freeze until firm; place sandwiches in zip-top plastic freezer bags, and freeze. Bake according to directions at 375° for 15 minutes.

Easy Calzones

Using refrigerated bread dough lets you assemble this meal in no time.

30 minutes or less
PREP: 15 MIN., COOK: 15 MIN.

¾ pound ground round
¼ cup chopped onion
3 garlic cloves, minced
1 (14-ounce) jar chunky spaghetti sauce, divided
½ teaspoon dried Italian seasoning
1 (11-ounce) can refrigerated crusty French loaf
4 (1-ounce) mozzarella cheese slices

1. Cook ground round, onion, and garlic in a large skillet over medium heat, stirring until beef crumbles and is no longer pink; drain well. Return to skillet; stir in ½ cup spaghetti sauce and Italian seasoning.
2. Unroll French loaf; press into a 16-inch square on a large lightly greased baking sheet. Cut into 4 squares; spoon ½ cup ground beef mixture off center of each square. Top each with a slice of mozzarella cheese. Fold over to form a triangle, pressing edges to seal. Separate calzones on baking sheet to allow for rising.
3. Bake at 400° for 12 to 15 minutes or until browned. Serve with remaining spaghetti sauce. **Makes** 4 servings.

Cheese-Steak Wraps

These meaty wraps rival the New England bun version. Wraps are easier to hold—and they're less messy. If you want some pizzazz, use flavored tortillas as your wrappers. Try dried tomato or avocado for a twist.

20 minutes or less
PREP: 7 MIN., COOK: 10 MIN.

4 (10-inch) flour tortillas
1 small onion, sliced
1 small green bell pepper, sliced
2 tablespoons vegetable oil
1 (1-pound) flank steak, cut diagonally across grain into thin slices
1 tablespoon cornstarch
6 ounces pasteurized prepared cheese product

1. Heat tortillas according to package directions; keep warm.
2. Sauté onion and bell pepper in hot oil in a large skillet over medium-high heat 3 to 4 minutes or until tender. Remove from skillet, and set aside; reserve drippings in skillet.
3. Toss together steak strips and cornstarch.
4. Sauté half of steak in drippings 2 to 3 minutes; remove from skillet, and repeat procedure with remaining half of steak.
5. Meanwhile, microwave cheese in a 1-quart glass bowl at HIGH 2 minutes or until melted, stirring once.
6. Place steak slices evenly down the center of each tortilla. Top with vegetables and cheese.
7. Roll up, and serve immediately. **Makes** 4 servings.

Easy Mushroom-Onion Burgers

Crispy French fried onions cook inside these burgers and crown a cheese and mushroom mixture slathered on top after grilling. Sandwich the bounty in kaiser rolls for burgers your family won't soon forget.

30 minutes or less
PREP: 8 MIN., COOK: 13 MIN.

1 pound ground chuck
2 tablespoons Worcestershire sauce, divided
2 teaspoons Dijon mustard, divided
½ teaspoon pepper
1 (2.8-ounce) can French fried onion rings, divided
1 (3-ounce) package cream cheese, softened
1 (4-ounce) can sliced mushrooms, drained
3 kaiser rolls

1. Combine ground chuck, 1 tablespoon Worcestershire sauce, 1 teaspoon mustard, pepper, and half of onion rings. Shape mixture into 3 patties. Grill, without grill lid, over medium heat (300° to 350°) 5 to 6 minutes on each side or until a meat thermometer inserted into thickest portion of 1 patty registers 160°.
2. Meanwhile, combine remaining 1 tablespoon Worcestershire sauce, remaining 1 teaspoon mustard, cream cheese, and mushrooms. Spread mixture on cooked patties. Top with remaining onions. Broil 3 inches from heat 1 minute. Serve on kaiser rolls. **Makes** 3 servings.

Italian Burgers With Fresh Basil

Serve this tasty sandwich alongside ovenbaked fries.

PREP: 20 MIN., COOK: 18 MIN.

1 pound lean ground beef
1 small onion, minced
¾ cup grated Parmesan cheese
¼ cup minced fresh parsley
1 large egg, lightly beaten
2 tablespoons dried Italian seasoning
¾ teaspoon pepper
½ teaspoon garlic salt
¼ teaspoon fennel seeds
4 (1-ounce) provolone cheese slices
4 English muffins, split
½ cup jarred pasta sauce
4 fresh basil sprigs

1. Combine first 9 ingredients; shape into 4 patties.
2. Grill, covered with grill lid, over medium-high heat (350° to 400°) 7 to 8 minutes on each side or until beef is no longer pink. Top patties with cheese, and grill 1 more minute or until cheese melts. Place muffins on grill, cut sides down, and grill 1 minute or until lightly toasted.
3. Top each muffin bottom with 2 tablespoons pasta sauce, a hamburger patty, a basil sprig, and a muffin top. **Makes** 4 servings.

Fiesta Burgers

Fiesta Burgers

*Burgers that taste this good can't be this easy. But they are! With the addition
of hot salsa, regular burgers turn into "Wow-burgers."*

30 minutes or less

PREP: 12 MIN., COOK: 12 MIN.

2 pounds extra-lean ground beef
1 small onion, finely chopped
⅓ cup soft breadcrumbs (fresh)
1 large egg, lightly beaten
2 tablespoons hot salsa
1 teaspoon salt
1 teaspoon prepared mustard
8 hamburger buns with sesame seeds
Toppings: shredded lettuce, tomato slices,
    red onion slices
Hot salsa

1. Combine first 7 ingredients in a bowl; shape into
8 (4½- to 5-inch) patties.
2. Grill, covered with grill lid, over medium-high heat
(350° to 400°) 5 to 6 minutes on each side or until
done. Place bottom half of each hamburger bun on
a plate; top with a patty. Add desired toppings, and
spoon additional salsa over toppings. Cover with bun
tops. **Makes** 8 servings.

Jack Cheeseburgers

Flavorful pockets of Monterey Jack cheese and ripe olives are nestled in these hearty burgers. Assemble these patties ahead. Cover and refrigerate up to 1 day. When you're ready for entertaining, just pop them on the grill, and cook according to directions.

PREP: 27 MIN., COOK: 12 MIN.

make ahead

1½ cups (6 ounces) shredded Monterey Jack cheese with peppers
⅓ cup chopped ripe olives
1¾ pounds lean ground chuck
¼ cup chopped onion
1 teaspoon salt
½ teaspoon black pepper
6 hamburger buns

1. Combine cheese and olives; stir well. Shape cheese mixture into 6 balls; set aside.
2. Combine ground chuck and next 3 ingredients in a large bowl; shape mixture into 12 patties.
3. Place a cheese ball in center of each of 6 patties; flatten cheese balls slightly. Top with remaining patties, pressing edges to seal.
4. Grill, covered with grill lid, over medium-high heat (350° to 400°) 5 to 6 minutes on each side or until done. Serve on buns. **Makes** 6 servings.

Giant Meatball Sandwich

PREP: 5 MIN., COOK: 32 MIN.

1 pound ground round
½ pound ground pork sausage
1 (28-ounce) jar spaghetti sauce with peppers and mushrooms
1 garlic clove, minced
1 (16-ounce) unsliced Italian bread loaf
1 (6-ounce) package sliced provolone cheese

1. Combine ground round and sausage; shape into 1-inch balls.
2. Cook meatballs in a large skillet over medium heat 10 to 15 minutes or until browned. Drain and return to skillet. Add spaghetti sauce and garlic; bring to a boil. Reduce heat, and simmer, stirring occasionally, 12 to 15 minutes or until meatballs are no longer pink in center.
3. Cut bread in half horizontally, and scoop out bottom, leaving a ½-inch-thick shell. Place bread shell and bread top, cut sides up, on a baking sheet. Broil 5½ inches from heat 1 to 2 minutes or until lightly toasted.
4. Spoon meatball mixture into toasted shell; top with provolone cheese slices. Cover with bread top. Cut sandwich into 6 pieces, and serve immediately. **Makes** 6 servings.

burger basics

- Rescue hands from the messy mixing of ground meats by combining patty ingredients in a zip-top plastic freezer bag; squeeze just until combined. Wearing latex gloves while mixing is another way to keep your hands clean.
- For consistent patty sizes, use a large spoon or ice-cream scoop to measure the meat mixture.
- Keep the meat from sticking to your fingers while forming the burger patties by wetting your hands with water.
- Allow patties to be a little loose rather than heavily packed. Compacted meat patties produce dense, solid burgers.
- For moist and juicy burgers, look for a coarse grind of meat. Avoid finely ground beef.
- Raw ground beef can be frozen up to 3 months or stored up to 2 days in the refrigerator.
- When grilling, resist the temptation to press the burgers flat. That squeezes out all the flavorful juices.

Grilled Bacon, Cheese, and Tomato Sandwiches

30 minutes or less
PREP: 16 MIN., COOK: 12 MIN.

12 bacon slices
8 (½-inch-thick) French bread slices
¼ cup butter or margarine, softened
16 (½-ounce) thin slices provolone cheese (we used Sargento)
3 plum tomatoes, thinly sliced
24 large fresh basil leaves

1. Microwave bacon, in batches, at HIGH 6 minutes or until crisp. Remove bacon, and drain on paper towels. Set bacon aside.
2. Spread 1 side of bread slices with butter; turn 4 slices, buttered side down, and top each with 2 cheese slices. Top cheese evenly with tomato slices, bacon, half of basil leaves, and remaining cheese slices; top with remaining basil leaves and bread slices, buttered side up.
3. Place a large skillet over medium heat until hot; add sandwiches, and cook, in batches, 3 minutes on each side or until golden. **Makes** 4 servings.

Double-Decker Egg Salad Sandwiches

A hearty helping of eggs, bacon, and spinach comes in each bite of these sandwiches. Hard-cook the eggs a day before, and chill overnight.

30 minutes or less
PREP: 10 MIN., COOK: 20 MIN.

4 large eggs
4 bacon slices
⅔ cup mayonnaise, divided
1 celery rib, diced
1 tablespoon minced sweet pickle relish
¼ teaspoon seasoned salt
½ teaspoon freshly ground pepper
12 very thin white or wheat sandwich bread slices, lightly toasted
1 cup packed fresh baby spinach

1. Place eggs in a saucepan; add water to 1 inch over eggs, and bring almost to a boil. Cover, remove from heat, and let stand 15 minutes. Rinse eggs in cold water, and peel; chop eggs.
2. While eggs cook, cook bacon in microwave at HIGH for 3 to 4 minutes or until done. Drain and crumble.
3. Meanwhile, stir together ⅓ cup mayonnaise, celery, relish, seasoned salt, and pepper. Stir in chopped eggs and crumbled bacon.
4. Spread remaining ⅓ cup mayonnaise evenly over 1 side of each bread slice.
5. Spread 4 bread slices, mayonnaise side up, evenly with half of egg salad. Top evenly with half of spinach and 4 bread slices.
6. Spread remaining egg salad on top of bread slice; top with spinach and remaining bread slices. Cut each sandwich into quarters. **Makes** 4 servings.

Deli-Stuffed
Sandwiches

Deli-Stuffed Sandwiches

Consider this colorful sandwich for your next tailgate party.

10 minutes or less

PREP: 10 MIN.

2 tablespoons olive oil

½ cup chopped ripe olives (see note)

1 tablespoon chopped fresh or 1 teaspoon dried
    oregano

1 tablespoon cider vinegar

½ teaspoon pepper

1 (16-ounce) round Italian bread loaf

¼ pound thinly sliced cooked turkey

¼ pound thinly sliced cooked ham

1 (8-ounce) package shredded Italian three-cheese
    blend

1. Stir together first 5 ingredients.

2. Cut bread loaf in half horizontally; remove center
of bread, and reserve for other uses, leaving a ½-inch-
thick shell.

3. Spoon half of olive mixture into bread shell. Top
with turkey, ham, cheese, and remaining olive mixture. Cover with bread top. Cut into wedges. Serve
immediately. **Makes** 8 servings.

Note: ½ cup chopped pimiento-stuffed Spanish olives
may be substituted.

Ham-Swiss-and-Asparagus Sandwiches

20 minutes or less
PREP: 13 MIN., COOK: 5 MIN.

12 fresh asparagus spears
3 tablespoons butter or margarine, softened
1 small garlic clove, minced
4 (6-inch) French rolls, split
3 tablespoons mayonnaise
¾ pound sliced cooked ham
2 (1½-ounce) Swiss cheese slices, cut in half
    diagonally
Green leaf lettuce leaves
3 plum tomatoes, sliced

1. Snap off tough ends of asparagus. Cook asparagus in boiling water to cover 3 minutes or until crisp-tender; drain. Rinse asparagus under cold water to stop the cooking process; drain and set aside.
2. Stir together butter and garlic; spread on bottom halves of rolls. Spread mayonnaise over garlic mixture. Layer ham, asparagus, and cheese over mayonnaise; place sandwiches on a baking sheet.
3. Broil 2 inches from heat 2 minutes or until cheese melts. Top with lettuce, tomato, and tops of rolls. Cut sandwiches in half diagonally. **Makes** 4 servings.

French Club Sandwiches

Tailgating takes a tasty turn when this winning cream cheese club sandwich is served. This sandwich wraps and travels nicely chilled in a cooler.

20 minutes or less
PREP: 13 MIN.

½ (8-ounce) container chive-and-onion
    cream cheese, softened
1 tablespoon mayonnaise
½ celery rib, chopped
¼ cup (1 ounce) shredded Cheddar cheese
1 (8-ounce) French baguette
½ pound thinly sliced cooked ham
3 dill pickle stackers (we used Vlasic)

1. Combine first 4 ingredients, stirring until blended.
2. Slice baguette in half horizontally, and spread cream cheese mixture evenly over cut sides of bread. Place

ham on bottom half of baguette, and top with pickles. Cover with top half of baguette. Cut baguette into 3 portions. **Makes** 3 servings.

Smoked Turkey Wraps

Pack these savory wraps filled with smoked turkey, bacon, arugula, and caramelized onions for a gourmet picnic.

20 minutes or less
PREP: 15 MIN.

2 (6.5-ounce) packages garlic-and-herb
    spreadable cheese, softened
8 (10-inch) whole grain pita bread rounds or flour
    tortillas
Caramelized Onions
1½ pounds thinly sliced smoked turkey
16 bacon slices, cooked and crumbled
4 cups loosely packed arugula or gourmet mixed
    baby salad greens

1. Spread garlic-and-herb cheese evenly over each pita round; top evenly with Caramelized Onions, sliced smoked turkey, crumbled bacon, and arugula. Roll up pitas, and wrap in parchment paper; chill up to 24 hours. Cut pitas in half to serve. **Makes** 8 servings.
Note: For testing purposes only, we used Alouette Garlic et Herbes Gourmet Spreadable Cheese for garlic-and-herb spreadable cheese.

Caramelized Onions:

PREP: 5 MIN., COOK: 20 MIN.

2 large sweet onions, diced
1 tablespoon sugar
2 tablespoons olive oil
2 teaspoons balsamic vinegar

1. Cook onions and sugar in hot oil in a skillet over medium-high heat, stirring often, 20 minutes or until onions are caramel colored. Stir in vinegar. **Makes** 2 cups.

Smoked Turkey Wraps

Open-Faced Southwestern
Chicken Sandwiches

Open-Faced Southwestern Chicken Sandwiches

Want a showy presentation when having guests over for lunch? This sandwich topped with colorful Black Bean Salsa (page 182) will do the trick.

PREP: 15 MIN., COOK: 20 MIN.

4 skinned and boned chicken breasts
2 tablespoons chopped fresh cilantro
2 tablespoons vegetable oil
2 teaspoons chili powder
¼ teaspoon ground red pepper
1 garlic clove, minced
1 cup (4 ounces) shredded Mexican four-cheese
    blend
⅓ cup mayonnaise
4 (1-inch-thick) French bread slices, lightly toasted
Black Bean Salsa (commercial or recipe on page 182)

1. Place chicken between 2 sheets of heavy-duty plastic wrap, and flatten to ½-inch thickness using a meat mallet or rolling pin.

2. Stir together cilantro and next 4 ingredients. Spread on chicken.

3. Grill, covered with grill lid, over medium-high heat (350° to 400°) 8 to 10 minutes on each side or until chicken is done.

4. Meanwhile, stir together cheese and mayonnaise. Spread on bread slices. Place bread, cheese mixture side up, on a baking sheet.

5. Broil 6 inches from heat 1 to 2 minutes or until cheese melts. Place chicken on bread, and serve with Black Bean Salsa. **Makes** 4 servings.

Grilled Chicken 'n' Cheese Sandwiches

20 minutes or less
PREP: 14 MIN., COOK: 6 MIN.

2 cups chopped cooked chicken
⅓ cup golden raisins
¼ cup slivered almonds, toasted
¼ cup diced celery
½ cup mayonnaise
12 (¾-ounce) Monterey Jack cheese slices
12 whole wheat bread slices
¼ cup butter or margarine, softened

1. Stir together first 5 ingredients. Place 1 cheese slice on each of 6 bread slices; spread evenly with chicken mixture, and top with remaining cheese and bread slices. Spread half of butter evenly on 1 side of each sandwich.

2. Cook sandwiches, buttered side down, in a nonstick skillet or griddle over medium heat about 3 minutes or until lightly browned. Spread remaining butter evenly on ungrilled sides; turn and cook 3 minutes or until lightly browned. **Makes** 6 servings.

Mango Chutney
Chicken Pitas

Mango Chutney Chicken Pitas

You can use turkey on this sandwich instead of chicken if you like.

20 minutes or less

PREP: 11 MIN.

1 (10-ounce) package finely shredded cabbage
1 Granny Smith apple, diced
1 (6-ounce) container fat-free yogurt
1 teaspoon grated lemon rind
½ teaspoon dry mustard
2 (6-ounce) packages grilled chicken strips
1 cup warm mango chutney
4 pita rounds, halved crosswise

1. Combine first 5 ingredients. Layer chicken, mango chutney, and slaw mixture evenly inside pita halves. **Makes** 4 servings.

Asparagus Hot Browns

To save time, cook the bacon while the bread is toasting.

PREP: 15 MIN., COOK: 35 MIN.

1 pound fresh asparagus
1 (2-pound) deli roasted whole chicken
4 (1½-inch-thick) French bread slices
4 plum tomatoes, cut into ¼-inch-thick slices
½ teaspoon freshly ground pepper
1 (10-ounce) container refrigerated Alfredo sauce
½ cup (2 ounces) shredded Cheddar cheese
6 bacon slices, cooked and crumbled

1. Snap off tough ends of asparagus, and remove scales with a vegetable peeler, if desired. Cook in boiling water to cover 1 minute or until crisp-tender; drain. Plunge asparagus into ice water to stop the cooking process; drain and set aside.

2. Skin and bone chicken, cutting meat into bite-size pieces. Set aside.

3. Place bread slices on a baking sheet. Bake at 400° for 8 to 10 minutes or until lightly browned. Remove from oven.

4. Arrange bread in a lightly greased 11- x 7-inch baking dish. Place tomato slices evenly over bread. Sprinkle evenly with ½ teaspoon pepper. Top evenly with chicken and asparagus. Spoon Alfredo sauce evenly over asparagus. Sprinkle with ½ cup shredded Cheddar cheese.

5. Bake sandwiches at 400° for 15 to 20 minutes or until thoroughly heated. Sprinkle with cooked bacon. **Makes** 4 servings.

Asparagus Hot Browns

Crab Cake
Sandwich

Crab Cake Sandwiches

For an elegant and effortless lunch, shape crab cakes the night before, and quickly fry the next day.

PREP: 20 MIN., COOK: 6 MIN. PER BATCH, OTHER: 1 HR.

make
ahead

1¼ cups Italian-seasoned breadcrumbs,
　　divided
1 large egg
3 tablespoons mayonnaise
1 tablespoon fresh lemon juice
1 teaspoon Dijon mustard
½ teaspoon salt
½ teaspoon ground red pepper
1 pound fresh lump crabmeat, drained
2 tablespoons butter or margarine
6 onion sandwich buns
Tartar sauce
Commercial coleslaw

1. Combine ¾ cup breadcrumbs, egg, and next 5 ingredients; gently fold in crabmeat. Shape crab mixture into 6 patties; dredge in remaining ½ cup breadcrumbs. Cover and chill 1 hour or overnight.
2. Melt butter in a large nonstick skillet over medium-high heat; cook crab cakes, in batches, 3 minutes on each side or until golden brown. Drain on paper towels. Serve on buns with tartar sauce and coleslaw. **Makes** 6 servings.

Open-Faced Crab Melts

This sandwich would be a great addition to a brunch menu.

10 minutes or less
PREP: 7 MIN., COOK: 3 MIN.

1 pound fresh lump crabmeat, drained (see note)
¼ to ⅓ cup mayonnaise
½ teaspoon salt
¼ teaspoon pepper
¼ teaspoon sugar
3 English muffins, split and toasted
1 cup (4 ounces) shredded sharp Cheddar cheese

1. Stir together first 5 ingredients. Spread mixture evenly over cut sides of muffin halves; sprinkle evenly with cheese.

2. Broil 5 inches from heat 2 to 3 minutes or until cheese is melted. Serve immediately. **Makes** 6 servings.
Note: 2 (6-ounce) cans lump crabmeat or 2 (6-ounce) cans solid white tuna in spring water, drained, may be substituted.

Zesty Fish Po'boys

20 minutes or less
PREP: 20 MIN.

2 (11-ounce) packages frozen breaded fish fillets (we
　　used Gorton's Southern Fried Country Style
　　Breaded Fish Fillets)
2 (12-inch) French bread loaves
1 cup mayonnaise
3 tablespoons lemon juice
1 tablespoon Creole mustard
1 tablespoon sweet pickle relish
1 teaspoon chopped fresh or ½ teaspoon
　　dried parsley
¼ teaspoon dried tarragon
½ teaspoon hot sauce
4 lettuce leaves

1. Bake fish fillets according to package directions. Set aside, and keep warm.
2. Meanwhile, cut bread in half crosswise. Split each half lengthwise, and toast.
3. Stir together mayonnaise and next 6 ingredients. Spread mixture evenly over cut sides of bread halves. Place lettuce and fish on bottom bread halves; top with remaining bread halves. Serve immediately. **Makes** 4 servings.

Curried Tuna-Apple Sandwiches

Curry powder puts a twist on traditional tuna salad, while apple, celery, and raisins add a sweet flavor and a bit of crunch.

10 minutes or less
PREP: 10 MIN.

¼ cup mayonnaise
1 tablespoon lemon juice
½ teaspoon curry powder
⅛ teaspoon garlic powder
1 (6-ounce) can albacore tuna in water, drained and flaked
1 small Granny Smith apple, chopped
1 celery rib, chopped
¼ cup raisins
2 tablespoons diced onion
6 whole grain bread slices

1. Stir together first 4 ingredients. Stir in tuna and next 4 ingredients.
2. Spread mixture on 3 bread slices; top with remaining bread slices. **Makes** 3 servings.

Fried Catfish Sandwiches

Crisp catfish is perfect sandwiched between savory onion buns. Serve the sandwiches with coleslaw and French fries.

30 minutes or less
PREP: 15 MIN., COOK: 10 MIN.

Vegetable oil
¾ cup yellow cornmeal
¼ cup all-purpose flour
2 teaspoons garlic salt
1 teaspoon ground red pepper
4 catfish fillets (about 1½ pounds)
4 onion sandwich buns, split and toasted
Cocktail or tartar sauce
Lettuce leaves
4 tomato slices (optional)

1. Pour oil to a depth of 3 inches in a Dutch oven; heat to 350°.
2. Combine cornmeal and next 3 ingredients in a large shallow dish.
3. Dredge fish in cornmeal mixture, coating well.
4. Fry fish in hot oil 4 to 5 minutes on each side or until golden brown. Drain on paper towels.
5. Serve on sandwich buns with cocktail sauce, lettuce, and, if desired, tomato. **Makes** 4 servings.

Grilled Shrimp Gyros With
Herbed Yogurt Spread

Grilled Shrimp Gyros With Herbed Yogurt Spread

PREP: 20 MIN., COOK: 10 MIN., OTHER: 30 MIN.

1½ pounds unpeeled, medium-size raw shrimp
2 tablespoons Greek seasoning
2 tablespoons olive oil
6 (12-inch) wooden skewers
4 (8-inch) pita or gyro bread rounds
Herbed Yogurt Spread
½ cup crumbled feta cheese
1 large tomato, chopped
1 cucumber, thinly sliced

1. Peel shrimp, and devein, if desired.
2. Combine seasoning and oil in a zip-top plastic freezer bag; add shrimp. Seal and chill 30 minutes; drain.
3. Soak skewers in water 30 minutes. Thread shrimp onto skewers.
4. Grill shrimp skewers, covered with grill lid, over medium heat (300° to 350°) about 5 minutes on each side or just until shrimp turn pink.

5. Wrap each pita round in a damp cloth. Microwave at HIGH 10 to 15 seconds or until soft. Spread 1 side of each pita round with Herbed Yogurt Spread. Top evenly with shrimp, feta cheese, tomato, and cucumber. Roll up, and serve immediately. **Makes** 4 servings.

Herbed Yogurt Spread:

PREP: 5 MIN.

½ cup low-fat plain yogurt
1 garlic clove, minced
1 tablespoon chopped fresh or ¾ teaspoon dried
    oregano
1 teaspoon chopped fresh mint
2 teaspoons lemon juice
¼ teaspoon pepper

1. Whisk together ½ cup yogurt and remaining ingredients. Chill spread until ready to serve. **Makes** about ½ cup.

Avocado Sandwiches Deluxe

Stir up a pitcher of iced tea, and take these sandwiches out to the patio on a pretty day. They're colorful and healthy vegetable sandwiches. Meat lovers, feel free to layer a slice or two of deli-sliced turkey or ham.

20 minutes or less
PREP: 20 MIN.

1 avocado, cut into 8 wedges
¼ cup Italian dressing
1 tablespoon mayonnaise
4 oatmeal or whole wheat bread slices,
    toasted
2 (1-ounce) processed American cheese
    slices
4 thin tomato slices
½ cup alfalfa sprouts

1. Toss avocado wedges gently with Italian dressing; drain well, reserving dressing.
2. Spread mayonnaise evenly over 1 side of each bread slice. Top 2 bread slices evenly with American cheese slices, tomato, avocado, and alfalfa sprouts.
3. Drizzle sandwiches evenly with reserved Italian dressing, and top with remaining 2 bread slices. Serve immediately. **Makes** 2 servings.

Double Cheese Grills

Cheddar and Monterey Jack with peppers are our favorite cheeses for this recipe. Go ahead and get creative and choose your two favorites for the right blend in your sandwich.

10 minutes or less
PREP: 5 MIN., COOK: 4 MIN.

½ cup (2 ounces) shredded Cheddar
    cheese
½ cup (2 ounces) shredded Monterey
    Jack cheese with peppers
2 tablespoons mayonnaise
8 sandwich bread slices
2 large eggs
3 tablespoons milk
3 tablespoons butter or margarine,
    divided

1. Combine cheeses and mayonnaise; spread evenly on 1 side of 4 bread slices; top with remaining bread slices.
2. Whisk together eggs and milk in a shallow dish; dip sandwiches into egg mixture, coating all sides.
3. Melt 2 tablespoons butter in a large skillet over medium heat; add 2 sandwiches, and cook 1 minute on each side or until golden. Repeat procedure with remaining sandwiches, using remaining butter. **Makes** 4 servings.

Cucumber Sandwiches

Cucumber Sandwiches

These petite sandwiches are a classic for showers and teas.

10 minutes or less
PREP: 10 MIN.

1 large cucumber, peeled, seeded, and
    grated
1 (8-ounce) package cream cheese,
    softened
1 tablespoon mayonnaise
1 small shallot, minced
¼ teaspoon seasoned salt
1 (16-ounce) loaf sandwich bread, crusts removed
Garnish: cucumber slices

1. Drain grated cucumber well, pressing between layers of paper towels.
2. Stir together grated cucumber and next 4 ingredients. Spread mixture evenly over half of bread slices. Top with remaining bread slices.
3. Cut sandwiches in half diagonally. Garnish, if desired. Store sandwiches in refrigerator in an airtight container. **Makes** 16 sandwiches.

Pimiento Cheese Finger Sandwiches

Sharp Cheddar and red pepper pack a nice punch in these dainty sandwiches. Be sure to shred your own cheese for pimiento cheese recipes. Freshly shredded cheese is more moist and bonds with other ingredients better.

10 minutes or less
PREP: 10 MIN.

12 ounces sharp Cheddar cheese, shredded
½ cup mayonnaise
2 (4-ounce) jars diced pimiento, drained
⅛ teaspoon ground red pepper
¼ teaspoon salt
20 thin white sandwich bread slices, crusts removed

1. Process first 5 ingredients in a food processor until smooth, stopping to scrape down sides. Spread mixture on half of bread slices; cover with remaining bread slices. Cut each sandwich into 4 strips. **Makes** 40 sandwiches.

French Onion Sandwiches

Accent these open-faced onion treats with tomato soup on the side.

20 minutes or less
PREP: 5 MIN., COOK: 10 MIN.

8 (1-ounce) French bread slices
2 teaspoons butter
1 large onion, very thinly sliced
1½ tablespoons brown sugar
1 cup (4 ounces) shredded Swiss cheese

1. Arrange bread slices on a baking sheet. Bake at 375° for 8 minutes or until lightly toasted. Remove from oven, and leave bread slices on baking sheet.
2. While bread toasts, coat a large heavy saucepan with cooking spray; add butter, and place over high heat until butter melts. Add onion, and cook, stirring constantly, 3 minutes or until onion is tender. Add brown sugar, and cook 5 more minutes or until onion is tender and browned, stirring often.
3. Spoon onion mixture evenly onto bread slices; top with cheese. Broil 5½ inches from heat 2 minutes. Serve immediately. **Makes** 8 sandwiches.

Honey-Pecan Pork
Chops, page 296

MAIN dishes
in minutes

Beef Fillets With
Orange Cream

Beef Fillets With Orange Cream

The slightly orange-colored sauce and orange rind curls make a pretty presentation and lend a hint to the flavor of these succulent fillets.

30 minutes or less
PREP: 5 MIN., COOK: 17 MIN.

4 (6- to 8-ounce) beef tenderloin fillets
½ teaspoon cracked pepper (optional)
1 cup whipping cream
2 tablespoons orange marmalade
1 to 2 tablespoons prepared horseradish
Garnish: orange rind curls

1. Sprinkle fillets with cracked pepper, if desired.
2. Grill, covered with grill lid, over medium-high heat (350° to 400°) 4 to 6 minutes on each side or to desired degree of doneness.
3. Bring whipping cream, marmalade, and horseradish to a boil over medium-high heat, stirring constantly; reduce heat, and simmer, stirring often, 5 minutes or until thickened. Serve immediately with fillets; garnish, if desired. **Makes** 4 servings.

Spicy Beef Fillets

A touch of bourbon adds depth of flavor to the juicy beef fillets.

30 minutes or less
PREP: 10 MIN., COOK: 20 MIN.

6 (6-ounce) beef tenderloin fillets (1½ inches thick)
¼ teaspoon salt
¼ teaspoon pepper
¼ cup butter or margarine
2 garlic cloves, pressed
2 tablespoons all-purpose flour
1 cup beef broth
1 cup dry red wine (see note)
¼ cup bourbon (see note)
2 tablespoons Dijon mustard
1 teaspoon Worcestershire sauce

1. Sprinkle fillets with salt and pepper.
2. Melt butter in a skillet over medium heat. Add fillets, and cook 5 to 7 minutes on each side or to desired degree of doneness. Remove fillets from pan, and keep warm.

3. Add garlic and flour to pan drippings; cook over medium heat, stirring constantly, 1 minute. Gradually add broth, wine, and bourbon, stirring to loosen particles from bottom of pan; bring to a boil. Stir in mustard and Worcestershire sauce; reduce heat, and simmer 5 minutes. Top steaks with sauce. **Makes** 6 servings.
Note: Substitute 1¼ cups beef broth or cranberry juice for red wine and bourbon.

Fillets With Tarragon Butter

A candlelight dinner for two is the perfect occasion to serve these elegant, yet simple, herbed fillets. Steamed asparagus is a great accompaniment with these beef fillets. Simply double the butter mixture to serve with the asparagus, if you'd like.

20 minutes or less
PREP: 3 MIN., COOK: 15 MIN.

2 (6-ounce) beef tenderloin fillets (1 inch thick)
¼ teaspoon salt
¼ teaspoon pepper
1 teaspoon olive oil
1 shallot, finely chopped
¼ cup butter, softened
⅛ teaspoon salt
2 tablespoons finely chopped fresh tarragon

1. Sprinkle fillets evenly with ¼ teaspoon salt and pepper. Place a 10-inch cast-iron skillet over medium-high heat until hot; add oil. Cook fillets in hot oil 2 minutes on each side. Place pan in oven, and bake, uncovered, at 400° for 10 minutes or to desired degree of doneness.
2. Meanwhile, cook shallot in 1 teaspoon butter in a small skillet over medium-high heat until tender, stirring often; cool 2 minutes. Combine shallot, remaining butter, ⅛ teaspoon salt, and tarragon in a small bowl. Top each fillet evenly with tarragon butter before serving. **Makes** 2 servings.

Filet Mignon With Horseradish Gravy

Filet Mignon With Horseradish Gravy

Serve this zippy entrée and its mushroom gravy with mashed potatoes.

30 minutes or less

PREP: 3 MIN., COOK: 26 MIN.

1 (³⁄₄-ounce) package brown gravy mix
2 tablespoons prepared horseradish
4 (5-ounce) beef tenderloin fillets
¼ teaspoon salt
¼ teaspoon pepper
2 tablespoons butter
1 (8-ounce) package sliced fresh mushrooms

1. Prepare gravy according to package directions; stir in horseradish. Set aside.
2. Coat a large nonstick skillet with cooking spray. Place skillet over medium-high heat until hot; add fillets, and cook 1 minute on each side. (Fillets will be rare.) Place in a lightly greased 1-quart baking dish; sprinkle with salt and pepper.
3. Melt butter in skillet over medium heat. Add mushrooms, and cook, stirring constantly, 5 minutes or until tender. Remove from heat, and stir in gravy. Pour gravy over fillets; bake, uncovered, at 350° for 15 minutes or to desired degree of doneness. **Makes** 4 servings.

Garlic-Herb Steaks

Minced garlic in a jar can be found in the produce area of your grocery store.

PREP: 10 MIN., COOK: 20 MIN., OTHER: 1 HR.

make ahead

4 (4-ounce) beef tenderloin fillets
¼ teaspoon salt
¼ teaspoon freshly ground pepper
¼ cup jarred minced garlic
1 tablespoon minced fresh rosemary

1. Sprinkle fillets with salt and pepper; coat with garlic and rosemary. Chill 1 to 24 hours.
2. Prepare a hot fire by piling charcoal or lava rocks on 1 side of grill, leaving other side empty; place rack on grill. Arrange fillets over empty side, and grill, covered with grill lid, over high heat (400° to 500°) 10 minutes on each side or to desired degree of doneness. **Makes** 4 servings.

Pan-Seared Steaks With Roasted Red Pepper Sauce

10 minutes or less
PREP: 4 MIN., COOK: 6 MIN.

1 teaspoon roasted garlic-pepper seasoning (see note)
½ teaspoon salt, divided
4 (4-ounce) beef tenderloin fillets (1 inch thick)
Olive oil cooking spray
1 (7-ounce) jar roasted red bell peppers, drained

1. Combine garlic-pepper and ¼ teaspoon salt. Rub both sides of fillets with pepper mixture.
2. Place a large nonstick skillet coated with olive oil cooking spray over medium-high heat until hot. Add fillets; cook 2 to 3 minutes on each side or to desired degree of doneness.
3. While fillets cook, place bell peppers and remaining ¼ teaspoon salt in a blender. Cover and process until smooth. Serve fillets with roasted red pepper sauce. **Makes** 4 servings.
Note: Can't find garlic-pepper seasoning? Use ½ teaspoon black pepper and ½ teaspoon garlic powder instead.

Grecian Skillet Rib-eyes

You'll find that this olive-feta-herb topping works great on chicken and lamb, too.

20 minutes or less
PREP: 5 MIN., COOK: 14 MIN.

1½ teaspoons garlic powder
1½ teaspoons dried basil, crushed
1½ teaspoons dried oregano, crushed
½ teaspoon salt
⅛ teaspoon pepper
2 (1-inch-thick) rib-eye steaks (1¾ to 2 pounds)
1 tablespoon olive oil
1 tablespoon fresh lemon juice
2 tablespoons crumbled feta cheese
1 tablespoon chopped kalamata or ripe olives

1. Combine first 5 ingredients; rub evenly onto all sides of steaks.
2. Add oil to a large nonstick skillet; place over medium heat until hot. Add steaks, and cook 10 to 14 minutes or to desired degree of doneness, turning once. Sprinkle with lemon juice; top with cheese and olives. **Makes** 2 to 4 servings.

Sirloin Steaks With Thyme Pesto

30 minutes or less
PREP: 3 MIN., COOK: 19 MIN.

2 tablespoons pine nuts
2 (12-ounce) boneless beef top loin steaks, trimmed
¾ teaspoon salt, divided
½ teaspoon coarsely ground pepper
⅓ cup fresh thyme leaves
½ cup chopped fresh parsley
1 garlic clove, chopped
¼ cup freshly grated Parmesan cheese
2 tablespoons olive oil

1. Bake pine nuts in a shallow pan at 350°, stirring occasionally, 5 minutes or until toasted; cool.
2. Coat steaks evenly with ½ teaspoon salt and pepper.
3. Grill, covered with grill lid, over medium-high heat (350° to 400°) 7 minutes on each side or to desired degree of doneness. Keep warm.
4. Process pine nuts, remaining ¼ teaspoon salt, thyme, and next 4 ingredients in a blender until smooth. Serve with steaks. **Makes** 4 to 6 servings.

Flank Steak With Tomato-Olive Relish

PREP: 10 MIN., COOK: 27 MIN.

1½ pounds flank steak
¾ teaspoon salt
¾ teaspoon coarsely ground pepper
3 tablespoons olive oil
2 garlic cloves, thinly sliced
½ cup red wine or chicken broth
1 (14½-ounce) can Italian-style diced tomatoes
½ cup pitted black olives, sliced
1 tablespoon balsamic vinegar
3 tablespoons minced fresh parsley

1. Sprinkle flank steak evenly with salt and pepper.
2. Cook steak in hot oil in a large skillet over medium-high heat 6 to 8 minutes on each side or to desired degree of doneness.
3. Drain, reserving 1 tablespoon drippings in skillet; add garlic, and sauté 1 minute. Add wine, tomatoes, olives, and vinegar; cook 10 minutes or until reduced by half. Stir in parsley. Cut steak diagonally across the grain into thin slices; serve with tomato mixture. **Makes** 6 servings.

Eye of Round Roast

The roast cooks for an hour, but this make-ahead recipe really saves you time. You prep the meat, cover and chill 8 hours or overnight, and then bake. A little work in advance delivers lots of flavor.

PREP: 15 MIN.; COOK: 1 HR.; OTHER: 8 HR., 30 MIN.

make ahead

1 (2.5-pound) eye of round roast
1 (5-ounce) jar Chinese sweet-hot mustard
3 tablespoons olive oil
2 garlic cloves, pressed
2 teaspoons lite soy sauce
1 teaspoon Worcestershire sauce
Roasted Potatoes, uncooked

1. Place roast on an 18- x 11-inch piece of heavy-duty aluminum foil.
2. Stir together mustard, olive oil, garlic, soy sauce, and Worcestershire sauce; spread over roast. Fold foil over roast to seal. Place in a shallow roasting pan, and chill at least 8 hours. Remove roast from foil; place in roasting pan. Let stand 15 minutes.
3. Bake, covered, at 450° for 20 minutes. Arrange uncooked Roasted Potatoes around roast, and bake, uncovered, 40 more minutes or until potatoes are tender and roast is desired degree of doneness. Remove pan from oven; lightly cover, and let stand 15 minutes before slicing. **Makes** 4 servings.

Roasted Potatoes:

PREP: 10 MIN., COOK: 25 MIN.

4 medium potatoes, cut into 8 wedges
2 medium onions, cut into wedges
2 tablespoons olive oil
2 garlic cloves, pressed
1 teaspoon salt
½ teaspoon pepper

1. Toss together all ingredients. **Makes** 4 servings.

Eye of Round Roast

Beef and Kraut Skillet Dinner

Tangy sauerkraut gives this beefy skillet entrée a German accent.

PREP: 5 MIN., COOK: 35 MIN.

1 tablespoon butter or margarine
1 (14-ounce) can sauerkraut, undrained
½ cup uncooked long-grain rice
½ cup water
1 medium onion, chopped
1 pound ground round, crumbled
½ teaspoon salt
¼ teaspoon pepper
1 (8-ounce) can tomato sauce

1. Melt butter in a large skillet over medium heat. Spread sauerkraut evenly in skillet; layer rice, ½ cup water, onion, and ground round over sauerkraut. Sprinkle evenly with salt and pepper; top with tomato sauce. Cover and cook over medium heat 35 minutes. Serve from skillet. **Makes** 4 to 6 servings.

Teriyaki Burgers

Cooking the burgers over medium-low heat keeps the honey in them from burning.

30 minutes or less
PREP: 5 MIN., COOK: 20 MIN.

1½ pounds ground beef
3 tablespoons teriyaki or soy sauce
1 tablespoon honey
1 teaspoon salt
¾ teaspoon ground ginger
2 garlic cloves, minced
4 sesame seed hamburger buns,
    toasted
Lettuce leaves
Red onion slices
Chinese sweet-hot mustard

1. Combine first 6 ingredients; shape into 4 patties. Cook patties in a large skillet over medium-low heat 20 minutes, turning once.
2. Place patties on buns with lettuce and onion; serve with Chinese mustard. **Makes** 4 servings.

Individual Meat Loaves

Individual Meat Loaves

You can reduce sodium by omitting seasoned salt and using only half a bottle of chili sauce.

PREP: 20 MIN., COOK: 1 HR., OTHER: 10 MIN.

2 pounds lean ground beef
1 tablespoon reduced-sodium Worcestershire sauce
½ teaspoon seasoned salt
½ teaspoon seasoned pepper
1 medium onion, minced
5 white bread slices, crusts removed
½ cup fat-free milk
¼ cup egg substitute
1½ cups soft breadcrumbs
1 (12-ounce) bottle chili sauce
½ cup boiling water

1. Combine ground beef and next 4 ingredients; set aside.

2. Cut bread into small pieces. Place bread, milk, and egg substitute in a large bowl. Beat at medium speed with an electric mixer until blended.

3. Stir meat mixture into egg mixture. Shape mixture into 6 loaves; roll in 1½ cups soft breadcrumbs.

4. Arrange loaves in a lightly greased 13- x 9-inch pan. Spread chili sauce over loaves. Pour ½ cup boiling water into pan.

5. Bake at 350° for 1 hour or until beef is no longer pink in center. Let stand 10 minutes before serving. **Makes** 6 servings.

Herbed Meat Loaf With
Tomato Gravy

Herbed Meat Loaf With Tomato Gravy
PREP: 30 MIN., COOK: 1 HR.

1 (8-ounce) jar dried tomatoes in oil
1 medium onion, diced
1 green bell pepper, diced
2 garlic cloves, pressed
1¾ pounds ground round
2 large eggs
1 whole wheat bread slice, torn into small pieces
½ cup (2 ounces) shredded sharp provolone cheese
2 teaspoons dried basil
1 teaspoon dried oregano
1 teaspoon pepper
½ teaspoon salt
½ teaspoon dried thyme
Tomato Gravy

1. Drain dried tomatoes, reserving 1 tablespoon oil. Reserve 6 tomatoes for Tomato Gravy. Chop remaining tomatoes.
2. Heat reserved 1 tablespoon tomato oil in a large skillet over medium-high heat; add onion, bell pepper, and garlic. Sauté 5 minutes or until tender. Stir in chopped tomatoes, ground round, and next 8 ingredients. Shape into a loaf, and place in a lightly greased 9- x 5-inch loaf pan.
3. Bake at 350° for 55 minutes or until beef is no longer pink in center. Remove from pan, reserving ¼ cup drippings for Tomato Gravy. Keep meat loaf warm, and serve with gravy. **Makes** 6 servings.

Tomato Gravy:
PREP: 15 MIN., COOK: 10 MIN.

1¼ cups milk
2½ tablespoons all-purpose flour
6 reserved dried tomatoes, chopped
¼ cup reserved meat loaf drippings
1 tablespoon diced green onions
¼ teaspoon salt
¼ teaspoon dried basil
⅛ teaspoon pepper

1. Whisk together 1¼ cups milk and flour in a saucepan until smooth. Whisk in remaining ingredients. Cook mixture over medium heat, whisking constantly, 10 minutes or until thickened. **Makes** 1½ cups.

Reuben Loaf
PREP: 20 MIN., COOK: 50 MIN.

2 (12-ounce) cans corned beef, crumbled
2 cups soft breadcrumbs
2 large eggs
2 tablespoons chopped fresh parsley
¼ teaspoon garlic salt
1 (14-ounce) can chopped sauerkraut, drained
1 cup (4 ounces) shredded Swiss cheese
½ teaspoon caraway seeds
3 (1-ounce) Swiss cheese slices, cut in half diagonally

1. Stir together crumbled corned beef, breadcrumbs, and next 3 ingredients in a bowl; shape into a 10-inch square on a sheet of heavy-duty plastic wrap. Wipe bowl clean.
2. Press sauerkraut between paper towels to remove excess moisture. Combine sauerkraut, shredded Swiss cheese, and caraway seeds in bowl; spoon down center of meat mixture.
3. Fold sides of meat mixture over sauerkraut mixture, lifting plastic wrap as needed. Remove plastic wrap. Press edges and ends of meat mixture to seal, and place, seam side down, in a lightly greased 13- x 9-inch pan.
4. Bake at 350° for 45 minutes or until beef is no longer pink in center. Arrange cheese slices on top, and bake 5 more minutes. Serve immediately. **Makes** 8 servings.

Veal in Lime Sauce

Complement these succulent cutlets by pairing with roasted asparagus drizzled with a bit of lime juice.

30 minutes or less
PREP: 13 MIN., COOK: 10 MIN.

1 pound veal cutlets (¼ inch thick)
¼ teaspoon salt
¼ teaspoon freshly ground pepper
Butter-flavored cooking spray
2 tablespoons fresh lime juice
2 tablespoons dry white wine
4 teaspoons all-purpose flour
½ cup chicken broth
⅔ cup fat-free evaporated milk

1. Sprinkle veal cutlets with salt and pepper. Coat a large nonstick skillet with butter-flavored cooking spray; place over medium-high heat until hot. Add cutlets; cook 1 minute on each side or until browned. Remove from skillet; set aside, and keep warm.
2. Add lime juice and wine to skillet; cook over high heat 1 minute or until mixture is reduced by half. Combine flour, broth, and milk; stir well. Add to lime juice mixture. Cook over medium heat, stirring constantly, 5 minutes or until thickened and bubbly. Return cutlets to skillet; cook until thoroughly heated. Transfer to a serving platter, and serve immediately.
Makes 4 servings.

Lamb and Vegetable Stir-fry

The thinner the lamb cutlets, the quicker and more evenly the strips of meat will cook.

20 minutes or less
PREP: 10 MIN., COOK: 8 MIN.

1½ pounds boneless leg of lamb top cutlets
    (½ inch thick)
2 tablespoons olive oil, divided
1 medium onion, sliced
1 red bell pepper, cut into thin strips
1 yellow bell pepper, cut into thin strips
1 teaspoon minced garlic
1 (6-ounce) package fresh baby spinach
¾ teaspoon salt
¾ teaspoon black pepper
¼ to ½ teaspoon dried crushed red pepper
Hot cooked rice

1. Cut lamb diagonally across the grain into wafer-thin slices.
2. Heat 1 tablespoon oil in a wok or Dutch oven over medium-high heat 1 minute. Add lamb; stir-fry 3 minutes. Remove from wok, and drain well.
3. Wipe wok with paper towels. Add remaining 1 tablespoon oil to wok, and heat over medium-high heat. Add onion and next 3 ingredients; stir-fry 2 minutes. Add spinach and lamb, and stir-fry 1 minute or until spinach wilts. Stir in salt, black pepper, and crushed red pepper. Serve over hot rice. **Makes** 4 servings.

Skillet Sausage, Peppers, and Mushrooms

Skillet Sausage, Peppers, and Mushrooms

This chunky blend doubles as a one-dish meal or as a sandwich filling spooned over French rolls.

PREP: 7 MIN., COOK: 38 MIN.

1 (1¼-pound) package link Italian sausage
1 cup dry white wine
1 medium onion, sliced
1 garlic clove, minced
2 medium-size green bell peppers, cut into strips
1 (8-ounce) package sliced fresh mushrooms
2 (8-ounce) cans tomato sauce

1. Brown sausage in a 10-inch cast-iron skillet; add wine. Bring to a boil; cover, reduce heat, and simmer 10 minutes or until sausage is done. Uncover, bring to a boil, and reduce wine by two-thirds. Remove sausage, reserving drippings in skillet; keep sausage warm.

2. Add onion, garlic, bell pepper, and mushrooms to skillet; sauté until tender. Return sausage to skillet; add tomato sauce. Simmer 8 minutes or to desired consistency. **Makes** 5 servings.

Peachy Pork Picante

Peachy Pork Picante

Taco seasoning and salsa team up with peach preserves to give chunks of pork a sweet-and-spicy persuasion. The taste this dish delivers belies the short cook time. Want more "picante" in your Peachy Pork? Use hot salsa instead of mild to kick the flavor up a notch.

20 minutes or less
PREP: 2 MIN., COOK: 18 MIN.

1 pound boneless pork, cubed
1 (1.25-ounce) package taco seasoning mix
1 tablespoon vegetable oil
¼ cup peach preserves
1 (8-ounce) jar mild salsa
Hot cooked rice
Garnish: fresh cilantro

1. Place pork in a large zip-top plastic freezer bag; add taco seasoning mix. Seal bag, and shake to coat pork.
2. Heat oil in a large skillet over medium-high heat. Add pork; cook, stirring constantly, until browned on all sides. Stir in preserves and salsa; cover, reduce heat, and simmer 15 minutes, stirring occasionally. Serve over rice. Garnish, if desired. **Makes** 4 servings.

Fruited Pork Chops

You can save on calories by using fat-free French dressing.

30 minutes or less
PREP: 3 MIN., COOK: 25 MIN.

4 (½-inch-thick) bone-in pork loin chops, trimmed
1 tablespoon vegetable oil
1 (8-ounce) can pineapple chunks, drained
1 cup pitted prunes
½ cup dried apricot halves
½ cup spicy sweet French dressing

1. Brown pork chops in hot oil in a large nonstick skillet over medium-high heat. Place pineapple, prunes, and apricots over pork chops. Pour dressing over fruit. Bring to a boil; cover, reduce heat, and simmer 20 minutes or until pork chops are done. **Makes** 4 servings.

Ginger-Glazed Pork Chops

It's best to use fresh ginger found in the produce section, but 1 teaspoon ground ginger may be substituted.

PREP: 10 MIN., COOK: 15 MIN., OTHER: 10 MIN.

6 (½-inch-thick) bone-in pork chops
½ teaspoon salt
⅓ cup apricot preserves
3 garlic cloves, minced
1 tablespoon water
1 tablespoon soy sauce
1 tablespoon grated fresh ginger

1. Place pork chops on a lightly greased rack in an aluminum foil-lined roasting pan. Sprinkle evenly with salt.
2. Combine preserves and next 4 ingredients. Spread evenly over pork.
3. Broil 6 inches from heat 5 minutes. Reduce oven temperature to 425°. Bake 8 to 10 minutes or until a meat thermometer inserted into thickest portion registers 155°. Remove from oven; cover and let stand 10 minutes or until thermometer registers 160°. **Makes** 6 servings.

Ginger-Glazed Pork Tenderloin: Substitute 1 (2-pound) pork tenderloin for pork chops. Prepare pork as directed. Do not broil. Bake at 425° for 25 minutes or until a meat thermometer inserted in thickest portion registers 155°. Remove from oven; cover and let stand 10 minutes or until thermometer registers 160°. **Makes** 6 servings. Prep: 10 min., Cook: 25 min., Other: 10 min.

Honey-Pecan Pork Chops

Honey-Pecan Pork Chops

*A seasoned honey-pecan mixture adds crunch and flavor. The pork chops will hiss as they
hit the pan—a telltale sign that the skillet and oil are hot enough.*

30 minutes or less

PREP: 7 MIN., COOK: 15 MIN.

4 (¼-inch-thick) bone-in pork loin chops
¼ cup all-purpose flour
1 tablespoon butter or margarine
¼ cup honey
¼ cup chopped pecans
½ teaspoon Greek seasoning
¼ teaspoon ground red pepper

1. Dredge pork chops in flour.
2. Melt butter in a large skillet over high heat; add
pork chops, and cook 4 minutes on each side or until
browned. Remove pork chops, and drain on paper
towels; keep warm.
3. Stir together honey and next 3 ingredients; add
mixture to skillet. Reduce heat to medium-low; cook,
covered, 7 minutes.
4. Serve pork chops with sauce. **Makes** 4 servings.

Balsamic Pork Chops

PREP: 10 MIN., COOK: 20 MIN.

1 (6.2-ounce) box quick-cooking long-grain and wild
  rice mix
3 tablespoons all-purpose flour
1 teaspoon chopped fresh rosemary
½ teaspoon salt
½ teaspoon pepper
6 (¾-inch-thick) boneless pork loin chops
2 tablespoons butter or margarine
2 tablespoons olive oil
2 garlic cloves, pressed
1 (14-ounce) can chicken broth
⅓ cup balsamic vinegar
Garnish: fresh rosemary sprigs

1. Cook rice according to package directions; keep
warm.
2. Combine flour, 1 teaspoon rosemary, ½ teaspoon
salt, and ½ teaspoon pepper. Dredge pork chops in
flour mixture.
3. Melt butter with oil in a large skillet over medium-
high heat; add garlic, and sauté 1 minute. Add pork
chops, and cook 4 minutes on each side or until
golden. Remove pork chops.
4. Add broth and vinegar, stirring to loosen particles
from bottom of skillet. Cook 6 minutes or until liquid
is reduced by half. Add pork chops, and cook 5 minutes or until done. Serve over rice. Garnish, if desired.
Makes 6 servings.

Balsamic Pork Chops

Fruity Baked Chicken

Fruity Baked Chicken

PREP: 20 MIN., COOK: 40 MIN.

2 (6-ounce) packages long-grain and wild rice mix
2 teaspoons salt, divided
⅓ cup all-purpose flour
½ teaspoon pepper
½ teaspoon paprika
6 skinned and boned chicken breasts
¼ cup vegetable oil
1 large sweet onion, diced
1 (7-ounce) package chopped mixed dried fruit (we used SunMaid FruitBits)
2 cups chicken broth
½ cup frozen orange juice concentrate, thawed
1 tablespoon grated fresh ginger
1 teaspoon chili-garlic paste
2 teaspoons cornstarch
¼ cup water

1. Prepare rice mix according to package directions, omitting seasoning packets; add 1 teaspoon salt. Set aside.
2. Combine flour, pepper, paprika, and remaining 1 teaspoon salt in a large bowl. Dredge chicken in flour mixture.
3. Cook chicken in hot oil in a skillet over medium heat about 2 minutes on each side. Remove from skillet; set aside. Add onion to skillet; sauté over medium-high heat, stirring often, 5 minutes. Stir in fruit and next 4 ingredients; bring to a boil.
4. Combine cornstarch and ¼ cup water. Stir into fruit mixture; cook 1 minute.
5. Spoon rice into a lightly greased 13- x 9-inch baking dish. Place chicken over rice. Spoon fruit mixture over chicken.
6. Bake, covered, at 350° for 30 minutes. **Makes** 6 servings.

Easy Chicken Cordon Bleu

PREP: 20 MIN., COOK: 25 MIN.

½ teaspoon salt
¼ teaspoon pepper
6 skinned and boned chicken breasts
1 (5.5-ounce) box seasoned croutons, crushed
⅓ cup shredded Parmesan cheese
2 egg whites
2 tablespoons water
12 thin slices smoked ham
6 Swiss cheese slices
Honey mustard dressing (optional)

1. Sprinkle salt and pepper over chicken; set aside.
2. Combine crouton crumbs and shredded Parmesan cheese in a large zip-top plastic bag. Whisk together egg whites and 2 tablespoons water in a shallow bowl.
3. Dip chicken in egg white mixture, and drain. Place 1 breast in bag; seal and shake to coat. Remove to a lightly greased aluminum foil-lined baking sheet, and repeat with remaining chicken.
4. Bake at 450° for 20 minutes or until chicken is done. Top each breast with 2 ham slices and 1 Swiss cheese slice. Bake 5 more minutes or until cheese melts. Serve with honey mustard dressing, if desired. **Makes** 6 servings.

Mushroom Chicken Bake

Mushroom soup and wine combine to create a savory sauce that's spooned over cheese-topped chicken breasts.

PREP: 5 MIN., COOK: 35 MIN.

make
ahead

8 skinned and boned chicken breasts
8 (1-ounce) Swiss cheese slices
1¼ cups sliced fresh mushrooms
1 (10¾-ounce) can cream of mushroom or cream of chicken soup, undiluted
¼ cup dry white wine
2 cups seasoned stuffing mix (we used Pepperidge Farm)
¼ cup butter or margarine, melted

1. Place chicken in a single layer in a lightly greased 13- x 9-inch baking dish. Top each breast with a cheese slice; sprinkle with mushrooms. Combine soup and wine in a bowl; pour over chicken. Sprinkle with stuffing; drizzle with butter. Bake, uncovered, at 350° for 35 minutes or until chicken is done. **Makes** 8 servings.

Chicken Parmesan

Chicken Parmesan

This can be put together in a large shallow dish or on individual ovenproof plates, if desired.

30 minutes or less
PREP: 12 MIN., COOK: 12 MIN.

8 ounces uncooked spaghetti
4 skinned and boned chicken breasts
½ cup Italian-seasoned breadcrumbs
¼ cup grated Parmesan cheese
⅓ cup all-purpose flour
1 egg, lightly beaten
1 tablespoon olive oil
3 cups pasta sauce, divided
1 cup (4 ounces) shredded part-skim mozzarella
    cheese

1. Cook pasta according to package directions, including salt. Drain pasta, and keep warm.
2. Meanwhile, place each chicken breast between 2 sheets of heavy-duty plastic wrap; flatten to ¼-inch thickness, using a meat mallet or rolling pin.
3. Combine breadcrumbs and Parmesan cheese in a shallow dish. Dredge 1 chicken breast in flour. Dip in egg; dredge in breadcrumb mixture. Repeat procedure with remaining chicken, flour, egg, and breadcrumb mixture.
4. Heat oil in a large nonstick skillet over medium-high heat. Add chicken; cook 4 minutes on each side or until done.
5. Place spaghetti evenly on each of 4 gratin dishes. Spoon ½ cup pasta sauce over each serving. Top each with 1 chicken breast half. Spoon ¼ cup sauce over each serving. Sprinkle each serving with ¼ cup mozzarella cheese.
6. Place gratin dishes on a baking sheet; broil 4 minutes or until cheese melts. **Makes** 4 servings.

Mediterranean Chicken Breasts on Eggplant

We like to leave the skin on the eggplant for texture and fiber, but you can peel it if you'd prefer. For more flavor, substitute basil-and-tomato-flavored feta cheese for regular feta cheese.

PREP: 8 MIN., COOK: 37 MIN.

1 small eggplant
¾ teaspoon salt, divided
½ teaspoon pepper, divided
¼ cup all-purpose flour
6 tablespoons olive oil, divided
4 skinned and boned chicken breasts
1 teaspoon minced garlic
1½ cups tomato and basil pasta sauce (we used
    Classico)
½ cup crumbled feta cheese

1. Cut eggplant into ¾-inch-thick slices.
2. Combine ¼ teaspoon each of salt and pepper with flour in a shallow dish. Dredge eggplant slices in flour mixture, shaking off excess flour mixture.
3. Heat 4 tablespoons olive oil in a large skillet over medium-high heat; add eggplant slices, and cook 2 to 3 minutes on each side or until golden. Drain on paper towels. Arrange in a single layer in a lightly greased 13- x 9-inch baking dish.
4. Sprinkle chicken with remaining ½ teaspoon salt and ¼ teaspoon pepper.
5. Brown chicken in remaining 2 tablespoons oil in a large skillet over medium-high heat 5 minutes on each side. Remove chicken, reserving drippings in skillet. Place chicken breasts on top of eggplant slices.
6. Cook garlic in pan drippings over medium-high heat 1 minute, stirring constantly. Add pasta sauce; cook 5 minutes, stirring often. Spoon over chicken; sprinkle with cheese. Bake, uncovered, at 425° for 15 minutes. Serve immediately. **Makes** 4 servings.

Chicken in Tomato
and Basil Cream

Chicken in Tomato and Basil Cream

We suggest serving this quick and easy dish over buttered penne pasta with a side of hot garlic bread.
Put the pot of water on as soon as you start the chicken.

PREP: 6 MIN., COOK: 35 MIN.

1 tablespoon butter
6 skinned and boned chicken breasts
½ cup finely chopped onion
1 tablespoon butter or margarine, melted
1 (16-ounce) can diced tomatoes, undrained
½ cup heavy whipping cream
½ cup shredded fresh basil
1 teaspoon salt
½ teaspoon freshly ground pepper
Hot cooked pasta (optional)
Garnish: basil sprigs

1. Melt butter in a large nonstick skillet over medium-high heat. Add chicken; cook 3 to 4 minutes on each side or until browned. Remove from skillet.
2. Cook chopped onion in melted butter in skillet over medium heat 5 minutes or until onion is tender. Increase heat to high, and add tomatoes; cook until liquid is almost absorbed. Add whipping cream, and cook until slightly thickened. Remove sauce from heat; add shredded basil, salt, and pepper.
3. Place chicken in an 11- x 7-inch baking dish; pour sauce over chicken. Bake, uncovered, at 450° for 10 minutes or until done. Serve over hot cooked pasta, if desired. Garnish, if desired. **Makes** 6 servings.

Tarragon Cream Chicken

Calling all tarragon lovers! With a rich tarragon-garlic sauce, this simple chicken dish is sure to make all mouths happy at the dinner table.

30 minutes or less
PREP: 9 MIN., COOK: 16 MIN.

4 skinned and boned chicken breasts
½ teaspoon salt
½ teaspoon ground white pepper
3 tablespoons butter or margarine
2 tablespoons lemon juice
1 cup whipping cream
⅓ cup minced green onions
2 tablespoons chopped fresh tarragon
½ teaspoon minced garlic
¼ teaspoon salt
¼ teaspoon ground white pepper
Garnishes: lemon slices, fresh tarragon sprigs

1. Place chicken between 2 sheets of heavy-duty plastic wrap; flatten to ¼-inch thickness, using a meat mallet or rolling pin.
2. Combine ½ teaspoon each of salt and white pepper; sprinkle over both sides of chicken.
3. Melt butter in a large nonstick skillet over medium-high heat. Add chicken; cook 5 minutes on each side or until done. Remove from skillet, and keep warm.
4. Add lemon juice to skillet, and cook over high heat 30 seconds, stirring to loosen particles from bottom of skillet.
5. Add cream and next 5 ingredients; bring to a boil. Cook, stirring constantly, 4 minutes or until slightly thickened. Pour over chicken. Garnish, if desired.
Makes 4 servings.

Chicken Piccata

Make less mess in the kitchen, and save time in cleanup, by dredging the chicken in a plastic bag.

30 minutes or less
PREP: 7 MIN., COOK: 14 MIN.

1 large egg, lightly beaten
1 tablespoon lemon juice
4 skinned and boned chicken breasts
⅓ cup all-purpose flour
¼ teaspoon salt
¼ teaspoon pepper
⅛ teaspoon garlic powder
¼ cup butter or margarine
½ cup hot water
2 teaspoons chicken bouillon granules
2 tablespoons lemon juice
Garnish: lemon slices

1. Combine egg and 1 tablespoon lemon juice. Dip chicken in egg mixture.
2. Combine flour and next 3 ingredients in a zip-top plastic freezer bag. Add chicken; seal bag, and shake to coat.
3. Melt butter in a large nonstick skillet over medium-high heat. Add chicken; cook 5 minutes on each side or until done. Remove from pan, and keep warm.
4. Combine ½ cup hot water, bouillon, and 2 tablespoons lemon juice, stirring until bouillon dissolves. Add bouillon mixture to skillet. Bring to boil, and cook over high heat 3 minutes or until mixture reduces to ¼ cup. Spoon sauce over chicken. Garnish, if desired.
Makes 4 servings.

Chicken Dijon

Chicken Dijon

Serve this family favorite with roasted potatoes and sweet peas.

PREP: 10 MIN., COOK: 25 MIN.

6 skinned and boned chicken breasts
1 teaspoon salt
½ teaspoon pepper
3 tablespoons butter
1 (14½-ounce) can chicken broth
1 medium-size sweet onion, diced
2 tablespoons all-purpose flour
3 tablespoons Dijon mustard

1. Sprinkle chicken evenly with salt and pepper.
2. Melt butter in a large skillet over medium-high heat; add chicken, and cook 2 minutes on each side or until golden brown.
3. Whisk together chicken broth and next 3 ingredients; pour over chicken. Cover, reduce heat to low, and simmer 20 minutes. **Makes** 6 servings.

Smothered Chicken

Tomato-Red Onion Salad (page 354) and mashed potatoes pair nicely with this entrée.

PREP: 20 MIN., COOK: 40 MIN.

4 skinned and boned chicken breasts
¾ teaspoon salt, divided
½ teaspoon pepper, divided
½ cup Italian-seasoned breadcrumbs
1 (8-ounce) package sliced fresh mushrooms
1 teaspoon olive oil
18 to 20 garlic cloves, crushed
2 tablespoons olive oil, divided
2 tablespoons butter or margarine, divided
1 (14-ounce) can chicken broth
1 tablespoon fresh lemon juice
½ teaspoon dried basil
¼ teaspoon dried oregano
3 tablespoons all-purpose flour
¼ cup water

1. Place chicken between 2 sheets of heavy-duty plastic wrap; flatten to a ¼-inch thickness, using a meat mallet or rolling pin. Sprinkle both sides of chicken evenly with ½ teaspoon salt and ¼ teaspoon pepper. Dredge in breadcrumbs. Set aside.

2. Sauté mushrooms in 1 teaspoon hot oil in a large nonstick skillet over medium-high heat 8 minutes or until edges are browned. Remove from skillet. Sprinkle with remaining ¼ teaspoon salt and ¼ teaspoon pepper; set aside.

3. Sauté garlic in 1 tablespoon hot oil over medium heat 5 to 10 minutes or until lightly browned and soft. Remove from skillet, and mash lightly with a fork or potato masher; set aside.

4. Melt 1 tablespoon butter with ½ tablespoon oil in skillet over medium heat; add 2 chicken breasts, and cook 4 minutes on each side or until done. Remove chicken to a wire rack in a jelly-roll pan. Keep chicken warm in a 225° oven. Repeat with remaining butter, oil, and chicken.

5. Stir chicken broth and next 3 ingredients into skillet, and cook 2 minutes, stirring to loosen particles from bottom of skillet. Stir in sautéed mushrooms and garlic.

6. Stir together 3 tablespoons flour and ¼ cup water; whisk into broth mixture over medium-high heat. Cook, whisking constantly, 3 minutes or until thickened. **Makes** 4 servings.

Smothered Chicken

Chicken Cakes With
Rémoulade Sauce

Chicken Cakes With Rémoulade Sauce

Make smaller patties for appetizer servings.

PREP: 10 MIN., COOK: 20 MIN.

2 tablespoons butter or margarine
½ red bell pepper, diced
4 green onions, thinly sliced
1 garlic clove, pressed
3 cups chopped cooked chicken
1 cup soft breadcrumbs
1 large egg, lightly beaten
2 tablespoons mayonnaise
1 tablespoon Creole mustard
2 teaspoons Creole seasoning
¼ cup vegetable oil
Rémoulade Sauce
Garnish: mixed baby greens

1. Melt butter in a large skillet over medium heat. Add bell pepper, green onions, and garlic, and sauté 3 to 4 minutes or until vegetables are tender.
2. Stir together bell pepper mixture, chicken, and next 5 ingredients. Shape mixture into 8 (3½-inch) patties.

3. Fry 4 patties in 2 tablespoons hot oil in a large skillet over medium heat 3 minutes on each side or until golden brown. Drain on paper towels. Repeat procedure with remaining 2 tablespoons oil and patties. Serve immediately with Rémoulade Sauce. Garnish, if desired. **Makes** 4 servings.

Rémoulade Sauce:

PREP: 5 MIN.

1 cup mayonnaise
3 green onions, sliced
2 garlic cloves, pressed
2 tablespoons Creole mustard
1 tablespoon chopped fresh parsley
¼ teaspoon ground red pepper
Garnish: sliced green onions

1. Stir together first 6 ingredients until well blended. Garnish, if desired. **Makes** 1¼ cups.

Lemon Chicken Stir-fry

The lemon zing of this dish is sure to make you pucker a little.

20 minutes or less
PREP: 10 MIN., COOK: 10 MIN.

2 tablespoons soy sauce
¼ cup water
1 tablespoon cornstarch
½ cup lemon juice
2 tablespoons sugar
2 tablespoons vegetable oil
1 pound chicken breast strips, cut into chunks
3 green onions, sliced
1 large carrot, sliced
1 large green bell pepper, cut into strips
2 garlic cloves, minced
Hot cooked rice

1. Combine soy sauce and next 4 ingredients in a small bowl. Set aside.
2. Heat oil in a large skillet over medium heat; add chicken, and stir-fry 3 to 4 minutes or until browned. Add green onions and next 3 ingredients to chicken; cook, stirring often, 2 to 3 minutes or until vegetables are tender. Stir in soy sauce mixture; cook 2 minutes or until sauce begins to thicken. Serve over hot cooked rice. **Makes** 2 to 3 servings.

Sweet-and-Sour Apricot Chicken

Apricot halves lend a juicy texture and pleasant sweetness to this quick stir-fry.

20 minutes or less
PREP: 5 MIN., COOK: 12 MIN.

2 tablespoons vegetable oil
4 skinned and boned chicken breasts
1 (15-ounce) can apricot halves, drained
1 (10-ounce) bottle sweet-and-sour sauce (we used La Choy)
1½ tablespoons rice wine vinegar
3 green onions, sliced
Hot cooked rice

1. Heat oil in a large nonstick skillet over medium-high heat. Add chicken; cook 5 minutes on each side or until done.
2. Add apricot halves; cook, stirring constantly, 1 minute. Add sweet-and-sour sauce and vinegar; cook, stirring constantly, 1 minute or until mixture thickens.
3. Sprinkle with green onions. Serve over hot cooked rice. **Makes** 4 servings.

Turkey-Basil Piccata

Turkey-Basil Piccata

A sauce made of white wine, lemon juice, and skillet drippings is drizzled over this extra-quick dish.

10 minutes or less

PREP: 5 MIN., COOK: 5 MIN.

2 tablespoons all-purpose flour
¼ teaspoon salt
¼ teaspoon pepper
1 (¾-pound) package turkey cutlets
2 tablespoons olive oil
4 garlic cloves, minced
1½ teaspoons dried or 1½ tablespoons chopped
    fresh basil
½ cup dry white wine
1½ tablespoons fresh lemon juice
1 lemon, sliced

1. Combine flour and next 2 ingredients in a shallow dish; dredge turkey cutlets in flour mixture, shaking off excess.
2. Cook turkey cutlets in hot oil in a large skillet over medium-high heat, 1½ minutes on each side or until done. Remove from skillet; keep warm.
3. Reduce heat to medium-low. Add minced garlic and basil to skillet, and sauté 45 seconds. Add wine, lemon juice, and lemon slices; cook, stirring to loosen particles from bottom of skillet. Return turkey cutlets to pan; cook just until thoroughly heated. Serve immediately. **Makes** 3 to 4 servings.

Sesame-Crusted Turkey Mignons

PREP: 20 MIN., COOK: 24 MIN.

½ cup sesame seeds, toasted
¼ cup olive oil
1 garlic clove, minced
1 tablespoon chopped fresh chives
1 tablespoon soy sauce
2 teaspoons fresh lemon juice
1 teaspoon grated fresh ginger
½ teaspoon dark sesame oil
2 (11-ounce) packages turkey mignons (see note)
Garnishes: halved lemon slices, chopped fresh parsley
  or cilantro
Creamy Wine Sauce (optional)
Hot cooked noodles (optional)

1. Stir together first 8 ingredients; dredge turkey in sesame seed mixture. Place on a greased rack in a broiler pan.
2. Broil 5½ inches from heat 12 minutes on each side or until done. Place turkey on a platter; garnish, if desired. Serve with Creamy Wine Sauce and hot cooked noodles, if desired. **Makes** 4 servings.

Note: 2 turkey tenderloins, cut in half, may be substituted for turkey mignons.

Creamy Wine Sauce:
This sauce is delicious served with Sesame-Crusted Turkey Mignons or just over pasta.

PREP: 5 MIN., COOK: 15 MIN.

1 cup fruity white wine (we used Liebfraumilch, see
  note)
2 teaspoons lemon juice
¼ cup whipping cream
⅓ cup butter or margarine
2 tablespoons soy sauce

1. Bring wine and lemon juice to a boil over medium-high heat. Boil 6 to 8 minutes or until mixture is reduced by half. Whisk in cream. Cook 3 to 4 minutes, whisking constantly, until thickened.
2. Reduce heat to a simmer; whisk in butter and soy sauce until butter is melted. **Makes** ¾ cup.
Note: 1 cup white grape juice may be substituted for fruity white wine.

Sesame-Crusted Turkey Mignons

Fish Florentine

Fish Florentine

Brown rice rounds out this meal nicely.

PREP: 10 MIN., COOK: 25 MIN.

2 (6-ounce) sea bass or other firm white fish fillets
1 (12-ounce) package frozen spinach soufflé, thawed
⅓ cup cracker crumbs (we used saltines)
3 tablespoons freshly grated Parmesan cheese

1. Place fish in a lightly greased 11- x 7-inch baking dish, or place 1 in each of 2 individual gratin dishes. Top with spinach soufflé.
2. Combine cracker crumbs and cheese; sprinkle evenly over spinach. Bake, uncovered, at 400° for 25 minutes or until fish flakes with a fork. **Makes** 2 servings.

Parmesan-Crusted Orange Roughy

Three ingredients are all it takes to make this crispy family favorite.

20 minutes or less
PREP: 5 MIN., COOK: 9 MIN.

4 (6-ounce) orange roughy fillets
    (1 inch thick)
3 tablespoons freshly shredded
    Parmesan cheese
1 teaspoon dried dillweed

1. Arrange fillets in a single layer in a lightly greased 15- x 10-inch jelly-roll pan. Combine Parmesan cheese and dillweed. Sprinkle evenly over fillets.
2. Bake at 450° for 7 to 9 minutes or until fish flakes with a fork. **Makes** 4 servings.

New England Stuffed Flounder

Stuffing these fillets is simple—rolling them up and securing them with wooden picks creates a nestling of breadcrumbs in the middle.

PREP: 18 MIN., COOK: 20 MIN.

1¼ cups soft breadcrumbs (fresh)
½ cup butter, melted and divided
⅓ cup grated onion
¼ cup chopped fresh parsley
1 tablespoon fresh lemon juice
1 tablespoon soy sauce
¼ teaspoon pepper
¼ teaspoon ground sage
8 (6-ounce) flounder fillets

1. Combine breadcrumbs, 6 tablespoons melted butter, and next 6 ingredients in a medium bowl.
2. Spoon 2 tablespoons breadcrumb mixture on top of each fillet. Roll up fillets, and secure each with a wooden pick. Place fillets in a lightly greased 13- x 9-inch baking dish; drizzle with remaining 2 tablespoons melted butter.
3. Bake at 400° for 20 minutes or until fish flakes with a fork. **Makes** 8 servings.

Broiled Salmon With Dijon-Caper
Cream Sauce

Broiled Salmon With Dijon-Caper Cream Sauce

20 minutes or less
PREP: 10 MIN., COOK: 7 MIN.

6 (6-ounce) salmon fillets
½ teaspoon salt
1 teaspoon pepper, divided
6 tablespoons coarse-grained Dijon mustard, divided
1 (8-ounce) container sour cream
1 (3-ounce) jar capers, well drained
Garnish: fresh parsley sprigs

1. Sprinkle salmon with salt and ½ teaspoon pepper; brush evenly with 2 tablespoons mustard. Place on a lightly greased rack in a broiler pan.
2. Broil 5½ inches from heat 7 minutes or until fish flakes with a fork.
3. Combine sour cream, capers, remaining ½ teaspoon pepper, and remaining 4 tablespoons mustard. Serve over salmon. Serve over fettuccine, if desired. Garnish, if desired. **Makes** 6 servings.

Tuna Steaks With Lemon Butter

Grilled tuna steaks are one of life's simple pleasures, satisfying even when unadorned. Here they're made better yet with a quick lemon sauce.

20 minutes or less
PREP: 10 MIN., COOK: 10 MIN.

¼ cup butter or margarine, softened
2 teaspoons lemon juice
4 (1-inch-thick) tuna steaks
½ teaspoon salt
½ teaspoon freshly ground pepper
2 tablespoons olive oil

1. Stir together butter and lemon juice.
2. Sprinkle tuna steaks evenly with salt and pepper.
3. Cook tuna in hot oil in a large nonstick skillet over medium-high heat 5 minutes on each side or until done. Serve immediately with butter mixture. **Makes** 4 servings.

Tuna With Sautéed Vegetables

PREP: 10 MIN., COOK: 20 MIN., OTHER: 1 HR.

½ cup olive oil
¼ cup dry white wine
2 tablespoons soy sauce
4 (4-ounce) tuna steaks
1 small onion, chopped
1 green bell pepper, chopped
1 medium tomato, chopped
1 garlic clove, minced
¼ teaspoon dried crushed red pepper
1 tablespoon olive oil

1. Combine first 3 ingredients in a shallow dish or large zip-top plastic bag; add tuna. Cover or seal, and chill 1 hour, turning occasionally. Remove tuna from marinade, discarding marinade.
2. Grill, without grill lid, over medium-high heat (350° to 400°) 3 to 4 minutes on each side or until fish flakes with a fork.
3. Sauté onion and next 4 ingredients in 1 tablespoon hot oil in a large skillet over medium-high heat until tender. Serve with tuna. **Makes** 4 servings.

Snappy Cajun Shrimp

Snappy Cajun Shrimp

The Cajun-style tomatoes give this recipe a bayou accent. If you want a little more spice with your shrimp,
add ½ teaspoon dried crushed red pepper in with the tomato.

20 minutes or less
PREP: 5 MIN., COOK: 13 MIN.

1 red bell pepper, chopped
1 green bell pepper, chopped
2 garlic cloves, minced
2 tablespoons olive oil
2 (14½-ounce) cans Cajun-style stewed tomatoes,
    undrained (we used Del Monte, see note)
1 (6-ounce) can tomato paste
1 teaspoon sugar
¾ pound cooked peeled, medium-size fresh shrimp
Hot cooked rice

1. Cook bell peppers and garlic in hot oil in a large skillet over medium-high heat until tender, stirring often.

2. Add tomatoes, tomato paste, and sugar. Bring to a boil; reduce heat, and simmer 8 minutes.

3. Add shrimp; cook until heated. Serve over hot cooked rice. **Makes** 4 servings.

Snappy Cajun Chicken: Substitute 2 cups chopped cooked chicken for shrimp.

Note: You can substitute 2 (14½-ounce) cans stewed tomatoes, 2 bay leaves, and 1 teaspoon Creole seasoning for the Cajun-style tomatoes. Discard bay leaves before serving.

Shrimp With Roasted Red Pepper Cream

30 minutes or less
PREP: 15 MIN., COOK: 10 MIN.

1 (7-ounce) package vermicelli
1 (12-ounce) jar roasted red bell peppers, drained (we used Alessi Sweet Pimento Italian-Style, Fire-Roasted Peppers)
1 (8-ounce) package ⅓-less-fat cream cheese, softened
½ cup low-sodium, fat-free chicken broth
3 garlic cloves, chopped
½ teaspoon ground red pepper
2 pounds cooked peeled, large fresh shrimp
¼ cup chopped fresh basil
Garnish: fresh basil sprigs

1. Prepare pasta according to package directions, omitting salt and fat. Keep warm.
2. Meanwhile, process bell peppers and next 4 ingredients in a blender or food processor until smooth, stopping to scrape down sides. Pour into a large skillet.
3. Cook over medium heat 5 minutes, stirring often, until thoroughly heated. Add shrimp, and cook, stirring occasionally, 2 minutes or until thoroughly heated. Remove from heat. Serve over hot cooked pasta. Sprinkle with chopped basil. Garnish, if desired. **Makes** 6 servings.

Lime Shrimp in Tortillas

30 minutes or less
PREP: 15 MIN., COOK: 9 MIN.

8 (6-inch) flour tortillas
1 small onion, sliced
½ green bell pepper, cut into strips
1 tablespoon olive oil
¾ pound cooked peeled, medium-size fresh shrimp
¼ cup fresh lime juice
2 teaspoons minced garlic
1 tablespoon minced fresh cilantro
½ teaspoon pepper
¼ teaspoon salt
Toppings: salsa, shredded Cheddar cheese, sour cream, lime wedges

1. Heat tortillas according to package directions; keep warm.
2. Cook onion and bell pepper in hot oil in a large skillet over medium-high heat, stirring constantly, 3 minutes or until tender. Add shrimp and next 5 ingredients to pan. Cook 3 minutes or just until shrimp are thoroughly heated.
3. Spoon mixture into warmed tortillas using a slotted spoon. Serve with desired toppings. **Makes** 4 servings.

Lemon-Garlic Shrimp

It's amazing how just a few simple ingredients can add so much flavor. This succulent shrimp sauté is a fine example.

20 minutes or less
PREP: 8 MIN., COOK: 8 MIN.

¾ pound peeled, large raw shrimp (see note)
3 tablespoons olive oil
2 large garlic cloves, minced
3 to 4 tablespoons fresh lemon juice
1 tablespoon finely chopped fresh parsley
½ teaspoon salt
⅛ teaspoon ground white pepper or ¼ teaspoon ground black pepper

1. Sauté shrimp in hot oil in a large skillet over medium-high heat just until shrimp turn pink; reduce heat to medium. Add garlic, lemon juice, and parsley; cook 1 minute. Sprinkle with salt and pepper. **Makes** 2 servings.
Note: Purchase 1 pound unpeeled, large raw shrimp if you want to peel your own.

Coconut Shrimp With Mustard Sauce

The crunchy coating on these shrimp serves as the perfect surface for soaking up the tangy mustard sauce.

30 minutes or less
PREP: 20 MIN., COOK: 2 MIN. PER BATCH

1½ pounds unpeeled, jumbo raw shrimp
2 cups all-purpose baking mix, divided
1 cup beer
½ teaspoon salt
⅛ to ¼ teaspoon ground red pepper
3 cups sweetened flaked coconut
Vegetable oil
Mustard Sauce

1. Peel shrimp, leaving tails intact; devein, if desired. Set aside.
2. Stir together 1 cup baking mix and 1 cup beer until smooth.
3. Stir together remaining 1 cup baking mix, salt, and pepper. Dredge shrimp in dry mixture, and dip in beer mixture, allowing excess coating to drip off. Gently roll shrimp in coconut.

4. Pour vegetable oil to a depth of 3 inches into a Dutch oven or heavy saucepan, and heat to 350°. Cook shrimp, in batches, 1 to 2 minutes or until golden; remove shrimp, and drain on paper towels. Serve immediately with Mustard Sauce. **Makes** 4 servings.

Mustard Sauce:
PREP: 5 MIN.

½ cup Dijon mustard
2 tablespoons light brown sugar
2 tablespoons beer
⅛ to ¼ teaspoon ground red pepper

1. Stir together all ingredients. **Makes** ⅔ cup.

Scallop-Veggie Skewers

The larger sea scallops are more common and easier to skewer than the smaller, more delicately flavored bay scallops.

PREP: 15 MIN., COOK: 20 MIN., OTHER: 30 MIN.

8 (12-inch) wooden skewers
¼ cup olive oil
3 tablespoons lemon juice
2 tablespoons chopped fresh parsley
½ teaspoon fennel seeds
½ teaspoon salt
2 garlic cloves, minced
1 pound large sea scallops, drained
1 zucchini, cut into ½-inch-thick slices
1 medium-size red onion, cut into 1-inch pieces
Lemon wedges (optional)

1. Soak 8 wooden skewers in warm water 30 minutes. Drain.
2. Combine oil and next 5 ingredients in a small bowl.
3. Place scallops, zucchini, and onion in a large zip-top plastic freezer bag. Add lemon juice mixture; seal bag, and marinate in refrigerator 20 minutes.
4. Remove scallops and vegetables from marinade, discarding marinade. Thread scallops and zucchini ¼-inch apart onto 4 skewers. Thread onion ¼-inch apart onto remaining 4 skewers.
5. Grill onion, covered with grill lid, over medium-high heat (350° to 400°) 5 minutes; add scallops. Grill, covered, 15 more minutes, turning once. Serve scallops and vegetables with lemon wedges, if desired. **Makes** 2 servings.

Scallop-Veggie Skewers

Mediterranean Frittata

Mediterranean Frittata

Serve this meatless main dish with crusty Italian bread.

30 minutes or less
PREP: 8 MIN., COOK: 22 MIN.

8 pitted kalamata olives, chopped (about ¼ cup)
1 medium zucchini, cut into ½-inch cubes (about
    2 cups)
1 red bell pepper, diced
½ cup chopped onion
¼ cup olive oil
9 large eggs, lightly beaten
½ (4-ounce) package crumbled feta cheese (about
    ½ cup)
⅓ cup thinly sliced fresh basil
½ teaspoon salt
⅓ cup freshly grated Parmesan cheese

1. Cook first 4 ingredients in hot oil in a 10-inch ovenproof skillet over medium-high heat, stirring constantly, until vegetables are tender.
2. Combine eggs and next 3 ingredients; pour into skillet over vegetables. Cover and cook over medium-low heat 10 to 12 minutes or until almost set. Remove from heat, and sprinkle with Parmesan cheese.
3. Broil 5½ inches from heat 2 to 3 minutes or until golden. Cut frittata into wedges. Serve warm or at room temperature. **Makes** 6 servings.

Bean-and-Cheese Chimichangas

To bake instead of frying, coat both sides of chimichangas with cooking spray, and place on a baking sheet. Bake at 425° for 8 minutes; turn chimichangas, and bake 5 more minutes.

30 minutes or less
PREP: 10 MIN., COOK: 20 MIN.

1 (16-ounce) can refried beans
1 cup (4 ounces) shredded Monterey Jack cheese
⅓ cup medium salsa
1 tablespoon taco seasoning mix
½ (5-ounce) package yellow rice mix, cooked
    (optional)
5 (10-inch) flour tortillas
2 cups vegetable oil
Shredded lettuce
Toppings: salsa, guacamole, sour cream

1. Stir together first 4 ingredients. Stir in rice, if desired. Place ⅓ cup mixture just below center of each tortilla. Fold opposite sides of tortillas over filling, forming rectangles; secure with wooden picks.
2. Pour oil into a large skillet; heat to 325°. Fry, in batches, 4 to 5 minutes on each side or until lightly browned. Drain on paper towels. Remove picks; arrange on lettuce. Serve with desired toppings. **Makes** 5 chimichangas.

Fresh Raspberry-Spinach
Salad, page 347

shortcut
SIDES 'n'
SALADS

Asian-Glazed
Asparagus

Asian-Glazed Asparagus

Toasted sesame seeds add to the Asian flair of this dish. To toast them, spread them out in a thin layer in a shallow pan. Bake at 350° for 4 to 6 minutes, stirring twice.

20 minutes or less
PREP: 3 MIN., COOK: 9 MIN.

1 tablespoon cornstarch
¾ cup chicken broth
3 tablespoons soy sauce
1 garlic clove, minced
2 pounds fresh asparagus
2 tablespoons olive oil
⅛ teaspoon pepper
1 tablespoon sesame seeds, toasted

1. Combine first 4 ingredients in a small saucepan. Bring to a boil; cook 1 minute, stirring constantly. Remove from heat; set aside.
2. Snap off tough ends of asparagus. Cook asparagus in hot olive oil in a large skillet over medium-high heat, stirring often, 6 minutes or until crisp-tender. Add chicken broth mixture to asparagus; cook, stirring constantly, 1 minute or until thoroughly heated. Stir in pepper. Sprinkle with sesame seeds. Serve immediately. **Makes** 4 to 6 servings.

Asparagus With Lemon Butter

How long to cook asparagus depends on the thickness of the stems. Just be sure not to overcook the asparagus so that it doesn't lose its flavor or nutrients.

20 minutes or less
PREP: 20 MIN.

2 pounds fresh asparagus
¼ cup butter or margarine
½ teaspoon salt
½ teaspoon freshly ground pepper
1 tablespoon grated lemon rind
¼ cup fresh lemon juice

1. Snap off tough ends of asparagus; remove scales with a vegetable peeler.
2. Melt butter in a skillet over medium-high heat; add asparagus, and sauté 3 minutes or until crisp-tender. Add salt and pepper; remove from heat. Toss with lemon rind and juice. **Makes** 4 to 6 servings.

Green Beans With Bacon and Mushrooms

To make preparation timely for this recipe, thaw the green beans in the refrigerator overnight so they'll be ready to cook when you are.

30 minutes or less
PREP: 3 MIN., COOK: 25 MIN.

1 (12-ounce) package sliced bacon
1 small onion, chopped
3 (9-ounce) packages frozen whole green beans, thawed
2 (4-ounce) cans sliced mushrooms, drained
1 tablespoon sugar

1. Cook bacon in a large skillet until crisp; remove bacon, and drain on paper towels, reserving 1 tablespoon drippings in skillet. Crumble bacon, and set aside.
2. Cook onion in reserved drippings, stirring constantly, until onion is tender. Stir in green beans, mushrooms, and sugar; cover and cook over medium heat 10 minutes. Spoon green beans into a serving dish; sprinkle with bacon. **Makes** 8 to 10 servings.

Green Beans Balsamic With Garlic

For added flavor, stir in toasted chopped walnuts or pecans.

30 minutes or less
PREP: 14 MIN., COOK: 12 MIN.
(pictured on page 331)

2 pounds fresh green beans, trimmed
1 garlic clove, minced
2 tablespoons olive oil
2 tablespoons balsamic vinegar
¼ teaspoon salt
¼ teaspoon pepper

1. Cook green beans in boiling salted water to cover 6 minutes; drain. Plunge beans into ice water to stop the cooking process; drain.
2. Sauté garlic in hot oil in a large skillet over medium-high heat 1 minute; add green beans, and sauté 3 to 4 minutes. Add balsamic vinegar, salt and pepper; sauté 1 minute. **Makes** 4 servings.

Green Beans With Garlic-Herb Butter

Green Beans With Garlic-Herb Butter

PREP: 10 MIN., COOK: 26 MIN.

1 pound fresh green beans, trimmed
¼ cup butter or margarine
1 small onion, minced
1 celery rib, minced
1½ teaspoons bottled minced garlic
¼ teaspoon chopped fresh or dried rosemary
¾ teaspoon salt
¼ cup chopped fresh parsley

1. Bring salted water to a boil in a large saucepan; add beans, cover, and cook 10 to 15 minutes or until crisp-tender. Drain. Plunge into ice water to stop the cooking process; drain.
2. Melt ¼ cup butter in a saucepan over medium-high heat; add onion and celery, and sauté 5 minutes. Add garlic, and sauté 2 minutes. Stir in beans, rosemary, salt, and parsley; sauté 4 minutes or until thoroughly heated. **Makes** 4 servings.

Sautéed Green Beans With Bacon

PREP: 25 MIN., COOK: 15 MIN.

1¾ pounds fresh green beans, trimmed (see note)
¼ cup water
8 bacon slices, chopped
5 green onions (white bottoms and light green parts
     of tops only), chopped
½ teaspoon salt
½ teaspoon pepper

1. Place beans and ¼ cup water in a large microwave-safe bowl. Cover with plastic wrap, and pierce plastic wrap with a fork. Microwave at HIGH 4 to 7 minutes or until beans are crisp-tender. Plunge green beans into ice water to stop the cooking process. Drain well, and set aside.

2. Cook chopped bacon in a large nonstick skillet over medium heat until crisp; remove bacon, and drain on paper towels, reserving 2 tablespoons drippings in a small bowl. Discard remaining drippings. Wipe skillet clean with a paper towel.

3. Sauté green onions in skillet in hot reserved drippings over medium-high heat 1 minute. Stir in green beans, salt, and pepper; sauté 2 to 3 minutes or until thoroughly heated. Stir in bacon. **Makes** 4 to 6 servings.

Note: Substitute 2 (12-ounce) packages ready-to-eat trimmed fresh green beans for the fresh green beans, omitting water. Pierce bags with a fork, and microwave at HIGH 4 to 5 minutes or until crisp-tender. Proceed with recipe as directed.

Smashed Pinto Beans

Keep these fiber-rich beans on hand to assemble quick breakfast burritos or veggie tacos. They're also great for a side dish for any Mexican meal or Texan cookout.

PREP: 15 MIN., COOK: 20 MIN.

1 medium onion, chopped
1 teaspoon olive oil
2 garlic cloves, minced
½ cup tomato sauce
2 (15-ounce) cans pinto beans, rinsed and
     drained
1 cup beef broth
1 tablespoon hot sauce
¼ teaspoon salt
¼ teaspoon ground cumin
½ teaspoon pepper
1 to 2 tablespoons red wine vinegar

1. Sauté onion in hot oil in a Dutch oven over medium-high heat 5 minutes or until tender. Add garlic, and sauté 1 minute. Stir in tomato sauce and remaining ingredients. Bring to a boil; reduce heat, and simmer 8 minutes.

2. Mash bean mixture with a potato masher until thickened, leaving some beans whole. **Makes** 8 servings.

Sesame Broccoli

Sesame Broccoli

Make everyday broccoli spiced with Asian flavors and sesame seeds.

30 minutes or less
PREP: 10 MIN., COOK: 12 MIN.

1 pound fresh broccoli
1 tablespoon sugar
1 tablespoon soy sauce
1 tablespoon vegetable oil
2 teaspoons vinegar
2 teaspoons sesame seeds, toasted

1. Cut broccoli into spears; arrange in a steamer basket over boiling water. Cover and steam 5 minutes or until crisp-tender. Place on a serving platter.
2. Stir together sugar and next 3 ingredients in a small saucepan over medium heat. Cook, stirring often, until sugar dissolves and mixture is thoroughly heated. Drizzle over broccoli, and sprinkle with sesame seeds.
Makes 4 servings.

Gratin of Broccoli in Béchamel

This fancy side combines broccoli with Gruyère cheese—sure to please any guest.

30 minutes or less
PREP: 10 MIN., COOK: 16 MIN.

2¼ pounds fresh broccoli crowns, cut into spears
3 tablespoons butter or margarine
3 tablespoons all-purpose flour
2 cups milk
2 tablespoons stone-ground mustard
⅛ teaspoon salt
⅛ teaspoon freshly grated or ground nutmeg
⅛ teaspoon pepper
1 cup (4 ounces) shredded Gruyère cheese

1. Arrange broccoli in a steamer basket over boiling water. Cover and steam 10 minutes or until crisp-tender. Remove from heat. Transfer broccoli to a lightly greased 13- x 9-inch baking dish.
2. Meanwhile, melt butter in a heavy saucepan over medium heat; whisk in flour until smooth. Cook 1 minute, whisking constantly. Gradually whisk in milk; cook over medium heat, whisking constantly, until mixture is thickened and bubbly. Stir in mustard and next 3 ingredients. Pour sauce over broccoli; sprinkle with cheese.
3. Broil 3 inches from heat 6 minutes or until lightly browned. Serve immediately. **Makes** 8 servings.

Honey-Tarragon Glazed Baby Carrots

Substitute another herb, such as dill or basil, for tarragon if you prefer.

20 minutes or less
PREP: 10 MIN., COOK: 12 MIN.
(pictured on page 331)

1 (2-pound) package peeled baby carrots
1 teaspoon lemon juice
½ teaspoon salt, divided
¼ cup butter or margarine
¼ cup honey
2 tablespoons chopped fresh tarragon or 2 teaspoons dried tarragon
¼ teaspoon pepper
Garnish: fresh tarragon sprigs

1. Cook baby carrots, 1 teaspoon lemon juice, and ¼ teaspoon salt in boiling water to cover 8 to 10 minutes; drain. Plunge into ice water to stop the cooking process; drain.
2. Heat butter and honey in a large saucepan over medium-high heat, stirring until butter melts. Stir in remaining ¼ teaspoon salt, carrots, tarragon, and pepper; cook 2 minutes or until thoroughly heated. Garnish, if desired. **Makes** 6 servings.

Sautéed Fennel and Carrots

Sautéed Fennel and Carrots

This recipe can easily be doubled for a larger yield.

30 minutes or less
PREP: 10 MIN., COOK: 13 MIN.

2 large fennel bulbs
4 medium carrots
2 tablespoons olive oil
½ cup dry white wine
½ cup water
2 tablespoons sugar
½ teaspoon salt, divided
½ teaspoon pepper

1. Cut a slice off fennel bulb bases. Trim stalks to within 1 inch of bulb. Reserve stalks for another use. Cut bulb lengthwise into thin slices. Cut slices into thin strips. Cut carrots in half crosswise, and cut into thin strips.

2. Sauté fennel and carrot in hot oil in a large skillet over medium-high heat 5 minutes or until lightly browned. Add wine and remaining ingredients. Bring to a boil; cover, reduce heat, and simmer 4 minutes. Uncover and cook 2 minutes or until almost all liquid evaporates and vegetables are glazed. **Makes** 3 to 4 servings.

Carrot-Sweet Potato Puree

This recipe requires no stovetop cooking; it's all done in the microwave. We reduced calories, fat, and cholesterol by using light butter (and less of it) and light sour cream.

PREP: 20 MIN., COOK: 17 MIN.

make ahead

5 carrots, sliced
¾ cup water
¼ cup light butter or margarine
1 (29-ounce) can sweet potatoes, drained
1 (16-ounce) can sweet potatoes, drained
1 (8-ounce) container light sour cream
1 tablespoon sugar
1 teaspoon grated lemon rind
½ teaspoon ground nutmeg
¼ teaspoon salt
¼ teaspoon ground black pepper
⅛ teaspoon ground red pepper

1. Microwave carrots and ¾ cup water in a glass bowl at HIGH 8 to 12 minutes or until tender. Drain.
2. Process carrots and butter in a food processor until mixture is smooth, stopping to scrape down sides. Add sweet potatoes; process until smooth.
3. Stir together sweet potato mixture, sour cream, and remaining ingredients.
4. Spoon mixture into a 1½-quart glass dish. Microwave at HIGH 4 to 5 minutes or until thoroughly heated. **Makes** 6 servings.
Note: To make ahead, prepare and stir together ingredients as directed; cover and chill up to 2 days. Let stand at room temperature 30 minutes; microwave as directed.

Frosted Cauliflower

Lose the fat but keep the taste of this creamy cauliflower side by substituting reduced-fat mayonnaise for regular.

30 minutes or less
PREP: 5 MIN., COOK: 25 MIN.

1 cauliflower, broken into large florets
¾ cup grated Parmesan cheese
½ cup mayonnaise
1 tablespoon lemon juice
2 tablespoons Dijon mustard
1 tablespoon minced fresh parsley
3 green onions, thinly sliced

1. Cook cauliflower, covered, in a saucepan over medium-high heat in a small amount of boiling water 8 to 10 minutes or until crisp-tender; drain. Place cauliflower in a lightly greased 2-quart baking dish.
2. Stir together Parmesan cheese and next 5 ingredients; spread evenly over cauliflower.
3. Bake at 375° for 15 minutes or until lightly browned. Serve immediately. **Makes** 6 servings.

Creamed Fresh Corn

Cutting the kernels off the corn is a snap when you have a sharp knife.

20 minutes or less
PREP: 8 MIN., COOK: 12 MIN.

4 ears fresh corn
1 teaspoon sugar (optional)
¼ cup butter or margarine
⅓ cup whipping cream
¼ teaspoon salt
½ teaspoon pepper

1. Remove husks and silks from corn. Cut corn from cobs, scraping cobs over bowl to remove milk. Stir in sugar, if desired.
2. Melt butter in medium saucepan over medium heat; add corn, and sauté 1 minute. Gradually stir in whipping cream; cook, stirring often, 10 to 12 minutes or until liquid is absorbed. Stir in salt and pepper. Serve immediately. **Makes** 2 cups.

Chili Corn on the Cob

If fresh corn is unavailable, use 8 half-ears of frozen corn instead. Just follow the package directions for cooking.

20 minutes or less
PREP: 10 MIN., COOK: 7 MIN.

4 ears fresh corn, husks removed
¼ cup butter or margarine, softened
1 tablespoon chopped fresh chives
1 teaspoon chili powder
¼ teaspoon salt
¼ teaspoon pepper

1. Wrap each ear of corn in plastic wrap; arrange, spoke fashion, on a glass plate.
2. Microwave at HIGH 7 minutes, turning corn after 3½ minutes. Let stand 2 minutes. Meanwhile, stir together butter, chives, and chili powder. Remove plastic wrap; brush corn with butter mixture. Sprinkle with salt and pepper. **Makes** 4 servings.

Mexican-Style Corn

Salsa verde is a green sauce typically made from tomatillos, green chiles, and cilantro. Look for it in the ethnic food section of your grocery store.

30 minutes or less
PREP: 15 MIN., COOK: 15 MIN.

1 small onion, diced
1 small green bell pepper, diced
1 small red bell pepper, diced
1 teaspoon minced garlic
1 tablespoon canola oil
1 (16-ounce) package frozen whole kernel corn, thawed
¼ cup salsa verde
1 teaspoon salt
½ teaspoon pepper
¼ teaspoon ground cumin
1 medium tomato, peeled, seeded, and diced
1 tablespoon chopped fresh cilantro
Garnish: fresh cilantro sprigs

1. Sauté first 4 ingredients in hot oil in a large skillet over medium heat 3 minutes; add corn, and sauté 3 minutes.
2. Stir in salsa verde and next 3 ingredients, and cook 1 minute. Stir in diced tomato and chopped cilantro; cook 2 minutes or until thoroughly heated. Garnish, if desired. **Makes** 4 servings.

Honey-Tarragon Glazed
Baby Carrots, page 327

Mexican-Style Corn

Green Beans Balsamic
With Garlic, page 323

Wilted Greens With Sweet-and-Sour Sauce

Wilted Greens With Sweet-and-Sour Sauce

The saltiness of the bacon contrasts with the sugar in the sauce, making these greens irresistible.

20 minutes or less
PREP: 4 MIN., COOK: 16 MIN.

4 bacon slices, cut into 1-inch pieces
½ cup chopped onion
½ cup sugar
⅓ cup white vinegar
2 (10-ounce) packages baby spinach
1 hard-cooked egg, chopped (optional)

1. Cook bacon in a large Dutch oven until crisp; remove bacon, and drain on paper towels, reserving drippings in pan. Crumble bacon, and set aside.
2. Add onion to drippings, and cook over medium heat 5 minutes, stirring occasionally. Add sugar and vinegar, and cook over high heat until sugar dissolves, stirring often. Add greens, and cook, stirring constantly, 3 minutes or until greens wilt. Sprinkle with bacon and, if desired, egg. Serve immediately. **Makes** 4 servings.

good news for greens

Despite how much we love cooked greens, our busy schedules may have virtually eliminated this Southern phenomenon from our diets had not so many prewashed, trimmed, and packaged varieties come on the market. Just a generation or two ago, anyone who wanted to enjoy this healthy side dish had to wash large volumes of the greens in several changes of water to remove dirt and sand. Cutting corners on the number of rinses made the greens come out gritty. Today, prewashed, trimmed, and bagged greens save you the washing step and the time spent trimming the stems. Be sure to check the use-by date on packaged greens before tossing them in your grocery cart to make sure you're getting the freshest greens available.

Braised Greens With Chipotle-Chile Vinaigrette

One chipotle chile spices up this dish—the perfect complement to wilted greens.

PREP: 10 MIN., COOK: 23 MIN.

2¼ cups low-sodium chicken broth, divided
2 tablespoons sherry vinegar
2 tablespoons fresh lime juice
1 tablespoon vegetable oil
½ teaspoon dried oregano
1 canned chipotle chile in adobo sauce
6 garlic cloves, minced
1 (1-pound) package prewashed chopped fresh mustard greens
1 (1-pound) package prewashed chopped fresh turnip greens

1. Combine ¼ cup broth, vinegar, and next 4 ingredients in a blender; process until smooth.
2. Bring 1 cup broth to a boil in a very large Dutch oven over medium-high heat. Add garlic; cook 2 minutes, stirring frequently. Add remaining 1 cup broth and greens; cover and cook 20 minutes or until wilted. Drain well. Serve with vinaigrette. **Makes** 8 servings.

Onion-Gruyère Gratin

We used Vidalia onions for this creamy gratin—their sweetness accentuates the flavor of the Gruyère cheese.

30 minutes or less
PREP: 5 MIN., COOK: 16 MIN.

6 medium onions, cut into ½-inch-thick slices (about 3 pounds)
3 tablespoons whipping cream
1 teaspoon all-purpose flour
½ teaspoon salt
⅛ teaspoon ground nutmeg
1 cup (4 ounces) shredded Gruyère cheese

1. Place onion slices in a lightly greased 11- x 7-inch baking dish. Cover tightly with heavy-duty plastic wrap; fold back a small corner to allow steam to escape. Microwave at HIGH 10 minutes or just until onion is tender. Drain onion; return to dish.
2. Whisk together whipping cream and next 3 ingredients in a small bowl. Pour cream mixture over onion, stirring to coat. Cover and microwave at HIGH 1 minute; stir. Sprinkle onion with cheese.
3. Broil 3 inches from heat 5 minutes or until cheese is golden. Serve immediately. **Makes** 6 servings.

Basic Mashed Potatoes

20 minutes or less
PREP: 5 MIN., COOK: 15 MIN.

4 medium-size baking potatoes, (1½ to 2 pounds)
3 tablespoons butter, cut up
½ cup milk or half-and-half
¾ teaspoon salt
¼ teaspoon pepper

1. Peel potatoes, and cut into eighths; cook in boiling water to cover 15 minutes or until tender; drain well. Return potatoes to pan. Add butter, and mash with a potato masher or fork. Stir in milk, salt, and pepper. Mash to achieve desired consistency. Serve hot. **Makes** 4 servings.

Garlic Mashed Potatoes

20 minutes or less
PREP: 6 MIN., COOK: 9 MIN.

3 tablespoons butter or margarine
4 garlic cloves, pressed
2⅔ cups frozen mashed potatoes (we used Ore Ida)
1⅓ cups milk
½ teaspoon salt
¼ teaspoon freshly ground pepper

1. Place butter in a 1½-quart microwave-safe bowl. Cover and microwave at HIGH 30 seconds or until butter melts. Add garlic; cover and microwave at HIGH 1½ minutes or until garlic is tender. Stir in potatoes, milk, salt, and pepper. Cover and microwave at HIGH 7 minutes or until thickened, stirring after 3 minutes. Serve immediately. **Makes** 4 servings.

Twice-Baked
Mashed Potatoes

Twice-Baked Mashed Potatoes

These potatoes are just as delicious when you substitute reduced-fat dairy products.
The potatoes can also be served family style in a 2-quart baking dish instead of individual ramekins.

PREP: 15 MIN., COOK: 20 MIN.

1 (22-ounce) package frozen mashed potatoes (we used Ore-Ida Frozen Mashed Potatoes)
½ (8-ounce) package cream cheese, softened
½ cup sour cream
¼ cup chopped fresh chives
4 bacon slices, cooked and crumbled
½ teaspoon seasoned pepper
¼ teaspoon salt
½ cup (2 ounces) shredded Cheddar cheese

1. Prepare potatoes according to package directions.
2. Stir in cream cheese and next 5 ingredients. Divide mixture evenly among 6 (6-ounce) lightly greased ramekins or custard cups. Sprinkle evenly with Cheddar cheese.
3. Bake at 350° for 20 minutes or until thoroughly heated. **Makes** 6 servings.

Cheesy Green Onion-and-Bacon Mashed Potatoes

Cook and crumble bacon ahead of time to make this dish much faster. You can also substitute 1 (22-ounce) package of frozen mashed potatoes for the baking potatoes. Prepare potatoes according to package directions; stir in cheese and remaining ingredients.

PREP: 15 MIN., COOK: 25 MIN.

4 large baking potatoes, peeled and cut into 2-inch pieces
2 cups (8 ounces) shredded colby-Jack cheese
6 to 8 bacon slices, cooked and crumbled
4 green onions, chopped
2 garlic cloves, pressed
½ cup sour cream
¼ cup butter
1½ teaspoons salt
½ teaspoon pepper

1. Bring potatoes and water to cover to a boil in a large Dutch oven; cook 25 minutes or until tender. Drain.
2. Mash potatoes with a fork or potato masher; stir in cheese and remaining ingredients. **Makes** 6 to 8 servings.

Balsamic-Roasted Potato Wedges

Balsamic vinegar is a bit expensive, but worth the cost. It's aged in wooden barrels to develop a rich color and unique flavor.

30 minutes or less
PREP: 5 MIN., COOK: 25 MIN.

2 tablespoons olive oil
1 tablespoon bottled minced garlic
1 tablespoon minced fresh rosemary
½ teaspoon salt
¼ teaspoon pepper
2 pounds red potatoes, cut into wedges
¼ cup balsamic vinegar

1. Combine first 5 ingredients in a large bowl, and stir well. Add potato wedges, tossing gently to coat. Arrange potato wedges in a single layer on a lightly greased baking sheet.
2. Bake, uncovered, at 450° for 20 minutes. Remove potatoes from oven; sprinkle with balsamic vinegar. Bake 5 more minutes. Serve immediately. **Makes** 4 servings.

whipped vs. mashed

Some folks like the convenience and light texture that results from whipping potatoes with an electric mixer. Just be careful not to overmix them, or you'll have gummy, gluey spuds. Mashing potatoes with a potato masher provides texture options for creamy or chunky spuds, depending on your preference. Be sure to use a durable masher with a stainless steel or wooden handle.

Balsamic-Roasted Potato Wedges

Easy Spinach

Easy Spinach

This side takes very little time to whip up and pairs perfectly with just about any entrée.

20 minutes or less
PREP: 5 MIN., COOK: 12 MIN.

2 (10-ounce) packages frozen chopped spinach,
    thawed and well drained
1 garlic clove, chopped
2 tablespoons olive oil
¼ cup Italian-seasoned breadcrumbs
¼ cup freshly grated Romano cheese
½ teaspoon salt
½ teaspoon pepper

1. Sauté spinach and garlic in hot oil in a large skillet over medium-high heat 10 to 12 minutes or until thoroughly heated and liquid evaporates. Add breadcrumbs and remaining ingredients, stirring well. Serve immediately. **Makes** 4 servings.

Spinach With Herbs

Rosemary lends an aromatic touch to everyday spinach. Find packages of fresh baby spinach in the produce section of your supermarket alongside packaged salad greens.

30 minutes or less
PREP: 14 MIN., COOK: 14 MIN.

3 bacon slices
1 small onion, thinly sliced
2 (7-ounce) packages fresh baby spinach
¼ cup chopped fresh parsley
1 tablespoon white wine vinegar
1 teaspoon chopped fresh rosemary
½ teaspoon salt
⅛ teaspoon pepper

1. Cook bacon in a large Dutch oven until crisp; remove bacon, and drain on paper towels, reserving 1 tablespoon drippings in pan. Crumble bacon; set aside.
2. Sauté onion in hot drippings in pan 4 minutes or until tender. Add spinach, parsley, and next 4 ingredients; sauté 3 to 5 minutes or just until spinach wilts. Top with crumbled bacon. Serve immediately. **Makes** 4 servings.

Southern Summer Squash

A touch of basil enhances the squash and tomato flavors in this side dish.

30 minutes or less
PREP: 10 MIN., COOK: 15 MIN.

¼ cup water
2 tablespoons butter or margarine
1 sweet onion, thinly sliced
1 pound small yellow squash, thinly sliced
1 pound small zucchini, thinly sliced
3 medium tomatoes, peeled, seeded, and chopped
    (see note)
1 tablespoon chopped fresh basil
½ teaspoon salt
¼ teaspoon pepper
1 cup (4 ounces) shredded Cheddar cheese

1. Bring ¼ cup water and butter to a boil in a large skillet over medium-high heat.
2. Add onion, squash, and zucchini; return to a boil. Cover, reduce heat, and simmer 5 minutes. Stir in tomato and next 3 ingredients; cover and simmer 5 minutes or until thoroughly heated. Sprinkle with cheese, and serve immediately. **Makes** 6 servings.
Note: Substitute 1 (14.5-ounce) can diced tomatoes, drained, if desired.

Summer Squash-
and-Corn Sauté

Summer Squash-and-Corn Sauté

This herby sauté gets a pungent kick from cumin seeds. It's easy to substitute fresh corn in this recipe. You'll need 4 ears. Simply position the pointed end of the cob into the center of a Bundt pan and slice down the cob. The kernels will fall in the pan.

20 minutes or less
PREP: 7 MIN., COOK: 12 MIN.

1 teaspoon olive oil
2 teaspoons cumin seeds
2 (15.25-ounce) cans sweet whole kernel corn
1 cup sliced onion
3 garlic cloves, minced
¾ pound diagonally sliced zucchini, cut ¼ inch thick
¾ pound diagonally sliced yellow squash, cut ¼ inch thick
½ teaspoon salt
1 (4.5-ounce) can chopped green chiles
2 tablespoons chopped fresh cilantro

1. Heat oil in a large nonstick skillet over medium-high heat; cook cumin seeds 30 seconds or until toasted, stirring frequently.
2. Add corn, onion, and garlic; sauté 5 minutes or until lightly browned. Add zucchini, yellow squash, salt, and chiles; sauté 6 minutes or until tender. Stir in cilantro. Remove from heat. **Makes** 6 servings.

Squash Casserole

This creamy Southern side gets a flavor boost from Ranch dressing mix.

PREP: 5 MIN., COOK: 33 MIN.

2 (16-ounce) packages frozen sliced yellow squash
1 cup chopped onion
1 cup mayonnaise or salad dressing
3 large eggs, lightly beaten
½ cup crushed unsalted saltine crackers
1 (0.4-ounce) envelope buttermilk Ranch dressing mix
1 cup (4 ounces) shredded sharp Cheddar cheese
1 cup soft breadcrumbs
1 tablespoon butter or margarine, melted

1. Cook squash with onion according to directions on squash package, omitting salt; drain well, pressing between paper towels. Combine squash mixture, mayonnaise, and next 4 ingredients in a lightly greased shallow 2-quart casserole.
2. Combine breadcrumbs and butter; sprinkle over top. Bake at 350° for 20 to 25 minutes. **Makes** 8 servings.

Zucchini-Parmesan Toss

Yellow squash works equally well in this quick summer squash recipe.

20 minutes or less
PREP: 10 MIN., COOK: 5 MIN.

2 pounds zucchini, cut into ¼-inch-thick slices
2 tablespoons olive oil
⅓ cup freshly grated Parmesan cheese
½ teaspoon grated lemon rind
½ teaspoon salt
½ teaspoon pepper

1. Sauté zucchini in hot oil in a large skillet over medium-high heat 5 minutes or until crisp-tender. Spoon into a serving dish.
2. Combine cheese and next 3 ingredients; reserve 2 tablespoons cheese mixture. Sprinkle remaining cheese mixture over squash; toss gently. Sprinkle reserved cheese mixture over top. Serve immediately. **Makes** 4 servings.

Tomato Napoleon

Tomato Napoleon

Tomato Napoleon—stacked with layers of in-season tomatoes, fresh mozzarella, and shredded basil—is the ideal accompaniment to a summer menu.

PREP: 20 MIN., OTHER: 1 HR.

make ahead

8 ounces fresh mozzarella cheese, cut into 8 slices
¾ cup Fresh Tomato Dressing (recipe on facing page)
3 large tomatoes, each cut into 4 slices
1 teaspoon salt
1 teaspoon pepper
24 fresh basil leaves, shredded

1. Place cheese in a shallow dish.
2. Pour Fresh Tomato Dressing over cheese; cover and chill 1 hour.
3. Remove cheese slices, reserving tomato dressing.
4. Sprinkle tomato slices evenly with salt and pepper.
5. Place 1 tomato slice on each of 4 salad plates; top each with 1 cheese slice and 2 shredded basil leaves. Repeat procedure with 1 tomato slice, 1 cheese slice, and 2 shredded basil leaves. Top with remaining tomato slices and basil. Drizzle evenly with reserved dressing. **Makes** 4 servings.

Fresh Tomato Dressing:

Serve this dressing over Tomato Napoleon or toss with your favorite greens.

PREP: 20 MIN., OTHER: 9 HR.

1 cup olive oil
½ cup balsamic vinegar
3 garlic cloves, sliced
1 tablespoon sugar
1 tablespoon salt
1 tablespoon pepper
4 large tomatoes, peeled and chopped
2 tablespoons fresh thyme leaves or 4 thyme sprigs

1. Whisk together first 6 ingredients in a large glass bowl.
2. Stir in chopped tomatoes and thyme. Cover and let stand at room temperature 1 hour, stirring occasionally. Cover and chill 8 hours. **Makes** 4 cups.
Note: Dressing may be stored in the refrigerator up to 1 month. Stir additional chopped fresh tomato into dressing after each use.

Italian-Topped Tomatoes

30 minutes or less
PREP: 7 MIN., COOK: 15 MIN.

2 tablespoons Dijon mustard
3 medium tomatoes, cut in half crosswise
⅛ teaspoon salt
¼ cup Italian-seasoned breadcrumbs
¼ cup shredded Parmesan cheese
2 tablespoons butter, melted
1 teaspoon chopped fresh parsley

1. Spread mustard evenly over cut side of each tomato half; sprinkle evenly with salt. Place tomato halves, cut sides up, in an 11- x 7-inch baking dish.
2. Combine breadcrumbs and next 3 ingredients in a small bowl. Gently spoon breadcrumb mixture evenly over each tomato. Bake at 450° for 12 to 15 minutes or until browned. Serve immediately. **Makes** 6 servings.

Honey-Baked Tomatoes

Prepare the crumb topping the day before you plan to serve these tasty tomatoes.

PREP: 10 MIN., COOK: 35 MIN.

make
ahead

8 medium tomatoes, cut into 1-inch
    slices
4 teaspoons honey
2 white bread slices
1 tablespoon dried tarragon
1½ teaspoons salt
2 teaspoons freshly ground pepper
4 teaspoons butter

1. Place tomato slices in a single layer in a lightly greased aluminum foil-lined 15- x 10-inch jelly-roll pan. Drizzle with honey, spreading honey into hollows.
2. Process bread in a blender or food processor until finely chopped.
3. Stir together breadcrumbs and next 3 ingredients; sprinkle evenly over tomato slices. Dot with butter.
4. Bake at 350° for 30 minutes or until tomato skins begin to wrinkle.
5. Broil 5 inches from heat 5 minutes or until tops are golden. Serve warm. **Makes** 8 servings.

Rice With Black Beans and Corn

While the rice simmers, prep the rest of the ingredients for this quick side.

30 minutes or less
PREP: 10 MIN., COOK: 20 MIN.

1 cup water
½ cup uncooked long-grain rice
4 plum tomatoes, chopped
1 (15-ounce) can black beans, rinsed and
    drained
1 (10-ounce) package frozen whole kernel
    corn, thawed
4 green onions, chopped
½ cup chopped fresh cilantro
¼ cup lime juice
1 teaspoon salt
¼ teaspoon pepper

1. Bring 1 cup water to a boil in a large saucepan; stir in rice. Cover, reduce heat, and simmer 20 minutes or until liquid is absorbed and rice is tender.
2. Add tomatoes and remaining ingredients. Cook over medium heat, stirring constantly until heated. **Makes** 8 servings.

Lemon Couscous

The tang of lemon rind and zing of freshly squeezed juice enhance this couscous.

20 minutes or less
PREP: 5 MIN., COOK: 2 MIN., OTHER: 5 MIN.

1 cup chicken broth
1 tablespoon grated lemon rind
2 tablespoons fresh lemon juice
1 tablespoon butter or margarine
¼ teaspoon salt
⅔ cup uncooked couscous
2 tablespoons pecan pieces, toasted
2 tablespoons chopped fresh parsley
1 (2-ounce) jar sliced pimiento, drained and
    chopped

1. Combine first 5 ingredients in a saucepan; bring to a boil. Add couscous, stirring well; cover, remove from heat, and let stand 5 minutes. Fluff couscous with a fork. Stir in pecans, parsley, and pimiento. **Makes** 2 servings.

Rice Pilaf

PREP: 5 MIN., COOK: 30 MIN.

1 tablespoon olive oil
1 cup uncooked long-grain rice
2½ cups chicken broth
½ cup coarsely chopped walnuts or pecans,
    toasted

1. Heat olive oil in a large skillet over medium-high heat until hot. Add rice; sauté 3 to 5 minutes or just until rice is lightly browned.
2. Meanwhile, bring broth to a boil in a large saucepan. Gradually add rice to broth; cover, reduce heat, and simmer 25 minutes or until liquid is absorbed and rice is tender. Stir in walnuts. **Makes** 4 servings.

Lemon Couscous

Fresh Raspberry-Spinach Salad

Fresh Raspberry-Spinach Salad

This recipe makes a large batch, perfect for big get-togethers. If you aren't planning for a huge crowd, the salad's ingredients can easily be halved.

20 minutes or less
PREP: 13 MIN.

5 (6-ounce) packages fresh baby spinach
1 (14.4-ounce) can hearts of palm, drained and thinly
    sliced
1 medium-size yellow bell pepper, coarsely chopped
Raspberry Vinaigrette or bottled vinaigrette
2 cups fresh raspberries
2 (4-ounce) packages goat cheese, crumbled

1. Combine first 3 ingredients in a large salad bowl. Pour vinaigrette over salad; toss gently. Top each serving evenly with raspberries; sprinkle with cheese. Serve immediately. **Makes** 10 servings.

Raspberry Vinaigrette:
PREP: 2 MIN., COOK: 5 MIN.

1 cup firmly packed light brown sugar
1 cup raspberry vinegar
1 (10-ounce) jar seedless raspberry fruit spread
¼ cup minced red onion
1 teaspoon minced garlic

1. Combine all ingredients in a small saucepan. Cook over low heat until smooth, stirring constantly; cool. **Makes** 2½ cups.

Apple-Spinach Salad

10 minutes or less
PREP: 5 MIN.

1 (6-ounce) package fresh baby spinach
2 small Granny Smith apples, chopped
½ cup cashews
¼ cup golden raisins
½ cup sweet and sour dressing (we used Old Dutch)

1. Combine first 4 ingredients in a bowl. Add dressing, tossing gently to coat. **Makes** 4 servings.

Cantaloupe-Spinach Salad

Buy cubed cantaloupe from your supermarket's produce section to make this refreshing salad in a snap.

10 minutes or less
PREP: 5 MIN.

make ahead

6 cups baby spinach leaves
1 large cantaloupe, cubed
½ cup pistachios, coarsely chopped
Pistachio-Lime Vinaigrette or bottled vinaigrette

1. Place spinach on individual serving plates; arrange cantaloupe on top, and sprinkle with pistachios. Serve with Pistachio-Lime Vinaigrette. **Makes** 6 to 8 servings.

Pistachio-Lime Vinaigrette:
This vinaigrette is spicy-sweet.

PREP: 3 MIN.

⅓ cup fresh lime juice
⅓ cup honey
¼ cup coarsely chopped red onion
1 teaspoon dried crushed red pepper
½ teaspoon salt
¼ cup fresh cilantro leaves
¾ cup vegetable oil
1 cup pistachios

1. Process first 6 ingredients in blender until smooth. With blender running, add oil in a slow, steady stream. Turn blender off; add pistachios, and pulse until pistachios are finely chopped. Cover and store in refrigerator. **Makes** about 2 cups.

Fruit Salad With Honey-Pecan Dressing

10 minutes or less
PREP: 5 MIN.

2½ cups fresh orange sections
2½ cups fresh grapefruit sections
1 avocado, sliced
3⅓ cups sliced strawberries
1 (16-ounce) package mixed salad greens
Honey-Pecan Dressing

1. Arrange fresh orange and grapefruit sections, sliced avocado, and sliced strawberries over mixed greens; drizzle with Honey-Pecan Dressing. **Makes** 4 servings.

Honey-Pecan Dressing:
PREP: 5 MIN.

2 tablespoons sugar
1 tablespoon chopped sweet onion
½ teaspoon dry mustard
½ teaspoon salt
¼ teaspoon pepper
¼ cup honey
⅓ cup red wine vinegar
1 cup vegetable oil
½ cup chopped pecans, toasted

1. Pulse first 7 ingredients in a blender 2 or 3 times until blended. With blender running, pour oil through food chute in a slow, steady stream; process until smooth. Stir in pecans. **Makes** 1¾ cups.

Pear-Walnut Salad

This autumn salad is proof positive that opposites attract. The natural sweetness of the ripe, tender pears plays off the tang of the blue cheese.

10 minutes or less
PREP: 8 MIN.

1 (5-ounce) package mixed salad greens, torn
1 (6-ounce) package walnut halves, toasted (about
    1½ cups)
1 cup jarred sliced Bartlett pears in light syrup,
    drained
½ cup crumbled blue cheese
½ cup sweet and sour dressing

1. Combine first 4 ingredients in a large bowl; toss gently. Pour dressing over salad mixture just before serving; toss. **Makes** 4 servings.

Quick Baby Blue Salad

30 minutes or less
PREP: 13 MIN., COOK: 15 MIN.

1½ cups pecan halves
2 tablespoons sugar
1 tablespoon Creole seasoning
2 (5-ounce) packages mixed salad greens (we used
    Dole Spring Mix)
1 (11-ounce) can mandarin oranges, drained
1 pint strawberries, quartered
¾ cup balsamic vinaigrette
1 (4-ounce) package crumbled blue cheese

1. Place pecans on a baking sheet. Coat pecans with cooking spray. Combine sugar and Creole seasoning. Sprinkle over pecans; toss gently.
2. Bake at 350° for 15 minutes or until pecans are golden brown, stirring once. Cool thoroughly.
3. While pecans are baking, gently toss together greens, mandarin oranges, strawberries, balsamic vinaigrette, and crumbled blue cheese. Top with pecans. **Makes** 7 servings.

Bacon-Mandarin Salad

Bacon-Mandarin Salad

PREP: 35 MIN.

1 (16-ounce) package bacon

½ cup olive oil

¼ cup red wine vinegar

¼ cup sugar

1 tablespoon chopped fresh basil

⅛ teaspoon hot sauce

2 (11-ounce) cans mandarin oranges, drained (see note)

1 head red leaf lettuce, torn

1 head romaine lettuce, torn

1 (4-ounce) package sliced almonds, toasted

1. Prepare bacon according to package directions; crumble.

2. Whisk together ½ cup oil and next 4 ingredients in a large bowl, blending well. Add mandarin oranges and lettuces, tossing gently to coat. Sprinkle with crumbled bacon and sliced almonds. Serve immediately. **Makes** 12 servings.

Note: Fresh orange segments may be substituted for canned mandarin oranges.

Layered Spinach
Tortellini Salad

Layered Spinach Tortellini Salad

Oooh la la! You will have your guests raving over the presentation of this salad. A trifle bowl gives this salad its flair. Just toss gently when you serve it in order to incorporate all of the ingredients.

PREP: 8 MIN., COOK: 16 MIN., OTHER: 3 HR.

1 (9-ounce) package refrigerated
    cheese-filled tortellini
8 bacon slices
1 (6-ounce) package fresh baby spinach, divided
2 cups shredded red cabbage
1 cup chopped tomatoes
1 bunch green onions, sliced (about 1 cup)
1 (8-ounce) bottle Ranch dressing

1. Cook pasta according to package directions. Drain; rinse with cold water, and drain again.
2. Meanwhile, cook bacon until crisp; drain and crumble.
3. Layer half of spinach, tortellini, cabbage, tomatoes, green onions, and remaining spinach in a 3-quart bowl. Top with dressing. Cover and chill 3 hours. Sprinkle with bacon. Toss gently before serving. **Makes** 6 servings.

pasta perfect

Never rinse pasta when serving it hot with a sauce because the starch that clings to cooked pasta helps the sauce adhere. Chilled pasta salads, on the other hand, will be sticky unless the pasta is rinsed. In these cases, rinse the cooked pasta in a colander to remove the excess starch and gently shake it to remove excess liquid before adding it to the recipe.

Macaroni and Cheese Salad

Diced ham and Cheddar cheese make this salad version of the classic Southern covered dish addictive.

PREP: 10 MIN., COOK: 10 MIN., OTHER: 1 HR.

1½ cups uncooked elbow macaroni
2 tablespoons vegetable oil
½ cup mayonnaise
1 tablespoon sugar
½ teaspoon salt
¼ teaspoon pepper
½ cup diced cooked ham
1 cup (4 ounces) shredded Cheddar cheese
¼ cup sliced green onions
½ cup frozen English peas, thawed

1. Cook macaroni according to package directions, including salt. Drain; rinse with cold water, and drain again. Toss macaroni with 2 tablespoons oil in a large bowl.
2. Meanwhile, stir together mayonnaise and next 3 ingredients; toss with ham and next 3 ingredients. Pour over macaroni, and toss gently. Cover and chill at least 1 hour. **Makes** 8 servings.

Roasted Onion Salad

Roasted Onion Salad

When broiling, be sure to check the onions after 5 minutes to prevent overbrowning.

30 minutes or less
PREP: 15 MIN., COOK: 10 MIN., OTHER: 5 MIN.

5 medium-size sweet onions, cut into ½-inch-thick
    slices
2 tablespoons olive oil
Salt and pepper to taste
8 cups gourmet mixed salad greens
½ cup chopped walnuts, toasted (optional)
1 (4-ounce) package crumbled blue cheese (optional)
Garlic Vinaigrette

1. Arrange onion slices on an aluminum foil-lined baking sheet. Brush evenly with olive oil. Sprinkle evenly with salt and pepper to taste.
2. Broil 5 inches from heat 10 minutes or until onion slices are lightly browned. Let onion slices stand 5 minutes.
3. Combine salad greens, and, if desired, walnuts and blue cheese; toss gently. Top with onion slices; drizzle with Garlic Vinaigrette. **Makes** 8 servings.

Garlic Vinaigrette:
PREP: 10 MIN.

3 garlic cloves, coarsely chopped
2 shallots, coarsely chopped
¼ cup chopped fresh parsley
2 tablespoons white wine vinegar
½ teaspoon dried crushed red pepper
½ teaspoon salt
½ teaspoon freshly ground black pepper
⅔ cup olive oil

1. Pulse chopped garlic and shallots in a food processor 3 or 4 times. Add chopped parsley and next 4 ingredients; process 20 seconds, stopping once to scrape down sides. With processor running, gradually pour ⅔ cup olive oil in a slow, steady stream through food chute until blended. **Makes** 1 cup.

Colorful Corn Salad

An abundance of colorful veggies sprinkles flavors throughout this vegetarian delicacy.

PREP: 7 MIN., OTHER: 2 HR.

1 (16-ounce) package frozen whole
    kernel corn, thawed
1 small sweet onion, chopped
1 large tomato, seeded and chopped
1 large green bell pepper, chopped
¼ cup mayonnaise
½ teaspoon salt
½ teaspoon coarsely ground black pepper
¼ cup seeded and chopped cucumber (optional)

1. Stir together corn and next 6 ingredients in a bowl, stirring until blended; cover and chill 2 hours. Serve salad with a slotted spoon.
2. Top each serving with chopped cucumber, if desired. **Makes** 5 cups.

Artichoke-Goat Cheese Salad

Serve this dressy salad with toasted baguette slices.

30 minutes or less
PREP: 10 MIN., OTHER: 20 MIN.

1 (4-ounce) package goat cheese
1 (3-ounce) package cream cheese, softened
3 tablespoons chopped fresh dill
½ teaspoon salt
¼ teaspoon freshly ground pepper
1 (12-ounce) jar marinated quartered artichoke
    hearts
7 cups gourmet mixed salad greens

1. Combine first 5 ingredients in a small bowl. Shape cheese mixture into a 5-inch log; cover and chill at least 20 minutes. Cut log diagonally into ½-inch-thick slices with a serrated knife, using a gentle sawing motion.
2. While cheese mixture chills, drain artichoke hearts, reserving liquid. Chop artichoke hearts.
3. Combine salad greens, artichoke, reserved artichoke liquid, and cheese slices in a large bowl, tossing gently to coat. **Makes** 7 servings.

Broccoli Salad

Capers deliver a bit of tang to this crunchy salad. If you don't have capers on hand, substitute 2 tablespoons chopped green olives instead. And ¼ cup pine nuts, toasted, in place of the pecans makes for a nutty variation.

PREP: 15 MIN., OTHER: 30 MIN.

4 cups chopped fresh broccoli
1 medium-size red onion, chopped
¼ cup chopped fresh dill
2 tablespoons capers, drained
Balsamic Vinaigrette or bottled vinaigrette
¼ cup chopped pecans, toasted

1. Toss together first 4 ingredients. Cover and chill at least 30 minutes. Drizzle with Balsamic Vinaigrette, and sprinkle with pecans just before serving. **Makes** about 5 cups.

Balsamic Vinaigrette:

This traditional vinaigrette also serves as a great staple for flavoring chicken and simple green salads.

10 minutes or less
PREP: 3 MIN.

⅓ cup balsamic vinegar
¼ cup olive oil
1 garlic clove, minced
½ tablespoon sugar
½ teaspoon salt
¼ teaspoon pepper

1. Whisk together all ingredients in a small bowl. Cover and store in the refrigerator. **Makes** about ⅔ cup.

Portobello Tossed Salad

Serve this tangy Italian salad with Parmesan cheese toast.
Enjoy the combo with a sprightly Sauvignon Blanc.

PREP: 5 MIN., COOK: 8 MIN., OTHER: 2 HR.

1 (8-ounce) bottle balsamic vinaigrette, divided (we
    used Newman's Own, see note)
4 medium portobello mushroom caps
4 cups gourmet salad greens
½ cup chopped walnuts or pecans, toasted
¼ cup crumbled goat cheese

1. Combine ½ cup balsamic vinaigrette and mushrooms in a large zip-top plastic freezer bag. Chill 2 to
3 hours. Drain mushrooms well, and place on a baking
sheet. Discard marinade.
2. Broil mushrooms 5 inches from heat 3 minutes; turn
mushrooms over, and broil 5 more minutes or until
tender.
3. Cut mushrooms into thick slices, cutting to, but not
through, opposite side.
4. Arrange salad greens on individual plates; top with
walnuts, goat cheese, and mushrooms. Drizzle evenly
with remaining ½ cup vinaigrette. **Makes** 4 servings.
Note: Substitute 1 (8-ounce) bottle Italian dressing, if
desired.

Black Bean 'n' Rice Salad

PREP: 20 MIN., OTHER: 1 HR.

2 tablespoons orange juice
2 tablespoons lemon juice
2 teaspoons olive oil
½ teaspoon salt
½ teaspoon ground cumin
½ teaspoon hot sauce
2 (15-ounce) cans black beans, rinsed and drained
1 cup cooked long-grain rice
3 plum tomatoes, seeded and chopped
1 green bell pepper, chopped
½ small red onion, chopped

1. Whisk together first 6 ingredients in a large bowl;
add beans and remaining ingredients, tossing gently
to coat. Cover and chill salad at least 1 hour. **Makes**
6 servings.

Tomato-Red Onion Salad

Create a variation of this salad by adding crumbled feta or
goat cheese, kalamata olives, and sliced cucumbers.

30 minutes or less
PREP: 15 MIN., OTHER: 10 MIN.

4 medium tomatoes, cut into ¼-inch-thick slices
¼ small red onion, thinly sliced
2 tablespoons chopped fresh oregano
2 tablespoons olive oil
1 tablespoon red wine vinegar
¼ teaspoon salt
⅛ teaspoon pepper

1. Layer tomatoes and onion slices on a serving platter.
Sprinkle evenly with chopped fresh oregano.
2. Whisk together oil, vinegar, salt, and pepper. Drizzle
evenly over tomato and onion slices. Let stand 10 minutes before serving. **Makes** 4 servings.

Cherry Tomato-Caper Salad

Cherry Tomato-Caper Salad

*Fresh basil leaves add a crisp herbal note to this colorful salad, and they're a snap to shred. Simply stack, roll, and slice.
The sliced leaves will fall from the roll in perfect-size pieces.*

30 minutes or less

PREP: 10 MIN., OTHER: 15 MIN.

make
ahead

2 tablespoons balsamic vinegar
1 tablespoon drained small capers
4 teaspoons olive oil
½ teaspoon freshly ground pepper
1 pint cherry or grape tomatoes, halved
6 fresh basil leaves, shredded
Bibb lettuce leaves

1. Combine first 4 ingredients. Drizzle over tomato halves, tossing to coat. Let stand at least 15 minutes or up to 1 hour. Sprinkle with basil. Serve over Bibb lettuce. **Makes** 4 servings.

Southwestern
Knots, page 364

no-fuss
BREADS

Tiny Cream Cheese Biscuits

The three simple ingredients below are worth committing to memory so you can stir up these gems without even looking at the recipe.

30 minutes or less
PREP: 8 MIN., COOK: 17 MIN.

1 (8-ounce) package cream cheese,
    softened
½ cup butter or margarine,
    softened
1 cup self-rising flour

1. Beat cream cheese and butter in a small mixing bowl at medium speed with an electric mixer 2 minutes or until creamy.
2. Gradually add flour to cream cheese mixture, beating at low speed just until blended.
3. Spoon dough into ungreased miniature (1¾-inch) muffin pans, filling full. Bake at 400° for 15 to 17 minutes or until golden. Remove from pans immediately. Serve hot. **Makes** 1½ dozen.

Biscuit Poppers

These unbelievably easy biscuits have a buttery, flaky texture like the ones Grandma used to bake.

30 minutes or less
PREP: 10 MIN., COOK: 20 MIN.

1 (8-ounce) container sour cream
½ cup butter, melted
2¼ cups all-purpose baking mix

1. Whisk together sour cream and butter until smooth. Stir in baking mix just until moistened. With floured hands, roll into 1½-inch balls. Place in lightly greased miniature muffin cups.
2. Bake at 350° for 18 to 20 minutes or until biscuits are golden brown. Remove from pans immediately. **Makes** 2 dozen.

Cheese Garlic Biscuits

The ¼ teaspoon garlic powder in this recipe equals 2 minced garlic cloves or 1 teaspoon jarred minced garlic. Take your pick.

20 minutes or less
PREP: 10 MIN., COOK: 10 MIN.

2 cups all-purpose baking mix
⅔ cup milk
½ cup (2 ounces) shredded Cheddar cheese
¼ cup butter, melted
¼ teaspoon garlic powder

1. Stir together first 3 ingredients until soft dough forms. Stir vigorously 30 seconds. Drop by tablespoonfuls onto an ungreased baking sheet.
2. Bake at 450° for 8 to 10 minutes.
3. Stir together butter and garlic powder; brush over warm biscuits. **Makes** 10 to 12 biscuits.

Biscuit Poppers

Streusel-Topped Pumpkin Muffins

Streusel-Topped Pumpkin Muffins

Muffin tops are indeed the best part of the bread, especially when it means a streusel packed with pecans and brown sugar. Muffin top pans allow you to indulge with this quick bread.

PREP: 10 MIN., COOK: 22 MIN., OTHER: 5 MIN.

make ahead

⅓ cup shortening
1 cup granulated sugar
2 large eggs
1⅔ cups all-purpose flour
1 teaspoon baking powder
¼ teaspoon baking soda
½ teaspoon salt
½ teaspoon ground cinnamon
¼ teaspoon ground cloves
1 cup canned, mashed pumpkin
⅓ cup water
½ cup chopped pecans
1 teaspoon vanilla extract
½ cup uncooked regular oats
½ cup all-purpose flour
½ cup firmly packed light brown sugar
¼ cup cold butter or margarine, cut into pieces
½ cup chopped pecans

1. Beat shortening at medium speed with an electric mixer until creamy; gradually add 1 cup sugar, beating well. Add eggs, 1 at a time, beating until blended after each addition.

2. Combine 1⅔ cups flour and next 5 ingredients; add to shortening mixture alternately with pumpkin and water, beginning and ending with flour mixture. Beat at low speed until blended after each addition. Stir in ½ cup pecans and vanilla. Spoon into greased muffin top pans, filling three-fourths full.

3. Combine oats, ½ cup flour, and brown sugar. Cut in butter with a pastry blender until crumbly; stir in ½ cup pecans. Sprinkle streusel over batter. Bake at 375° for 22 minutes or until a wooden pick inserted in center comes out clean. Cool in pans on a wire rack 5 minutes. Remove from pans, and cool on wire racks. **Makes** 1 dozen.

Note: If you don't have a muffin top pan, spoon batter into regular 2½-inch muffin pans, filling two-thirds full. Bake at 375° for 20 minutes or until a wooden pick inserted in center comes out clean. **Makes** 1½ dozen.

Raspberry-Streusel Muffins

The streusel (German for "sprinkle") makes a delicious crown for these sweet muffins. It's a crumbly topping of flour, butter, sugar, and, in this recipe, chopped pecans.

PREP: 15 MIN., COOK: 25 MIN.

1¾ cups all-purpose flour, divided
2 teaspoons baking powder
½ cup granulated sugar
1 large egg, lightly beaten
½ cup milk
½ cup plus 2 tablespoons butter, melted
    and divided
1 cup frozen unsweetened raspberries
¼ cup chopped pecans
¼ cup firmly packed brown sugar

1. Combine 1½ cups flour, baking powder, and sugar in a large bowl; make a well in center of mixture.
2. Combine egg, milk, and ½ cup butter; add to dry ingredients, stirring just until dry ingredients are moistened. Fold in raspberries. Spoon into a lightly greased muffin pan, filling two-thirds full.
3. Combine remaining ¼ cup flour, remaining 2 tablespoons butter, pecans, and brown sugar; sprinkle over muffins.
4. Bake at 375° for 20 to 25 minutes. Remove muffins from pan immediately. **Makes** 1 dozen.

White Chocolate-Macadamia Nut Muffins

Chunks of melted white chocolate make little pockets of sweetness in these muffins.

30 minutes or less
PREP: 10 MIN., COOK: 12 MIN.

2½ cups all-purpose baking mix
½ cup sugar
¾ cup coarsely chopped white chocolate (we used
    Baker's Premium)
½ cup coarsely chopped macadamia nuts
¾ cup half-and-half
3 tablespoons vegetable oil
2 teaspoons vanilla extract
1 large egg, lightly beaten

1. Combine baking mix and sugar in a large bowl; stir in chocolate and nuts. Make a well in center of mixture. Combine half-and-half and remaining 3 ingredients; add to dry ingredients, stirring just until dry ingredients are moistened.
2. Spoon batter into a lightly greased muffin pan, filling two-thirds full. Bake at 400° for 11 to 12 minutes or until a wooden pick inserted into center comes out clean. Remove from pan immediately. **Makes** 1 dozen.

Broccoli Cornbread Muffins

PREP: 20 MIN., COOK: 20 MIN., OTHER: 3 MIN.

1 (8½-ounce) package corn muffin mix
1 (10-ounce) package frozen chopped
    broccoli, thawed
1 cup (4 ounces) shredded Cheddar cheese
1 small onion, chopped
2 large eggs
½ cup butter or margarine, melted and slightly
    cooled

1. Combine first 4 ingredients in a large bowl; make a well in center of mixture.
2. Stir together eggs and butter, blending well; add to broccoli mixture, stirring just until dry ingredients are moistened.
3. Spoon into lightly greased mini muffin pans, filling three-fourths full.
4. Bake at 325° for 15 to 20 minutes or until golden. Let stand 2 to 3 minutes before removing from pans. **Makes** 2 dozen.

Cheese Muffins

The buttery, fluffy texture of these cheesy muffins makes them simply irresistible. We like sharp Cheddar in these golden muffins to maximize the cheese flavor.

30 minutes or less
PREP: 10 MIN., COOK: 12 MIN.

2 tablespoons butter or margarine,
    divided
½ cup chopped onion
1½ cups all-purpose baking mix
1 cup (4 ounces) shredded sharp Cheddar cheese,
    divided
1 large egg, lightly beaten
½ cup milk
1 tablespoon sesame seeds

1. Melt 1 tablespoon butter in a large skillet over medium-high heat; add onion, and sauté until tender. Remove from heat.
2. Add baking mix and ½ cup cheese to onion mixture in skillet. Combine egg and milk; add to onion mixture, stirring just until moistened. Spoon into a lightly greased muffin pan, filling half full. Sprinkle

with remaining ½ cup cheese and sesame seeds; dot with remaining 1 tablespoon butter.
3. Bake at 400° for 12 minutes or until golden. Remove from pan immediately, and serve warm. **Makes** 1 dozen.

Peanut Butter Bread

Slather honey and butter on toasted slices of this delicious bread.

PREP: 15 MIN., COOK: 1 HR.

2 cups all-purpose flour
½ cup sugar
2 teaspoons baking powder
1 teaspoon salt
¾ cup creamy or crunchy peanut butter
1 large egg
1 cup milk

1. Stir together first 4 ingredients in a medium bowl.
2. Cut in peanut butter with a fork or pastry blender until crumbly.
3. Stir together egg and milk; stir into dry ingredients just until moistened. Pour batter into a greased 9- x 5-inch loaf pan.
4. Bake at 350° for 1 hour or until a wooden pick inserted in center of bread comes out clean. Remove from pan immediately, and cool on a wire rack. **Makes** 1 (9-inch) loaf.

Peanut Butter Muffins: Spoon batter into greased muffin pans, filling two-thirds full. Stir together ½ cup uncooked regular oats; 2 tablespoons golden raisins, chopped; 2 tablespoons honey; and 1 tablespoon butter or margarine, melted. Spoon oats mixture evenly over batter. Bake at 350° for 25 to 30 minutes. **Makes** 1 dozen. Prep: 20 min., Cook: 30 min.

Peanut Butter Bread

Southwestern Knots

Southwestern Knots

*Just three ingredients—butter, chili powder, and cumin—are brushed
onto refrigerated breadsticks to make Southwestern Knots.*

30 minutes or less
PREP: 15 MIN., COOK: 15 MIN.

2½ tablespoons butter or margarine, melted
¼ teaspoon chili powder
¼ teaspoon ground cumin
1 (11-ounce) can refrigerated breadsticks

1. Stir together first 3 ingredients until blended.
2. Unroll breadsticks. Loosely tie each breadstick into a
knot, and place, 1 inch apart, on an ungreased baking
sheet. Brush evenly with butter mixture.

3. Bake at 350° for 15 minutes or until breadsticks are
golden. **Makes** 1 dozen.

Italian Bread Knots: Substitute ¼ teaspoon Italian
seasoning for chili powder and cumin. Sprinkle bread
knots with 1 tablespoon grated Parmesan cheese.
Proceed as directed.

Cajun Bread Knots: Substitute ½ teaspoon Cajun
seasoning for chili powder and cumin. Add ¼ teaspoon dried thyme, if desired. Proceed as directed.

Blue Cheese Bread

The strong flavor and aroma of this toasted bread is a nice complement to many of the salads in the previous chapter.

20 minutes or less
PREP: 10 MIN., COOK: 7 MIN.

1 (12-ounce) crusty French bread loaf
½ cup butter, softened
1 (4-ounce) package crumbled blue cheese

1. Cut French bread loaf into ¾-inch-thick slices, cutting to, but not through, opposite side.
2. Stir together ½ cup butter and crumbled blue cheese; spread evenly on both sides of each bread slice. Wrap bread loaf in aluminum foil, and place on a baking sheet.
3. Bake at 375° for 7 minutes or until bread is toasted. **Makes** 8 servings.

Buttery Garlic Bread

This garlicky treat is the perfect match for spaghetti with meat sauce.

20 minutes or less
PREP: 10 MIN., COOK: 7 MIN.

½ cup butter or margarine
4 garlic cloves, pressed
½ teaspoon salt
1 (16-ounce) Italian bread loaf
1½ teaspoons Italian seasoning
¼ cup freshly grated Parmesan cheese

1. Melt butter in a skillet over medium-high heat; add garlic and salt, and sauté 2 minutes.
2. Cut bread into 1½-inch slices, and dip into butter mixture, coating both sides. Place on a baking sheet.
3. Stir together Italian seasoning and Parmesan cheese; sprinkle on 1 side of each bread slice.
4. Broil 5 inches from heat 4 minutes or until cheese melts. **Makes**: 8 servings.

Herb Bread

A medley of herbs creates a savory bread suitable for any entrée or soup.

PREP: 10 MIN., COOK: 25 MIN.

make ahead

1 (16-ounce) French bread loaf
1 cup butter or margarine, softened
1 (2¼-ounce) can chopped ripe olives
½ cup chopped fresh parsley
⅓ cup chopped green onions
1½ teaspoons dried basil
½ teaspoon garlic powder
½ teaspoon dried tarragon
¼ teaspoon celery seeds

1. Slice bread in half horizontally.
2. Combine butter and remaining 7 ingredients; spread evenly over cut sides of bread. Place halves together; wrap in aluminum foil. Store in refrigerator until ready to bake.
3. Bake at 350° for 25 minutes or until thoroughly heated. Cut into slices to serve. **Makes** 12 servings.

Pesto-and-Tomato
Focaccia

Pesto-and-Tomato Focaccia

Mix up a simple homemade pesto while the crust prebakes, and you can have this unbelievable focaccia in 23 minutes flat. Substitute ½ cup store-bought pesto for our homemade version, if you'd like.

30 minutes or less
PREP: 10 MIN., COOK: 13 MIN.

2 tablespoons stone-ground yellow cornmeal
1 (13.8-ounce) can refrigerated pizza crust
1 cup fresh basil leaves
½ cup pine nuts
1 tablespoon olive oil
1 large garlic clove
½ teaspoon salt
¼ teaspoon pepper
¾ cup (3 ounces) shredded provolone cheese, divided
2 plum tomatoes, cut into ¼-inch-thick slices

1. Sprinkle cornmeal onto a lightly greased baking sheet. Unroll pizza crust on baking sheet into a 12- x 10-inch rectangle. Bake at 450° for 8 minutes or until crust is golden.
2. Meanwhile, process basil and next 5 ingredients in a blender or food processor until blended, stopping to scrape down sides.
3. Spread pesto over crust. Sprinkle with ½ cup cheese. Arrange tomato slices evenly over cheese. Sprinkle with remaining ¼ cup cheese.
4. Bake at 450° for 3 to 5 minutes or until cheese melts. Serve immediately. **Makes** 8 servings.

Fast Rosemary-Dried Tomato Flatbread

This yummy flatbread is laced with pockets of flavorful rosemary, garlic, and tomato. Frozen bread dough keeps it easy to make. The package of frozen dough comes as two loaves, so use one loaf and leave the second one frozen for the next time you prepare this recipe.

PREP: 8 MIN., COOK: 16 MIN., OTHER: 15 MIN.

¼ cup chopped fresh rosemary
2 tablespoons dried tomatoes in oil, drained and chopped
1 garlic clove, minced
½ (32-ounce) package frozen bread dough, thawed
1 teaspoon olive oil
1 tablespoon freshly grated Parmesan cheese

1. Combine first 3 ingredients. Turn dough out onto a lightly floured surface; knead in rosemary mixture. Place dough on a lightly greased baking sheet. Press into a 9-inch circle.
2. Cover and let rise in a warm place (85°), free from drafts, 15 minutes. Brush loaf with oil. Sprinkle with cheese.
3. Bake at 400° for 16 minutes or until golden. **Makes** 8 servings.

Pecan Crescent Twists

30 minutes or less
PREP: 18 MIN., COOK: 12 MIN.

2 (8-ounce) cans refrigerated crescent rolls
3 tablespoons butter or margarine, melted and
　　divided
½ cup chopped pecans
¼ cup granulated sugar
1 teaspoon ground cinnamon
⅛ teaspoon ground nutmeg
½ cup powdered sugar
2½ teaspoons maple syrup or milk

1. Unroll crescent rolls, and separate each can into 2 rectangles, pressing perforations to seal. Brush evenly with 2 tablespoons melted butter.
2. Stir together chopped pecans and next 3 ingredients; sprinkle 3 tablespoons pecan mixture onto buttered side of each rectangle, pressing in gently.
3. Roll up, starting at 1 long side, and twist. Cut 6 shallow ½-inch-long diagonal slits in each roll.
4. Shape rolls into rings, pressing ends together; place on a lightly greased baking sheet. Brush rings evenly with remaining 1 tablespoon butter.
5. Bake at 375° for 12 minutes or until rings are golden.
6. Stir together powdered sugar and maple syrup until glaze is smooth; drizzle evenly over warm rings. Cut rings in half, and serve. **Makes** 8 servings.

Italian Cheese Breadsticks

Dip these pizza-flavored sticks into your favorite brand of marinara sauce.

20 minutes or less
PREP: 5 MIN., COOK: 12 MIN.

1 (11-ounce) can refrigerated soft breadsticks
1 to 2 tablespoons olive oil
1½ teaspoons garlic powder
1 teaspoon dried Italian seasoning
1 cup (4 ounces) shredded mozzarella cheese

1. Unroll breadstick dough; twist breadsticks, and place 1 inch apart on a lightly greased aluminum foil-lined baking sheet. Brush breadsticks with oil.

Combine garlic powder and Italian seasoning; sprinkle over breadsticks.
2. Bake at 400° for 9 to 10 minutes or until golden. Sprinkle with cheese; bake 1 to 2 minutes or until cheese melts. Serve immediately. **Makes** 8 breadsticks.

Spicy Breadsticks

Spicy seasoned pepper blend makes these crisp breadsticks perfect for pairing with robust gumbo or stew.

30 minutes or less
PREP: 15 MIN., COOK: 12 MIN.

1 (11-ounce) can refrigerated soft breadsticks
1 large egg, lightly beaten
2 tablespoons paprika
2 tablespoons seasoned pepper blend (we used
　　McCormick, see note)

1. Separate breadsticks; working with 2 at a time, roll each breadstick into a 12-inch rope. Brush ropes with egg. Twist ropes together, pinching ends to seal. Repeat with remaining breadsticks.
2. Combine paprika and pepper blend; spread mixture on a paper plate. Roll breadsticks in pepper mixture, pressing gently to coat. (Wash hands between rolling each breadstick, if necessary.)
3. Place breadsticks on a lightly greased baking sheet. Bake at 375° for 10 to 12 minutes. **Makes** 4 servings.
Note: If you can't find seasoned pepper blend, combine equal portions of cracked black pepper, red bell pepper flakes, and salt.

Spicy Breadsticks

Cinnamon-Apple Breakfast Buns

30 minutes or less
PREP: 4 MIN., COOK: 22 MIN.

1 (12.4-ounce) can refrigerated cinnamon rolls
1 (1.62-ounce) package instant cinnamon and spice
    oatmeal
¼ cup firmly packed brown sugar
¼ cup chopped pecans
¼ teaspoon ground cinnamon
Dash of ground nutmeg
1 tablespoon butter or margarine, melted
1 Granny Smith apple, peeled, cored, and cut into
    8 rings

1. Separate cinnamon rolls, and place in a lightly
greased 8- or 9-inch round cake pan; set icing aside.
Bake rolls according to package directions.
2. Meanwhile, stir together oatmeal and next 5
ingredients. Place 1 apple ring on each cinnamon roll;
sprinkle oatmeal mixture evenly over cinnamon rolls.
3. Bake at 400° for 20 to 22 minutes.
4. Remove top to icing. Microwave icing at LOW
(10% power) for 20 seconds; drizzle evenly over rolls.
Makes 8 rolls.

Caramel-Nut Pull-Apart Bread

*This warm, gooey bread is swimming in sweet caramel. To
enjoy it at its best, serve immediately.*

PREP: 10 MIN., COOK: 30 MIN.

1 cup plus 2 tablespoons firmly packed brown sugar
1 cup chopped walnuts
¾ cup butter, melted
3 (10-ounce) cans refrigerated cinnamon and sugar
    biscuits (we used Pillsbury Hungry Jack)

1. Combine brown sugar and walnuts in a small bowl.
Stir in butter. Spoon half of sugar mixture into a
lightly greased Bundt pan.
2. Cut each biscuit in half. Place half of biscuit halves
over sugar mixture. Spoon remaining sugar mixture
evenly over biscuits in pan, and top with remaining
biscuit halves.
3. Bake at 350° for 30 minutes or until browned. Invert
bread onto a serving platter immediately, spooning
any brown sugar sauce left in pan over bread. **Makes**
12 servings.

Easy Caramel-Chocolate Sticky Buns

*Everyone will clamor for these sticky buns when they discover
hidden chocolate in the center of each! It's a good thing these
serve a crowd.*

PREP: 12 MIN., COOK: 30 MIN.

1 (15-ounce) container ready-to-spread coconut-
    pecan frosting
1 cup pecan halves
2 (10-ounce) cans refrigerated buttermilk biscuits
20 milk chocolate kisses, unwrapped

1. Spread frosting in bottom of a lightly greased 9-inch
square pan. Sprinkle pecan halves over frosting.
2. Separate biscuits; flatten each to about ¼-inch
thickness. Place a chocolate kiss to 1 side of center of
each biscuit. Fold biscuit in half, forming a semicircle;
press edges of biscuit gently to seal. Repeat procedure
with remaining biscuits and chocolate kisses. Arrange
biscuits over pecans, placing flat sides down.
3. Bake at 375° for 28 to 30 minutes or until lightly
browned. Cool in pan on a wire rack 3 minutes; invert
onto serving plate, and serve immediately. **Makes**
20 buns.

Caramel-Nut Pull-Apart Bread

Veggie Pancakes

Veggie Pancakes

For something out of the ordinary, serve these pancakes with sour cream and salsa.

30 minutes or less
PREP: 5 MIN., COOK: 20 MIN.

1 (6-ounce) package self-rising white cornmeal mix
1 (11-ounce) can whole kernel corn, drained
½ large red bell pepper, chopped
7 green onions, thinly sliced
1 large carrot, shredded
⅔ cup buttermilk
1 large egg, lightly beaten
½ cup all-purpose flour
½ teaspoon dried crushed red pepper
¼ cup vegetable oil, divided
Toppings: sour cream, salsa
Garnishes: chopped fresh cilantro, leaf lettuce

1. Stir together first 9 ingredients.
2. Heat 2 tablespoons oil in a large nonstick skillet. Drop half of batter by ⅓ cupfuls into hot oil, and cook 3 to 4 minutes on each side or until golden. Keep warm.
3. Repeat procedure with remaining oil and batter. Serve pancakes with desired toppings. Garnish, if desired. **Makes** 12 pancakes.

Pumpkin Pancakes

These spiced pumpkin pancakes are a true autumn treat when served with apple butter on top.

30 minutes or less
PREP: 8 MIN., COOK: 4 MIN. PER BATCH

1 cup all-purpose flour
2 teaspoons baking powder
½ teaspoon salt
1 tablespoon sugar
½ teaspoon ground cinnamon or pumpkin
    pie spice
2 large eggs, separated
¾ cup milk
½ cup canned pumpkin
¼ cup butter or margarine, melted

1. Combine first 5 ingredients in a large bowl; make a well in center of mixture.

2. Combine egg yolks, milk, pumpkin, and butter; add to flour mixture, stirring just until dry ingredients are moistened.
3. Beat egg whites at high speed with an electric mixer until stiff peaks form. Gently fold beaten whites into pumpkin mixture.
4. Pour about ¼ cup batter for each pancake onto a hot, lightly greased griddle. Cook pancakes until tops are covered with bubbles and edges look cooked; turn and cook other side. **Makes** 12 (4-inch) pancakes.

Easy Banana Pancakes

These airy cakes come together in a flash, thanks to baking mix and mashed bananas.

30 minutes or less
PREP: 5 MIN., COOK: 4 MIN. PER BATCH

2 cups all-purpose baking mix
1 cup milk
2 ripe bananas, mashed
2 large eggs, lightly beaten
Maple syrup or fruit topping

1. Combine first 4 ingredients in a medium bowl, stirring just until dry ingredients are moistened.
2. Pour about ¼ cup batter for each pancake onto a hot, lightly greased griddle. Cook pancakes 2 minutes or until tops are covered with bubbles and edges look cooked; turn and cook other side. Serve immediately with syrup or fruit topping. **Makes** 16 pancakes.

Blueberry Pancakes

30 minutes or less
PREP: 5 MIN., COOK: 25 MIN.

1½ cups all-purpose flour
¼ cup sugar
1 teaspoon baking powder
⅛ teaspoon salt
¾ cup milk
1 large egg
1 tablespoon vegetable oil
½ cup fresh or frozen blueberries
Maple syrup

1. Stir together first 4 ingredients; make a well in center of mixture.
2. Stir together milk, egg, and oil; add to dry ingredients, stirring just until moistened. Fold in blueberries.
3. Pour about ¼ cup batter for each pancake onto a hot, lightly greased griddle. Cook pancakes until tops are covered with bubbles and edges look cooked; turn and cook other side. Serve with maple syrup. **Makes** 8 to 10 pancakes.

Waffles

Serve this family favorite in the evening alongside fresh fruit and bacon for a fast and delicious dinner.

20 minutes or less
PREP: 5 MIN., COOK: 15 MIN.

2 cups all-purpose baking mix
½ cup vegetable oil
2 large eggs
1 cup club soda

1. Stir together first 3 ingredients in a large bowl; add club soda, stirring until batter is blended.
2. Cook in a preheated, greased waffle iron until golden. **Makes** 10 (4-inch) waffles.

Cornbread Waffles

Freeze any leftover waffles up to a month in a zip-top plastic freezer bag. Crisp them in a toaster oven to reheat them. No need to thaw.

30 minutes or less
PREP: 10 MIN., COOK: 20 MIN.

make
ahead

1½ cups plain white cornmeal
½ cup all-purpose flour
2 tablespoons sugar
2½ teaspoons baking powder
¾ teaspoon salt
1 large egg
1½ cups milk

1. Stir together first 5 ingredients in a large bowl. Stir together egg and milk; add to cornmeal mixture, stirring just until dry ingredients are moistened.
2. Cook in a preheated, oiled waffle iron just until crisp. **Makes** 12 (4-inch) waffles.

Waffles

Corn Spoonbread

Corn Spoonbread

Sweet nuggets of corn pack rich flavor in this buttery bread.

PREP: 6 MIN., COOK: 35 MIN.

1 (8½-ounce) package corn muffin mix (we used Jiffy)
1 (8¼-ounce) can cream-style corn
1 (8¾-ounce) can sweet whole kernel corn, drained
1 (8-ounce) container sour cream
½ cup butter or margarine, melted
2 large eggs

1. Stir together all ingredients, and pour into a lightly greased 11- x 7-inch baking dish.
2. Bake at 350° for 35 minutes or until golden. **Makes** 12 servings.

Green Chile Cornbread

30 minutes or less

PREP: 5 MIN., COOK: 20 MIN.

2 (8½-ounce) packages corn muffin mix
1 (8¼-ounce) can cream-style corn
1 (4.5-ounce) can chopped green chiles, drained
1 cup (4 ounces) shredded Cheddar cheese
½ cup plain yogurt
¼ cup milk
2 large eggs, lightly beaten

1. Combine all ingredients, stirring just until dry ingredients are moistened. Pour batter into a lightly greased 13- x 9-inch pan. Bake at 450° for 20 minutes or until golden. **Makes** 15 servings.

Southern traditions

Southern cooking doesn't get more down-home than spoonbread and cornbread. They're both made from cornmeal, but their textures seem a world apart.

- Spoonbread is a puddinglike bread made from cornmeal, butter, milk, and eggs. It's so light and creamy that it requires a spoon. One bite and this soufflélike dish could become a new favorite. Serve spoonbread warm from the oven; it becomes dense as it cools. It's great for breakfast, lunch, or dinner. Also, try it warmed in the microwave with just a kiss of butter and a crack of fresh black pepper. Spoonbread invites a host of accompaniments—our favorite is any braised meat smothered in gravy, especially when flavored with smoked bacon drippings.
- Cornbread's crisp edge and slightly gritty texture make it a popular staple in the South—all by itself, crumbled over chili, or smeared with butter and honey. Traditionally, cornbread is prepared in a well-seasoned cast-iron skillet. The base of cornbread is cornmeal, which is sold as plain meal, self-rising meal, and as a mix. Cornmeal can be made from either white or yellow corn, and white and yellow cornmeal can be used interchangeably. (Cornbread made with yellow meal tends to be slightly coarser.) Cornbread batter should be fairly thin and easy to pour. If it seems too thick, add a little more liquid. Pouring the batter into a very hot pan with a dab of melted fat yields a crisp crust when baked.

Apple Shortbread Crisp,
page 391

DESSERTS
in a dash

Pecan-Chocolate Chip Cookies

Ultimate Chocolate Chip Cookies

PREP: 30 MIN., COOK: 14 MIN. PER BATCH

make ahead

¾ cup butter, softened
¾ cup granulated sugar
¾ cup firmly packed dark brown sugar
2 large eggs
1½ teaspoons vanilla extract
2¼ cups plus 2 tablespoons all-purpose flour
1 teaspoon baking soda
¾ teaspoon salt
1 (12-ounce) package semisweet chocolate morsels

1. Beat butter and sugars at medium speed with an electric mixer until creamy. Add eggs and vanilla, beating until blended.
2. Combine flour, baking soda, and salt in a small bowl; gradually add to butter mixture, beating well. Stir in morsels. Drop by tablespoonfuls onto lightly greased baking sheets.
3. Bake at 350° for 8 to 14 minutes or to desired degree of doneness. Remove to wire racks to cool completely.
Makes about 5 dozen.

Pecan-Chocolate Chip Cookies: Add 1½ cups chopped, toasted pecans with chocolate morsels. Proceed with recipe as directed.

Oatmeal-Raisin-Chocolate Chip Cookies: Reduce flour to 2 cups. Add 1 cup uncooked quick-cooking oats to dry ingredients and 1 cup raisins with chocolate morsels. Proceed with recipe as directed.

Almond-Toffee-Chocolate Chip Cookies: Reduce chocolate morsels to 1 cup. Add ½ cup slivered toasted almonds and 1 cup toffee bits. Proceed with recipe as directed.
Note: For testing purposes only, we used Hershey's Heath Bits O'Brickle Toffee Bits.

Coconut-Macadamia-Chocolate Chunk Cookies: Substitute 1 (12-ounce) package semisweet chocolate chunks for morsels. Add 1 cup white chocolate morsels, ½ cup sweetened flaked coconut, and ½ cup macadamia nuts with chocolate chunks. Proceed with recipe as directed.

Nutty Oatmeal-Chocolate Chunk Cookies

PREP: 10 MIN., COOK: 8 MIN. PER BATCH

make
ahead

2½ cups uncooked regular oats
1 cup butter or margarine, softened
1 cup granulated sugar
1 cup firmly packed brown sugar
2 large eggs
1 tablespoon vanilla extract
2 cups all-purpose flour
1 teaspoon baking powder
1 teaspoon baking soda
½ teaspoon salt
3 (1.55-ounce) milk chocolate candy bars, chopped
1½ cups chopped pecans

1. Process oats in a blender or food processor until ground; set aside.

2. Beat 1 cup butter and sugars at medium speed with an electric mixer until fluffy. Add eggs and vanilla, and beat until blended.

3. Combine ground oats, flour, and next 3 ingredients. Add to butter mixture, beating until blended. Stir in chocolate and pecans. Drop dough by tablespoonfuls onto ungreased baking sheets.

4. Bake at 375° for 7 to 8 minutes or until golden brown; remove to wire racks to cool. **Makes** 6 dozen.

Nutty Oatmeal-Chocolate
Chunk Cookies

Coconut-Macadamia Cookies

PREP: 15 MIN., COOK: 10 MIN. PER BATCH

½ cup granulated sugar
½ cup firmly packed light brown sugar
½ cup butter or margarine, softened
1 large egg
1 teaspoon vanilla extract
1¼ cups all-purpose flour
1 cup uncooked quick-cooking oats
½ cup sweetened flaked coconut
½ teaspoon baking soda
¼ teaspoon salt
1 cup coarsely chopped macadamia nuts

1. Beat first 5 ingredients at medium speed with an electric mixer until fluffy.
2. Combine flour and next 5 ingredients. Add half of flour mixture at a time to sugar mixture, beating at low speed until blended after each addition.
3. Drop dough by heaping teaspoonfuls 2 inches apart onto lightly greased baking sheets.
4. Bake at 350° for 7 to 10 minutes or until edges are golden brown. Cool on baking sheets 1 minute. Remove to wire racks to cool. **Makes** 3 dozen.

Peanut Blossom Cookies

PREP: 10 MIN., COOK: 10 MIN. PER BATCH

1 (14-ounce) can sweetened
    condensed milk
¾ cup creamy peanut butter
1 teaspoon vanilla extract
2 cups all-purpose baking mix
⅓ cup sugar
1 (9-ounce) package milk chocolate kisses

1. Stir together condensed milk, peanut butter, and vanilla, stirring until smooth. Add baking mix, stirring well.
2. Shape dough into 1-inch balls; roll in sugar, and place on ungreased baking sheets. Make an indentation in center of each ball with thumb or spoon handle.
3. Bake at 375° for 8 to 10 minutes or until lightly browned. Remove cookies from oven, and press a chocolate kiss in center of each cookie. Transfer to wire racks to cool completely. **Makes** 4 dozen.

Chocolate-Pecan Cookies

If you love cookies but are short on time, try making these chocolaty treats that start with a cake mix.

PREP: 5 MIN., COOK: 10 MIN. PER BATCH

1 (18.25-ounce) package chocolate or
    yellow cake mix
½ cup vegetable oil
2 large eggs
1 cup (6 ounces) semisweet chocolate morsels
½ cup chopped pecans

1. Beat first 3 ingredients at medium speed with an electric mixer until batter is smooth. Stir in chocolate morsels and pecans. Drop by heaping teaspoonfuls onto ungreased baking sheets.
2. Bake at 350° for 8 to 10 minutes. Remove to wire racks to cool. **Makes** 4½ dozen.

Peanut Blossom Cookies

Lemon Squares

Lemon Squares

PREP: 20 MIN., COOK: 40 MIN.

make
ahead

1 cup all-purpose flour
⅓ cup powdered sugar
⅓ cup butter or margarine, cut into small pieces
1 cup granulated sugar
2 tablespoons all-purpose flour
½ teaspoon baking powder
¼ teaspoon salt
3 egg whites
1 large egg
½ cup frozen lemon juice, thawed (see note)
1½ teaspoons grated lemon rind
¼ teaspoon butter extract
2 tablespoons powdered sugar

1. Combine 1 cup flour and ⅓ cup powdered sugar; cut in butter with a pastry blender until crumbly. Press firmly into bottom of a lightly greased 11- x 7-inch baking dish.
2. Bake at 350° for 20 minutes or until lightly browned.
3. Whisk together granulated sugar and next 8 ingredients until blended; pour over crust.
4. Bake at 350° for 20 minutes or until set. Cool on a wire rack. Cut into squares, and sprinkle evenly with 2 tablespoons powdered sugar. **Makes** 2 dozen.
Note: For testing purposes only, we used Minute Maid Premium 100% Pure Lemon Juice From Concentrate found in the freezer section. ½ cup fresh lemon juice may be substituted for frozen lemon juice.

Double Chocolate Brownies

PREP: 15 MIN., COOK: 40 MIN.

make ahead

2 (1-ounce) squares unsweetened
    chocolate
2 (1-ounce) squares semisweet chocolate
1 cup butter, softened
2 cups sugar
4 large eggs
1 cup all-purpose flour
½ teaspoon salt
1 teaspoon vanilla extract
¾ cup toasted chopped pecans
¾ cup semisweet chocolate morsels

1. Microwave chocolate squares in a small microwave-safe bowl at MEDIUM (50% power) for 30-second intervals until melted (about 1½ minutes total time). Stir chocolate until smooth.
2. Beat butter and sugar at medium speed with an electric mixer until light and fluffy. Add eggs, 1 at a time, beating just until blended after each addition. Add melted chocolate, beating just until blended.
3. Add flour and salt, beating at low speed just until blended. Stir in vanilla, ½ cup pecans, and ½ cup chocolate morsels. Spread batter into a greased and floured 13- x 9-inch baking pan. Sprinkle with remaining ¼ cup pecans and ¼ cup chocolate morsels.
4. Bake at 350° for 40 minutes or until set. Cool completely on a wire rack. **Makes** 32 brownies.

Double Chocolate Brownies With Caramel Frosting:
Prepare Double Chocolate Brownies as directed. Melt ¾ cup butter in a large saucepan over low heat. Stir in 2 cups sugar, ½ cup buttermilk, 12 large marshmallows, 1 tablespoon light corn syrup, and ½ teaspoon baking soda. Cook over medium heat, stirring occasionally, 20 to 25 minutes or until a candy thermometer registers 234° (soft-ball stage). Remove from heat, and pour mixture immediately into a large mixing bowl. Beat mixture with an electric mixer at high speed 5 minutes or until mixture thickens and begins to lose its gloss. Spread frosting evenly over brownies.

Gooey Turtle Bars

PREP: 10 MIN., COOK: 15 MIN., OTHER: 30 MIN.

make ahead

½ cup butter, melted
1½ cups vanilla wafer crumbs
1 (12-ounce) package semisweet chocolate
    morsels (2 cups)
1 cup pecan pieces
1 (12-ounce) jar caramel topping

1. Combine butter and wafer crumbs in a 13- x 9-inch pan; press into bottom of pan. Sprinkle with morsels and pecans.
2. Remove lid from caramel topping; microwave at HIGH 1 to 1½ minutes or until hot, stirring after 30 seconds. Drizzle evenly over pecans.
3. Bake at 350° for 12 to 15 minutes or until morsels melt; cool in pan on a wire rack. Cover and chill at least 30 minutes; cut into bars. **Makes** 2 dozen.

Creamy No-Bake Bars

Once these ice-cream sandwiches freeze, cut them into bars, and wrap individually with plastic wrap for ready-made treats.

PREP: 12 MIN.; OTHER: 8 HR., 30 MIN.

1 cup chopped pecans
1 cup sweetened flaked coconut
2½ cups crisp rice cereal, crushed
1 cup firmly packed light brown sugar
½ cup butter or margarine
1 quart vanilla ice cream, softened

1. Bake pecans and coconut separately in shallow pans at 350°, stirring occasionally, 5 to 10 minutes or until toasted. Combine pecans, coconut, and cereal in a medium bowl.
2. Bring brown sugar and butter to a boil in a small saucepan over medium heat, stirring constantly; boil, stirring constantly, 1 minute. Pour sugar mixture over cereal mixture, stirring until coated.
3. Press half of cereal mixture into a 9-inch square pan lined with plastic wrap; freeze until firm. Spread with ice cream; press remaining cereal mixture over ice cream. Cover and freeze 8 hours or until firm; freeze until ready to serve. **Makes** 16 bars.

Butter-Mint Shortbread

These cookies are like a dessert and after-dinner mint in one. They're especially tasty with hot tea.

PREP: 10 MIN., COOK: 20 MIN., OTHER: 10 MIN.

1 cup butter, softened
¾ cup powdered sugar
½ teaspoon mint extract
½ teaspoon vanilla extract
2 cups all-purpose flour
Powdered sugar

1. Beat butter and ¾ cup powdered sugar at medium speed with an electric mixer until light and fluffy. Add extracts, beating until blended. Gradually add flour, beating at low speed until blended after each addition. Pat dough into a 15- x 10-inch rectangle on a large baking sheet lined with parchment paper.
2. Bake at 325° for 18 to 20 minutes or until lightly browned. Cool on pan on a wire rack 10 minutes. Cut into squares; sprinkle with powdered sugar. Remove from pan; cool on wire rack. **Makes** 3 dozen.

Butter-Mint Shortbread

Texas Millionaires

Texas Millionaires

PREP: 25 MIN., OTHER: 1 HR., 5 MIN.

1 (14-ounce) package caramels
2 tablespoons butter or margarine
2 tablespoons water
3 cups pecan halves
1 cup semisweet chocolate morsels
8 (2-ounce) vanilla candy coating squares

1. Cook first 3 ingredients in a heavy saucepan over low heat, stirring constantly until smooth. Stir in pecan halves. Cool in pan 5 minutes.
2. Drop by tablespoonfuls onto lightly greased wax paper. Chill 1 hour, or freeze 20 minutes until firm.
3. Melt morsels and candy coating in a heavy saucepan over low heat, stirring until smooth. Dip caramel candies into chocolate mixture, allowing excess to drip; place on lightly greased wax paper. Let stand until firm. **Makes** 2 dozen.

Rocky Road Clusters

Crunchy almonds and soft marshmallows nestle in a bed of chocolate—a three-ingredient miracle.

30 minutes or less

PREP: 15 MIN., OTHER: 15 MIN.

1 (12-ounce) package semisweet
    chocolate morsels
1 cup miniature marshmallows
½ cup slivered almonds, toasted

1. Heat chocolate in a medium-size heavy saucepan over low heat until melted, stirring occasionally. Set aside, and cool.
2. Add marshmallows and almonds to chocolate; stir well. Drop by teaspoonfuls onto wax paper. Chill 15 minutes or until firm. Store in an airtight container in refrigerator. **Makes** 3 dozen.

Orange-Nut Balls

PREP: 30 MIN., OTHER: 1 HR.

½ cup butter or margarine, melted
1 (16-ounce) package powdered sugar, sifted
1 (6-ounce) can frozen orange juice concentrate,
    thawed
1 (12-ounce) package vanilla wafers, crushed
1 cup finely chopped pecans
1 (14-ounce) package sweetened flaked coconut

1. Stir together first 5 ingredients. Form into 1-inch balls; roll in coconut. Cover and chill 1 hour or until firm. Store in refrigerator up to 3 weeks. **Makes** 5 dozen.

Peanut Butter Fudge

20 minutes or less

PREP: 10 MIN., COOK: 5 MIN.

⅔ cup evaporated milk
1⅔ cups sugar
½ teaspoon salt
1½ cups miniature marshmallows
1 (10-ounce) package peanut butter morsels
½ cup chopped peanuts
1 teaspoon vanilla extract

1. Bring first 3 ingredients to a boil in a large saucepan. Cook over medium heat, stirring constantly, 5 minutes; remove from heat. Add marshmallows and remaining ingredients; stir until smooth. Pour into a greased 9-inch square pan; cool. Cut into squares. **Makes** 1¾ pounds.

Speedy Blackberry Cobbler

Sugar cookie dough is put to clever use to form a crispy crust atop this cobbler.

PREP: 6 MIN., COOK: 28 MIN.

4 cups fresh blackberries
¾ cup sugar
¼ cup all-purpose flour
1 teaspoon lemon zest
1 teaspoon fresh lemon juice
9 (¼-inch-thick) slices refrigerated sugar cookie
    dough (we used Pillsbury Sugar Cookie dough)
1 tablespoon sugar

1. Combine first 5 ingredients in a medium bowl; pour into a lightly greased 8-inch baking dish. Microwave at HIGH 8 minutes or until bubbly, stirring once.
2. Place cookie slices over berries; sprinkle evenly with 1 tablespoon sugar. Bake at 375° for 20 minutes or until golden. **Makes** 6 servings.

Apple-Blueberry Crunch

PREP: 10 MIN., COOK: 50 MIN.

1 (21-ounce) can apple pie filling
1 (14-ounce) package frozen blueberries
1 cup sugar
1 (18.25-ounce) package white cake mix
½ cup butter or margarine, melted
1 cup chopped walnuts, toasted
Ice cream or whipped topping

1. Spread pie filling in a lightly greased 13- x 9-inch pan.
2. Toss together frozen blueberries and ¾ cup sugar, and spoon over apple pie filling. Sprinkle cake mix evenly over fruit, and drizzle with melted butter. Sprinkle with chopped walnuts and remaining ¼ cup sugar.
3. Bake at 350° for 45 to 50 minutes or until golden and bubbly. Serve with ice cream. **Makes** 8 to 10 servings.

Black Forest Crisp

This is our one-pan interpretation of the attractive Black Forest torte.

PREP: 15 MIN., COOK: 50 MIN.

1 (21-ounce) can cherry pie filling
1 (8¼-ounce) can crushed pineapple, undrained
½ cup slivered almonds, toasted
1 cup semisweet chocolate morsels
1 cup sweetened flaked coconut
1 (18.25-ounce) package devil's food cake mix
½ cup butter or margarine, cut up
Ice cream or whipped topping

1. Layer cherry pie filling, crushed pineapple, slivered almonds, chocolate morsels, and flaked coconut in a lightly greased 13- x 9-inch baking dish. Sprinkle cake mix over layers, and dot evenly with butter.
2. Bake at 350° for 45 to 50 minutes or until golden and bubbly. Serve with ice cream. **Makes** 8 to 10 servings.

Apple Shortbread Crisp

Apple Shortbread Crisp

The buttery, crispy shortbread cookie topping on this dessert will leave you wanting more.

PREP: 7 MIN., COOK: 36 MIN.

2 (12-ounce) packages frozen apple chunks (we used
    Stouffer's Harvest Apples)
6 tablespoons butter or margarine
20 shortbread cookies, crushed (we used Keebler
    Sandies Simply Shortbread)
½ cup chopped walnuts
¼ cup firmly packed light brown sugar
1 teaspoon ground cinnamon, divided
¼ teaspoon ground nutmeg
2 tablespoons light brown sugar
Vanilla ice cream

1. Prick plastic wrap covering apple chunks several times with a fork; microwave at MEDIUM (50% power) 7 minutes or until apple is thawed. Let stand 2 minutes.

2. Meanwhile, melt butter in a large skillet over medium heat; add cookie crumbs and walnuts. Cook, stirring constantly, 2 minutes. Remove from heat, and stir in ¼ cup brown sugar, ½ teaspoon cinnamon, and nutmeg.

3. Combine 2 tablespoons brown sugar and remaining ½ teaspoon cinnamon; sprinkle in a lightly greased 1-quart baking dish. Sprinkle half of apple over brown sugar mixture; top with half of cookie crumb mixture. Repeat layers with remaining apple and crumb mixture.

4. Bake at 375° for 25 minutes or until cookie mixture is golden. Serve warm with vanilla ice cream. **Makes** 6 servings.

Fresh Fruit Pizza

The lemon curd not only holds the fruit in place, it also serves as an exquisite anchor for all the flavors. You may have never imagined such a pizza. Now you'll never forget it. Serve any leftover sauce over cut fruit or pound cake.

PREP: 23 MIN., COOK: 13 MIN.

make
ahead

1 (16-ounce) package refrigerated
    sugar cookie dough
2 tablespoons seedless raspberry jam, melted
¾ cup Lemon Curd
2 cups fresh raspberries
2 cups fresh blackberries
2 cups fresh sliced strawberries

1. Press cookie dough into a 12-inch pizza pan coated with cooking spray. Bake at 350° for 13 minutes or until golden brown. Cool completely on a wire rack.
2. Spread jam over crust. Spread Lemon Curd over jam; arrange raspberries, blackberries, and strawberry slices on top. Serve immediately. **Makes** 12 servings.

Lemon Curd:

PREP: 6 MIN., COOK: 7 MIN.

¾ cup sugar
1 tablespoon grated lemon rind
2 large eggs
⅔ cup fresh lemon juice (about 3 large lemons)
1 tablespoon butter or margarine

1. Whisk together first 3 ingredients in a saucepan over medium heat; cook, stirring frequently, until sugar dissolves and mixture is light in color (about 3 minutes).
2. Stir in lemon juice and butter; cook 4 minutes or until mixture thinly coats the back of a spoon, stirring constantly with whisk. Cool. Cover and chill (mixture will thicken as it cools). **Makes** 1⅓ cups.
Note: Store Lemon Curd in the refrigerator for up to 1 week. Or freeze it in a zip-top plastic freezer bag. Thaw in the refrigerator, and use within 1 week of thawing.

Caramel-Apple Shortcakes

Substitute store-bought sponge cake cups for the Cinnamon-Crunch Shortcakes, if desired.

PREP: 15 MIN., COOK: 18 MIN.

1 tablespoon butter
5 Gala apples, peeled and sliced
½ cup apple juice
3 tablespoons brown sugar
¼ teaspoon ground cinnamon
Bottled caramel sauce
1 recipe Cinnamon-Crunch Shortcakes
Whipped cream

1. Melt butter in a large skillet over medium-high heat; add apple, tossing to coat. Stir in apple juice, brown sugar, and cinnamon. Bring to a boil; reduce heat to low, and simmer 10 to 15 minutes or until apple slices are tender.
2. Pour ½ cup caramel sauce over apples, tossing to coat. Split Cinnamon-Crunch Shortcakes in half. Layer half of shortcake halves with apple mixture and whipped cream. Top with remaining shortcake halves. Drizzle with additional caramel sauce. **Makes** 12 servings.

Cinnamon-Crunch Shortcakes:

These sweet shortcakes form a lovely base for any kind of fruit.

PREP: 20 MIN., COOK: 15 MIN.

2½ cups all-purpose baking mix
3 tablespoons granulated sugar
½ cup milk
4 tablespoons butter, melted and divided
¼ cup chopped pecans
2 tablespoons brown sugar
¼ teaspoon ground cinnamon

1. Stir together baking mix, granulated sugar, milk, and 3 tablespoons butter until a soft dough forms. Turn out onto a lightly floured surface; knead 3 or 4 times.
2. Pat dough to a ¼-inch thickness; cut with a 2¾-inch round biscuit cutter. Place on lightly greased baking sheets.
3. Combine pecans, brown sugar, cinnamon, and remaining tablespoon butter; pat onto biscuit tops.
4. Bake at 375° for 12 to 15 minutes or until lightly browned. **Makes** 12 servings.

Streusel Blueberry Shortcake

PREP: 15 MIN., COOK: 18 MIN., OTHER: 10 MIN.

make ahead

3 cups all-purpose baking mix
⅔ cup milk
¼ cup butter or margarine, melted
½ cup firmly packed brown sugar
½ cup chopped pecans
¼ cup butter or margarine
1 (8-ounce) container frozen whipped topping, thawed
2 pints fresh blueberries

1. Combine first 3 ingredients in a large bowl; stir until a soft dough forms. Spread dough evenly into 2 lightly greased 8-inch square pans.
2. Combine brown sugar and pecans; cut in ¼ cup butter with a pastry blender until mixture is crumbly. Sprinkle nut mixture over dough.
3. Bake, uncovered, at 400° for 18 minutes or until a wooden pick inserted in center comes out clean. Cool in pans on wire racks 10 minutes; remove from pans, and cool completely on wire racks.
4. Place 1 cake layer on a serving plate. Spread half of whipped topping over layer, and arrange half of blueberries on top. Repeat procedure with remaining cake layer, whipped topping, and blueberries. Chill cake until ready to serve. **Makes** 1 (8-inch) cake.

Berry-Amaretto
Summer Trifle

Berry-Amaretto Summer Trifle

Any combination of berries will work in this stunning trifle. Use what's most available in your area.

30 minutes or less
PREP: 15 MIN., OTHER: 10 MIN.

1½ cups sliced strawberries
¾ cup blueberries
2 tablespoons almond liqueur
1 cup frozen whipped topping, thawed
1½ cups (1-inch) cubed angel food cake
1 tablespoon frozen whipped topping, thawed

1. Combine first 3 ingredients in a medium bowl; stir gently. Let stand 10 minutes.
2. Spoon ⅓ cup berry mixture into each of 2 (12-ounce) parfait glasses; top each with ¼ cup whipped topping and about ⅓ cup cake cubes. Repeat layers with remaining ingredients, ending with berry mixture. Top each parfait with ½ tablespoon whipped topping before serving. **Makes** 2 servings.

Strawberry Trifle

Make the custard the night before for easy assembly.

PREP: 45 MIN.

make ahead

5 cups sliced fresh strawberries
2 (10-ounce) angel food cakes, cut into 1-inch cubes
6 tablespoons strawberry liqueur (see note)
Custard
½ cup strawberry preserves
2 cups whipping cream
¼ cup powdered sugar
Garnishes: whole strawberry, toasted sliced almonds

1. Arrange ½ cup strawberry slices along lower edge of a 14-cup trifle bowl. Place half of cake cubes in bowl. Drizzle with 2 tablespoons liqueur. Top cake cubes with 2 cups strawberries; drizzle with 2 tablespoons liqueur. Spoon 2 cups Custard over strawberries.
2. Arrange ½ cup strawberries along edge of bowl. Top with remaining cake cubes. Drizzle with remaining 2 tablespoons liqueur. Spoon remaining 2 cups strawberries over cake cubes. Spread preserves over strawberries; spoon remaining 2 cups Custard over preserves.

3. Beat whipping cream until foamy; gradually add powdered sugar, beating until soft peaks form. Spread over trifle. Garnish, if desired. Serve immediately. **Makes** 14 servings.
Note: Strawberry syrup may be substituted.

Custard:

PREP: 10 MIN., COOK: 15 MIN.

1¾ cups milk
⅓ cup cornstarch
2 cups half-and-half
4 egg yolks
¾ cup sugar
2 teaspoons vanilla extract

1. Cook ½ cup milk and cornstarch in a large saucepan over medium heat, stirring well. Add half-and half and remaining 1¼ cups milk; cook, stirring constantly, until thickened.
2. Beat egg yolks and ¾ cup sugar at medium speed with an electric mixer until thick and pale. Gradually stir about one-fourth of hot mixture into egg mixture; add to remaining hot mixture, stirring constantly. Cook over low heat, stirring constantly, 1 to 2 minutes or until thickened. Remove from heat; stir in 2 teaspoons vanilla, and cool. Cover and chill custard until ready to serve. **Makes** 4 cups.

Molten Chocolate Cakes

Molten Chocolate Cakes

These yummy little cakes ooze soft chocolate from the center when you spoon into them.

PREP: 19 MIN., COOK: 11 MIN., OTHER: 1 HR.

2 tablespoons butter, melted
2 tablespoons unsweetened cocoa
¾ cup butter, cut into pieces
3 (4-ounce) bars premium semisweet chocolate,
    broken into chunks (we used Ghirardelli)
½ cup whipping cream
1¼ cups egg substitute (see note)
¾ cup granulated sugar
⅔ cup all-purpose flour
Powdered sugar

1. Brush 16 muffin cups with 2 tablespoons melted butter. Sprinkle evenly with cocoa, shaking out excess. Place in refrigerator to firm butter.
2. Place ¾ cup butter and chocolate in a large heavy saucepan. Cook over low heat, stirring often, until butter and chocolate melt. Slowly whisk in cream; set mixture aside.
3. Combine egg substitute and granulated sugar in a large mixing bowl. Beat at medium speed with an electric mixer 5 to 7 minutes or until slightly thickened; add chocolate cream and flour, beating until blended. Pour batter into muffin cups, filling to within ¼-inch from tops. Cover and chill at least 1 hour or up to 24 hours, or cover and freeze up to 1 month. If frozen, thaw overnight in refrigerator before baking.
4. Bake at 450° for 10 to 11 minutes or just until edges of cakes spring back when lightly touched, but centers are still soft. Let stand 3 minutes before loosening edges with a knife. Quickly invert cakes onto a baking sheet. Transfer to dessert plates using a spatula. Sprinkle with powdered sugar. Serve immediately. **Makes** 16 servings.
Note: The recipe uses egg substitute instead of real eggs because the cakes aren't in the oven long enough for eggs to cook thoroughly for safety.

Chocolate Éclair Cake

One box of graham crackers contains 3 individually wrapped packages of crackers; use 1 package for each layer of this indulgent dessert.

PREP: 15 MIN., OTHER: 8 HR.

1 (14.4-ounce) box honey graham
    crackers
2 (3.4-ounce) packages French vanilla instant
    pudding mix
3 cups milk
1 (12-ounce) container frozen whipped topping,
    thawed
1 (16-ounce) container ready-to-spread chocolate
    frosting

1. Line bottom of an ungreased 13- x 9-inch baking dish with one-third of honey graham crackers.
2. Whisk together pudding mix and milk; add whipped topping, stirring until mixture thickens. Spread half of pudding mixture over graham crackers. Repeat layers with one-third of graham crackers and remaining pudding mixture. Top with remaining graham crackers. Spread with chocolate frosting. Cover and chill 8 hours. **Makes** 12 servings.
Note: To lighten, use reduced-fat graham crackers, sugar-free pudding mix, fat-free milk, and fat-free frozen whipped topping.

Turtle Cake

No one would guess that this scrumptious cake begins with a cake mix.

PREP: 15 MIN., COOK: 28 MIN.

1 (18.25-ounce) package German
    chocolate cake mix with pudding
3 cups chopped pecans, divided
¾ cup butter, melted
⅓ cup evaporated milk
1 (14-ounce) package caramels (about 50 caramels)
½ cup evaporated milk
2 cups (12 ounces) semisweet chocolate morsels

1. Combine cake mix, 2 cups pecans, butter, and ⅓ cup evaporated milk in a large bowl; stir until well combined. Reserve half of cake mix mixture for topping. Press remaining half into a greased and floured 13- x 9-inch pan.
2. Bake at 350° for 8 minutes. Remove pan from oven.
3. Microwave caramels and ½ cup evaporated milk in a large microwave-safe bowl at HIGH 2½ to 3 minutes, stirring mixture every 30 seconds until smooth.
4. Sprinkle remaining 1 cup pecans and chocolate morsels evenly over cake. Drizzle caramel mixture over pecans and chocolate morsels. Crumble reserved cake mix mixture evenly over caramel mixture.
5. Bake at 350° for 20 more minutes. Let cool in pan on a wire rack. **Makes** 12 servings.

Birthday Party Brownie Cakes

This festive twist on traditional cupcakes comes complete with colorful toppings instead of typical icing.

PREP: 10 MIN., COOK: 30 MIN.

1 (21-ounce) package brownie mix
½ cup vegetable oil
¼ cup cranberry juice
2 large eggs
Toppings: semisweet chocolate morsels, candy-coated chocolate pieces, chopped pecans, candy sprinkles

1. Stir together first 4 ingredients until smooth. Spoon batter into 12 lightly greased muffin cups. Sprinkle with desired toppings.
2. Bake at 375° for 30 minutes or until a wooden pick inserted in center comes out clean. Remove from pan, and cool on a wire rack. **Makes** 12 servings.

German Chocolate Snack Cake

This moist and delicious cake is mixed right in the pan.

PREP: 15 MIN., COOK: 1 HR.

1 (18.25-ounce) package German
    chocolate cake mix
4 large eggs, divided
½ cup chopped pecans, toasted
½ cup butter or margarine, melted
1 (16-ounce) package powdered sugar
1 (8-ounce) package cream cheese, softened
Ice cream or whipped topping

1. Stir together cake mix, 1 egg, pecans, and butter; press mixture into bottom of a lightly greased 13- x 9-inch pan.
2. Beat powdered sugar, cream cheese, and remaining 3 eggs at medium speed with an electric mixer until creamy. Spoon powdered sugar mixture over batter in pan.
3. Bake at 300° for 1 hour. Cool and cut into 2½- to 3-inch squares. Serve with ice cream. **Makes** 18 servings.

Mississippi Mud Cake

Mississippi Mud Cake

PREP: 20 MIN., COOK: 30 MIN.

make
ahead

1 cup butter, melted
2 cups sugar
½ cup unsweetened cocoa
4 large eggs, lightly beaten
1 teaspoon vanilla extract
⅛ teaspoon salt
1½ cups all-purpose flour
1½ cups coarsely chopped pecans, toasted
1 (10.5-ounce) bag miniature marshmallows
Chocolate Frosting

1. Whisk together melted butter and next 5 ingredients in a large bowl. Stir in flour and chopped pecans. Pour batter into a greased and floured 15- x 10-inch jelly-roll pan.
2. Bake at 350° for 20 to 25 minutes or until a wooden pick inserted in center comes out clean. Remove from oven; top warm cake evenly with marshmallows.

Return to oven, and bake 5 more minutes. Drizzle Chocolate Frosting over warm cake. Cool completely. **Makes** 15 servings.
Note: Two (19.5-ounce) packages brownie mix, prepared according to package directions, may be substituted for first 7 ingredients. Stir in chopped pecans. Bake at 350° for 30 minutes. Proceed with marshmallows and Chocolate Frosting as directed.

Chocolate Frosting:

PREP: 10 MIN.

1 (16-ounce) package powdered sugar,
    sifted
½ cup milk
¼ cup butter, softened
⅓ cup unsweetened cocoa

1. Beat all ingredients at medium speed with an electric mixer until smooth. **Makes** 2 cups.

Quick Italian Cream Cakes

Whether in loaf pans or as a layer cake, the result is traditional flavor in about half the time.

make ahead

1 (18.5-ounce) package white cake mix
 with pudding
3 large eggs
1¼ cups buttermilk
¼ cup vegetable oil
1 (3½-ounce) can sweetened flaked coconut
⅔ cup chopped pecans, toasted
Cream Cheese Frosting

1. Beat first 4 ingredients at medium speed with an electric mixer 2 minutes. Stir in coconut and pecans. Pour into 4 greased and floured 5¾- x 3¼-inch miniature disposable loaf pans.

2. Bake at 350° for 33 to 35 minutes or until a wooden pick inserted in center comes out clean. Cool in pans on wire racks 10 minutes. Remove from pans, and cool completely on wire racks.

3. Spread Cream Cheese Frosting on top of cakes. Cover and chill 2 hours before slicing. **Makes** 4 mini loaf cakes.

Cream Cheese Frosting:

1 (8-ounce) package cream cheese,
 softened
½ cup butter, softened
6 cups powdered sugar
1 teaspoon vanilla extract

1. Beat cream cheese and butter at medium speed with an electric mixer until creamy; gradually add sugar, beating well. Stir in vanilla. **Makes** 4 cups.

Quick Italian Cream Layer Cake: Pour batter into 3 greased and floured 9-inch round cake pans. Bake at 350° for 15 to 17 minutes or until a wooden pick inserted in center comes out clean. Cool in pans on wire racks 10 minutes. Remove from pans, and cool completely on wire racks. Spread Cream Cheese Frosting between layers and on top and sides of cake. Cover and chill 2 hours before slicing. Prep: 10 min., Cook: 17 min., Other: 2 hr.

Quick Italian
Cream Cakes

Tropical Dump Cake

Tropical Dump Cake

PREP: 10 MIN., COOK: 50 MIN.

make
ahead

2 (20-ounce) cans crushed pineapple,
    undrained
1 (18.25-ounce) package white cake mix
½ cup butter or margarine, cut up
2 cups pecans, toasted
Ice cream or whipped topping (optional)

1. Drain 1 can crushed pineapple. Spread both the drained and undrained pineapple in a lightly greased 13- x 9-inch pan. Sprinkle cake mix over fruit. Dot evenly with butter; sprinkle with pecans.
2. Bake at 350° for 45 to 50 minutes or until golden and bubbly. Serve with ice cream, if desired. **Makes** 8 to 10 servings.

Sour Cream Pound Cake

Bake this delicious cake, and store at room temperature up to 3 days; or place it in a large zip-top plastic freezer bag, and store in the freezer up to 2 months.

PREP: 20 MIN.; COOK: 1 HR., 30 MIN.; OTHER: 10 MIN.

1½ cups butter, softened
3 cups sugar
6 large eggs
3 cups all-purpose flour
½ teaspoon salt
¼ teaspoon baking soda
1 (8-ounce) container sour cream
1 teaspoon lemon extract
¼ teaspoon almond extract
Whipped Cream
Simple Syrup
Sliced peaches

1. Beat butter at medium speed with an electric mixer until creamy. Gradually add sugar, beating at medium speed until light and fluffy. Add eggs, 1 at a time, beating just until the yolk disappears.
2. Sift together flour, salt, and soda. Add to butter mixture alternately with sour cream, beginning and ending with flour mixture. Beat batter at low speed just until blended after each addition. Stir in extracts. Pour into a greased and floured 12-cup tube pan.
3. Bake at 325° for 1 hour and 20 minutes to 1 hour and 30 minutes or until a long wooden pick inserted in center of cake comes out clean. Cool in pan on a wire rack 10 minutes. Remove cake from pan, and cool completely on wire rack. Serve with Whipped Cream, Simple Syrup, and sliced peaches. **Makes** 10 to 12 servings.

Whipped Cream:

Try replacing the teaspoon of vanilla extract with a tablespoon of your favorite liqueur. Almond-flavored liqueur is a perfect match for peaches, while orange liqueur pairs especially well with berries.

PREP: 5 MIN.

1 cup whipping cream
2 tablespoons powdered sugar
1 teaspoon vanilla extract

1. Beat whipping cream at low speed with an electric mixer until foamy; increase speed to medium-high, and gradually add powdered sugar, beating until soft peaks form. Stir in vanilla. **Makes** about 2 cups.

Simple Syrup:

PREP: 5 MIN., COOK: 5 MIN.

1 cup water
1 cup sugar
6 strawberries, sliced (optional)

1. Bring water, sugar, and, if desired, strawberries to a boil in a saucepan, stirring until sugar dissolves; boil 1 minute. Remove from heat. If necessary, pour syrup through a wire-mesh strainer into a bowl, discarding fruit; cool. **Makes** about 1½ cups.

Peanut Butter Pudding

PREP: 5 MIN., COOK: 6 MIN., OTHER: 2 HR.

½ cup sugar
2 tablespoons cornstarch
¼ teaspoon salt
1½ cups milk
½ cup half-and-half
¾ cup creamy peanut butter
1 teaspoon vanilla extract

1. Combine first 3 ingredients in a medium-size heavy saucepan; gradually whisk in milk and half-and-half.
2. Bring to a boil over medium heat, whisking constantly. Boil, whisking constantly, 1 minute. Remove from heat. (Pudding will be thin.)
3. Add peanut butter and vanilla, whisking until smooth. Pour into a bowl; place plastic wrap directly over pudding. Chill at least 2 hours. **Makes** 2½ cups.

Chocolate Cookie Pudding

Chocolate Cookie Pudding

This creamy concoction gets a crunchy surprise from chocolate sandwich cookies and pecans.

20 minutes or less

PREP: 15 MIN., OTHER: 5 MIN.

make ahead

1 (5.9-ounce) package chocolate
    instant pudding mix

2 cups milk

1 (3-ounce) package cream cheese, softened

1 (8-ounce) container frozen whipped topping,
    thawed

16 double-stuffed cream-filled chocolate sandwich
    cookies, crushed (about 2 cups) (we used Oreo
    Double Stuf)

¾ cup chopped pecans, toasted

1. Whisk together pudding mix and milk for 2 minutes. Cover and chill 5 minutes.

2. Stir together cream cheese and whipped topping, blending well.

3. Place 1 cup crushed cookies evenly in an 8-cup bowl. Spread half of cream cheese mixture over crushed cookies; sprinkle with half of pecans. Spread all of pudding evenly over top; spread remaining cream cheese mixture evenly over pudding. Sprinkle with remaining cookies and pecans. Chill until ready to serve. **Makes** 6 to 8 servings.

Blackberry Custard

This chilled, berry-topped custard won top honors in our Test Kitchens.

PREP: 15 MIN. COOK: 7 MIN., OTHER: 2 HR.

¾ cup sugar
⅓ cup all-purpose flour
Dash of salt
4 egg yolks
2 cups milk
½ teaspoon vanilla extract
1 cup whipping cream
2 tablespoons sugar
2 cups fresh blackberries

1. Combine first 3 ingredients in a heavy saucepan; whisk in egg yolks and milk. Cook over medium heat, whisking constantly, 5 to 7 minutes or until thickened. Remove from heat; stir in vanilla. Pour into a serving dish; cool. Cover and chill 2 hours.
2. Beat whipping cream at medium speed with an electric mixer until foamy; gradually add 2 tablespoons sugar, beating until soft peaks form. Spread over custard. Top with fresh blackberries. **Makes** 4 servings.

Cinnamon-Chocolate Chip Ice-Cream Balls

We used vanilla ice cream for this delicious dessert. You can substitute your favorite flavor.

PREP: 25 MIN., OTHER: 2 HR.

1½ cups cinnamon-sugar whole
    wheat-and-rice cereal, crushed (we used
    Cinnamon Toast Crunch)
½ cup semisweet chocolate mini-morsels
1 cup finely chopped pecans (optional)
1 quart ice cream
Caramel syrup

1. Combine crushed cereal, morsels, and, if desired, pecans in a large bowl.
2. Scoop out ice cream, and shape into 6 (2½-inch) balls. Roll balls in cereal mixture, coating evenly. Place in a 9-inch square pan; freeze at least 2 hours or until firm. Drizzle with caramel syrup before serving. **Makes** 6 servings.

Soft-Serve Chocolate Ice Cream

Cool off on triple-digit summer days with this frozen chocolate delight. Serve it with either a spoon or a straw.

30 minutes or less
PREP: 5 MIN., OTHER: 25 MIN.

1 (14-ounce) can sweetened condensed
    milk
½ cup instant malted milk powder
1 cup chocolate syrup
6 cups chocolate milk
1 (16-ounce) container frozen whipped topping,
    thawed

1. Combine first 4 ingredients; fold in whipped topping. Pour mixture into freezer container of a 1-gallon hand-turned or electric freezer. Freeze according to manufacturer's instructions. **Makes** about 4 quarts.

Ginger Grilled Pineapple
With Ice Cream

Ginger Grilled Pineapple With Ice Cream

Buy pineapple already peeled and cored in a plastic container to save time.

30 minutes or less
PREP: 10 MIN., COOK: 12 MIN.

1 pineapple, peeled and cored
3 tablespoons light brown sugar
½ teaspoon ground cinnamon
1 tablespoon grated fresh ginger
Vanilla ice cream
Ground cinnamon

1. Cut pineapple in half lengthwise. Combine brown sugar, ½ teaspoon cinnamon, and ginger; rub evenly over pineapple.
2. Coat a food rack with cooking spray; place on grill over medium-high heat (350° to 400°). Place pineapple on rack. Grill, covered with grill lid, 6 minutes on each side. Remove pineapple from grill; cut into ¼-inch-thick slices. Serve with ice cream; sprinkle lightly with cinnamon. **Makes** 6 servings.

Index

Appetizers
Biscuit Cups, Bacon, 201
Biscuits, Savory Tomato-Bacon, 202
Caviar, Carolina, 182
Caviar, Texas, 184
Cheese
  Brie, Coffee-Kissed Pecan, 177
  Brie, Warmed Cranberry, 177
  Cheesecake, Cheddar-Chili, 181
  Crisps, Blue Cheese, 201
  Crisps, Spicy Jack Cheese, 201
  Green Chile Cheddar Cheese
    With Avocado-Mango Salsa,
    Smoky, 198
  Marinated Cheese, Olives, and
    Peppers, 199
  Ring, Cherry-Cheese, 180
  Rounds, Bacon-Cheese, 200
Chicken Strips, Barbecue-Battered, 20
Chicken Strips, Sesame, 206
Chicken Wings, Sweet-and-Spicy, 207
Chicken Won Tons With Hoisin-Peanut
  Dipping Sauce, 208
Crackers, Snack, 193
Crostini, Easy Egg Salad, 202
Crostini, Tomato, 202
Deviled Eggs, Basic, 197
Dips
  Artichoke Dip, Florentine, 186
  Bacon-Blue Cheese Dip, 189
  Bean Dip, Cinco de Mayo, 189
  Cheese Dip, Meaty, 185
  Curry Dip, 191
  Fiesta Dip, Quick, 187
  Hoisin-Peanut Dipping Sauce, 209
  Hummus, 110
  Hummus, Black-eyed Pea, 188
  Nacho Dip, Layered, 185
  Pizza Dip, 185
  Swiss-Onion Dip, 187
  Vegetable Dip, Quick Creamy, 189
  Vidalia Onion Dip, 187
Meatballs, Bourbon, 209
Meatballs, Cocktail, 209
Mix, Mexicali Snack, 191
Mix, Starry Snack, 192
Mix, Sweet 'n' Savory Snack, 191
Olives, Balsamic Marinated, 195
Olives, Lemon-Garlic, 195
Pecans, Citrusy, 195
Pecans, Spiced, 195
Pinwheels, Pepperoni Pizza, 212
Quesadillas, Barbecue, 204
Quesadillas, Quick Fiesta, 204
Quesadillas, Santa Fe Chicken, 204
Sandwiches, Green Chile Pimiento
  Cheese Tea, 197
Spreads
  Cheese Spread, Mexican, 181
  Cucumber-Yogurt Spread, 179

Feta Cheese Spread, Garlic-and-
  Dill, 177
Feta Spread, Herbed, 179
Goat Cheese Spread, Pesto-, 179
Pimiento Cheese, Green Chile, 197
Tapenade, 178
Tomatoes, Stuffed Cherry, 197
Wraps, Thai Green Apple Pork
  Lettuce, 203
Apples
Crisp, Apple Shortbread, 391
Crunch, Apple-Blueberry, 390
Grunt, Apple, 173
Salad, Apple-Spinach, 347
Shortcakes, Caramel-Apple, 393
Artichokes
Dip, Florentine Artichoke, 186
Pasta, Artichoke, 229
Salad, Artichoke-Goat Cheese, 353
Asparagus
Glazed Asparagus, Asian-, 323
Hot Browns, Asparagus, 271
Lemon Butter, Asparagus With, 323
Avocados
Salsa, Avocado-Corn, 182
Salsa, Avocado-Mango, 198
Sandwiches Deluxe, Avocado, 277

Bacon
Biscuit Cups, Bacon, 201
Cheese Rounds, Bacon-, 200
Penne Alfredo, Bacon, 221
Pizza, Breakfast, 54
Salad, Bacon-Mandarin, 349
Banana Pancakes, Easy, 373
Banana Pudding, New-Fashioned, 47
Barbecue. See also Grilled.
Beef
  Chuck Roast Barbecue, 151
  Flank Barbecue, Peppery, 154
  Pot Roast, Zippy Barbecue, 151
Chicken
  Barbecue, Chicken, 165
  Honey Barbecue Chicken, 132
  Pizza, Quick 'n' Easy Chicken
    Barbecue, 217
  Strips, Barbecue-Battered
    Chicken, 20
Dressing, Barbecue, 20
Pork Chops, Barbecue-Battered, 20
Quesadillas, Barbecue, 204
Salad, Warm Barbecue, 20
Sauce, Honey Barbecue, 132
Beans. See also Salads, Soups.
Baked Beans, Hearty, 161
Black Bean Salsa, 182
Black Beans and Corn, Rice
  With, 344
Butterbeans, Bacon 'n' Herb, 33
Chimichangas, Bean-and-Cheese, 319
Dip, Cinco de Mayo Bean, 189
Green
  Bacon and Mushrooms, Green Beans
    With, 323

Balsamic With Garlic, Green
  Beans, 323
Garlic-Herb Butter, Green Beans
  With, 324
Saucy Green Beans, 32
Sautéed Green Beans With
  Bacon, 325
Hummus, 110
Hummus, Traditional, 188
Pinto Beans, Smashed, 325
Pinto Beans With Ham, 161
Beef. See also Beef, Ground; Grilled/Beef.
Brisket in Beer, Peppered Beef, 157
Corned Beef
  Reuben Loaf, 291
  Reubens, Golden-Baked Mini, 259
  Reuben Soup, Cream of, 250
Roasts
  Chili, Slow-cooker Chunky
    Beef, 153
  Chuck Roast Barbecue, 151
  Eye of Round Roast, 286
  Horseradish Sauce, Roast Beef
    With, 154
  Pot Roast, Company, 152
  Pot Roast, Savory, 150
  Pot Roast, Zippy Barbecue, 151
  Salad, Roast Beef-Blue Cheese, 71
  Sauerbraten, 151
  Stew, Company Beef, 247
Steaks
  Burgundy, Beef, 154
  Chicken-fried Steak 'n' Country
    Gravy, 25
  Country Steak With Gravy, 157
  Fajitas, Slow-cooker, 155
  Filet Mignon With Horseradish
    Gravy, 284
  Fillets, Spicy Beef, 283
  Fillets With Tarragon Butter, 283
  Flank Barbecue, Peppery, 154
  Flank Steak With Tomato-Olive
    Relish, 286
  Ginger, Beef With, 68
  Pan-Seared Steaks With Roasted Red
    Pepper Sauce, 285
  Rib-eyes, Grecian Skillet, 285
  Salad Niçoise, Steak, 122
  Salad With Cilantro, Beef, 70
  Salad With Hot Pan Dressing,
    Steak-and-Spinach, 71
  Stew, Skillet Beef Burgundy, 67
  Stir-fry, Steak, 69
  Wraps, Cheese-Steak, 260
Beef, Ground
Burgers
  Cheeseburgers, Jack, 263
  Cheeseburgers, Jalapeño, 143
  Feta Burgers, Greek, 140
  Fiesta Burgers, 262
  Italian Burgers With Fresh Basil, 261
  Mozzarella-Basil Burgers, 143
  Mushroom-Onion Burgers, Easy, 260
  Stuffed Southwestern Burgers, 142
  Teriyaki Burgers, 288
Calzones, Easy, 259

Casseroles
    Easy Beef Casserole, 67
    Lombardi, Beef, 67
    Lombardi, Light Beef, 67
    Noodle Casserole, Beefy, 60
    Pizza Casserole, Weeknight, 61
Chili, Chunky Beef, 42
Chimichangas, Beef-and-Bean, 65
Dip, Meaty Cheese, 185
Mac and Cheese, Taco Dinner, 63
Meatball Sandwich, Giant, 263
Meatballs, Cocktail, 209
Meat Loaf With Tomato Gravy,
    Herbed, 291
Meat Loaves, Individual, 289
Pie, Corn Chip Chili, 61
Pie, Shepherd's, 63
Pizza, Cheeseburger, 219
Pizza, Hamburger-Mushroom, 218
Salad, Beef-and-Lime Rice, 64
Sauce, Beefy Pasta, 157
Skillet Dinner, Beef and Kraut, 288
Soup, Chunky Italian, 247
Soup, Taco, 249
Spaghetti, Easy, 223
Spaghetti, One-Skillet, 222
Spaghetti, Zucchini-Beef, 105
Stew, Meatball, 249
Tacos, Easy Skillet, 63
Taco Squares, Deep-Dish, 61
Tostadas, 65
Biscuits
    Bowls, Biscuit, 78
    Buttermilk Biscuits, Best-Ever, 112
    Cheese Garlic Biscuits, 358
    Cream Cheese Biscuits, Tiny, 358
    Cups, Bacon Biscuit, 201
    Green Chile Biscuits, 245
    Poppers, Biscuit, 358
    Tomato-Bacon Biscuits, Savory, 202
Blackberry Cobbler, Speedy, 390
Blackberry Custard, 404
Blueberries
    Cheesecake, Blueberry, 115
    Cobbler, Blueberry-Pecan, 45
    Pancakes, Blueberry, 374
    Sherbet, Blueberry, 115
    Shortcake, Streusel Blueberry, 393
Breads. See also Biscuits, Cornbreads,
    Muffins, Pancakes, Rolls and Buns,
    Waffles.
    Blue Cheese Bread, 365
    Breadsticks, Italian Cheese, 368
    Breadsticks, Spicy, 368
    Flatbread, Fast Rosemary-Dried
      Tomato, 367
    Focaccia, Pesto-and-Tomato, 367
    Garlic Bread, Buttery, 365
    Herb Bread, 365
    Peanut Butter Bread, 362
    Pizza Dough, 101
    Pull-Apart Bread, Caramel-Nut, 370
    Spoonbread, Corn, 377
    Toast, Basil Pesto, 254
    Toasts, Parmesan, 71
    Twists, Pecan Crescent, 368

Broccoli
    Gratin of Broccoli in Béchamel, 327
    Salad, Broccoli, 353
    Sesame Broccoli, 326
    Stir-fry, Broccoli-Ginger, 101
Burritos, Breakfast, 53
Burritos, Chicken, 85
Butter
    Basil Butter, Swordfish Steaks
      With, 134
    Garlic-Herb Butter, Green Beans
      With, 324
    Jalapeño-Lime Butter, Grilled Corn
      With, 147
    Lemon Butter, Asparagus With, 323
    Lemon Butter, Tuna Steaks With, 313
    Tarragon Butter, Fillets With, 283

Cakes
    Cheesecake, Blueberry, 115
    Cheesecake, Cheddar-Chili, 181
    Chocolate
      Brownie Cakes, Birthday Party, 398
      Éclair Cake, Chocolate, 397
      German Chocolate Snack Cake, 398
      Mississippi Mud Cake, 399
      Molten Chocolate Cakes, 397
      Turtle Cake, 398
    Dump Cake, Tropical, 401
    Italian Cream Cakes, Quick, 400
    Italian Cream Layer Cake, Quick, 400
    Pound Cake, Sour Cream, 402
    Shortcakes
      Caramel-Apple Shortcakes, 393
      Cinnamon-Crunch Shortcakes, 393
      Streusel Blueberry Shortcake, 393
Candies
    Fudge, Peanut Butter, 389
    Orange-Nut Balls, 389
    Rocky Road Clusters, 389
    Texas Millionaires, 389
Carrots
    Glazed Baby Carrots, Honey-
      Tarragon, 327
    Puree, Carrot-Sweet Potato, 329
    Sautéed Fennel and Carrots, 328
Casseroles
    Beef Casserole, Easy, 67
    Beef Lombardi, 67
    Beef Lombardi, Light, 67
    Chicken-and-Broccoli Casserole, 77
    Chicken-and-Wild Rice Casserole,
      Leslie's Favorite, 81
    Chicken Cannelloni With Roasted Red
      Bell Pepper Sauce, 83
    Chicken Casserole, Cheesy, 81
    Chicken Casserole, King Ranch, 19
    Chicken Tetrazzini, 79
    Egg Casserole, Southwest, 54
    Enchilada Casserole, 169
    Enchilada Casserole, Easy, 85
    Ham Casserole, Creamy, 56
    Mac-and-Cheese, Veggie, 235
    Macaroni and Cheese, 99

    Mushroom Chicken Bake, 299
    Noodle Casserole, Beefy, 60
    Pizza Casserole, Weeknight, 61
    Shells, Spinach-Stuffed, 222
    Squash Casserole, 341
Cauliflower, Frosted, 329
Cheese. See also Appetizers/Cheese;
    Breads.
    Cauliflower, Frosted, 329
    Chicken Parmesan, 301
    Chicken Penne, Cheesy, 225
    Chops, Blue Cheese-Stuffed, 125
    Frosting, Cream Cheese, 400
    Gratin, Onion-Gruyère, 334
    Grits, Garlic-and-Herb Cheese, 110
    Grits, Parmesan Cheese, 124
    Grits, Quick Double-Cheese, 27
    Mac and Cheese, Taco Dinner, 63
    Mac-and-Cheese, Veggie, 235
    Macaroni and Cheese, 99
    Noodles, Blue Cheese, 231
    Pizza, Fresh Mozzarella and Basil, 100
    Pizzas, Chicken-and-Three-Cheese
      French Bread, 213
    Rib-eye Steaks, Grilled Gorgonzola, 121
    Ring, Cherry-Cheese, 180
    Sandwiches
      Cheeseburgers, Jack, 263
      Cheeseburgers, Jalapeño, 143
      Cheeseburgers, Turkey, 141
      Grills, Double Cheese, 277
      Pimiento Cheese Finger
        Sandwiches, 279
      Wraps, Cheese-Steak, 260
    Soup, Blue Satin, 252
    Soup, Herbed Cheese, 252
    Tomato Napoleon, 342
    Tortellini in Jalapeño Tomato Sauce,
      Cheese, 235
    Tortellini Pasta Salad, Cheese, 238
    Zucchini-Parmesan Toss, 341
Chicken. See also Grilled/Poultry; Salads/
    Chicken.
    Apricot Chicken, Sweet-and-Sour, 307
    Baked Chicken, Fruity, 299
    Bake, Mushroom Chicken, 299
    Barbecue-Battered Chicken Strips, 20
    Barbecue, Chicken, 165
    Barbecue Chicken, Honey, 132
    Benne Seed Chicken, 14
    Braised Chicken Thighs With Rosemary
      and Potatoes, 165
    Burritos, Chicken, 85
    Cacciatore, Chicken, 224
    Cajun Chicken Pasta, 225
    Cajun Chicken, Snappy, 314
    Cakes With Rémoulade Sauce,
      Chicken, 306
    Cannelloni With Roasted Red Bell
      Pepper Sauce, Chicken, 83
    Casserole, Cheesy Chicken, 81
    Casserole, Chicken-and-Broccoli, 77
    Casserole, King Ranch Chicken, 19
    Casserole, Leslie's Favorite Chicken-
      and-Wild Rice, 81
    Cordon Bleu, Easy Chicken, 299

Chicken (*continued*)

Creamed Chicken in Biscuit Bowls, 78
Deviled Chicken Breasts, 106
Dijon, Chicken, 304
Dressing, Santa Fe Chicken and, 19
Drumsticks and Thighs, Saucy, 162
Dumplings, Light Chicken and, 19
Dumplings, Quick Chicken and, 19
Fried
    Garlic Fried Chicken Breasts, 17
    Italian-Seasoned Fried Chicken, 15
    Oven-Fried Chicken, Crispy, 17
    Simple Fried Chicken, 16
Gumbo, Chicken-Sausage, 22
Herbs and Vegetables, Chicken With Fresh, 74
Honey-Pecan Chicken Thighs, 15
Hot Browns, Asparagus, 271
Hot Dish, Chicken-and-Wild Rice, 164
Lasagna, Heavenly Chicken, 82
Mediterranean Chicken Breasts on Eggplant, 301
Parmesan, Chicken, 301
Pecan Chicken, 17
Penne, Cheesy Chicken, 225
Pepper Pot, Chicken, 165
Peppers With Chicken and Corn, Stuffed, 77
Pesto Chicken, Fettuccine With, 225
Piccata, Chicken, 303
Pilaf, Chicken-Vegetable, 75
Pitas, Mango Chutney Chicken, 270
Pizza, Bistro Grilled Chicken, 218
Pizza, Quick 'n' Easy Chicken Barbecue, 217
Pizzas, Chicken-and-Three-Cheese French Bread, 213
Pizzas, Roasted Chicken-and-White Bean, 216
Poblano Chicken, Creamy, 85
Pot Pie in Biscuit Bowls, Chicken, 78
Pot Pie, Pronto Chicken, 80
Provençale Chicken Supper, 162
Quesadillas, Santa Fe Chicken, 204
Sandwiches, Grilled Chicken 'n' Cheese, 269
Sesame Chicken Strips, 206
Smothered Chicken, 305
Soup, Chicken Noodle, 244
Spaghetti, Chicken, 75
Stir-fry, Chicken-and-Snow Pea, 73
Stir-fry, Chicken-Vegetable, 72
Stir-fry, Lemon Chicken, 307
Sweet-and-Sour Chicken and Rice, 75
Tacos, Chicken-and-Refried Bean, 84
Tarragon Cream Chicken, 303
Tetrazzini, Chicken, 79
Tomato and Basil Cream, Chicken in, 302
Wings, Sweet-and-Spicy Chicken, 207
Won Tons With Hoisin-Peanut Dipping Sauce, Chicken, 208
Chili
Beef Chili, Chunky, 42
Beef Chili, Slow-cooker Chunky, 153
Pie, Corn Chip Chili, 61

Chimichangas, Bean-and-Cheese, 319
Chimichangas, Beef-and-Bean, 65
Chocolate
Bars and Cookies
    Almond-Toffee-Chocolate Chip Cookies, 380
    Brownies, Double Chocolate, 385
    Brownies With Caramel Frosting, Double Chocolate, 385
    Coconut-Macadamia-Chocolate Chunk Cookies, 380
    Oatmeal-Chocolate Chunk Cookies, Nutty, 381
    Oatmeal-Raisin-Chocolate Chip Cookies, 380
    Pecan-Chocolate Chip Cookies, 380
    Pecan Cookies, Chocolate-, 382
    Turtle Bars, Gooey, 385
    Ultimate Chocolate Chip Cookies, 380
Buns, Easy Caramel-Chocolate Sticky, 370
Cakes
    Brownie Cakes, Birthday Party, 398
    Éclair Cake, Chocolate, 397
    German Chocolate Snack Cake, 398
    Mississippi Mud Cake, 399
    Molten Chocolate Cakes, 397
    Turtle Cake, 398
Candies
    Rocky Road Clusters, 389
    Texas Millionaires, 389
Crisp, Black Forest, 390
Frosting, Chocolate, 399
Ice-Cream Balls, Cinnamon-Chocolate Chip, 404
Ice Cream, Soft-Serve Chocolate, 404
Muffins, White Chocolate-Macadamia Nut, 361
Pudding, Chocolate Cookie, 403
Chowder, Quick Shrimp, 252
Chowder, So-Quick Seafood, 250
Coconut
Cookies, Coconut-Macadamia, 382
Cookies, Coconut-Macadamia-Chocolate Chunk, 380
Pie, Coconut Cream, 46
Shrimp and Rice, Thai Coconut, 166
Shrimp With Mustard Sauce, Coconut, 316
Cookies
Bars and Squares
    Brownies, Double Chocolate, 385
    Brownies With Caramel Frosting, Double Chocolate, 385
    Lemon Squares, 384
    No-Bake Bars, Creamy, 386
    Pecan Squares, 46
    Turtle Bars, Gooey, 385
Drop
    Almond-Toffee-Chocolate Chip Cookies, 380
    Chocolate Chip Cookies, Ultimate, 380
    Chocolate-Pecan Cookies, 382

Coconut-Macadamia-Chocolate Chunk Cookies, 380
Coconut-Macadamia Cookies, 382
Oatmeal-Chocolate Chunk Cookies, Nutty, 381
Oatmeal-Raisin-Chocolate Chip Cookies, 380
Oatmeal-Raisin Cookies, 117
Pecan-Chocolate Chip Cookies, 380
Peanut Blossom Cookies, 382
Shortbread, Butter-Mint, 386
Corn
Caviar, Carolina, 182
Cob, Chili Corn on the, 330
Creamed Fresh Corn, 330
Dip, Quick Fiesta, 187
Grilled Corn With Jalapeño-Lime Butter, 147
Mexican-Style Corn, 330
Pudding, Corn, 32
Salad, Colorful Corn, 353
Spoonbread, Corn, 377
Cornbreads
Green Chile Cornbread, 377
Jalapeño Cornbread, 113
Muffins, Broccoli Cornbread, 362
Muffins, Broccoli Cornbread Mini-, 43
Muffins, Parmesan Corn, 113
Skillet Cornbread, Old-Fashioned, 43
Waffles, Cornbread, 374
Couscous, Lemon, 344
Couscous, Spinach-and-Onion, 235
Crab Cake Sandwiches, 273
Crab Melts, Open-Faced, 273
Cranberry Brie, Warmed, 177
Crawfish Étouffée, 90
Crawfish Omelet, Easy, 53
Cucumbers
Gazpacho, Instant, 256
Salad With Cucumbers and Tomatoes, Potato, 38
Sandwiches, Cucumber, 279
Sauce, Cucumber-Dill, 140
Spread, Cucumber-Yogurt, 179
Custard, 395
Custard, Blackberry, 404

Desserts. *See also* Cakes, Custard, Pies and Pastries, Puddings.
Apple Grunt, 173
Frozen
    Ice-Cream Balls, Cinnamon-Chocolate Chip, 404
    Ice Cream, Soft-Serve Chocolate, 404
    Sherbet, Blueberry, 115
Pears With Raspberry Sherbet, 117
Pineapple, Sautéed, 117
Pineapple With Ice Cream, Ginger Grilled, 405
Pizza, Fresh Fruit, 392
Trifle, Berry-Amaretto Summer, 395
Trifle, Strawberry, 395
Dressing, Santa Fe Chicken and, 19

Dumplings
    Chicken and Dumplings, Light, 19
    Chicken and Dumplings, Quick, 19
    Pork Dumplings, 102

Eggplant
    Chicken Breasts on Eggplant,
        Mediterranean, 301
    Parmigiana, Eggplant and
        Artichoke, 169
    Ravioli, Mediterranean, 98
Eggs. *See also* Omelets.
    Benedict, Traditional Eggs, 55
    Casserole, Southwest Egg, 54
    Deviled Eggs, Basic, 197
    Frittata, Mediterranean, 319
    Green Eggs and Ham, 50
    Salad Crostini, Easy Egg, 202
    Salad Sandwiches, Double-Decker
        Egg, 264
    Scramble, Veggie, 50
Enchilada Casserole, 169
Enchilada Casserole, Easy, 85
Étouffée, Crawfish, 90

Fajitas, Slow-cooker, 155
Fennel and Carrots, Sautéed, 328
Fettuccine
    Chicken, Fettuccine With Pesto, 225
    Cream, Basil, and Romano, Fettuccine
        With, 229
    Primavera, Fettuccine, 98
    Scallop Fettuccine, Saucy, 227
Fish. *See also* Crab; Crawfish; Grilled/Fish
        and Shellfish; Salmon; Scallop;
        Seafood; Shrimp; Tuna.
    Catfish
        Fried Catfish, Crispy, 22
        Oven-Fried Catfish, 106
        Sandwiches, Fried Catfish, 274
    Dinner, Fish and Vegetable, 90
    Florentine, Fish, 311
    Flounder, New England Stuffed, 311
    Orange Roughy, Parmesan-Crusted, 311
    Orange Roughy, Pesto-Crusted, 108
    Po'boys, Zesty Fish, 273
Frittata, Mediterranean, 319
Fritters, Okra, 30
Frostings
    Caramel Frosting, Double Chocolate
        Brownies With, 385
    Chocolate Frosting, 399
    Cream Cheese Frosting, 400
Fruit. *See also* specific types and Salads.
    Pizza, Fresh Fruit, 392
    Trifle, Berry-Amaretto Summer, 395

Garlic
    Bread, Buttery Garlic, 365
    Chicken-and-Wild Rice Hot Dish, 164

Chicken, Smothered, 305
Flank Steaks, Peppered, 121
Jambalaya, Shrimp, 23
Olives, Lemon-Garlic, 195
Pasta, Artichoke, 229
Pizza, Mediterranean Garlic, 213
Pizza, Roasted Vegetable, 215
Potatoes, Garlic Mashed, 334
Roasted Garlic-and-Basil Tomato
    Soup, 254
Salad, Peanut-Noodle, 238
Scampi, Speedy, 227
Soup, Sausage, Spinach, and Bean, 249
Steaks, Garlic-Herb, 285
Vermicelli, Tomato-Jalapeño, 233
Vinaigrette, Garlic, 352
Zucchini-Beef Spaghetti, 105
Gravies
    Country Gravy, Chicken-fried
        Steak 'n', 25
    Horseradish Gravy, Filet Mignon
        With, 284
    Pork Chops and Gravy, 159
    Steak With Gravy, Country, 157
    Tomato Gravy, 291
Greens
    Braised Greens With Chipotle-Chile
        Vinaigrette, 333
    Collard Stew, 41
    Grits and Greens, 28
    Turnip Greens Stew, 41
    Wilted Greens With Sweet-and-Sour
        Sauce, 333
Grilled. *See also* Barbecue.
    Beef
        Burgers, Easy Mushroom-Onion, 260
        Burgers, Fiesta, 262
        Burgers, Mozzarella-Basil, 143
        Burgers, Stuffed Southwestern, 142
        Burgers With Fresh Basil, Italian, 261
        Cheeseburgers, Jack, 263
        Fillets With Orange Cream, Beef, 283
        Flank Steak, Asian Grilled, 121
        Flank Steaks, Peppered, 121
        Flank Steak With Molasses Barbecue
            Glaze, Grilled, 105
        London Broil, Marinated, 104
        Rib-eye Steaks, Grilled
            Gorgonzola, 121
        Rib-eye Steaks, Peppered, 120
        Sirloin and Serrano Chile Salsa, Texas
            Grilled, 123
        Sirloin Steaks With Thyme Pesto, 286
        Steak, Italian Grilled, 123
        Steaks, Garlic-Herb, 285
    Fish and Shellfish
        Mahimahi, Honey-Macadamia, 136
        Salmon With Nectarine-Onion
            Relish, Grilled, 137
        Salmon With Sweet Soy Slaw and
            Dipping Sauce, Grilled, 130
        Scallop-Veggie Skewers, 316
        Shrimp Gyros With Herbed Yogurt
            Spread, Grilled, 275
        Shrimp Skewers With Cilantro
            Salsa, 138

Skewers, Fish, 138
Swordfish Steaks With Basil
    Butter, 134
Trout, Grilled, 136
Tuna Sandwiches, Grilled, 108
Tuna Steaks, Pacific Rim, 134
Tuna Steaks With Green Peppercorn
    Sauce, 134
Tuna With Sautéed Vegetables, 313
Peaches, Grilled Balsamic-Glazed, 109
Pineapple With Ice Cream, Ginger
    Grilled, 405
Pork
    Chops, Blue Cheese-Stuffed, 125
    Chops With Pistachio Pesto and
        Parmesan Cheese Grits, Grilled
        Pork, 124
    Medallions in Mustard Sauce,
        Pork, 126
    Salad, Grilled Pork
        Cosmopolitan, 127
    Tenderloin With Red Wine Sauce,
        Molasses Pork, 127
Poultry
    Chicken, Garlic-Lime, 129
    Chicken Pizza, Bistro Grilled, 218
    Chicken Sandwiches, Open-Faced
        Southwestern, 269
    Chicken, Sesame-Ginger, 131
    Chicken Thighs, Teriyaki Grilled, 129
    Chicken With Lemon-Yogurt
        Coleslaw, Grilled, 133
    Chicken With Pineapple Salsa,
        Grilled Southwestern, 133
    Chicken With Sweet Soy Slaw and
        Dipping Sauce, Grilled, 130
    Turkey Cheeseburgers, 141
Vegetables
    Corn With Jalapeño-Lime Butter,
        Grilled, 147
    Okra and Tomatoes, Grilled, 147
    Portobello Burgers, Grilled, 143
    Portobello Pizzas, Grilled, 214
    Red Onions, Grilled, 145
    Sandwiches, Grilled Vegetable, 144
    Squash, Marinated Grilled, 147
    Tomatoes, Grilled, 144
Grits
    Cheese Grits, Quick Double-, 27
    Creamy Grits, 27
    Garlic-and-Herb Cheese
        Grits, 110
    Greens, Grits and, 28
    Parmesan Cheese Grits, 124
    Shrimp and Grits, 92
    Tomato Grits, Hot, 27
Gumbo, Chicken-Sausage, 22

Ham. *See also* Bacon, Pork, Sandwiches.
    Casserole, Creamy Ham, 56
    Eggs and Ham, Green, 50
    Glazed Ham, Pineapple-, 24
    Omelet, Ham-and-Broccoli, 51
    Omelets, Ham 'n' Cheddar, 50

Ham (*continued*)

Potatoes, Double-Stuffed Ham-and-
Broccoli, 57
Pot Pie, Chunky Ham, 58
Quesadillas, Quick Fiesta, 204
Salad, Ham-and-Pasta, 238
Hummus
Black-eyed Pea Hummus, 188
Hummus, 110
Traditional Hummus, 188
Hush Puppies, Baked, 113
Hush Puppies, Jalapeño, 43

Jambalaya, Shrimp, 23

Lamb and Vegetable Stir-fry, 292
Lamb Meatballs With Chutney Sauce, 162
Lasagna, Heavenly Chicken, 82
Lemon
Chicken Piccata, 303
Chicken Stir-fry, Lemon, 307
Couscous, Lemon, 344
Curd, Lemon, 392
Mayonnaise, Lemon, 141
Olives, Lemon-Garlic, 195
Shrimp, Lemon-Garlic, 316
Squares, Lemon, 384
Turkey-Basil Piccata, 308
Lime
Chicken, Garlic-Lime, 129
Sauce, Veal in Lime, 292
Shrimp in Tortillas, Lime, 315
Vinaigrette, Pistachio-Lime, 347
Linguine, Sautéed Shrimp and, 108

Macaroni
Cheese, Macaroni and, 99
Cheese, Taco Dinner Mac and, 63
Cheese, Veggie Mac-and-, 235
Salad, Macaroni and Cheese, 351
Make Ahead
Appetizers
Caviar, Carolina, 182
Caviar, Texas, 184
Cheese Crisps, Spicy Jack, 201
Cheese, Olives, and Peppers,
Marinated, 199
Cheese With Avocado-Mango Salsa,
Smoky Green Chile Cheddar, 198
Crackers, Snack, 193
Crostini, Easy Egg Salad, 202
Deviled Eggs, Basic, 197
Dip, Curry, 191
Dip, Layered Nacho, 185
Dip, Quick Creamy Vegetable, 189
Hummus, 110
Hummus, Black-eyed Pea, 188
Lettuce Wraps, Thai Green Apple
Pork, 203

Mix, Mexicali Snack, 191
Mix, Sweet 'n' Savory Snack, 191
Olives, Balsamic Marinated, 195
Olives, Lemon-Garlic, 195
Pecans, Citrusy, 195
Pecans, Spiced, 195
Pimiento Cheese, Green Chile, 197
Pork Dumplings, 102
Ring, Cherry-Cheese, 180
Salsa, Avocado-Corn, 182
Salsa, Black Bean, 182
Salsa, Five-Minute, 182
Spread, Cucumber-Yogurt, 179
Spread, Garlic-and-Dill Feta
Cheese, 177
Spread, Herbed Feta, 179
Spread, Mexican Cheese, 181
Spread, Pesto-Goat Cheese, 179
Tapenade, 178
Beans, Hearty Baked, 161
Breads
Biscuit Poppers, 358
Biscuits, Best-Ever Buttermilk, 112
Biscuits, Cheese Garlic, 358
Biscuits, Tiny Cream Cheese, 358
Herb Bread, 365
Hush Puppies, Jalapeño, 43
Muffins, Broccoli Cornbread, 362
Muffins, Cheese, 362
Muffins, Parmesan Corn, 113
Muffins, Raspberry-Streusel, 361
Muffins, Streusel-Topped
Pumpkin, 360
Muffins, White Chocolate-
Macadamia Nut, 361
Peanut Butter Bread, 362
Pizza Dough, 101
Waffles, Cornbread, 374
Desserts
Apple Grunt, 173
Balls, Orange-Nut, 389
Bars, Creamy No-Bake, 386
Bars, Gooey Turtle, 385
Brownies, Double Chocolate, 385
Cake, Chocolate Éclair, 397
Cake, German Chocolate Snack, 398
Cake, Mississippi Mud, 399
Cakes, Birthday Party Brownie, 398
Cakes, Molten Chocolate, 397
Cakes, Quick Italian Cream, 400
Cake, Sour Cream Pound, 402
Cake, Tropical Dump, 401
Cake, Turtle, 398
Cheesecake, Blueberry, 115
Clusters, Rocky Road, 389
Cookies, Chocolate-Pecan, 382
Cookies, Coconut-Macadamia, 382
Cookies, Nutty Oatmeal-Chocolate
Chunk, 381
Cookies, Oatmeal-Raisin, 117
Cookies, Peanut Blossom, 382
Cookies, Ultimate Chocolate
Chip, 380
Curd, Lemon, 392
Custard, Blackberry, 404
Fudge, Peanut Butter, 389

Ice-Cream Balls, Cinnamon-
Chocolate Chip, 404
Ice Cream, Soft-Serve Chocolate, 404
Pie, Caramel, 173
Pie, Coconut Cream, 46
Pie Fingers, Honey-Pecan, 46
Pie, Texas Star Pecan, 45
Pizza, Fresh Fruit, 392
Pudding, Chocolate Cookie, 403
Pudding, Peanut Butter, 402
Sherbet, Blueberry, 115
Shortbread, Butter-Mint, 386
Shortcake, Streusel Blueberry, 393
Squares, Lemon, 384
Squares, Pecan, 46
Texas Millionaires, 389
Trifle, Strawberry, 395
Grits, Quick Double-Cheese, 27
Main Dishes
Barbecue, Chuck Roast, 151
Beef Brisket in Beer, Peppered, 157
Beef Burgundy, 154
Beef Lombardi, 67
Casserole, Chicken-and-Broccoli, 77
Casserole, Easy Beef, 67
Casserole, Enchilada, 169
Casserole, King Ranch Chicken, 19
Casserole, Leslie's Favorite Chicken-
and-Wild Rice, 81
Casserole, Southwest Egg, 54
Chicken and Dumplings, Quick, 19
Chicken-and-Wild Rice Hot
Dish, 164
Chicken Bake, Mushroom, 299
Chicken Barbecue, 165
Chicken, Benne Seed, 14
Chicken Cannelloni With Roasted
Red Bell Pepper Sauce, 83
Chicken, Honey Barbecue, 132
Chicken Lasagna, Heavenly, 82
Chicken Pepper Pot, 165
Chicken Supper, Provençale, 162
Chicken Tetrazzini, 79
Chicken Thighs, Honey-Pecan, 15
Chicken Thighs, Teriyaki Grilled, 129
Chicken Thighs With Rosemary and
Potatoes, Braised, 165
Chicken With Pineapple Salsa,
Grilled Southwestern, 133
Chicken With Sweet Soy Slaw and
Dipping Sauce, Grilled, 130
Drumsticks and Thighs, Saucy, 162
Eggplant and Artichoke
Parmigiana, 169
Eye of Round Roast, 286
Fajitas, Slow-cooker, 155
Flank Barbecue, Peppery, 154
Flank Steak, Asian Grilled, 121
Flank Steaks, Peppered, 121
Ham, Pineapple-Glazed, 24
London Broil, Marinated, 104
Mac-and-Cheese, Veggie, 235
Meatballs With Chutney Sauce,
Lamb, 162
Pasta Toss, Garden, 236
Pinto Beans With Ham, 161

Pork and Vegetables, Apple
  Cider, 159
Pork, Caribbean-Style, 158
Pork Chops and Gravy, 159
Pork Dumplings, 102
Pork Medallions in Mustard
  Sauce, 126
Pork, Spiced, 159
Pork Tenderloin With Red Wine
  Sauce, Molasses, 127
Pot Pie, Chunky Ham, 58
Pot Roast, Company, 152
Pot Roast, Savory, 150
Pot Roast, Zippy Barbecue, 151
Rib-eye Steaks, Peppered, 120
Ribs and Beans, Spicy-Sweet, 161
Roast Beef With Horseradish
  Sauce, 154
Salmon With Nectarine-Onion
  Relish, Grilled, 137
Sauerbraten, 151
Shells, Spinach-Stuffed, 222
Shrimp and Rice, Thai Coconut, 166
Spaghetti, Easy, 223
Steaks, Garlic-Herb, 285
Steak With Gravy, Country, 157
Swordfish Steaks With Basil
  Butter, 134
Tuna Steaks, Pacific Rim, 134
Turkey and Sweet Potatoes, Apricot-
  Glazed, 166
Mayonnaise, Béarnaise, 179
Salads and Salad Dressings
  Beef-and-Lime Rice Salad, 64
  Black Bean 'n' Rice Salad, 354
  Broccoli Salad, 353
  Cantaloupe-Spinach Salad, 347
  Cherry Tomato-Caper Salad, 355
  Chicken-Black Bean Salad, 88
  Chicken-Pasta Salad, Zesty, 241
  Chicken Salad, Fruity, 89
  Chicken Salad, Greek, 87
  Chicken Salad, Southwestern, 87
  Coleslaw, Colorful, 35
  Coleslaw, Jalapeño, 35
  Corn Salad, Colorful, 353
  Macaroni and Cheese Salad, 351
  Mozzarella-Tomato-Basil Salad,
    Fresh, 37
  Pasta Salad, Greek, 237
  Peanut-Noodle Salad, 238
  Potato Salad, Creole, 37
  Potato Salad, Dilled, 39
  Potato Salad With Cucumbers and
    Tomatoes, 38
  Shrimp Salad, Marinated, 93
  Spinach Tortellini Salad, Layered, 351
  Tabbouleh Salad, Southwestern, 110
  Tomato Salad, Blackened, 37
  Tortellini Pasta Salad, Cheese, 238
  Tuna-and-White Bean Salad, 90
Sandwiches
  Burgers, Greek Feta, 140
  Cheeseburgers, Jack, 263
  Cheeseburgers, Turkey, 141
  Club Sandwiches, French, 266

Crab Cake Sandwiches, 273
  Pork Dip Sandwiches, Easy
    Spanish, 160
  Reubens, Golden-Baked Mini, 259
  Wraps, Smoked Turkey, 266
Sauce, Beefy Pasta, 157
Soups and Stews
  Beef Stew, Company, 247
  Black Bean Soup, 171
  Chili, Chunky Beef, 42
  Chili, Slow-cooker Chunky
    Beef, 153
  French Onion Soup,
    Caramelized, 170
  Gazpacho, Instant, 256
  Italian Soup, Chunky, 247
  Noodle Soup, Chicken, 244
  Potato Soup, Homestyle, 171
  Reuben Soup, Cream of, 250
  Roasted Garlic-and-Basil Tomato
    Soup, 254
  Tomato-Basil Cream Soup, 40
  Turnip Greens Stew, 41
  Vegetable Soup, Spicy, 171
Vegetables
  Carrot-Sweet Potato Puree, 329
  Onions, Grilled Red, 145
  Tomatoes, Honey-Baked, 343
  Tomato Napoleon, 342
Mango Chutney Chicken Pitas, 270
Mango Salsa, Avocado-, 198
Marinade, Cheese, 199
Mayonnaise
  Béarnaise Mayonnaise, 179
  Gremolata Mayonnaise, 179
  Lemon Mayonnaise, 141
  Tomato-Basil Mayonnaise, 179
Meatless Products
  Pizzas, Veggie Sausage, 214
Microwave
  Appetizers
    Dip, Cinco de Mayo Bean, 189
    Dip, Quick Fiesta, 187
    Dip, Vidalia Onion, 187
    Meatballs, Bourbon, 209
  Desserts
    Cobbler, Speedy Blackberry, 390
    Crisp, Apple Shortbread, 391
  Main Dishes
    Burritos, Breakfast, 53
    Casserole, Beefy Noodle, 60
    Fish and Vegetable Dinner, 90
    Pie, Corn Chip Chili, 61
  Sandwiches
    Bacon, Cheese, and Tomato
      Sandwiches, Grilled, 264
    Egg Salad Sandwiches, Double-
      Decker, 264
    Wraps, Cheese-Steak, 260
  Vegetables
    Carrot-Sweet Potato Puree, 329
    Corn on the Cob, Chili, 330
    Green Beans With Bacon,
      Sautéed, 325
    Onion-Gruyère Gratin, 334
    Potatoes, Garlic Mashed, 334

Muffins
  Broccoli Cornbread Muffins, 362
  Cheese Muffins, 362
  Cornbread Mini-Muffins,
    Broccoli, 43
  Corn Muffins, Parmesan, 113
  Peanut Butter Muffins, 362
  Pumpkin Muffins, Streusel-Topped, 360
  Raspberry-Streusel Muffins, 361
  White Chocolate-Macadamia Nut
    Muffins, 361
Mushrooms
  Bake, Mushroom Chicken, 299
  Burgers, Easy Mushroom-Onion, 260
  Portobello Burgers, Grilled, 143
  Portobello Pizzas, Grilled, 214
  Portobello Tossed Salad, 354

Nectarine-Onion Relish, 137
Noodles, Blue Cheese, 231
Noodles, Thai, 231

Okra
  Basil Okra 'n' Tomatoes, 30
  Creole, Okra, 32
  Fried Okra, Crunchy, 31
  Fritters, Okra, 30
  Grilled Okra and Tomatoes, 147
Olives
  Lemon-Garlic Olives, 195
  Marinated Cheese, Olives, and
    Peppers, 199
  Marinated Olives, Balsamic, 195
  Tapenade, 178
Omelets
  Easy Crawfish Omelet, 53
  Ham-and-Broccoli Omelet, 51
  Ham 'n' Cheddar Omelets, 50
Onions
  Caramelized Onions, 170, 266
  Dip, Swiss-Onion, 187
  Gratin, Onion-Gruyère, 334
  Green Onion-and-Bacon Mashed
    Potatoes, Cheesy, 336
  Red Onions, Grilled, 145
  Roasted Onion Salad, 352
  Sandwiches, French Onion, 279
  Soup, Caramelized French
    Onion, 170
  Vidalia Onion Dip, 187
Oranges
  Balls, Orange-Nut, 389
  Cream, Beef Fillets With Orange, 283
  Salad, Bacon-Mandarin, 349

Pancakes
  Banana Pancakes, Easy, 373
  Blueberry Pancakes, 374
  Pumpkin Pancakes, 373
  Veggie Pancakes, 373

Pasta. *See also* Couscous, Fettuccine, Lasagna, Linguine, Macaroni, Noodles, Spaghetti.
Artichoke Pasta, 229
Bow Tie Pasta Salad, Chicken and, 241
Cannelloni With Roasted Red Bell Pepper Sauce, Chicken, 83
Chicken Pasta, Cajun, 225
Dinner, One-Pot Pasta, 233
Penne Alfredo, Bacon, 221
Penne, Cheesy Chicken, 225
Penne, Spicy Vegetables With, 228
Salad, Greek Pasta, 237
Salad, Ham-and-Pasta, 238
Salad, Hoisin Chicken-and-Pasta, 240
Salad, Pasta-Veggie, 237
Salad, Zesty Chicken-Pasta, 241
Sauce, Beefy Pasta, 157
Shells, Creamy Tomato-Sausage Sauce With, 222
Shells, Spinach-Stuffed, 222
Tortellini Carbonara, 58
Tortellini in Jalapeño Tomato Sauce, Cheese, 235
Tortellini Pasta Salad, Cheese, 238
Tortellini Salad, Layered Spinach, 351
Tortellini, Shrimp and, 93
Toss, Garden Pasta, 236
Vegetable Pasta, 96
Vermicelli, Shrimp and Feta, 227
Vermicelli, Tomato-Jalapeño, 233
Vermicelli With Chunky Vegetable Sauce, 234
Ziti With Mozzarella and Tomato, 229
Ziti With Sausage and Broccoli, 221
Peaches
Cobbler, Quick Peach, 45
Glazed Peaches, Grilled Balsamic-, 109
Pork Picante, Peachy, 295
Peanut Butter
Bread, Peanut Butter, 362
Cookies, Peanut Blossom, 382
Fudge, Peanut Butter, 389
Muffins, Peanut Butter, 362
Pudding, Peanut Butter, 402
Pears With Raspberry Sherbet, 117
Pear-Walnut Salad, 348
Peas
Black-eyed
Cakes, Black-Eyed Pea, 35
Caviar, Carolina, 182
Caviar, Texas, 184
Ham, Quick Black-Eyed Peas 'n', 34
Hummus, Black-eyed Pea, 188
Snow Pea Stir-fry, Chicken-and-, 73
Pecans
Chicken, Pecan, 17
Citrusy Pecans, 195
Crescent Twists, Pecan, 368
Desserts
Pie Fingers, Honey-Pecan, 46
Pie, Texas Star Pecan, 45
Squares, Pecan, 46
Dressing, Honey-Pecan, 348
Spiced Pecans, 195

Peppers
Chicken Pepper Pot, 165
Chile
Chipotle-Chile Vinaigrette, Braised Greens With, 333
Green Chile Biscuits, 245
Green Chile Cheddar Cheese With Avocado-Mango Salsa, Smoky, 198
Green Chile Cornbread, 377
Green Chile Pimiento Cheese, 197
Green Chile Pimiento Cheese Tea Sandwiches, 197
Poblano Chicken, Creamy, 85
Serrano Chile Salsa, 123
Jalapeño
Butter, Grilled Corn With Jalapeño-Lime, 147
Cheeseburgers, Jalapeño, 143
Coleslaw, Jalapeño, 35
Cornbread, Jalapeño, 113
Hush Puppies, Jalapeño, 43
Sauce, Cheese Tortellini in Jalapeño Tomato, 235
Red
Roasted Red Bell Pepper Sauce, 83
Roasted Red Pepper Cream, Shrimp With, 315
Roasted Red Pepper Sauce, Pan-Seared Steaks With, 285
Salsa Verde, 65
Stuffed Peppers With Chicken and Corn, 77
Pesto, Sirloin Steaks With Thyme, 286
Pesto With Sun-dried Tomatoes, Pistachio, 124
Pies and Pastries
Caramel Pie, 173
Cobblers and Crisps
Apple-Blueberry Crunch, 390
Apple Shortbread Crisp, 391
Blackberry Cobbler, Speedy, 390
Black Forest Crisp, 390
Blueberry-Pecan Cobbler, 45
Peach Cobbler, Quick, 45
Coconut Cream Pie, 46
Honey-Pecan Pie Fingers, 46
Main Dish
Chicken Pot Pie, Pronto, 80
Corn Chip Chili Pie, 61
Ham Pot Pie, Chunky, 58
Shepherd's Pie, 63
Pecan Pie, Texas Star, 45
Pineapple
Cake, Tropical Dump, 401
Grilled Pineapple With Ice Cream, Ginger, 405
Salsa, Pineapple, 133
Sautéed Pineapple, 117
Pizza
Breakfast Pizza, 54
Casserole, Weeknight Pizza, 61
Cheeseburger Pizza, 219
Chicken-and-Three-Cheese French Bread Pizzas, 213
Chicken Barbecue Pizza, Quick 'n' Easy, 217

Chicken Pizza, Bistro Grilled, 218
Dip, Pizza, 185
Dough, Pizza, 101
Fruit Pizza, Fresh, 392
Garlic Pizza, Mediterranean, 213
Hamburger-Mushroom Pizza, 218
Mozzarella and Basil Pizza, Fresh, 100
Pesto-Tomato Pizza, 214
Pinwheels, Pepperoni Pizza, 212
Portobello Pizzas, Grilled, 214
Roasted Chicken-and-White Bean Pizzas, 216
Roasted Vegetable Pizza, 215
Rollups, Pizza, 213
Veggie Sausage Pizzas, 214
Pork. *See also* Bacon; Grilled/Pork; Ham; Sausage.
Apple Cider Pork and Vegetables, 159
Chops
Balsamic Pork Chops, 297
Barbecue-Battered Pork Chops, 20
Caribbean-Style Pork, 158
Dumplings, Pork, 102
Fruited Pork Chops, 295
Glazed Pork Chops, Ginger-, 295
Gravy, Pork Chops and, 159
Honey-Pecan Pork Chops, 296
Skillet, Pork-and-Pepper, 102
Lettuce Wraps, Thai Green Apple Pork, 203
Picante, Peachy Pork, 295
Quesadillas, Barbecue, 204
Ribs and Beans, Spicy-Sweet, 161
Sandwiches, Easy Spanish Pork Dip, 160
Spiced Pork, 159
Tenderloin, Ginger-Glazed Pork, 295
Potatoes. *See also* Salads/Potato; Sweet Potatoes.
Mashed
Basic Mashed Potatoes, 334
Garlic Mashed Potatoes, 334
Green Onion-and-Bacon Mashed Potatoes, Cheesy, 336
Twice-Baked Mashed Potatoes, 335
Roasted Potatoes, 286
Roasted Potato Wedges, Balsamic-, 336
Soup, Homestyle Potato, 171
Soup, Roasted Garlic-Potato, 110
Soup With Ham, Potato, 250
Stuffed Ham-and-Broccoli Potatoes, Double-, 57
Puddings. *See also* Custard.
Banana Pudding, New-Fashioned, 47
Chocolate Cookie Pudding, 403
Corn Pudding, 32
Peanut Butter Pudding, 402
Pumpkin Muffins, Streusel-Topped, 360
Pumpkin Pancakes, 373

Quesadillas
Barbecue Quesadillas, 204
Chicken Quesadillas, Santa Fe, 204
Fiesta Quesadillas, Quick, 204

Raspberries
Muffins, Raspberry-Streusel, 361
Salad, Fresh Raspberry-Spinach, 347
Sherbet, Pears With Raspberry, 117
Vinaigrette, Raspberry, 347
Ravioli, Mediterranean, 98
Relish, Flank Steak With Tomato-Olive, 286
Relish, Nectarine-Onion, 137
Rice
Black Beans and Corn, Rice With, 344
Chicken and Rice, Sweet-and-Sour, 75
Pilaf, Rice, 344
Salad, Beef-and-Lime Rice, 64
Salad, Black Bean 'n' Rice, 354
Shrimp and Rice, Thai Coconut, 166
White Rice, Fluffy, 68
Wild Rice Casserole, Leslie's Favorite Chicken-and-, 81
Wild Rice Hot Dish, Chicken-and-, 164
Rolls and Buns
Caramel-Chocolate Sticky Buns, Easy, 370
Cinnamon-Apple Breakfast Buns, 370
Knots, Cajun Bread, 364
Knots, Italian Bread, 364
Knots, Southwestern, 364

Salad Dressings
Barbecue Dressing, 20
Honey-Pecan Dressing, 348
Pan Dressing, Steak-and-Spinach Salad With Hot, 71
Tomato Dressing, Fresh, 343
Vinaigrette
Balsamic Vinaigrette, 353
Chipotle-Chile Vinaigrette, Braised Greens With, 333
Garlic Vinaigrette, 352
Pistachio-Lime Vinaigrette, 347
Raspberry Vinaigrette, 347
Salads
Artichoke-Goat Cheese Salad, 353
Baby Blue Salad, Quick, 348
Bacon-Mandarin Salad, 349
Barbecue Salad, Warm, 20
Beef-and-Lime Rice Salad, 64
Beef Salad With Cilantro, 70
Black Bean 'n' Rice Salad, 354
Broccoli Salad, 353
Cherry Tomato-Caper Salad, 355
Chicken
Black Bean Salad, Chicken-, 88
Fruity Chicken Salad, 89
Greek Chicken Salad, 87
Hoisin Chicken-and-Pasta Salad, 240
Pasta Salad, Chicken and Bow Tie, 241
Pasta Salad, Zesty Chicken-, 241
Southwestern Chicken Salad, 87
Spicy Chicken Salad, 87
Corn Salad, Colorful, 353
Egg Salad Crostini, Easy, 202

Egg Salad Sandwiches, Double-Decker, 264
Fruit Salad With Honey-Pecan Dressing, 348
Ham-and-Pasta Salad, 238
Macaroni and Cheese Salad, 351
Mozzarella-Tomato-Basil Salad, Fresh, 37
Niçoise, Steak Salad, 122
Pasta Salad, Greek, 237
Pasta-Veggie Salad, 237
Peanut-Noodle Salad, 238
Pear-Walnut Salad, 348
Pork Cosmopolitan Salad, Grilled, 127
Portobello Tossed Salad, 354
Potato
Creole Potato Salad, 37
Cucumbers and Tomatoes, Potato Salad With, 38
Dilled Potato Salad, 39
Roast Beef-Blue Cheese Salad, 71
Roasted Onion Salad, 352
Shrimp Salad, Marinated, 93
Spinach
Apple-Spinach Salad, 347
Cantaloupe-Spinach Salad, 347
Layered Spinach Tortellini Salad, 351
Raspberry-Spinach Salad, Fresh, 347
Steak-and-Spinach Salad With Hot Pan Dressing, 71
Tabbouleh Salad, Southwestern, 110
Tomato Napoleon, 342
Tomato-Red Onion Salad, 354
Tomato Salad, Blackened, 37
Tortellini Pasta Salad, Cheese, 238
Tuna-and-White Bean Salad, 90
Salmon
Broiled Salmon With Dijon-Caper Cream Sauce, 313
Grilled Salmon With Nectarine-Onion Relish, 137
Grilled Salmon With Sweet Soy Slaw and Dipping Sauce, 130
Salsas. *See also* Pesto, Relish, Sauces, Toppings.
Avocado-Corn Salsa, 182
Avocado-Mango Salsa, 198
Black Bean Salsa, 182
Cilantro Salsa, Shrimp Skewers With, 138
Five-Minute Salsa, 182
Pineapple Salsa, 133
Serrano Chile Salsa, 123
Verde, Salsa, 65
Sandwiches
Avocado Sandwiches Deluxe, 277
BLTs, "Fried" Green Tomato, 29
Calzones, Easy, 259
Calzones, Spinach-and-Cheese, 97
Chicken Sandwiches, Open-Faced Southwestern, 269
Club Sandwiches, French, 266
Crab Cake Sandwiches, 273
Cucumber Sandwiches, 279
Egg Salad Sandwiches, Double-Decker, 264

French Onion Sandwiches, 279
Fried Catfish Sandwiches, 274
Grilled Bacon, Cheese, and Tomato Sandwiches, 264
Grilled Chicken 'n' Cheese Sandwiches, 269
Grilled Tuna Sandwiches, 108
Grills, Double Cheese, 277
Gyros With Herbed Yogurt Spread, Grilled Shrimp, 275
Ham-Swiss-and-Asparagus Sandwiches, 266
Hot Browns, Asparagus, 271
Meatball Sandwich, Giant, 263
Melts, Open-Faced Crab, 273
Melts, Vegetable-Cheese, 97
Pimiento Cheese Finger Sandwiches, 279
Pimiento Cheese Tea Sandwiches, Green Chile, 197
Pitas, Mango Chutney Chicken, 270
Po'boys, Zesty Fish, 273
Pork Dip Sandwiches, Easy Spanish, 160
Reubens, Golden-Baked Mini, 259
Rollups, Pizza, 213
Stuffed Sandwiches, Deli-, 265
Tuna-Apple Sandwiches, Curried, 274
Vegetable Sandwiches, Grilled, 144
Wraps, Cheese-Steak, 260
Wraps, Smoked Turkey, 266
Sauces. *See also* Gravies, Pesto, Relish, Salsas, Syrup, Toppings.
Alfredo Sauce, 233
Barbecue Sauce, Honey, 132
Béchamel, Gratin of Broccoli in, 327
Chutney Sauce, Lamb Meatballs With, 162
Cucumber-Dill Sauce, 140
Dijon-Caper Cream Sauce, Broiled Salmon With, 313
Dipping Sauce, Grilled Chicken With Sweet Soy Slaw and, 130
Ginger Dipping Sauce, 102
Green Peppercorn Sauce, Tuna Steaks With, 134
Hollandaise Sauce, 55
Horseradish Sauce, 154
Jalapeño Tomato Sauce, Cheese Tortellini in, 235
Lime Sauce, Veal in, 292
Mustard Sauce, 126, 316
Pasta Sauce, Beefy, 157
Peanut Dipping Sauce, Hoisin-, 209
Red Wine Sauce, 127
Rémoulade Sauce, 306
Roasted Red Bell Pepper Sauce, 83
Roasted Red Pepper Sauce, Pan-Seared Steaks With, 285
Sweet-and-Sour Sauce, Wilted Greens With, 333
Tomato-Sausage Sauce With Shells, Creamy, 222
Vegetable Sauce, Vermicelli With Chunky, 234
Wine Sauce, Creamy, 309

Sausage
    Dip, Meaty Cheese, 185
    Gumbo, Chicken-Sausage, 22
    Meatless
        Pizzas, Veggie Sausage, 214
    Sauce With Shells, Creamy Tomato-
        Sausage, 222
    Skillet Sausage, Peppers, and
        Mushrooms, 293
    Soup, Sausage, Spinach, and Bean, 249
    Ziti With Sausage and Broccoli, 221
Scallop Fettuccine, Saucy, 227
Scallop-Veggie Skewers, 316
Seafood. See also Crab, Crawfish, Fish,
        Salmon, Scallop, Shrimp, Tuna.
    Chowder, So-Quick Seafood, 250
Seasonings
    Hoisin Mixture, 241
    Spicy Seasoning, 87
Shrimp. See also Grilled/Fish and Shellfish.
    Cajun Shrimp, Snappy, 314
    Chowder, Quick Shrimp, 252
    Coconut Shrimp and Rice, Thai, 166
    Coconut Shrimp With Mustard
        Sauce, 316
    Destin, Shrimp, 91
    Grits, Shrimp and, 92
    Jambalaya, Shrimp, 23
    Lemon-Garlic Shrimp, 316
    Lime Shrimp in Tortillas, 315
    Oriental, Shrimp, 93
    Roasted Red Pepper Cream, Shrimp
        With, 315
    Salad, Marinated Shrimp, 93
    Sautéed Shrimp and Linguine, 108
    Scampi, Speedy, 227
    Tortellini, Shrimp and, 93
    Vermicelli, Shrimp and Feta, 227
Slaws
    Colorful Coleslaw, 35
    Jalapeño Coleslaw, 35
    Lemon-Yogurt Coleslaw, Grilled
        Chicken With, 133
    Soy Slaw and Dipping Sauce, Grilled
        Chicken With Sweet, 130
Slow Cooker
    Apple Grunt, 173
    Beans, Hearty Baked, 161
    Main Dishes
        Beef Brisket in Beer, Peppered, 157
        Beef Burgundy, 154
        Chicken-and-Wild Rice Hot
            Dish, 164
        Chicken Barbecue, 165
        Chicken Pepper Pot, 165
        Chicken Supper, Provençale, 162
        Chicken Thighs With Rosemary and
            Potatoes, Braised, 165
        Chuck Roast Barbecue, 151
        Country Steak With Gravy, 157
        Drumsticks and Thighs, Saucy, 162
        Eggplant and Artichoke
            Parmigiana, 169
        Enchilada Casserole, 169
        Fajitas, Slow-cooker, 155
        Flank Barbecue, Peppery, 154

Lamb Meatballs With Chutney
        Sauce, 162
Pinto Beans With Ham, 161
Pork and Vegetables, Apple
    Cider, 159
Pork, Caribbean-Style, 158
Pork Chops and Gravy, 159
Pork, Spiced, 159
Pot Roast, Company, 152
Pot Roast, Savory, 150
Pot Roast, Zippy Barbecue, 151
Ribs and Beans, Spicy-Sweet, 161
Roast Beef With Horseradish
    Sauce, 154
Sauerbraten, 151
Shrimp and Rice, Thai Coconut, 166
Turkey and Sweet Potatoes, Apricot-
    Glazed, 166
Onions, Caramelized, 170
Pie, Caramel, 173
Sandwiches, Easy Spanish Pork
    Dip, 160
Sauce, Beefy Pasta, 157
Soups and Stews
    Black Bean Soup, 171
    Chili, Slow-cooker Chunky Beef, 153
    French Onion Soup,
        Caramelized, 170
    Potato Soup, Homestyle, 171
    Vegetable Soup, Spicy, 171
Soups. See also Chili, Chowder, Gumbo,
        Jambalaya, Stews.
    Bean
        Black Bean Soup, 171, 256
        Quick Bean Soup, 257
        White Bean Soup, 41
    Bisque, Tomato-Basil, 255
    Blue Satin Soup, 252
    Cheese Soup, Herbed, 252
    Chicken Noodle Soup, 244
    French Onion Soup, Caramelized, 170
    Gazpacho, Instant, 256
    Italian Soup, Chunky, 247
    Potato Soup, Homestyle, 171
    Potato Soup, Roasted Garlic-, 110
    Potato Soup With Ham, 250
    Reuben Soup, Cream of, 250
    Sausage, Spinach, and Bean Soup, 249
    Taco Soup, 249
    Tomato-Basil Cream Soup, 40
    Tomato Soup, Roasted Garlic-and-
        Basil, 254
    Tortilla Soup, Spicy, 41
    Turkey Soup With Green Chile Biscuits,
        Fiesta, 245
    Vegetable Soup, Spicy, 171
Spaghetti
    Chicken Spaghetti, 75
    Easy Spaghetti, 223
    Skillet Spaghetti, One-, 222
    Tetrazzini, Chicken, 79
    Zucchini-Beef Spaghetti, 105
Spinach. See also Salads/Spinach.
    Calzones, Spinach-and-Cheese, 97
    Couscous, Spinach-and-Onion, 235
    Dip, Florentine Artichoke, 186

Easy Spinach, 339
Fish Florentine, 311
Herbs, Spinach With, 339
Shells, Spinach-Stuffed, 222
Spreads. See also Butter, Mayonnaise.
    Cheese
        Feta Cheese Spread, Garlic-and-
            Dill, 177
        Feta Spread, Herbed, 179
        Goat Cheese Spread, Pesto-, 179
        Mexican Cheese Spread, 181
        Pimiento Cheese, Green Chile, 197
    Cucumber-Yogurt Spread, 179
    Yogurt Spread, Herbed, 275
Squash. See also Zucchini.
    Casserole, Squash, 341
    Grilled Squash, Marinated, 147
    Summer Squash-and-Corn
        Sauté, 341
    Summer Squash, Southern, 339
Stews. See also Chili, Chowder, Gumbo,
        Jambalaya, Soups.
    Beef Burgundy Stew, Skillet, 67
    Beef Stew, Company, 247
    Collard Stew, 41
    Meatball Stew, 249
    Turnip Greens Stew, 41
Strawberry Trifle, 395
Sweet Potatoes, Apricot-Glazed Turkey
    and, 166
Sweet Potato Puree, Carrot-, 329
Syrup, Simple, 402

Tabbouleh Salad, Southwestern, 110
Tacos
    Chicken-and-Refried Bean Tacos, 84
    Skillet Tacos, Easy, 63
    Soup, Taco, 249
    Squares, Deep-Dish Taco, 61
Tapenade, 178
10 Minutes or Less
    Appetizers
        Hummus, 110
        Mix, Starry Snack, 192
        Salsa, Five-Minute, 182
        Tapenade, 178
    Grits, Garlic-and-Herb Cheese, 110
    Pineapple, Sautéed, 117
    Salads and Salad Dressings
        Apple-Spinach Salad, 347
        Balsamic Vinaigrette, 353
        Cantaloupe-Spinach Salad, 347
        Coleslaw, Colorful, 35
        Coleslaw, Jalapeño, 35
        Fruit Salad With Honey-Pecan
            Dressing, 348
        Pear-Walnut Salad, 348
        Roast Beef-Blue Cheese Salad, 71
    Sandwiches
        Cucumber Sandwiches, 279
        Grills, Double Cheese, 277
        Melts, Open-Faced Crab, 273
        Pimiento Cheese Finger
            Sandwiches, 279

Stuffed Sandwiches, Deli-, 265
Tuna-Apple Sandwiches,
    Curried, 274
Sauce, Alfredo, 233
Spread, Herbed Feta, 179
Steaks With Roasted Red Pepper Sauce,
    Pan-Seared, 285
Tomatoes, Grilled, 144
Tomatoes, Savory Stuffed, 29
Turkey-Basil Piccata, 308
30 Minutes or Less
  Appetizers
    Biscuits, Savory Tomato-Bacon, 202
    Chicken Strips, Sesame, 206
    Deviled Eggs, Basic, 197
    Dip, Pizza, 185
    Dip, Swiss-Onion, 187
    Dip, Vidalia Onion, 187
    Meatballs, Bourbon, 209
    Mix, Mexicali Snack, 191
    Pinwheels, Pepperoni Pizza, 212
    Quesadillas, Barbecue, 204
    Quesadillas, Quick Fiesta, 204
    Rounds, Bacon-Cheese, 200
  Breads
    Biscuit Poppers, 358
    Biscuits, Tiny Cream Cheese, 358
    Breadsticks, Spicy, 368
    Buns, Cinnamon-Apple
        Breakfast, 370
    Cornbread, Green Chile, 377
    Cornbread, Old-Fashioned Skillet, 43
    Focaccia, Pesto-and-Tomato, 367
    Knots, Southwestern, 364
    Muffins, Broccoli Cornbread
        Mini-, 43
    Muffins, Cheese, 362
    Muffins, Parmesan Corn, 113
    Muffins, White Chocolate-
        Macadamia Nut, 361
    Pancakes, Blueberry, 374
    Pancakes, Easy Banana, 373
    Pancakes, Pumpkin, 373
    Pancakes, Veggie, 373
    Twists, Pecan Crescent, 368
    Waffles, Cornbread, 374
  Couscous, Spinach-and-Onion, 235
  Desserts
    Ice Cream, Soft-Serve Chocolate, 404
    Pineapple With Ice Cream, Ginger
        Grilled, 405
    Rocky Road Clusters, 389
    Trifle, Berry-Amaretto Summer, 395
  Main Dishes
    Beef Fillets, Spicy, 283
    Beef With Ginger, 68
    Casserole, Beefy Noodle, 60
    Catfish, Oven-Fried, 106
    Chicken and Dumplings, Quick, 19
    Chicken Breasts, Deviled, 106
    Chicken Breasts, Garlic Fried, 17
    Chicken in Biscuit Bowls,
        Creamed, 78
    Chicken Parmesan, 301
    Chicken, Pecan, 17
    Chicken Piccata, 303

    Chicken, Sesame-Ginger, 131
    Chicken, Tarragon Cream, 303
    Chicken With Fresh Herbs and
        Vegetables, 74
    Chicken With Lemon-Yogurt
        Coleslaw, Grilled, 133
    Chimichangas, Bean-and-
        Cheese, 319
    Chimichangas, Beef-and-Bean, 65
    Fettuccine Primavera, 98
    Fettuccine With Cream, Basil, and
        Romano, 229
    Filet Mignon With Horseradish
        Gravy, 284
    Fillets With Orange Cream, Beef, 283
    Fish and Vegetable Dinner, 90
    Frittata, Mediterranean, 319
    Pasta Dinner, One-Pot, 233
    Pasta, Vegetable, 96
    Penne Alfredo, Bacon, 221
    Pizza, Bistro Grilled Chicken, 218
    Pizza, Breakfast, 54
    Pizza, Hamburger-Mushroom, 218
    Pizza, Mediterranean Garlic, 213
    Pizza, Pesto-Tomato, 214
    Pizzas, Roasted Chicken-and-White
        Bean, 216
    Pizzas, Veggie Sausage, 214
    Pork Chops, Fruited, 295
    Pork Chops, Honey-Pecan, 296
    Pork Chops With Pistachio
        Pesto and Parmesan Cheese Grits,
        Grilled, 124
    Rib-eye Steaks, Grilled
        Gorgonzola, 121
    Shrimp and Grits, 92
    Shrimp and Linguine, Sautéed, 108
    Shrimp in Tortillas, Lime, 315
    Shrimp With Mustard Sauce,
        Coconut, 316
    Shrimp With Roasted Red Pepper
        Cream, 315
    Sirloin Steaks With Thyme Pesto, 286
    Spaghetti, One-Skillet, 222
    Steak 'n' Country Gravy, Chicken-
        fried, 25
    Tacos, Chicken-and-Refried Bean, 84
    Trout, Grilled, 136
    Veal in Lime Sauce, 292
  Rice With Black Beans and Corn, 344
  Salads and Salad Dressings
    Artichoke-Goat Cheese Salad, 353
    Baby Blue Salad, Quick, 348
    Cherry Tomato-Caper Salad, 355
    Chicken-Black Bean Salad, 88
    Peanut-Noodle Salad, 238
    Potato Salad, Creole, 37
    Roasted Onion Salad, 352
    Tomato-Red Onion Salad, 354
  Sandwiches
    Burgers, Easy Mushroom-Onion, 260
    Burgers, Fiesta, 262
    Burgers, Mozzarella-Basil, 143
    Burgers, Teriyaki, 288
    Calzones, Easy, 259
    Catfish Sandwiches, Fried, 274

    Cheeseburgers, Jalapeño, 143
    Egg Salad Sandwiches, Double-
        Decker, 264
    Grilled Bacon, Cheese, and Tomato
        Sandwiches, 264
    Grilled Tuna Sandwiches, 108
    Reubens, Golden-Baked Mini, 259
  Soups and Stew
    Bean Soup, Quick, 257
    Blue Satin Soup, 252
    Meatball Stew, 249
    Potato Soup With Ham, 250
    Sausage, Spinach, and Bean
        Soup, 249
    Seafood Chowder, So-Quick, 250
    Taco Soup, 249
    Tortilla Soup, Spicy, 41
  Vegetables
    Black-Eyed Peas 'n' Ham, Quick, 34
    Broccoli in Béchamel, Gratin of, 327
    Broccoli, Sesame, 326
    Cauliflower, Frosted, 329
    Corn, Mexican-Style, 330
    Corn Pudding, 32
    Corn With Jalapeño-Lime Butter,
        Grilled, 147
    Fennel and Carrots, Sautéed, 328
    Green Beans Balsamic With
        Garlic, 323
    Green Beans, Saucy, 32
    Green Beans With Bacon and
        Mushrooms, 323
    Okra Fritters, 30
    Okra 'n' Tomatoes, Basil, 30
    Onion-Gruyère Gratin, 334
    Potato Wedges, Balsamic-
        Roasted, 336
    Spinach With Herbs, 339
    Squash, Southern Summer, 339
    Tomatoes, Fried Green, 29
    Tomatoes, Italian-Topped, 343
Tomatoes. See also Salads, Soups.
  Baked Tomatoes, Honey-, 343
  Biscuits, Savory Tomato-Bacon, 202
  Cherry Tomatoes, Stuffed, 197
  Cream, Chicken in Tomato and
      Basil, 302
  Crostini, Tomato, 202
  Dressing, Fresh Tomato, 343
  Flatbread, Fast Rosemary-Dried
      Tomato, 367
  Focaccia, Pesto-and-Tomato, 367
  "Fried" Green Tomato BLTs, 29
  Fried Green Tomatoes, 29
  Gravy, Tomato, 291
  Grilled Tomatoes, 144
  Grits, Hot Tomato, 27
  Italian-Topped Tomatoes, 343
  Mayonnaise, Tomato-Basil, 179
  Okra 'n' Tomatoes, Basil, 30
  Pizza, Pesto-Tomato, 214
  Relish, Flank Steak With Tomato-
      Olive, 286
  Salsa, Five-Minute, 182
  Sauce, Cheese Tortellini in Jalapeño
      Tomato, 235

Tomatoes (*continued*)
Sauce With Shells, Creamy Tomato-
Sausage, 222
Stuffed Tomatoes, Savory, 29
Vermicelli, Tomato-Jalapeño, 233
Toppings. *See also* Frostings, Pesto, Relish,
Salsas, Sauces, Syrup.
Savory
Molasses Barbecue Glaze, Grilled
Flank Steak With, 105
Orange Cream, Beef Fillets With, 283
Roasted Red Pepper Cream, Shrimp
With, 315
Sweet
Lemon Curd, 392
Whipped Cream, 402
Tuna. *See also* Grilled/Fish and Shellfish.
Salad, Tuna-and-White Bean, 90
Sandwiches, Curried Tuna-Apple, 274
Steaks With Lemon Butter, Tuna, 313
Turkey
Cheeseburgers, Turkey, 141
Glazed Turkey and Sweet Potatoes,
Apricot-, 166
Mignons, Sesame-Crusted Turkey, 309
Piccata, Turkey-Basil, 308
Sandwiches, Deli-Stuffed, 265
Soup With Green Chile Biscuits, Fiesta
Turkey, 245
Wraps, Smoked Turkey, 266
20 Minutes or Less
Appetizers
Blue Cheese Crisps, 201
Brie, Coffee-Kissed Pecan, 177
Brie, Warmed Cranberry, 177
Caviar, Texas, 184
Crackers, Snack, 193
Crostini, Tomato, 202
Dip, Bacon-Blue Cheese, 189
Dip, Cinco de Mayo Bean, 189
Dip, Layered Nacho, 185
Dip, Meaty Cheese, 185
Mix, Sweet 'n' Savory Snack, 191
Pimiento Cheese, Green Chile, 197
Quesadillas, Santa Fe Chicken, 204
Salsa, Black Bean, 182
Tomatoes, Stuffed Cherry, 197
Breads
Biscuits, Best-Ever Buttermilk, 112
Biscuits, Cheese Garlic, 358
Blue Cheese Bread, 365
Breadsticks, Italian Cheese, 368
Garlic Bread, Buttery, 365
Waffles, 374
Couscous, Lemon, 344
Desserts
Fudge, Peanut Butter, 389
Pears With Raspberry Sherbet, 117
Pudding, Chocolate Cookie, 403
Grits, Creamy, 27
Grits, Quick Double-Cheese, 27
Main Dishes
Burritos, Breakfast, 53
Catfish, Crispy Fried, 22
Chicken Penne, Cheesy, 225

Chicken Stir-fry, Lemon, 307
Chicken, Sweet-and-Sour Apricot, 307
Chicken-Vegetable Stir-fry, 72
Chicken With Pineapple Salsa,
Grilled Southwestern, 133
Eggs and Ham, Green, 50
Eggs Benedict, Traditional, 55
Fettuccine With Pesto Chicken, 225
Fillets With Tarragon Butter, 283
Lamb and Vegetable Stir-fry, 292
Mahimahi, Honey-Macadamia, 136
Noodles, Blue Cheese, 231
Noodles, Thai, 231
Omelet, Easy Crawfish, 53
Omelets, Ham 'n' Cheddar, 50
Orange Roughy, Parmesan-
Crusted, 311
Orange Roughy, Pesto-Crusted, 108
Pasta, Artichoke, 229
Pie, Corn Chip Chili, 61
Pizza, Cheeseburger, 219
Pizzas, Chicken-and-Three-Cheese
French Bread, 213
Pizzas, Grilled Portobello, 214
Pork-and-Pepper Skillet, 102
Pork Picante, Peachy, 295
Ravioli, Mediterranean, 98
Rib-eyes, Grecian Skillet, 285
Salmon With Dijon-Caper Cream
Sauce, Broiled, 313
Salmon With Nectarine-Onion
Relish, Grilled, 137
Scallop Fettuccine, Saucy, 227
Scampi, Speedy, 227
Scramble, Veggie, 50
Shells, Creamy Tomato-Sausage
Sauce With, 222
Shrimp and Feta Vermicelli, 227
Shrimp and Tortellini, 93
Shrimp, Lemon-Garlic, 316
Shrimp, Snappy Cajun, 314
Tortellini Carbonara, 58
Tortellini in Jalapeño Tomato Sauce,
Cheese, 235
Tostadas, 65
Tuna Steaks With Green Peppercorn
Sauce, 134
Tuna Steaks With Lemon Butter, 313
Vermicelli, Tomato-Jalapeño, 233
Ziti With Mozzarella and Tomato, 229
Ziti With Sausage and Broccoli, 221
Mayonnaise, Béarnaise, 179
Pecans, Spiced, 195
Salads
Chicken Salad, Fruity, 89
Chicken Salad, Greek, 87
Ham-and-Pasta Salad, 238
Pasta-Veggie Salad, 237
Raspberry-Spinach Salad, Fresh, 347
Tortellini Pasta Salad, Cheese, 238
Sandwiches
Avocado Sandwiches Deluxe, 277
BLTs, "Fried" Green Tomato, 29
Burgers, Greek Feta, 140
Club Sandwiches, French, 266
French Onion Sandwiches, 279

Grilled Chicken 'n' Cheese
Sandwiches, 269
Ham-Swiss-and-Asparagus
Sandwiches, 266
Melts, Vegetable-Cheese, 97
Pitas, Mango Chutney Chicken, 270
Po'boys, Zesty Fish, 273
Rollups, Pizza, 213
Wraps, Cheese-Steak, 260
Wraps, Smoked Turkey, 266
Soups and Stews
Cheese Soup, Herbed, 252
Gazpacho, Instant, 256
Potato Soup, Roasted Garlic-, 110
Tomato-Basil Bisque, 255
White Bean Soup, 41
Spread, Mexican Cheese, 181
Vegetables
Asparagus, Asian-Glazed, 323
Asparagus With Lemon Butter, 323
Broccoli-Ginger Stir-fry, 101
Carrots, Honey-Tarragon Glazed
Baby, 327
Corn, Creamed Fresh, 330
Corn on the Cob, Chili, 330
Greens With Sweet-and-Sour Sauce,
Wilted, 333
Okra and Tomatoes, Grilled, 147
Okra, Crunchy Fried, 31
Potatoes, Basic Mashed, 334
Potatoes, Garlic Mashed, 334
Spinach, Easy, 339
Squash-and-Corn Sauté, Summer, 341
Zucchini-Parmesan Toss, 341

Veal in Lime Sauce, 292
Vegetables. *See also* specific types.
Dip, Quick Creamy Vegetable, 189
Fish and Vegetable Dinner, 90
Frittata, Mediterranean, 319
Mac-and-Cheese, Veggie, 235
Melts, Vegetable-Cheese, 97
Pancakes, Veggie, 373
Pasta Toss, Garden, 236
Pasta, Vegetable, 96
Penne, Spicy Vegetables With, 228
Primavera, Fettuccine, 98
Roasted Vegetable Pizza, 215
Salad, Pasta-Veggie, 237
Sandwiches, Grilled Vegetable, 144
Sauce, Vermicelli With Chunky
Vegetable, 234
Scramble, Veggie, 50
Soup, Spicy Vegetable, 171

Waffles, 374
Waffles, Cornbread, 374

Zucchini-Beef Spaghetti, 105
Zucchini-Parmesan Toss, 341